# The Handbook of Journal Publi

*The Handbook of Journal Publishing* is a comprehensive reference work written by experienced professionals, covering all aspects of journal publishing, both online and in print. Journals are crucial to scholarly communication, but changes in recent years in the way journals are produced, financed, and used make this an especially turbulent and challenging time for journal publishers – and for authors, readers, and librarians. The *Handbook* offers a thorough guide to the journal publishing process, from editing and production through marketing, sales, and fulfillment, with chapters on journal management, finances, metrics, copyright, and ethical issues. It provides a wealth of practical tools, including checklists, sample documents, worked examples, alternative scenarios, and extensive lists of resources, which readers can use in their day-to-day work. Between them, the authors have been involved in every aspect of journal publishing over several decades and bring to the text their experience working for a wide range of publishers in both the not-for-profit and commercial sectors.

**Sally Morris** has worked in journal and book publishing for over forty years, for presses including Oxford University Press, Churchill Livingstone, and John Wiley & Sons, and as CEO of the Association of Learned and Professional Society Publishers. She has herself edited a peer-reviewed journal: *Learned Publishing*. She has played a leading role in many industry and publisher/library groups and has written and lectured widely on copyright and journal publishing.

**Ed Barnas** has worked in journal publishing for over thirty-five years. His expertise covers submission through publication, print and online, the sciences and the humanities. Ed's experience covers both not-for-profit and for-profit sectors at Cambridge University Press, Raven Press, John Wiley & Sons, and the American Institute of Physics. Ed has been active in various publishing groups and served a term as President of the Society for Scholarly Publishing (SSP).

**Douglas LaFrenier** has held a variety of advertising, marketing, and sales positions at Macmillan, McGraw-Hill, W. H. Freeman and Company, the consulting firm Robert Ubell Associates, and the American Institute of Physics. He is a former Board member of SSP, and a frequent speaker about online publishing issues at meetings of SSP, the Special Libraries Association, the Council of Engineering and Scientific Society Executives, and the Charleston Conference.

**Margaret Reich** has been working in scholarly publishing for over twenty-five years. Most of her experience is with non-profit society publishers, including the American Physiological Society and the American Heart Association. A past President of SSP, Margaret has also served on its Board of Directors and has performed Committee service for SSP and the Council of Science Editors (CSE).

# The Handbook of
# Journal Publishing

Sally Morris
Ed Barnas
Douglas LaFrenier
Margaret Reich

CAMBRIDGE
UNIVERSITY PRESS

CAMBRIDGE UNIVERSITY PRESS

Cambridge, New York, Melbourne, Madrid, Cape Town,
Singapore, São Paulo, Delhi, Mexico City

Cambridge University Press
The Edinburgh Building, Cambridge CB2 8RU, UK

Published in the United States of America by Cambridge University Press,
New York

www.cambridge.org
Information on this title: www.cambridge.org/9781107020856

First published 2013

Printed and bound in the United Kingdom by the MPG Books Group

*A catalog record for this publication is available from the British Library*

*Library of Congress Cataloging in Publication data*
The handbook of journal publishing / Sally Morris . . . [et al.].
    p.   cm.
Includes bibliographical references and index.
ISBN 978-1-107-02085-6 (Hardback) – ISBN 978-1-107-65360-3 (pbk.)
1. Scholarly periodicals – Publishing.   2. Electronic
journals – Publishing.   3. Periodicals – Publishing.   I. Morris, Sally, 1948–
Z286.S37H35   2012
070.5–dc23   2012023156

ISBN 978-1-107-02085-6 hardback
ISBN 978-1-107-65360-3 paperback

# CONTENTS

# PREFACE AND ACKNOWLEDGMENTS

We, the authors, have all spent many years involved with scholarly and professional journals in the course of our respective publishing careers. And we have all found journals to be one of the most fascinating areas of publishing. Maybe it is because journals are so important to authors; particularly in the sciences, being published promptly in the best available journal is key to a researcher's future career. Maybe it is because journals represent the cutting edge, where new findings and new ideas are first reported. Maybe it is because journals are not static, but more like a living entity; the publisher can make adjustments to every aspect of a journal, as frequently as necessary, and observe what difference they make (whereas a book publisher has only one chance to make changes – the publication of a new edition – if any!). Maybe it is because journals have been for decades – and still are – in the vanguard of all kinds of exciting developments enabled by the web: developments not just in how journals are produced, delivered, and used, but also in how they are financed. Maybe it is because journals have been at the forefront of significant cultural changes affecting academia, scientific research, publishing, and scholarly communication in general. Probably it is a combination of all these reasons, and more besides.

Whether you, the reader, have come to journals publishing after a spell with books, or are completely new to publishing – or, indeed, if you have some journals experience and want to refresh your knowledge and ideas – we hope that you will find this book a useful resource. You may or may not want to read it from cover to cover; more likely, you will refer to particular sections as you need them. However you use our book, we hope that it will help you to enjoy your experience of journals publishing as much as we have done. Good luck!

We could not have written this book without the help of many people, including the innumerable colleagues and mentors from whom we have learned so much over the years; indeed, we have learned greatly from each other in the course of writing this book. Friends and colleagues too numerous to mention have patiently provided information and answered questions. In particular, we should like to thank the following for their suggestions, comments, and advice: Aravind Akella, Susann Brailey, Lori Carlin, Kevin Cohn, Ed Colleran, Phil Davis, Elizabeth Ennis (for redrawing the diagrams), Will Farnam, Robert Finnegan, Norman Frankel, Hugh Jones, Elizabeth Just, Bill Kasdorf, Andrea Lopez, Judy Luther, Wayne Manos, David Marshall, Cliff Morgan, Margaret Morgan, Christine Orr, Lynette Owen, Jan Peterson, Charlie Rapple, Tom Sanville, Mark Seeley, Peter Shepherd, Louise Tutton, Eunice Walford, and Stuart Wortzman. Special thanks are due to Jo Cross, who contributed much of Chapter 5, Journal metrics.

# 1 Introduction to journals

Journals have been, for more than 350 years, a key part of the fabric of scholarly communication. They enable scholars to communicate their ideas and discoveries across time as well as space; thus the sum of human knowledge and understanding is gradually increased, as others are able to integrate, question, and build on the work of their predecessors (as in Newton's famous remark "if I have seen further it is by standing on $y^e$ sholders of giants" [Newton, 1676]).[1]

In November 2012, there were 28,714 active peer-reviewed, scholarly journals listed in the Ulrichsweb database (Ulrichsweb, 2012) and there are certainly many more, particularly in languages other than English; this number has been increasing steadily by around 3% per annum, and will no doubt continue to do so.[2] Jinha estimated that by 2009, some 50 million individual articles had been published since the first journals appeared in 1665 (Jinha, 2010); for about every 100 additional articles written, a new journal is created (Mabe, 2003).

No accurate estimates are available for the global value of the scholarly journals market; in 2011, the global market for all scholarly, peer-reviewed journals was variously estimated at $9.4bn (Outsell, 2012) to $10.3bn for science, technology, and medicine (STM) alone (Simba Information, 2012). This is not large in the overall scheme of things – in 2010, the market for chocolate and confectionery in the UK alone was estimated at approximately $7.72bn (KeyNote, 2011)!

Scholarly journals have seen more change in the past few decades than in the previous three centuries, triggered by the developments in (and convergence between) information and communications technology, which enabled the electronic journal to become a practical reality. How

---

[1] Newton was actually quoting a much earlier author, the twelfth-century Richard of Salisbury, though even he may not have been the originator of the phrase.
[2] The figure for all serials (which also includes proceedings, monographic series, etc.) was even higher, at 32,033 (Ulrichsweb, 2012).

journals are delivered, how they are bought and sold, and in particular how they are used have all changed dramatically. And there are unprecedented challenges from the library and scholarly communities to the dominance of publishers (particularly commercial publishers) and indeed to the prevailing economic model of reader-side payment (usually paid by librarians) for subscriptions or licenses. Yet, essentially, the journal still performs the same function for author and reader – that of facilitating scholarly communication through the valuable filters of peer review and editing.

## What is a journal?

*The concise Oxford English dictionary* has as its first definition of "journal": "a newspaper or magazine that deals with a particular subject or professional activity." More particularly, in the case of the scholarly journals with which this book is concerned, most of the articles report original research in the field, having been evaluated before publication (i.e., peer reviewed) by several relevant experts. However, there may also be review articles (summarizing work in a specific area), case reports, educational articles, historical articles, reviews of books or other media, letters to the Editor, features, and news reports.

But a journal is more than the sum of its articles. It attracts articles of interest to a particular community (well known to its Editor and Editorial Board), assembles them in a structured, navigable collection, and makes them available to readers with links to further study (i.e., citations). In that sense, it is a database like any other.[3]

The journal adds value to the articles it contains, in a number of ways.

### Selection

Research articles are selected from among those submitted to the journal. First, they are considered by the journal's Editor-in-Chief or a member of the Editorial team, to establish whether or not they are appropriate to the scope of the journal (i.e., the interests of its community of readers). Then,

---

[3] The European Database Directive defines a database as "a collection of independent works, data or other materials arranged in a systematic or methodical way and individually accessible by electronic or other means"; this sounds just like a journal!

those that pass this first hurdle are evaluated by several experts (the author's "peers"), not only to establish the validity of the research being reported, but also to judge whether or not the work is interesting and important enough to warrant inclusion in the journal (see Chapter 3, Editing, for more on peer review). Equally, nonresearch items – which are usually commissioned – are selected with just as much care to fit the readers' interests and to respect their time.

In preonline days, selection also entailed ensuring that the total number of pages did not exceed what had been allowed for in the annual page budget – otherwise, the journal's finances would suffer. For electronic journals, "page budgets" are less of an issue (although the available staff resources to edit and prepare articles for publication are still finite), but that does not mean that the reader's time is any less pressured – rather, the reverse (Tenopir et al., 2009). So in fact "quantity control" remains just as important a service for readers as "quality control." Whether this is still achieved by the individual journal itself, however, or by the tools that the reader uses to find relevant articles, is an interesting question; some journals are now so enormous that no one reader could even browse their complete contents, but publishers and others are providing ever more refined tools to enable readers to make their own selections of articles.

## *Preparation*

Those articles which are accepted (usually after a certain amount of modification by the author – it is rare for an article to be accepted without any changes at all) must then be prepared for publication. These days, typesetting no longer needs to be carried out from scratch – most authors provide an electronic script which can be used without further rekeying. However, few authors write with complete clarity, even if they are writing in their own language, which many are not. The all-important process of editing makes the text as clear, unambiguous, and consistent as possible. References (citations of other journal articles, book chapters, etc.) are linked whenever possible to the original source – this is a particularly highly valued feature of online journals (Swan, 2002). Online, it is possible to supplement the article itself with links to much more information than could be included in print – the full text of surveys, for example, or even full datasets or video material. The author's charts and diagrams are very likely professionally edited or redrawn. And the author's script is given the visual appearance of the particular journal, which has been chosen for ease of reading (as well as elegance).

## Collection

Gathering articles together in a usable collection is still, we would maintain, an immensely valuable service for the reader. Even if the reader no longer receives print issues – or browses them in the library – and searches multiple journals online instead, the "branding" conferred by the title of a given journal carries many useful signals about the content; this can be all the more helpful when confronted with a long list of search results. This "branding" not only indicates the area covered, but also (once the reader is familiar with the journal and its reputation) the editorial "flavor" imparted by the journal's Editor and Editorial team. In addition, there are a number of measures which provide at least proxy indicators of the journal's popularity, and thus – if only by implication – its quality: impact factor, circulation, downloads, even rejection rate (see Chapter 5, Journal metrics, for more details).

## Navigation

Once the articles have been gathered together in a journal, the publisher may add many features to aid the reader's navigation. In a print journal, these consist of the table of contents; abstracts, with or without keywords; a helpful hierarchy of headings and subheadings within the article; running heads; references; and a professionally compiled index. Electronic journals make possible many more sophisticated navigational aids as well, from fielded fulltext searching, through internal linking to sections within an article, to linking from citations to their original (online) sources, wherever they may be. Even more possibilities are being worked on, including text and data mining, and linking to subject databases (for example, see Strickland et al., 2008).

## Preservation

"Homeless" articles on the web are highly likely to become un-findable in fairly short order. An individual author is unlikely to be able to ensure his or her article's ongoing availability through job moves, retirement, or other life changes. The short- and long-term preservation of print journals was seen to be the responsibility of libraries; in addition to the processing costs involved in acquiring, shelving, binding, and preserving journals, this incurs the cost of space – and all these costs are multiplied over many libraries. For online journals, both publishers and libraries are taking some of the responsibility. Many publishers are both digitizing preelectronic issues, and undertaking to make a permanent preservation arrangement (often in association with one or more libraries – for example, Elsevier is working with the national library of the Netherlands, de Koninklijke Bibliotheek). Nonprofit organizations such as JSTOR (www.jstor.org), OCLC (www.oclc.org/digitalarchive), Portico (www.portico.org/digital-preservation), and LOCKSS/CLOCKSS (www.lockss.org, www.clockss.org) – often involving publisher/library collaborations – are working to ensure ongoing access and availability in the short to medium term. And national libraries are urgently looking at the requirements for truly long-term preservation (e.g., beyond the lifetime of current hardware, media, and software). For more on archiving and preservation of journal content, see Chapter 4, The production process.

## The purpose of journals

The answer to the question "What is a journal for?" depends on your role. For the author, it carries out a number of important functions (many of them irrespective of whether or not anyone actually reads his or her article). From the perspective of the reader, its functions are rather different.

### For the author

Publishing an article is the way that the author is connected (via the publisher and the library) with the reader. This can be a cyclical process (see Figure 1.1), with the reader digesting what is read and in turn building on it in his or her own next article. (However, in the majority of fields – particularly applied fields, such as medicine and engineering – the number of readers [practitioners] vastly exceeds the number of authors [researchers].) The appropriateness of the readership is one of the key factors for authors when choosing where to submit their work (CIBER, 2004).

Michael Mabe (Ware and Mabe, 2009) has outlined the canonical functions of a journal (from the perspective of the author) as follows:

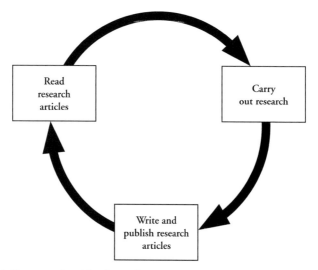

**Figure 1.1** The research publication cycle

- Registration – establishing the author's precedence and ownership of an idea.
- Dissemination – communicating the findings to the intended audience.
- Certification – both ensuring quality control through peer review, and rewarding authors (through enhanced reputation – though usually not financially).
- Archival record – preserving a fixed version of the paper for future reference and citation.[4]

As pressure grows on university faculty appointments, a track record of publishing articles in well-regarded journals is increasingly important to authors. It can be key both to obtaining funding and to career progression – it really is a matter of "publish or perish."

### For the reader

Journals provide readers with easy access to all the relevant research in their field.[5] Today, they can use powerful search engines both to find

---

[4] These were originally described by Henry Oldenburg, who founded the first English-language journal, *Philosophical Transactions*, in 1665.

[5] As early as the seventeenth century, the German philosopher, mathematician, inventor, and librarian Gottfried Wilhelm von Leibniz declared that "a treatise of

articles of whose existence they already know, and to discover ones unknown to them. They can also use a variety of current awareness services such as publisher email alerts to browse or to be alerted to newly published content in their favorite journals or on a specific topic.

Many journals also provide a wealth of information to readers other than research findings. There are editorial opinions, review articles that survey entire fields of study, educational articles with instructional guidance, reviews of new publications, and news on recent developments in the field.

## The development of journals

### The first journals

The two earliest scientific journals were both launched in 1665 – *Le journal des sçavans* on January 5 in Paris, and *Philosophical Transactions* on March 6 in London (Figure 1.2).[6] Both covered a comprehensive area of what we now know as science, and by publishing written accounts of the latest discoveries, they enabled far wider dissemination of those findings than was possible through private correspondence or at meetings.

The first learned societies were formed in the seventeenth century (the Royal Society of London, for example, arose out of meetings of "natural philosophers" [i.e., scientists] held from the mid-1640s to discuss their observations and experiments, and was officially founded on November 28, 1660). Many of the oldest leading journals were founded by such societies, operating on a "not-for-profit"[7] basis (e.g., the

architecture or a collection of periodicals … is worth a hundred volumes of literary classics" (quoted in Escolar, 1985).

[6] Although *Philosophical Transactions* is sometimes thought to have been published from the outset by the Royal Society of London, in fact it was initially a private venture by the Society's Secretary, Henry Oldenburg, and only became a publication of the Society after Oldenburg's death in 1677.

[7] "Not-for-profit" (or "nonprofit") is, strictly speaking, a tax-exempt status; to qualify, an organization must be devoted to the public good and must reinvest any money made by its activities into the furtherance of its mission, rather than paying out dividends to shareholders as a commercial company might do. It does not mean that individual activities – including publishing – are necessarily unprofitable, but those profits (or "surpluses" as they are known) must be reinvested; many societies support a range of member services, including educational and other activities, with the surpluses produced by their journals.

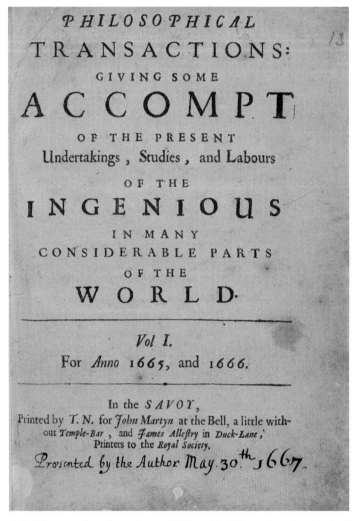

**Figure 1.2** Title page of the first volume of *Philosophical Transactions*. Reprinted with the permission of the Royal Society, London.

*Transactions of the American Philosophical Society*, first published in 1771). At the same time, some notable journals were launched independently of societies: the *Philosophical Magazine* in 1798, *The Lancet* in 1825, and *Nature* in 1865. The number of journals published increased very steadily until World War II; in some subjects, such as chemistry, mathematics, and physics, German research and thus the German language was predominant.

## After World War II

After the war, there was a significant increase in government expenditure on science and technology. This resulted, naturally enough, in increased output of research articles, and the existing society journals could no longer cope. New subjects were springing up, either by subdivision (sometimes called "twigging") of existing disciplines, or in the areas of overlap between them (for example, biochemistry). Existing societies, even if they had the resources, were unable to launch new journals which lay outside their defined scope.

This was the period, therefore, when commercial publishers started to play a more active role. They were not constrained to a single discipline in the same way as societies, and many commercial publishers, most notably Robert Maxwell,[8] saw the huge potential for launching new journals to accommodate the increased output of research articles. As a result, the number of new journals increased dramatically in the years immediately following the war (although the rate of growth subsequently settled back to much the same level as before, as shown in Figure 1.3) (Mabe, 2003).

English became increasingly dominant as the language of international scholarly communication. The practice of translating at least the article abstracts into several major European languages fell increasingly

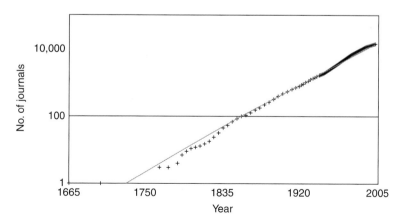

**Figure 1.3** The growth of active, peer-reviewed learned journals since 1665. Reprinted from Ware and Mabe, 2009, with the permission of STM.

[8] The founder of Pergamon Press (now part of Elsevier).

out of use; some non-English-language journals introduced an English-language edition, while others abandoned their local language in favor of English.

Although libraries have never been able to buy everything they wanted, for a while they were sufficiently well funded to be able more or less to keep pace with this steady expansion in the number and, thus, the cost of journals. However, this could not continue indefinitely, and by the 1970s, they were experiencing what became known as the "serials crisis" – the gap was widening uncomfortably between the journals libraries could afford to purchase and those to which their patrons required access, and even interlibrary loan (see Chapter 11, Copyright and other legal aspects) was not enough to compensate. In 1990, the Association of Research Libraries (ARL) published data showing that journal prices were increasing at a far greater rate than increases to the universities' periodicals budgets – that is, the rising cost of journal subscriptions was making it impossible for the typical ARL library to expand, or even to maintain, its journal portfolio (ARL, 1990). As librarians became increasingly conscious both of above-inflation price increases and of the high absolute prices of some journals, they began to work together by forming consortia in order to negotiate more favorable deals with publishers.

Because the academic market was relatively static for many years – with few new institutional subscribers – every time a customer canceled, the publisher had to recover lost revenue from the remaining subscribers in order to stay in business. Thus, cancellations led to higher prices, and higher prices led to more cancellations – a "downward spiral."

## *Electronic publishing*

Science and technology journals were the first to move to the World Wide Web, beginning in the mid-1990s; in the arts and humanities, some disciplines took rather longer, perhaps because their readers spent less time working on computers than did scientists. Now, the vast majority of journals are online (Cox and Cox, 2008), and a growing number have either no print equivalent, or produce on-demand copies of a single volume at the end of the year. (For more on the development of electronic journals, see Chapter 4, The production process.)

When electronic journals first appeared on the scene in the mid-1990s, they were hailed by both librarians and publishers as a possible solution to the problem of the "serials crisis." However, although online publication has changed many aspects of journal publishing, it has not fulfilled all the initial expectations of either librarians or publishers.

## What online didn't do

Librarians and, in many cases, publishers anticipated useful cost savings with the move to online publishing. Sure enough, there are some savings for both the publisher and the library – but only if print is given up altogether; and these savings can be more than offset by new costs.

The full extent of cost increases was perhaps not foreseen by either publishers or librarians. Some publishing costs (e.g., prepress) remain unchanged, while myriad new costs arise in the creation, hosting, and preservation of the online journal. And libraries incur new costs for computer systems and staff. The new staff required by both publishers and libraries tend to be computer-skilled, and thus expensive. User support is another completely new cost for both parties; no one, in the days of print-only journals, would phone up the publisher in the middle of the night because they were unable to open the journal, but now technical experts need to be available at all times. The production and analysis of the new forms of data which online journals can generate, such as comparable usage statistics, requires sophisticated programing by both publishers and librarians. And the negotiation of licenses is another completely new cost for both publishers and libraries, requiring a new level of (expensive) legal expertise.

The other area of potential saving which librarians, perhaps unrealistically, hoped for was in the cost of purchasing journals; they expected subscription prices to fall, and consortial purchasing to reduce the costs still further by sharing resources. However, it wasn't quite that simple. From the library point of view, one online subscription could indeed service an entire institution (or consortium or even country, for that matter), potentially replacing a number of print subscriptions serving different departments. Yet, from the publisher's viewpoint, this could be a financial disaster – perhaps hundreds of subscriptions canceled, with no comparable reduction in expenses.

This meant that establishing appropriate pricing for online journals was not simply a matter of applying (or discounting) the price for a single print subscription. Some publishers offered online "free" with a print subscription, others charged the same price for the online version as they did for print, and others felt that subscribers should pay more for the online version, given its greater functionality.

In print-only days, the number of copies purchased provided a – very broad-brush – proxy for the number of users. For purely practical reasons, it was difficult, if not impossible, to share the same print subscription across multiple sites, even within the same institution, let alone throughout a wider consortium.[9] With an online journal, however, a single license can indeed serve many institutions in a consortium, or even nationwide, and – unlike with print journals – all those users could, in theory, access the same article simultaneously. But at the same time, it is possible to be much more precise about the number of users being served.

The new ability to track downloads and other uses of the online content quickly showed huge variations from institution to institution. This raised an important question: why should an institution with 100 downloads a year pay the same price as an institution with 10,000 downloads a year? The value to the latter institution is clearly much greater, so why shouldn't it pay more? Put another way, why should an institution with little research activity pay the same price as a research-intensive institution?[10]

Licenses for electronic journals therefore tend to be priced on a customer-by-customer basis, to reflect not only the size of the community being served, but – increasingly – usage[11] as well; it is very difficult to make comparisons with the price of print subscriptions. Publishers found this as unnerving as did librarians, and tried various approaches to ensure

---

[9]  Though, as times became harder, most libraries had to eliminate duplicate subscriptions despite the resultant inconvenience to users; the consequent erosion of publishers' revenues contributed to the price spiral mentioned above.

[10]  In 2001, the American Physical Society introduced tiered pricing for its current journals, based mainly on the Carnegie Foundation classifications for US universities, and equivalent classifications (or, failing those, download ranges) for universities abroad (Chesler and King, 2009). (JSTOR had already adopted tiered pricing for its online backlist collections.)

[11]  The development of standards for the recording and measurement of usage (see www.projectcounter.org) has made this much more feasible.

that their revenues did not take an unintended nosedive with the move to online journals.

An initial step adopted by some publishers (which understandably became more unpopular with libraries as the years passed) was to base the price on what the library (or libraries, in the case of a consortium or national license) was previously paying for the publisher's or publishers' journals, but to include in the package many other journals that were not previously subscribed to. (See Chapter 8, Journal finances, for more on pricing.)

The additional journals in these packages were found to receive surprisingly high usage (see, for example, Sanville, 2001, and Bucknell, 2008), with the effect of both widening patrons' reading and reducing the cost to the library of interlibrary loan or document delivery fees. However, this does not alter the fact that the overall amount spent by libraries on journals has continued to rise, often at the expense of other types of publication – monographs in particular. As the amount spent by governments and corporations on research and development (R&D) continues to grow, driving up the number of researchers and thus the number of research articles, it is hard to envisage library funding ever being able to keep pace. This is a fundamental problem to which no one has yet found a complete solution; the Open Access (OA) movement described below is one attempt to address it.

## What online did do

On the other hand, electronic journals did make an enormous difference in a huge number of areas.

*Costs.* Some of the costs, for both publishers and libraries, have certainly fallen, although the benefits are only felt if print copies are abandoned altogether. Without any print copies, publishers save on printing, distribution, and storage costs; libraries, too, save on space, physical handling, and binding costs. One reason for the saving for libraries is that the responsibility for, and cost of, preserving and ensuring access to both current and past journals has moved *de facto* from the library to the publisher. (At the same time, however – as mentioned above – other new costs have arisen.)

Most journal publishers would dearly love to drop print altogether, thus eliminating not only costs but also a great deal of duplication of cost and effort. However, the move to online only has been surprisingly slow. Many librarians are reluctant to abandon print because they still lack confidence in the long-term preservation and accessibility of online journals, even though publishers and librarians have worked together to arrive at a number of workable medium-term solutions, and national libraries are grappling with the more fundamental issues raised by truly long-term preservation, as mentioned above. Many librarians are still also concerned about losing ongoing access if the subscription ceases (whereas previously subscribed-to print copies would, of course, remain on the library shelves); however, many publishers have now modified their licenses to permit continuing access to previously subscribed material.[12]

Another obstacle to giving up print, in the UK and some other European countries, is the European Value Added Tax (VAT) regime, which allows a lower rate (currently zero in the UK) to be charged on printed publications, while the full rate must be charged on electronic publications; publishers have tended to minimize the impact for libraries by selling their journals as print publications with a free online version (even where the local VAT officer objects to this – and, curiously, there is no central locus of decision-making – the publisher can allocate just a portion of the price to the online version).[13]

However, as King and Tenopir have conclusively demonstrated (King, 2007), the savings to all parties are so substantial that it can only be a matter of time before print issues cease to be produced at all. Print-on-demand technology means that those who really want a paper copy could still obtain one; some publishers of online-only journals already offer an annual volume on this basis.

And although the cost of journals acquisition did not fall, as librarians had hoped, there was a dramatic increase both in the number of journals acquired, through package deals of various kinds, and in the level of usage. Various analyses (e.g., Montgomery and King, 2002; King et al., 2004;

---

[12] Providing and supporting continuing access does have some cost to the publisher; one approach is to make backfiles freely accessible after a certain period, thus at least removing the need to manage access controls. Some publishers do make a charge either for the complete backfile (which may include all the older print volumes, retrodigitized by the publisher – a costly operation, but hugely valuable to researchers) or for continuing access to the previously subscribed volumes.

[13] Current European Union proposals may impose the full rate of VAT on printed, as well as online, publications in the near future.

CIBER, 2011) have shown that both the cost per journal and the cost per download have reduced dramatically through licensing arrangements such as these.

*Ways of selling and buying journals.* As mentioned above, electronic journals made it possible for large numbers of customers to join forces in a consortium to get a more favorable deal from the publisher; for the first time, this gave library customers significant negotiating power over publishers (particularly smaller publishers, many of whom have banded together themselves to offer larger aggregations of content). And large numbers of publications can also be brought together (sometimes called "bundling") and sold as a single package from one or a group of publishers.[14]

The bundling of both customers and publications has created a discontinuity in the way that publishers can count the number of journals sold, and librarians can count the number of journals acquired: while it is, of course, perfectly possible to count the number of journals in a package and the number of libraries in a consortium, multiplying the one by the other does not give a figure which is in any way comparable with previous subscription statistics for either party. (For more on this, see Chapter 7, Fulfillment.)

Both forms of bundling have also had a major impact on the role of the subscription agent. Traditionally, agents had a vital intermediary role, helping librarians to buy many different journals from many different publishers in many different countries, and helping publishers to sell to many different customers, also in many different countries. Now, subscription agents are reinventing their role in a number of imaginative ways – helping multiple publishers to put together packages of journals, for instance (such as the ALPSP Learned Journals Collection, http://aljc. swets.com/) or working with national licensing bodies. (For more on the changing role of the subscription agent, see Chapter 6, Marketing and sales, and Chapter 7, Fulfillment.)

*Ways of using journals.* Online journals enable readers to search rapidly and efficiently at their desktops for unknown articles, simply by using search terms to define the topic of interest. Readers can use a variety of entry points, including Google Scholar, which is specific to scholarly

---

[14] In 1996, Academic Press (now an imprint of Elsevier) signed a pioneering licensing agreement with the statewide consortium OhioLINK. Other early library consortia included CAPES in Brazil and HEAL-Link in Greece.

publications, or a wide range of more specialized subject gateways;[15] however, many students and a surprising number of older researchers tend to rely on the most familiar basic search engines (e.g., Google, Bing, and Yahoo!). Once they have found an article of interest – through whatever route they choose – readers can print out copies, if they wish, without stirring from their chairs. One effect of this unprecedented ability to search across the widest possible range of literature (provided it is online – and the publisher has enabled indexing by search engines) is to increase the breadth of reading or, from the publisher's perspective, to increase usage of less-known titles. It has also led to increased usage overall. And that usage can be accurately measured, in a way that was impossible with print publications; publishers can, for the first time, not only see what articles are actually being read, but also glean a better understanding of how researchers interact with the content.

One of the most significant new features made possible by online journals (and correctly predicted as long ago as 1999 by the SuperJournal project, www.superjournal.ac.uk) is that of citation linking – whereby the reader can click on a citation within a journal article, and go directly to the original cited item (generally via its abstract page). The CrossRef project, www.crossref.org (development of which was funded by a consortium of publishers) has put in place the infrastructure and standards which make this possible, and it is being increasingly widely adopted by publishers and eagerly used by readers (see Box 1.1). And, once again, this use (in this case, the resolution of Digital Object Identifier [DOI] links) can actually be measured and has the potential to produce valuable statistics – more meaningful, in some ways, than those produced by the *Journal Citation Reports* (which is discussed in Chapter 5, Journal metrics).

*Added features.* With online journals, it is not only possible to do the same things in new and more efficient ways; it is also possible to do completely new things. Publishers have added a variety of new features and services to their online journals, and are continuing to learn from experience what readers want and what they don't. It is possible to publish articles ahead of the print issue (if there is one), or even immediately after

---

[15] These were the natural online successors to the specialized abstracting and indexing databases which previously flourished in many areas, providing valuable finding aids, but which now have largely fallen into disuse.

**Box 1.1 CrossRef**

CrossRef uses the DOI system, which assigns a unique identifier to each digital object (in this case, journal articles) (for details see Box 3.3 in Chapter 3, Editing).

Each DOI is associated in a powerful database with both a set of basic metadata (information about the digital object) and one or more URLs for the location of the full text.

It is the responsibility of the participating publishers (who pay a small fee) to register each new item, and to provide update information if these URLs change (e.g., if a journal changes platform or publisher).

For more information, see www.crossref.org

acceptance (but before copy-editing and composition). It is possible to provide additional content: data supplemental to particular articles, more extensive versions of articles (as in the *BMJ*'s [formerly *British Medical Journal*] "e-long, p-short" approach), or content which is only made available in the online version, such as online-only supplements or letters to the Editor. It is possible to include nontextual content, such as audio, video, or animations. It is possible to carry out online polls on pertinent topics. It is possible to provide convenient tools for readers, for example enabling them to bookmark, automatically create citations for, or email links to articles of particular interest. It is possible to provide related material via podcasts. It is possible to provide a variety of electronic fora for readers to communicate with each other – such as blogs and other social media (see, for example, the range of options offered by *Nature*, www.nature.com/).

*Unforeseen consequences.* A number of the changes brought about by the migration to online journals were not foreseen by either publishers or librarians. As a consequence of the ability to search for articles rather than being limited to browsing in known journals, emphasis has shifted away from the journal itself and toward the individual article as the primary unit of information (which is not to say that the journal does not remain an important "envelope" for all the reasons outlined at the beginning of this chapter).

Not all the changes have been desirable. Searching for content is extremely easy, but it may not be obvious to the reader which of the documents in the search results has or has not been "quality controlled" through peer review. And because content arrives at the reader's desktop without apparent barriers, the distinction becomes blurred in the reader's mind between content that has been subscribed to and content that is freely available to all – he or she may come to think that everything is free on the web, ignoring the library's role in acquisition. Equally, the reader can lose sight of the value of the services that the library provides in assisting users to find and navigate content; indeed, he or she may seldom if ever need to visit the physical library at all. Thus, it is all too easy for readers to remain ignorant of the value provided by both libraries and publishers.

It is also all too easy for readers to "cut and paste" content from online sources. This can lead to copyright infringements, ranging from unattributed quotations to full-scale plagiarism (though tools have also been developed to detect this – see Chapter 12, Ethical issues); it can also lead to a lazy approach to literature-based research.

For publishers, there has been an impact on the already declining sales of offprints or reprints – that is, single (print) copies of journal articles. Most publishers do offer single articles for sale online (see Chapter 9, Subsidiary income), but the online equivalent of bulk sales of journal articles (for example, to pharmaceutical companies) is much harder to price and control.

When a publisher seeks (or grants) permission for use of another's material in an online journal, the issues can become much more complex than they were for print. This is particularly the case with illustrations, especially reproductions of works of art; the owner may be extremely reluctant to make the image available online, where it might be cut and pasted (and perhaps degraded or distorted). Often, rights owners may want to grant far more limited rights (sometimes impractically so) than would apply for reproduction in print, and the resultant negotiations can be protracted and the outcome costly.

The full complexity of the issues involved in truly long-term archiving and preservation has only gradually become apparent. In years to come, the original content may no longer be accessible because the software and/or the hardware have become obsolete. Thus, it needs to be extracted in a "medium-neutral" format (which may not be able to cope with the full richness of images, links, and associated tools and services); alternatively the software and/or hardware will need to be emulated in future on the equipment of the day. Much highly technical research still needs to be done, and all of this will have substantial costs attached; the biggest question of all is "who will pay?"

## Open access

Online publication has made possible one completely new approach to the dissemination of research, which has gained a great deal of publicity and support: that of open access. The creation of the Public Library of Science (PLoS) in 2000 (www.plos.org) was particularly significant. At its most fundamental, open access simply means providing unrestricted access to (in our context) research articles.[16] Some supporters have mistakenly assumed that it is a way of saving money by getting access to journal articles free, but that was not the intention of its original advocates. And although it is sometimes seen as an attack on publishers, that was not their aim either; rather, it was the universal availability of scholarly research information, so that every article would be available, at least in "preprint" form, for those readers to whom the published journal version was not available (Okerson and O'Donnell, 1995).

There are two ways of providing free access to research journal articles. The first (sometimes called "Green" open access) depends on authors placing copies of their own articles in freely accessible web locations; this is often referred to as "self-archiving." The second ("Gold" open access) refers to articles which are published in the usual way, but in journals which are freely accessible to readers. In most cases, the costs of "Gold" publication (most of which are, of course, no different from the costs of publishing a subscription-based journal) are covered by a flat author-side publication charge, although some journals split this into a submission element (which also applies to articles subsequently rejected) and a pub-lication element; grants and institutional subscriptions can also play a part. (See Chapter 8, Journal finances, for more on OA pricing models.)

[16] Although people's understanding varies as to what "open" means – see Grubb and Easterbrook, 2011. Some OA enthusiasts insist that the term is synonymous with the Budapest (www.soros.org/openaccess/read.shtml), Bethesda (www.earlham.edu/~peters/fos/bethesda.htm), or Berlin (www.zim.mpg.de/openaccess-berlin/berlindeclaration.html) definitions, all of which include freedom of reuse as well as access. However, in general use, the term is rarely so specific; Peter Suber (www.earlham.edu/~peters/fos/overview.htm) makes the useful distinction between "gratis OA" (access only) and "libre OA" (access and – at least some – reuse).

In a variant on "Gold" open access, some subscription-based journals offer authors the option to pay a fee to make their own articles freely accessible, while the rest of the content is accessible only to subscribers (these are generally referred to as "hybrid" journals).[17] A large number of publishers, including all of the largest ones, offer this option in those of their journals that are not fully OA; most of them report rather low uptake by authors so far, despite the fact that many funders and some institutions are prepared to pay the publication charge (Björk, 2012).

Another variant, adopted by a growing number of publishers, is to make all content freely available after a relatively short period, most commonly six, twelve, or twenty-four months; this is sometimes called "delayed OA." (It can even be done the other way round, making research articles freely available for an initial period only – for example, the Institute of Physics makes all research articles freely available for thirty days after publication.)

## "Green" open access

"Green" open access, or self-archiving, can be done in a variety of ways, some of which are more helpful to potential readers than others. Some authors simply place their articles on their own personal web pages. Others place them in a repository organized by their institution (indeed, a growing number of universities mandate that their faculty do so). In other cases, the repository of choice is a subject-based one (like the very first electronic preprint database, arXiv, a repository for papers in theoretical physics and related disciplines – http://arxiv.org). And some funders, notably the US National Institutes of Health (NIH), require grant recipients to place articles in their own repository (PubMed Central in the case of NIH – www.ncbi.nlm.nih.gov/pmc). Tools have been developed to help readers search across multiple repositories – although, as with traditional journals, readers may in fact prefer to rely on the basic search engines for access.

The percentage of researchers who do, in fact, self-archive their articles has remained relatively low (estimated at 11.9% of articles published in 2008) (Björk et al., 2010) despite years of energetic campaigning by OA's

---

[17] A number of publishers make an explicit commitment to reduce each year's subscription/license prices to reflect the contribution of the previous year's OA fees.

most vocal advocate, Stevan Harnad, and others (http://users.ecs.soton.ac. uk/harnad/intpub.html). Various reasons for this are put forward by the researchers themselves (Thorn et al., 2009). A surprisingly high percentage simply does not know, or does not clearly understand, what open access and self-archiving are. Although a growing number of publishers allow some form of self-archiving, many authors are unaware that they are permitted to do so (Morris, 2009); others think that it is just too much effort.

Publishers initially expressed concern that self-archiving by authors ran the risk – when it reached critical mass – of providing an apparently free substitute for paid-for journal subscriptions or licenses, and thus destroying their market. Indeed, studies (such as Beckett and Inger, 2006, and Ware, 2006) showed that many librarians felt that once most of the journal literature was freely available in repositories, they would consider canceling subscriptions. However, to date this has not happened. For one thing, the proportion of articles being self-archived has remained fairly steady for a number of years (Björk et al., 2010). In addition, readers evidently prefer, whenever possible, to access the "definitive" version – that published in the journal, with the benefit of editing (Thatcher, 2011), and all the associated functionality such as links to data, cited articles, and errata or updates.

A growing majority of publishers therefore allow at least some form of self-archiving, though they may place restrictions on what version may be deposited, where it may be deposited, when it may be deposited, or the form of reference (or link) to be included to the final published version (Cox and Cox, 2008). Publishers are more likely to permit informal self-archiving by authors in either subject-based or institutional repositories (particularly if mandated by the institution or funder) than systematic archiving by the institution on behalf of all its authors, which has the potential to be much more threatening. At the current level of uptake of self-archiving, sales of journal licenses or subscriptions are perhaps unlikely to suffer, but if uptake were ever to increase substantially, that situation could change – and no one knows for sure what the "tipping point" would be.

One issue which has arisen with self-archiving is the question of what version of an article the reader may be looking at. Indeed, more than one version of an article may well be present on the Internet. Many publishers have specified which version the author may self-archive (usually a version at a prepublication stage, before value has been added by the publisher's own editing and preparation), although authors often do not clearly understand this (Morris, 2009). Useful standards for defining and referring to journal versions (www.niso.org/publications/rp/RP-8-2008.pdf) have been developed under the auspices of the US National Information Standards Agency (NISO), but while publishers may be expected to use these, it is unlikely that individual authors will ever do so. Thus, the reader may not easily be able to discover that the version he or she is looking at is not the final published version, nor to find the published version for checking and perhaps citation. In addition, the version that the author deposits may or may not be fully searchable; if it is in a proprietary format, such as PDF, search engines may not be able to index the text (or even the abstract). (For more on the "version of record" see Chapter 4, The production process.)

Of course, self-archiving itself is not free of cost. Some of the cost may be invisible, involving the time of the author in depositing the article; the bulk of the cost lies in the creation, hosting, and day-to-day maintenance of the repositories. Long-term preservation of the content of repositories also remains a major unresolved issue.

## *"Gold" open access*

Unlike "Green," "Gold" open access does seem to be on the increase. Some publishers have established themselves from the first as, or have become, OA-only publishers, several of them publishing large numbers of journals; others, including the largest commercial publishers, offer OA journals alongside their traditionally funded titles. The number of journals listed in the Directory of Open Access Journals (DOAJ) (www.doaj.org/)[18] keeps growing, and the number of articles being published under an open access model has continued to increase (Laakso and Björk, 2012, estimated that in 2011, 11% of articles indexed in Scopus were immediately available in Gold OA journals, 0.7% in hybrid journals, and a further 5% available within twelve months).

Some OA journals have rapidly become extremely prestigious; however, not all those listed by the DOAJ would survive as journals in the regular marketplace, and indeed some publish very little or have ceased publication altogether. The total number of DOAJ-listed journals remains a small percentage of the total number of journals, and so does the percentage of all articles that are published in "Gold" OA journals

---

[18] DOAJ only lists fully OA journals; "hybrid" journals are not included.

(Laakso et al., 2011, estimated that 7.7% of articles published during 2009, in journals listed in the Ulrich's database, were in journals also included in the DOAJ).

OA enables a different approach to acceptance criteria, since (unlike journals funded by reader-side subscriptions or licenses) the more papers published, the greater the revenue. Some OA journals, such as *PLoS One*, which have broad multidisciplinary subject coverage, accept all articles judged to be technically sound, and offer only the lightest possible editing; this is becoming an increasingly popular model. These journals are attracting many authors; indeed, *PLoS One* recently became the largest journal in the area of STM, in terms of the number of papers published.

A related issue is that of Open Data. Many publishers feel that it is desirable to make freely available the research data on which authors have based their findings; this makes it possible for other researchers to examine the data for themselves, and perhaps to "mine" it or combine it with other data for completely new purposes. However, while researchers seem to be keen to have unfettered access to other researchers' data, some are less enthusiastic about releasing their own (ALPSP/STM, 2006).

## *Journals today*

In November 2012, Ulrichsweb (the online version of *Ulrich's Periodicals Directory*) listed 28,903 active peer-reviewed/refereed journals; of these, 28,714 were specifically designated as academic/scholarly (Ulrichsweb, 2012). However, even this directory is not comprehensive, particularly with regard to non-English-language and open access journals, so the true total number of journals must be even higher.

In 2007, the comparable figure of active, peer-reviewed, scholarly journals was 23,588; an analysis at that time (Morris, 2007) showed that most of the 9,883 publishers listed were small – the mean number of journals per publisher was just 2.39, with the median being considerably lower. More than half of these journals were published by (or on behalf of) nonprofit organizations. About a quarter of the total were published by the four leading publishers: Elsevier, Springer, Wiley-Blackwell, and Taylor and Francis; of these four publishers' titles, just over a quarter were published on behalf of societies and other nonprofit organizations. Although, as in other industries, smaller players are regularly absorbed into larger ones, and even large ones periodically merge, new journals and

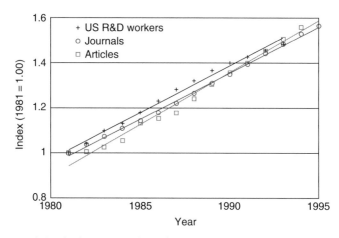

**Figure 1.4** Relationship between numbers of researchers, journals, and articles (1981–1995). Reprinted from Ware and Mabe, 2009, with the permission of STM.

journal publishers continue to appear on the scene regularly; indeed, being unhampered by any historical baggage, they are freer than others to adopt new business models and new ways of doing things.

But things are changing. The annual growth in the number of researchers, the number of journal articles they write, and the resultant growth in the number of journals in which they are published has been almost unchanged since 1665, apart from a brief spurt after World War II (Mabe, 2003 – see Figure 1.4). But now we are seeing unprecedented increases in the amount of money devoted to research and development in countries whose economies are growing rapidly, such as India and China. This is resulting not only in a steep increase in the number of journals published in those countries (many of them, in order to reach a worldwide readership, published in English), but also in an increase in the number of authors from those countries submitting their articles to journals in the USA, UK, and elsewhere. This puts new pressures on the system, not only because of the overall increase in quantity, but also because English-language articles by non-native speakers generally require more editorial intervention (and thus cost). Authors from countries where formal scholarly publication is relatively new may also be unfamiliar with Western publishing norms, for example on acknowledgment and plagiarism; some publishers are addressing this by setting up workshops in developing countries both for authors (on how to write and get published) and for journals (on how to attract papers and how to publish).

Libraries and publishers are seeing their roles changing and even converging. Publishers are having to take on some of the former role of libraries, in storing, providing access to, and preserving journals. Libraries are becoming closely involved in the creation and maintenance of institutional repositories for the work of faculty, and in digitizing and making available their own special collections, which brings them close to the traditional role of a publisher; increased demands are being placed on librarians to help authors with formal publication, too. And helping readers to navigate the ever vaster amount of available information, and to find what is really valuable to them, has become a task which may be handled by publisher, librarian, or indeed another entity entirely (think of Google!).

But being published in a well-regarded scholarly journal remains a key objective for researchers worldwide. Though the form of the journal, and the technologies which support its processes, have changed out of all recognition, the service that it provides to scholars has not.

## REFERENCES

Association of Learned and Professional Society Publishers (ALPSP) and International Association of Scientific, Technical & Medical Publishers (STM) joint position statement, 2006, *Databases, data sets and data accessibility – views and practices of scholarly publishers*, June (www.alpsp.org/Ebusiness/AboutALPSP/ALPSPStatements/Statementdetails.aspx?ID=55)

Association of Research Libraries (ARL), 1990, *ARL statistics 1988–89*, Washington, DC, Association of Research Libraries (www.arl.org/stats/annualsurveys/arlstats/preveds.shtml)

Beckett, Chris, and Simon Inger, 2006, *Self-archiving and journal subscription: co-existence or competition?*, London, Publishing Research Consortium (www.publishingresearch.net/self_archiving2.htm)

Björk, Bo-Christer, 2012, The hybrid model for open access publication of scholarly articles – a failed experiment?, *Journal of the American Society for Information Science and Technology* 63: 1496–1504 (http://dx.doi.org/10.1002/asi.22709)

Björk, Bo-Christer, Patrik Welling, Mikael Laakso, Peter Majlender, Turid Hedlund, and Guðni Guðnason, 2010, Open access to the scientific journal literature: situation 2009, *PLoS One* 5(6): e11273 (http://dx.doi.org/10.1371/journal.pone.0011273)

Bucknell, Terry, 2008, Usage statistics for Big Deals: supporting library decision-making, *Learned Publishing* 21: 198–9 (http://dx.doi.org/10.1087/095315108x323893)

Chesler, Adam, and Susan King, 2009, Tier-based pricing for institutions: a new, e-based pricing model, *Learned Publishing* 22: 42–9 (http://dx.doi.org/10.1087/095315108X378768)

CIBER, 2004, *Scholarly communication in the digital environment: what do authors want?*, London, Publishers Association (www.homepages.ucl.ac.uk/~uczciro/ciber-pa-report.pdf)

2011, *E-journals: their use, value and impact*, London, Research Information Network (www.rin.ac.uk/our-work/communicating-and-disseminating-research/e-jour nals-their-use-value-and-impact)

Cox, John, and Laura Cox, 2008, *Scholarly publishing practice 3*, Worthing, Association of Learned and Professional Society Publishers (www.alpsp.org/Ebusiness/ ProductCatalog/Product/aspx?ID=44)

Escolar, Hipólito, 1985, *Historia de las bibliotecas*, Madrid, Fundación German Sánchez Ruipérez

Grubb, Alicia M, and Steve M Easterbrook, 2011, On the lack of consensus over the meaning of openness: an empirical study, *PLoS One* 6(8): e23420 (http://dx.doi. org/10.1371/journal.pone.0023420)

Jinha, Arif E, 2010, Article 50 million: an estimate of the number of scholarly articles in existence, *Learned Publishing* 23: 258–63 (http://dx.doi.org/10.1087/20100308)

Keynote, 2011, *KeyNote Confectionery Market Report Plus 2011*, London, KeyNote (www.keynote.co.uk/market-intelligence/view/product/10421/confectionery)

King, Donald W, 2007, The cost of journal publishing: a literature review and commentary, *Learned Publishing* 20: 85–106 (http://dx.doi.org/10.1087/ 174148507X183551)

King, Donald W, Sarah Aerni, Fern Brody, Matt Herbison, and Paul Kohberger, 2004, *Comparative cost of the University of Pittsburgh electronic and print libraries collections*, Pittsburgh, Sara Fine Institute for Interpersonal Behavior and Technology (web.utk.edu/~tenopir/research/pitts/Pitt_Cost_Final.pdf)

Laakso, Mikael, and Bo-Christer Björk, 2012, Anatomy of open access publishing, *BMC Medicine* 10: 124 (http://dx.doi.org/10.1186/1741–7015–10–124)

Laakso, Mikael, Patrik Welling, Helena Bukvova, Linus Nyman, Bo-Christer Björk, and Turid Hedlund, 2011, The development of open access journal publishing from 1993 to 2009, *PLoS One* 6(6): e20961 (http://dx.doi.org/10.1371/jour nal.pone.0020961)

Mabe, Michael, 2003, The growth and number of journals, *Serials* 16: 191–7 (http:// uksg.metapress.com/content/f195g8ak0eu21muh/fulltext.pdf)

Montgomery, Carol Hansen, and Donald W King, 2002, Comparing library and user related costs of print and electronic journal collections: a first step towards a comprehensive analysis, *D-Lib Magazine* 8(2), October (www.dlib.org/dlib/ october02/montgomery/10montgomery.html)

Morris, Sally, 2007, Mapping the journal publishing landscape: how much do we know?, *Learned Publishing* 20: 299–310 (http://dx.doi.org/10.1087/095315107X239654)

2009, *Journal authors' rights: perception and reality*, London, Publishing Research Consortium (www.publishingresearch.net/author_rights.htm)

Newton, Isaac, 1676, letter to Robert Hooke, February 5, in H W Turnbull (ed.), *Correspondence of Isaac Newton*, Vol. II (1676–1687), Cambridge University Press, 1960

Okerson, Ann, and James O'Donnell (eds.), 1995, *Scholarly journals at the crossroads: a subversive proposal*, Washington, DC, Association of Research Libraries (www.arl. org/scomm/subversive/toc.html)

Outsell, 2012, *Scientific, technical & medical information 2012: market size share, forecast, and trend report*, Burlingame, CA, Outsell, Inc.

Richardson, Martin J, 1997, A system for the publication of biomedical journals in multiple formats, *Learned Publishing* 10: 221–5 (http://dx.doi.org/10.1087/09531519750146923)

Sanville, Thomas J, 2001, A method out of the madness: OhioLINK's collaborative response to the serials crisis, *Serials* 14: 163–77 (http://uksg.metapress.com/content/n1mbcw2rugk8pkj2/fulltext.pdf)

Simba Information, 2012 (in press), *Global STM Publishing 2012–2013* (personal communication, Dan Strempel, Senior Analyst)

Strickland, Peter R, Brian McMahon, and John R Helliwell, 2008, Integrating research articles and supporting data in crystallography, *Learned Publishing* 21: 63–72 (http://dx.doi.org/10.1087/095315108X248347)

Swan, Alma, 2002, *Authors and electronic publishing*, Worthing, Association of Learned and Professional Society Publishers (www.alpsp.org/Ebusiness/ProductCatalog/Product.aspx?ID=30)

Tenopir, Carol, Donald W King, Sheri Edwards, and Lei Wu, 2009, Electronic journals and changes in scholarly article seeking and reading patterns, *ASLIB Proceedings* 61: 5–32 (http://dx.doi.org/10.1108/00012530910932267)

Thatcher, Sanford, 2011, Copyediting's role in an open access world, *Against the Grain* 23: 30–4 (www.psupress.org/news/pdf/fea_Thatcher_v23-2.pdf)

Thorn, Sue, Sally Morris, and Ron Fraser, 2009, Learned societies and open access: key results from surveys of bioscience societies and researchers, *Serials* 22: 39–48 (http://dx.doi.org/10.1629/2239)

Ulrichsweb, 2012, *Ulrichsweb.com™*, Copyright © 2012 Seattle, WA, ProQuest LLC, 2011, all rights reserved (www.ulrichsweb.com) (accessed November 5, 2012)

Ware, Mark, 2006, *ALPSP survey of librarians on factors in journal cancellation*, Worthing, Association of Learned and Professional Society Publishers (www.alpsp.org/Ebusiness/ProductCatalog/Product.aspx?ID=26)

Ware, Mark, and Michael Mabe, 2009, *The STM report*, London, International Association of Scientific, Technical & Medical Publishers (www.stm-assoc.org/2009_10_13_MWC_STM_Report.pdf)

## FURTHER READING

Page, Gillian, Robert Campbell, and Jack Meadows, 1997, *Journal publishing*, Cambridge University Press

Tenopir, Carol, and Donald King, 2000, *Towards electronic journals*, Alexandria, VA, Special Libraries Association

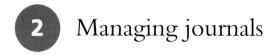

# 2 Managing journals

## Introduction – what is management?

Management is the process of gathering a team of people to work together in order to accomplish a desired goal both effectively and efficiently with available resources. The effective manager does not need to know every detail of the process involved in attaining the goal; rather, he or she must know what needs to be done, who knows how to do it, what resources are needed, and how to get everyone to work together to get the job done.

It has been said that we learn to manage by the way we have been managed. While we all may consciously emulate aspects of the style of managers we admire and avoid the style of those we do not, it is important to recognize that we may have unconsciously absorbed other aspects of their management approach, of which we are unaware. Anyone aspiring to management should consider taking a basic management course, or at least read a basic management text (see "Further reading" at the end of this chapter), in order to gain an overview of what is entailed in managing a project and to be exposed to a variety of management methods.

While much has been written about the science of management, there is a large component of art involved as well. Some aspects can be taught, but others are best learned by observation and practice. One of these is the ability to recognize the strengths (and weaknesses) of the individuals in the team; another consists of learning how best to get each person to "buy in" to the goal and work together with the rest of the team. Two additional interpersonal skills are essential: (1) knowing when to leave someone alone to do a job and when to intervene to get the job done and (2) knowing how to be an effective buffer between your staff and your own manager, allowing each to concentrate on the task at hand and not to interfere unduly with each other. These skills are not limited to an individual's direct reports. Journal publishing involves many different actors, both inside and outside the publishing house, and the effective manager must be able to get all of them to work together.[1]

Note that this chapter is geared primarily to the in-house individual who is directly responsible for managing one or more journals, whether his or her title is Commissioning/Acquisitions Editor,[2] Managing Editor, Publisher, or something else.

## Publishing policy

Policy is needed to guide decision-making by identifying what an enterprise does and why. It is formulated at the senior governance level of an organization and implemented by senior executives, who translate policy into short- and long-term strategies for who needs to do what, how it is to be done and when, and what resources will be made available, getting more and more detailed as the strategy moves further into the enterprise to the tactical level. The main issues that need to be addressed by a publishing policy are what is to be published, how, and why.

### What is to be published: the content

Does the publisher concentrate on any given subject area, or is it open to a wide range of potential subjects? If concentrating on a specific subject area, how broad is the scope of that area and how would the intersection with related areas be addressed? Is the purpose to cover specific segments (e.g., basic research) or to cover the entire field (in medical parlance, from lab bench to bedside)? A society publisher may limit its coverage to the interests of its members.[3] A commercial publisher may cover one or a few

---

[1] While how one gets the various departments and personalities involved to work together is beyond the scope of this book, the reader might also review some of the "management" trade books that gain popular attention. While primarily light and anecdotal in nature, these books do offer useful commentary on contemporary organizational structures and management issues. Examples include Parkinson's Law in the 1950s, the Peter Principle in the 1970s, and the Dilbert Principle in the 1990s. (See "Further reading" at the end of the chapter.)

[2] Commissioning/Acquisitions Editors are sometimes known as Developmental Editors; see Chapter 3, Editing, for more on the various types of "Editor," both at the publisher and in the Editorial office of the journal.

[3] Although some large societies may offer publishing services to societies in related fields as well.

broad subject areas (e.g., psychology), or may cover a multitude of subjects in science, technology, and medicine (STM) and/or the humanities and social sciences (HSS). A University Press, depending on its size, may focus on a few areas of strength (possibly those with local faculty expertise) or a wider range.

### How the content is to be published: the medium

While the subject of this handbook is the scholarly and professional journal, whether in print or electronic form, many publishers also publish books (monographs and trade books), magazines, and other information products (e.g., databases) in the same or related subject areas. The policy guides how these different types of publications balance each other and how resources are allocated among them. Policy will also guide product development.

### Why it is being published helps determine the what and how

The "why" usually is a combination of several factors. Making a surplus of revenue over expenses is not limited to the for-profit sector, just as serving the growth of a field is not limited to the not-for-profit sector.

A for-profit publisher needs to provide a return to investors. It can do so by a conservative publication policy, holding off on investment in new technology and platforms until others have led the way. Or it can adopt a more active stance, developing its own new platforms and features in order to dominate its chosen areas and attract a greater market share. A nonprofit publisher may publish a journal as a service to the field or, in the case of a society, also to produce a surplus which helps subsidize the society and its activities.

Knowing the publishing policy, and how it filters through the organization and is implemented, is just as important as knowing the financial targets and how they are applied (see Chapter 8, Journal finances). How they work together is also important. Consider the implications in the following areas:

- *Staffing*: What are the staffing levels and are they appropriate to the volume of work, both current and planned? Is there a tendency to hold headcounts steady as the volume of work increases? Are there "trigger events" that must occur to justify adding staff when needed? How do these vary for different job functions? What is the policy regarding the interim utilization of contract workers[4] or freelancers to cover shortages of full-time staff?

- *Marketing and sales*: Is this area properly valued – or is it the first line to be reduced when budgets need to be trimmed?
- *Customer relations and support*: Is this recognized as part of every employee's job?
- *Technical support services*: With the preponderance of electronic publishing products, what level of technical support does the publisher provide, both to in-house staff and to its "electronic" customers?
- *Research and development*: Does the publisher have an active R&D program in-house for product development? Is the program reactive, evaluating what others have already done, or proactive, seeking to develop new approaches and features? Is the tendency to buy or to build the necessary software platforms?
- *Financial resources*: Is there money available to invest in growing the list – for product development, journal launches (start-up costs) or purchases?
- *Intellectual property*: How does the publisher strike a balance between controlling the distribution of content and being responsive to the changing needs of authors and readers? For example, what are the policies with regard to self-archiving, institutional repositories, and transfer of copyright vs license to publish?
- *Contingency planning*: What plans are in place to deal with a disruption in service to online customers (authors and subscribers)? Are mirror systems in place? Have third-party dark archives been established (e.g., Portico, OCLC, CLOCKSS) or does the publisher participate in a distributed effort (e.g., LOCKSS)? Recent events both natural and man-made highlight the need for disaster-recovery plans to be in place for the enterprise itself as well as for its primary vendors.

---

[4] Full- and part-time staff are included in the headcount while contract workers and freelancers usually are not included. Generally, freelancers work off site as independent contractors; labor laws in some jurisdictions limit the amount of time they can spend on site in the publisher's office. Contract workers are engaged for a specific project or function and for a set time period under a written contract that may also provide some of traditional employee benefits. They may work on site or off.

## Managing the list

The "list" in this context can refer to the publisher's entire list of journals or to that segment handled by an individual Commissioning or Managing Editor. The majority of publishers have only a small number of journals (see Chapter 1, Introduction to journals). For larger publishers, however, the overall list may be diverse but ideally would contain enough "mass" in each of the areas covered to allow synergies to exist between titles, enabling efficient cooperative marketing efforts. If both books and journals are published, the subject coverage of these product lines should be complementary, permitting further efficiencies in marketing and sales as well as achieving a greater market share.

## Growing the list

In the present environment, a publisher cannot simply maintain a list of titles at their present levels of content or revenue. The volume of scholarly research is ever increasing, generating more content worthy of publication (see Chapter 1, Introduction to journals). If the list does not grow in response to the increased volume of research, authors – and readers – will shift to other journals, reducing the publisher's share of the market and negatively impacting the revenues needed to sustain the program. The list needs to grow just to maintain its current share of the market.

Growth can be accomplished by developing existing titles, by adding new ones, or by adopting new approaches to the list as a whole:

- Journals can increase the amount of content published, with prices adjusted to cover the added cost.
- Publisher-owned journals can become affiliated with societies in the field, adding member subscriptions and expanding their community of authors and reviewers.
- Journals can raise their rejection rate, thus increasing the quality of their content, raising their profile with prospective authors, generating more citations, and attracting more subscription income.[5]

---

[5] This strategy would not be as attractive for an OA journal, whose income is tied to the number of published papers.

- If the journal's content grows rapidly, a journal may split into multiple sections devoted to the various subdisciplines or give rise to the launch of a new title (both sometimes known as "twigging").
- The publisher can launch additional titles, either in new or developing subjects or where there is new activity at the intersection of existing areas.
- The publisher can purchase titles from another publisher.
- The publisher can publish journals on behalf of learned societies.
- The list may be prestigious and/or large enough to make an attractive package for licensing to larger libraries and consortia.
- The publisher can explore other business models (e.g., OA).
- Subsidiary income streams, such as pay-per-view downloads, sponsored supplements, etc., can be developed (see Chapter 9, Subsidiary income).

While the above tactics focus on growing a list of titles or growing revenue, at the same time it is important to defend the existing list against the competition:

- Current journals must remain attractive to customers, delivering quality content regularly and on time to the reader, and keeping authors happy with prompt peer-review and publication times.
- Journals published on behalf of societies must be well managed, and communications and relationships with the societies must be properly attended to, so that contract renewal is assured.
- Journal Editors-in-Chief must be attuned to developments in their fields.
- The editorial areas covered must be monitored to ensure that the publisher's journals continue to address the changing needs of those in the field.
- The competition must be monitored to make sure that the publisher's journals provide at least as good, if not better, content and service to customers.
- The online publishing platform must be reviewed and upgraded periodically to remain current technologically, with emphasis placed on adding features that users want (not just what the developer thinks is "cool").
- Systems supporting online submission and peer review, content processing, fulfillment, etc., should also be reviewed and upgraded periodically to maintain currency and efficiency.

And, contradictory as it may sound, periodic pruning of the list is advised:

- Titles may be merged where fields are shrinking.
- The publisher may not wish to renew a contract with a society if the editorial policy or focus of either party changes.
- Journals that are underperforming, or that no longer fit with the editorial focus of the list, may be sold or even closed down.

## Managing relationships and maintaining communications

One of the most important roles as an in-house Editor managing a list is to actively monitor the status of each journal on a regular basis and to communicate regularly, not just with the in-house staff, but also with the journal Editor and any society partners or other sponsors. (See Chapter 3, Editing, and Chapter 10, Contract publishing, for more on these relationships and contractual arrangements.)

Regular telephone contact with each journal's Editor-in-Chief is important in order to monitor the front end of the operation and to identify problems and/or opportunities early. It is important to provide support for an annual Editorial Board meeting, usually in conjunction with a related society meeting that most Board members would normally attend. Such a meeting offers an opportunity for both the Publisher and the Editor-in-Chief to report to the Board on the health of the journal, discuss planned developments and publication policy, and solicit input on developments in the field, marketing opportunities, and problems or opportunities that need to be addressed. The occasion can also serve to recognize the work of members rotating off the Board, and to introduce new Board or staff members to the group. For larger journals, inclusion of representatives from the production and marketing groups at the Editorial Board meeting can be quite effective. (See Chapter 3, Editing, for more on the Editorial Board.)

In the case of contract publishing for a society, regular contact with the society officers, the Publication Committee Chair, and the society's management group, if any, is also vital. This will ensure that any problems that arise are addressed – and resolved – promptly and efficiently. In addition to attending the Editorial Board meeting, it is important to attend the annual meeting of the society and meet with current and incoming officers, present a comprehensive publisher's report to the appropriate Board or Committee, and review marketing and financial plans as necessary. An essential goal of this multipronged contact approach is to ensure that the publisher's message is getting through to all the right parties, and that a blockage created by any one individual does not jeopardize the future relationship with the society.

## Managing existing journals

A journal has a definite growth pattern. No journal springs fully formed from a publisher, like Athena from the head of Zeus. It will move from conception through birth, early development, and adolescence, evolving into a long period of mature growth. Some journals appear to go on forever while others eventually come to a close. It is important to recognize where a journal is in its life, if it is to be properly managed and to achieve its full potential.

In its early years, a journal will require significant editorial and marketing resources to develop its community of authors and readers. As this community grows and stabilizes, these efforts can be scaled back, but must be continually monitored to assure prompt responses to external or internal influences in the field (e.g., rapid growth in one subdiscipline, collapse of funding in another, competition from a new title). Even a well-respected mature journal, highly ranked in its field, can face challenges. The most recent of such "mid-life crises" were the significant changes wrought by online publishing in the late 1990s and the subsequent growth of the open access journal model in the 2000s. We will look at some of these factors below.

### Growing a journal's content with the field

As a field grows, so will the number of submissions to the journal. For a subscription-based journal, the Editor-in-Chief can tighten the peer-review criteria to keep the number of accepted papers within the agreed page budget for the journal, but this can only be a temporary measure.[6] If the journal needs to grow in size to accommodate the increase in

---

[6] This will also have the effect of improving overall quality. However, if submission criteria are tightened too much, there is the risk of their becoming viewed as arbitrary or unrealistic by authors and having a negative impact both on submissions and on the perception of the journal.

publishable submissions, there are several options available, each of which has associated costs that must be factored into the pricing of the journal if margins are to be maintained.

The journal could be redesigned to increase marginally the amount of copy on each page in the print edition, for example by changing to a more compact typeface, decreasing page margins, and/or increasing the trim size of the page.

The number of pages in the volume could be increased by adding pages to each issue or increasing the number of issues per volume[7] (or both). The costs associated with added content will scale linearly for the online edition. For the print edition, however, given the same increase in total content per volume, increasing the size of the printed issues is less costly than increasing the number of issues, because of the additional printing press setup and mailing costs for each issue. Nevertheless, it is often easier to justify increased subscription rates to cover an increased number of issues than it is to explain an increase based on extra pages per issue (which are not so obvious) – either way, the total number of articles will increase and the price per article can easily be measured. If the journal accepts advertising, added issues provide an opportunity to increase the amount of advertising space sold.[8]

The above assumes that the journal has both print and electronic editions and that any additional pages are added to both. Another possibility is to create a two-tiered structure for accepted papers, selecting one tier to appear "full text" in both print and electronic editions and another tier to appear in full online, with only the article titles and abstracts in the print edition.

In the case of a full or hybrid open access journal (discussed in more detail below), the increase in accepted papers would be fully or partially supported by the author-side publication fees (assuming that they have been set at an appropriate level). What still needs to be considered, however, is whether existing systems for submission, peer review, and online publication are robust enough to support the increase in volume.

---

[7] Care should be taken, when increasing the number of issues of a print journal, to ensure that the increase in available copy is real and not the result of a transient spike in submissions. It has been known for a journal to increase frequency to accommodate more copy and then have to scramble to fill the extra issues.

[8] The increase in advertising revenue is usually not linear, given that advertising budgets are fixed in advance and may take a year or more to adjust to the higher frequency.

## Growing a journal's circulation with the field

While one would expect the circulation of a subscription-based journal to grow as the size of the field it covers grows, this is not always the case. A growing field will often tend to see an increase in the number of individual researchers and scholars without any corresponding increase in the number of institutions employing them – or in the number of libraries willing to subscribe. Consequently, growing the institutional subscriber base for a mature journal is difficult, with continuous marketing efforts needed to keep existing institutional subscriptions from being siphoned off by competing journals.

Potential for growth does exist among individual subscribers, but this varies depending on a number of factors. On the whole, HSS journals are less expensive than STM titles (see Chapter 8, Journal finances) and thus the individual subscription rates are more attractive to individuals. Furthermore, while online access may be available for these journals from the institution, the length and discursive nature of many HSS articles makes them much easier to read on paper than on-screen, encouraging humanities scholars to take a personal subscription.[9] On the STM side, fields where the number of researchers is small compared with the number of practitioners (clinical medicine and engineering, for instance) also offer potential for individual subscriptions. However, in this case, the regular structure of most STM articles[10] makes them much more amenable to online search and access than HSS articles. In both cases, it may be possible to increase paid circulation by exploring a relationship with related societies – either a formal one, with all members of the society becoming subscribers, or an informal one, simply offering members a reduced rate.[11]

In the case of an open access journal, "circulation" as such is not a meaningful term. In its place, download statistics provide a measure of the journal's usage and, indirectly, distribution. High download data can be used to attract additional authors; in turn, their publication fees provide

---

[9] For a discussion of journal use by faculty, see King et al., 2003.

[10] Many STM articles follow the "IMRAD" structure (Introduction, Materials & Methods, Results, and Discussion) and a more succinct writing style that makes articles easier to search and scan than the less standardized humanities formats.

[11] A formal arrangement would usually entail a lower member rate than an informal one, but would usually bring the benefits of both an increased number of subscribers and the reduced handling costs of a bulk order and payment.

support for the journal. (See the discussion of the "virtuous circle" in Chapter 6, Marketing and sales.)

## Improving editorial impact

The best way to improve the editorial quality of a journal is to publish better papers. Unfortunately, identifying what papers will have a significant impact when published is not an easy task. This is further complicated in the early years of a journal, when copy flow may be tenuous and there may be a tendency to publish papers that are "acceptable" but not outstanding, in order to get the issues out on schedule and establish the title. Care should be taken to make sure that the Editor-in-Chief is cognizant of this problem, and takes steps to encourage better submissions and to raise review standards to an appropriate level.

Publication of comprehensive review articles summarizing the current "state of the art" in a specific area is a useful means to raise the impact of a journal. Properly prepared, these serve the discipline by providing an evaluative summary of the field with references to the primary sources, and provide scholars with a single reference to cite in setting the context for their own work. The drawbacks of a review article are that it must generally be invited (and often paid for), the author must be carefully chosen, and the review will generally take a lot of time to prepare.

In addition, ancillary products can be developed which drive traffic and usage to the journal. One example of such a product is a "subject portal," a website offering a "one-stop shop" for information about a given subject (as, for example, Bone and Joint (www.boneandjoint.org.uk) from the British *Journal of Bone and Joint Surgery*). It may comprise a number of online resources such as journals, books, and databases, as well as a user-friendly navigation system to access all this information along with links to various other online resources.

### Increasing financial return on a journal

The financial return on a subscription-based journal can be increased in several ways. Prices can be increased above the rate of increase in costs, but this runs the risk of eroding the subscriber base unless there are tangible (to the purchaser) benefits in return for the higher prices (e.g., more articles or features). Costs can be reduced by periodically conducting production audits to maximize efficiencies, and reviewing bids from other suppliers to make sure prices are competitive. Marketing efforts may also be able to increase paid circulation.

For an OA journal, similar strategies apply. The author publication fee can be increased, but must remain competitive with other OA titles in the field. Institutional memberships can be solicited, gaining up-front income in exchange for discounts or waivers on fees for authors from the sponsoring institutions. And, of course, marketing efforts aimed at increasing submissions are important (see Chapter 6, Marketing and sales).

## To print or not to print

With the growth of electronic publishing platforms there has been much discussion of the "death of print," and the potential cost saving that may arise from eliminating the print edition. However, while there would be savings from eliminating the cost of paper, printing, binding, and mailing,[12] the costs of content acquisition and preparation would still exist, as well as the cost of maintaining and continually improving the electronic platform.

As the number of print subscriptions to a journal decreases, the average cost of printing each issue increases owing to the fixed costs of traditional printing press setup and make-ready. As the printrun decreases to a few hundred, it may be more economical to shift to a print-on-demand process, which is usually more cost-effective for runs of less than 250 copies.

Before making a decision to eliminate the print edition of a journal, it is necessary to research how the market would react. There is still a market for print in various countries and in various disciplines – and not just with those who fear a future loss of electronic access. If a decision is made to eliminate the print edition, provision may need to be made for producing an annual print compilation for these customers.

### Replacing the Editor-in-Chief

The Editor-in-Chief is the public face of the journal, and will usually already be in place when the publisher's in-house Commissioning or

---

[12] The "savings" that can be realized from discontinuing a print edition in favor of online-only publication vary with a number of factors (number of issues and pages printed, number of color illustrations, printrun, geographic distribution of print subscribers, etc.). They have been estimated to average 15–20% of costs (Tenopir and King, 2000).

Managing Editor is assigned responsibility for managing an existing journal. Difficulties may arise if the incumbent Editor-in-Chief's performance is not satisfactory, in light of either the needs of the journal or the publisher's plans for its future. If efforts to remedy the situation have not succeeded, it will be necessary to seek a replacement. Provided that a good level of communication has been maintained with the Editor-in-Chief, he or she should be aware that a change is coming and not be surprised that the contract is not renewed or that it may be ended prematurely. Special care should be taken in managing this kind of editorial transition, to ensure that there is no ill will and that the reputation of the journal is not negatively impacted by the transition.

It is essential to seek advice on an Editor-in-Chief's replacement both internally, from relevant colleagues commissioning in the field, and externally, from the Editorial Board and from the Commissioning/Managing Editor's own connections in the field. If the Editor-in-Chief is retiring voluntarily, he or she will usually also have some candidates to suggest. The transition must be carefully managed, as outlined in Chapter 3, Editing.

### Modifying the journal's business model

With the growth of the Open Access movement and the propagation of OA mandates by various government and funding agencies, many journal publishers have adopted a hybrid business model for their subscription-based journals, giving authors of accepted papers the option to pay a publication fee to make their papers open access on publication. This option is viable in fields (such as biomedicine) that have sufficient funding to provide authors with the necessary fees. However, while the number of "Gold" OA journals continues to increase (see Chapter 1, Introduction to journals), the number of authors who choose the OA option in hybrid journals remains relatively low (Oxford University Press, 2010). (When a hybrid journal is published both in print and online, the OA articles usually appear in both editions.)

If a journal is published only in an online edition and the field is supportive of OA (i.e., funding exists and authors are willing), the publisher may consider converting from a subscription-based or hybrid model to a fully OA business model, or even launching a fully OA journal as a complement to the existing subscription-based journal. How successful this strategy would be depends on the strength of the journal's brand compared with the existing OA journals in the field. Such a move should be undertaken with care, particularly if the publisher has not been perceived as receptive to OA in the past.

## Starting a journal

The Biblical admonition "of making many books there is no end; and much study is a weariness of the flesh" (Ecclesiastes 12:12, KJV) applies just as well to periodicals. Nevertheless, new specialty journals continue to be launched to meet the expanding needs of the ever-growing scholarly and professional community, despite the plethora of existing journals and the competition for limited funds on both the author and the reader side.

A proposal for a new journal may come from an outside source (an individual academic or a society's Request for Proposal [RFP]), or the idea may germinate from a regular review of developments in the fields covered by the publisher (book Acquisitions Editors, as well as current journal Editors-in-Chief, are good sources of ideas). If it comes from outside, the proposal will generally be fleshed out, but there may be strings attached (the proposer wants to be the Editor-in-Chief, the society wants to own it).

### What to ask when considering a new journal proposal

A new journal launch requires a significant commitment of resources and is not to be undertaken lightly. The following is a list of questions and points to address to establish both the nature of the new journal and its environment.

### *Why launch this journal?*

- What is special about this proposal?
- What is wrong with/missing from the existing journals?
- Is there a need for a new journal for this content? Why can't it be accommodated in existing titles?
- Are current journals too broad, or do they have too large a backlog of accepted papers?
- Where do authors currently publish work in this subject area?

## *Who is proposing this project?*

- Internal initiative – either from in-house staff or suggestion from journal Editor.
- External proposal from an individual (need to evaluate proposer's affiliation and curriculum vitae).
- Proposal from a sponsoring society.

## *What does the proposer want?*

- Financial return.
- Individual may want to be the Editor-in-Chief.
- Society may want to own the journal.

## *Description of the new journal*

- Tentative title (is it too narrow/broad or too close to that of an existing journal?).[13]
- Aims and scope (one to two pages), detailing the purpose of the new publication and what topics would be covered (and, if relevant, what would not be covered).
- Types of content: original research articles, review articles, letters, book/other media reviews, conference proceedings, etc.
- Suggested/proposed Editor(s)-in-Chief and affiliations(s).
- Editorial Board: composition and role of the Board (are they work-horses or window dressing?).[14] List of potential members (and whether any have been informally or formally approached).
- Editorial operations: who would oversee the review process? What kind of peer-review system would be employed (open, closed, single or double blind)?

---

[13] See, for example, the FAQ *What's in a name? Presentation guidelines for serial publications* (www.loc.gov/issn/whats.html).

[14] Some Editorial Boards are composed of members who actively work to solicit papers and form the majority of the reviewers. In other cases, the Board is composed of a number of well-known names whose presence on the Board serves to lend stature to the journal and to attract submissions simply by their association with the title.

- List of fifteen to twenty previously published papers (with bibliographic information) that would have been appropriate for the new journal.
- List of fifteen to twenty topics or "dream papers" that would be appropriate for the new journal.

## *Where will the content come from?*

- Who are the potential authors and how large is that pool?
- Where do potential authors publish now?
- What features are important to potential authors (e.g., speed of review and publication, need for enhanced online features)?
- How important is abstracting and indexing (A&I) coverage to the authors? (New titles are normally not indexed until at least a complete volume has appeared for evaluation.)
- Have papers already been invited/promised for the journal?
- How many papers do the proposers expect to be submitted annually? And what percentage of these would be accepted?

## *Who would read/buy this journal?*

- Who would need to read this journal?
- What number and kind of libraries or other institutions would be potential subscribers (if subscription-based)?
- What number and kind of individuals would be potential subscribers?
- What is the geographic spread of the target market?
- Are there any professional or scholarly societies that might formally or informally adopt the journal?
- To the members of what organizations and professional or scholarly societies should marketing information and calls for papers be sent in order to reach individuals who might contribute and/or subscribe?

## *What is the funding environment?*

- Is there a preprint or OA culture in this field?
- Is funding available to support author-side publication fees?
- Are there existing OA or hybrid journals in the field?

## *What is the competitive environment?*

- What are the existing journals in the field (with details of ranking, circulation, frequency, and price if available)?
- How well do they meet the author/reader needs?
- What sort of competition, for both contributors and subscribers, would they pose?
- What other publication channels are regularly used by this author pool (e.g., books, working papers, institutional repositories, etc.)?

## *Media*

- Is a print edition necessary? Is an online edition sufficient?
- Are there any preferences for the print edition (frequency, trim size, design points, etc.)?
- Are there any preferences for the online edition (e.g., publication by "issue" or as individual articles are ready)?

## *Subsidiary income*

- Is there potential for supplements to the journal? Would these be sponsored?
- Is there potential for advertising income?

### Evaluation

The primary question to address is how well the scope of the proposed journal fits within the existing list and the publisher's current plans for expansion or growth. If it is not a fit, move on to another project. The next two questions to address are bound together: is there really a need for a new publication in this area and, if so, is the need great enough to support the launch of a new journal financially?

Determining the need for a new title requires an analysis of both the proposed scope and the market (see also Chapter 6, Marketing and sales). While in-house expertise in the subject area will be helpful, most proposals tend to be very specialized in scope and it is important to seek advice from outside experts – in effect, subjecting the journal proposal to peer review. As with the review of an article, in addition to seeking an overall recommendation to publish or not, it is important to ask the reviewers to respond to specific questions about the journal as it has been proposed (Does it fill a need? How would it compare with the existing journals? Would there be enough submissions to support it? Who might read it? What changes might they suggest? Is there a similar title in development elsewhere? etc.). As a new journal is a long-term financial commitment, more reviews are usually sought than for a single book project – at least four or five completed reviews (which may mean sending out ten or more requests).[15] To help develop the project, some of the issues raised in these reviews may be shared (anonymously, of course) with the proposers.

If the general subject area is already covered by the publisher's list, existing market research will need to be fine-tuned to address the specialized nature of the proposal. Properly phrased searches of subject databases can help to quantify how many papers are published within the proposed scope and in which journals they appear. Data about these journals from the *Journal Citation Reports* (impact factors, number of items published, citation half-life, etc. – see Chapter 5, Journal metrics) will help to give a clearer picture of the environment (as will data on societies and associations in the field). Circulation data may be difficult to obtain, but unit sales data for books in the field may be helpful.

As the need and market data are clarified, the parameters of the journal (media, extent, business model) will need to be determined and refined (see detailed discussion in Chapter 8, Journal finances). Subscription price data from existing journals, divided by the number of items published annually, will give an idea of the going "price per article" which, coupled with in-house pricing strategy, will help determine initial subscription rates. If the journal is to be fully OA or a hybrid OA/subscription title, data on existing OA author publication fees, coupled with an analysis of current costs, will help to decide on the appropriate author fees.

Estimating the size of the market for a new journal, how many members of the various segments will subscribe (or have access to author-side funds, in the case of an OA model), and how long it will take to achieve those numbers, is a mixture of art and science. Past experience with prior launches of similar titles will help to provide a baseline, but must be tempered with informed speculation as to how the market is evolving.

---

[15] It is customary to provide a small honorarium to these reviewers and, as a courtesy, to advise them of the ultimate decision.

With constrained budgets (of which a large proportion may be tied up in bundles and consortia packages), library decisions to acquire subscriptions to new titles are taking longer.[16] In general, circulation for a new subscription-based title will generally be low in the first year, grow slowly in the subsequent years with hopes of reaching a financially viable level by year five, and (as noted in Chapter 8, Journal finances) it will generally take several more years before the journal recoups the losses of the early years. In the case of a new OA journal being added to an existing online platform, the financial risks are lower, but it may still take several years to build up a sufficient author community to support the ongoing existence of the journal.[17]

The parameters of the journal – its subscription rates and circulation projections (or OA fee and projected percentage acceptance rate) – will then be input to the publisher's financial model for new launches. The model will most likely go through several refinement iterations until the financial projections coalesce with internal targets. (See Tables 8.6 through 8.9 and the accompanying discussion in Chapter 8, Journal finances.) The model must include realistic costs for Editorial office support (including start-up costs), adequate marketing outlay (heavier investment in the early years), any requisite return to the proposer/ owner, and an informed evaluation of the impact on overheads. The formulae incorporated in the model must be accurate within the range of the journal's parameters and adjust revenues and costs properly as parameters are tweaked.[18]

Concurrent with all this must be the identification and evaluation of qualified candidates for the journal Editor-in-Chief and the Editorial Board (external proposals usually come complete with a candidate). The Editor-in-Chief of a new journal must both be well known in the field and have sufficient stature effectively to solicit contributions to the journal

---

[16] Although inclusion in "Big Deals" and similar packages will help.

[17] If the new journal is the first online publication for the publisher, the investment in the online platform – whether internally developed or from a third party – will add significantly to the start-up costs.

[18] For example, models built to project print-related costs for journals within a specific range of circulation may not work if the circulation deviates above or below the range. Some elements may scale linearly, but others (such as the need to shift from a sheet-fed to a web press) will change drastically as certain benchmarks are reached. In addition, inflation will affect different lines at different rates.

(and must be sufficiently experienced to understand the amount of work involved in a new launch). (See Chapter 3, Editing, for more about the Editor-in-Chief and Editorial Board.)

Each publisher will have its own formal internal protocols for reviewing proposals to launch new titles and deciding whether to go ahead. Not all viable proposals are approved. Another proposal with a higher or more immediate return may be preferred, or there may simply not be enough resources (cash or staff) to undertake all the proposals under consideration.

### The launch process

Once a decision is made to launch a new journal, the Editor-in-Chief has been appointed, and all contracts have been signed, it is important to schedule a formal meeting involving representatives of all relevant departments to distribute firm information about the title, review what needs to be done prior to publication, assign responsibility for each task, identify critical events and sequences, and determine a timetable for completion (see Box 2.1 for a starter list of topics). Many of these tasks will need to be carried out concurrently, while others require a specific sequence: the initial announcement of the journal to libraries and subscription agents should include the ISSN,[19] which must therefore be applied for at the earliest possible stage (print and electronic editions must each have their own ISSN). A Call for Papers[20] should include the Instructions for Contributors (sometimes called Instructions to Authors) (Box 2.2),[21] and the online submission system should be up and running, ready to process papers. Once a journal design has been determined, elements of it should be incorporated into marketing efforts to help build the journal brand.

---

[19] The International Standard Serial Number (ISSN) is the standard international identifier for serials such as journals and is administered through a network of eighty-eight National Centers (see www.issn.org). Given that a journal may have several editions and thus several ISSNs, a new identifier, the ISSN-L, has been introduced as a unique identifier for the journal in all its editions. See Box 4.2 in Chapter 4, The production process, for more on the ISSN and how to obtain one.

[20] See discussion in Chapter 6, Marketing and sales.

[21] An examination of the Instructions for Contributors for similar journals in the same subject area is often useful to identify relevant style points to address.

**Box 2.1** Some items to assign, address, and/or schedule at a formal kick-off meeting for a new journal launch

- Identify who will be the primary contact from each of the various internal departments, and whether these individuals would have direct contact with the Editor-in-Chief and/or society sponsor or would go through the in-house Managing/Commissioning Editor (e.g., marketing and production would need direct contact but finance and fulfillment might not).
- Meet with the Editor-in-Chief to get his or her input on marketing, editorial, and production issues.
- Identify the journal "brand" and how it is to relate to that of the publisher.
- Set the date for publication of the first issue (this may need to coincide with a related society or professional meeting).
- Obtain the relevant bibliographic identifiers (ISSNs for print and online editions, ISSN-L, DOI prefix – see Box 4.2 in Chapter 4, The production process) and communicate to the relevant entities and databases (e.g., CrossRef).
- Issue an announcement of the journal via relevant media (direct mail, online discussion lists, email campaigns, etc.) to the targeted author, institutional, individual, and society markets as well as to subscription agents (if subscription-based).
- Prepare Instructions for Contributors in consultation with the Editor-in-Chief (see Box 2.2 below), and customize the requisite forms (e.g., Copyright Transfer or License to Publish – see Chapter 11, Copyright and other legal aspects).
- Issue a Call for Papers (see Chapter 6, Marketing and sales).
- Design the journal cover and page layout for the print edition, and home page and format(s) for the online version.
- Confirm vendors for all outsourced work, communicate specifications, and confirm prices if there have been any changes in specifications since the initial bid.
- Assign in-house staff and identify out-of-house freelance or contract staff as needed.
- Establish production schedules, including deadlines for receipt of accepted copy, and communicate these to the Editor-in-Chief (note that added time should always be built into the schedule for the first issue, to cover unforeseen eventualities).

**Box 2.1** (continued)

• Complete journal-specific setups for various internal department systems and databases (e.g., production workflow, fulfillment, finance, and marketing).
• Complete journal-specific setups for external or third-party systems (e.g., online submission and peer-review system, electronic platform if outsourced, etc.).

**Box 2.2** Items to include in the Instructions for Contributors

• A statement of the scope of the journal (subject areas to be covered, intended readers).
• The types of article that will be considered (research articles, letters, book reviews, etc.).
• The type of peer review (single blind, double blind, and/or open) and to which submissions it applies.
• The format for submission (paper or electronic; specify acceptable file formats for both text and artwork).
• The preferred style to follow in preparing the submission (preferably specify a standard existing style guide such as the *Chicago manual of style*, the *APA style guide*, or *ICMJE uniform requirements for manuscripts submitted to biomedical journals*; include sample model references and figure and table citations, and note any preferred abbreviation style).
• What forms must be included with the submission (Copyright Transfer/License to Publish, conflict of interest, permissions, human or animal subject protocols).
• Whether there are any mandatory or optional fees associated with submission or publication (e.g., whether color or page charges are levied, and if so on what basis; whether an author-side publication fee is required [OA journal] or optional [hybrid journal]).
• Where submissions are to be sent (postal address, email, or website).
• Whom to contact with queries about submitted papers.
• The procedure for proof correction.
• Journal policy on Copyright Transfer or License to Publish.
• Journal policy on self-archiving (what version, if any, may be deposited, when, and where, and under what conditions – e.g., a link to the published version).

It is essential to circulate formal minutes of the launch meeting and to schedule regular follow-up meetings to monitor progress and, if necessary, revise deadlines. Challenges may arise if submissions are running light or late, or if the content includes unplanned elements which need to be designed and specified. After the first issue is published, it is equally essential to schedule a meeting to review formally what went well and not so well, and to modify future actions in response.

The "launch" process does not end with the publication of the first issue. It continues through the marketing and renewal cycles for the first few volumes, until the journal brand has been established.

## Acquiring an existing journal

This section deals with the question of acquiring ownership of an existing journal from another publisher. The topic of contract publishing – publishing a journal on behalf of another party, usually a scholarly or professional society or association, which owns the title – is discussed in Chapter 10, Contract publishing.

While one can identify journals owned by other publishers that would be useful additions to the publisher's list and make an offer for them, it is more common to be approached with a (generally confidential) invitation to consider purchasing a specific journal. If discussions are to proceed, the next step is the signing of a nondisclosure agreement (NDA), before the full prospectus containing confidential information will be provided. Signing a nondisclosure agreement is not a matter to be taken lightly, as it imposes legal obligations on the publisher. Each publisher will have its own guidelines regarding what terms it will accept in such an agreement,[22] who needs to be advised and approve it, and who within the publishing house is authorized to sign an NDA on behalf of the publisher.

If the journal looks like a good fit with the existing list and the terms of the NDA are acceptable, it is time to move forward. The full prospectus should include a comprehensive description of the journal (Box 2.3) and specify exactly what is being sold (Box 2.4). Many of the items in Box 2.3 are familiar from the listing of items to consider when evaluating a new

---

[22] For example, would the "confidentiality" clause of the NDA prevent the publisher from taking expert advice from outside individuals?

**Box 2.3** Journal information needed for initial evaluation of a potential journal acquisition

*Description of the journal*

- Title.
- Copyright holder(s) (may differ over life of journal).
- Published aims and scope.
- Types of content: original research articles, reviews, dialogues, letters, book/other media reviews, conference proceedings, etc.
- Editor(s)-in-Chief, affiliation(s), and term of appointment.
- Editorial Board: composition and role of the Board. List of members, with affiliations and terms of appointment.
- Overview of Editorial office operations: who oversees the review process? What kind of peer review is employed (open, closed, single or double blind)? What software platform, if any, is used?
- Copy flow and acceptance/revision/rejection data – is there a backlog of accepted but unpublished papers?
- How is it published – print, electronic, or both; frequency/page budget, online platform, etc.
- Business model (subscription/license-based, advertising, subsidy, OA, etc.).
- Pricing data for subscriptions, advertising, publication fees, etc.
- Data regarding supplements/special issues currently published.

*Who are the authors?*

- Demographic data and size of author community.
- Other publication channels regularly used by this author community (e.g., books, working papers, institutional repositories, etc.).
- Level of support for institutional repositories or OA culture among authors in this field.
- Authors' access to funding to support OA publication fees.

*Who are the customers/readers?*

- Circulation data broken down by type of subscribers, media purchased, and geographic distribution.
- Available demographic data for institutional and individual subscribers.
- List of societies or other groups with special subscription rates for members.
- Data on inclusion in consortia packages; list of consortia customers.

**Box 2.3** (continued)

*Financial data*

- Subscription revenue data broken down by type (institutional, individual, print/online, etc.).
- Subsidiary income data.
- Profit/loss statement (at least to gross profit if not net).
- Level of support for journal Editors and Editorial office operations.

**Box 2.4** Items that may be included in the sale of a journal

*What is being offered for sale*

- Journal title and full copyright.
- Trademarks and design rights associated with the journal.
- Lists of current and past subscribers (including consortia).
- Lists of current and past advertisers.
- Lists of other journal-related customers.
- Current and back stock of print edition.
- Content of electronic edition (whether online or in other media, including full technical specifications and any back-volume legacy data).
- Revenues collected for product/services to be delivered after the sale (e.g., prepaid subscriptions).
- Services of the Editor(s)-in-Chief (is the contract transferred/assigned with the sale?).

*Obligations assumed by the purchaser*

- Ongoing contractual obligations to the Editor(s)-in-Chief and Editorial team.
- Ongoing obligations to present and past subscribers and/or consortia members (e.g., for online access).
- Ongoing contractual obligations with third parties (sales representatives, vendors of technology platforms, etc.).
- Contractual obligations for future special issues or supplements.
- Possible limitations on copyright in existing content (e.g., as a result of differences between seller's and purchaser's Copyright Transfer/License to Publish or permissions agreements, institutional repository policies, etc.).

> **Box 2.4** (continued)
>
> • Possible obligation to take on existing staff.
>
> *Obligations/rights retained by the seller*
>
> • License to continue to service existing online customers during transition period.

journal proposal but in this instance actual data will be available; several years' worth of data should be made available for analysis.

One of the most important questions to consider is "why is this journal being offered for sale?" There are a number of possible reasons: there has been a shift in focus of the seller's list, the journal is not performing up to the seller's expectations, the journal is part of a recent acquisition whose list the seller is pruning, etc. The stated reasons may not be the actual ones.

Judging the fit of the journal within the existing list involves more than just looking at the scope of coverage:

• Will this acquisition complement or compete with existing titles (this is an especially worrisome point for contract publishers, who may risk losing an existing society journal contract if they acquire a major competitor)?

• As an existing title, the journal will have its own unique "brand"; can this brand coexist with the publisher's brand, or is there a need to rebrand?

• Does the current pricing model or structure conflict with that of the publisher?[23] If so, could it be adjusted, and what might the financial consequences be?

As with a new journal launch, the competitive environment for the journal (see above) needs to be evaluated as well, including available metrics for the title up for sale (see Chapter 5, Journal metrics, and Chapter 6, Marketing and sales).

---

[23] For example, the journal may have had a single flat institutional online subscription rate and the acquiring publisher may have tiered prices based on the size of the institution or the number of users. Or the rates may be noticeably higher or lower than similar journals published by the publisher.

With actual current and historical financial and production data in hand, the task of creating a financial model is somewhat easier than when evaluating a proposal for a new journal launch. A useful exercise is to use the journal parameters and price and circulation data for the last complete year, to calculate what the financial picture would have been had it been part of the acquiring publisher's list, and then to compare that "retrocast" with the selling publisher's reported revenues and return.

When projecting the potential return on this journal, consider all the relevant cost factors involved in moving the title:

- Online submission and peer-review system: does the seller use the same platform/system as the buyer? If different, what would be the costs and benefits of keeping the seller's system vs converting over to the buyer's system?
- Online publishing platform: if this is different from the buyer's platform, what is the cost of converting existing files? Even if the same platform is used by both publishers, there will still be the cost of bringing the journal's current features in line with the buyer's implementation on that platform, as well as the cost of redesigning the journal's website to fit the buyer's brand.
- Subscriber data: how compatible are the data formats between the two fulfillment systems?
- Retrodigitized back volumes: does the seller or buyer offer online access to retrodigitized print back volumes? Are files available for this journal? If not, are print copies available for scanning?
- Inflation/volume adjustments in journal Editor(s) existing contract(s). If the payments to the journal Editors are linked to inflation, what is the inflation metric specified in the contract (and which geographic area is it tied to)? Is the financial support tied directly to the volume of submissions or of accepted papers?

The review will also need to consider what the journal does well, and what needs improvement. (Consideration should also be given to the performance of the Editor-in-Chief and Editorial Board.) The price structure for future volumes will need to be projected in line with the buying publisher's pricing strategy for subscription rates and/or OA author publication fees, and the effect of any significant changes on paid circulation or author-supported submissions will need to be calculated.

When the editorial, environmental, and financial analysis is done, it is time to consider whether the cost is worth the benefit to the publisher. The asking price is usually based on some multiplier of the annual revenue or the net profit. The multipliers are based on various rules of thumb based on the type of journal (e.g., "2 × revenue" or "8 × net profit/surplus"). Given the vagaries of costs, a multiplier on the net profit/surplus is generally a more useful valuation. Note that each publisher will generally have established guidelines for what it would expect to pay[24] and specific benchmarks for the return (e.g., 60% gross profit/surplus).

If, after review at the appropriate management levels, it is decided to make an offer and the seller accepts the bid in principle, a period of "due diligence" should ensue. Due diligence is simply the process by which the buyer conducts audits of various aspects of the journal to be sold, to satisfy itself that the information in the prospectus it has received is accurate and complete. This may entail detailed examination of the journal's accounts, subscriber lists, existing contracts, and/or interviews with individuals involved with the journal. The results of due diligence may lead to modification of the offer or, in rare cases, its withdrawal.

Assuming that the due diligence process is satisfactory and a formal contract of sale is drawn up and signed, the next step is managing the transition.

### The transition process

As with the launch of a brand-new journal, it is important to schedule a formal meeting to initiate the integration of the acquired journal within the publishing house. As before, this meeting should involve representatives of all relevant departments, and the agenda should include distribution of firm information about the title, a review of what needs to be done during the transfer, assignment of responsibility for each task, identification of critical events and sequences, and setting of a timetable for completion (see Box 2.5 for a starter list of topics). Many of these tasks will need to be carried out concurrently, while others require a specific sequence: for example, the fulfillment system setup for the journal must be complete before subscriber data can be entered; and online files may need

---

[24] For example, a not-for-profit publisher may not want to offer more than 5 × net profit/surplus, while a for-profit company may offer up to twice that.

**Box 2.5** Some items to assign, address, and/or schedule at a formal meeting to integrate a new journal acquisition

- Identify who will be the primary contacts from the various internal departments, with their counterparts in the seller's organization.
- Issue an announcement of the journal's change of publisher via the relevant media (direct mail, online discussion lists, email campaigns, etc.), both to existing institutional, individual, and society subscribers and to subscription agents.
- Arrange a meeting with the Editor-in-Chief and relevant staff to plan the transition (include a review of copy deadlines).
- Complete journal-specific setup for the various internal department systems and databases (e.g., production workflow, fulfillment, finance, and marketing).
- Arrange for the transfer of subscription lists and data entry into the acquiring publisher's fulfillment system.
- Arrange for the transfer of all revenues due to the acquiring publisher.
- Schedule a marketing meeting with the Editor-in-Chief to obtain his or her suggestions for relevant meetings/exhibits.
- Schedule a launch event at a relevant meeting/exhibition.
- Communicate information about the transfer to all relevant entities and databases (e.g., CrossRef, ISSN registry) and establish any necessary redirection of links.
- Set the production schedule.
- Schedule the transfer of all "work in progress" (i.e., accepted papers forwarded to the selling publisher, whether still in composition, at proof stage, or returned for correction).
- Complete journal-specific setup for any external or third-party systems (e.g., online submission and peer-review system, electronic platform, etc.).
- Arrange for the conversion/transition of the online submission and peer-review system.
- Arrange for the transfer/conversion and integration of files to the acquiring publisher's online publishing platform.
- Arrange for the activation of access for existing online customers.
- Schedule renewal efforts for existing customers.
- Revise designs as needed to incorporate the acquiring publisher's "brand" (journal cover and page layout in print; home page and format[s] online).

> **Box 2.5** (continued)
>
> * Integrate the journal "brand" with that of the acquiring publisher.
> * Revise the Instructions for Contributors and customize requisite forms as needed (e.g., Copyright Transfer/License to Publish).
> * Assign vendors for all outsourced work; communicate final specifications and schedules.
> * Assign in-house staff and/or identify out-of-house contractors/free-lances as needed.
> * Arrange for the transfer of print back-issue stock to the acquiring publisher's warehouse.
> * Arrange for the transfer/conversion and integration of electronic back-issue files, if available.

to be converted before they can be mounted and made accessible to subscribers. Formal minutes of this meeting should be circulated, and regular follow-up meetings scheduled to monitor progress and, if necessary, to revise deadlines.

The goal of the process is to ensure a seamless transition of content from one publisher to the other, with minimal disruption to customers, whether subscribers or authors. This will often require both seller and buyer to provide online access to the journal for a sufficient overlap period while customers migrate their access protocols, for example by establishing new linking targets in their electronic resource management systems. The Transfer Code of Practice, which was developed by the UKSG (formerly known as the UK Serials Group) is designed to provide consistent guidelines to help publishers ensure that journal content remains easily accessible by librarians and readers when there is a transfer from one publisher to another (see UKSG, 2008).[25]

It is important to remember that the transfer process does not end with the publication of the first issue. It continues through the completion of the first year's volume(s) under the buyer's imprint, and into the next renewal cycle.

---

[25] One thing which must be done by the transferring, rather than the acquiring, publisher is to notify CrossRef of the change of publisher in order that replacement URLs can be set up for each DOI (see Box 4.2 in Chapter 4, The production process, for more on DOIs).

## Auditing

Periodic internal audits of each journal in the publisher's list are essential in order to identify potential problems, as well as to ensure that each journal is performing to its full potential.[26] The audit should examine how well the journal is performing against internal benchmarks and targets as well as how well it is doing compared with the competition. The scope of the audit should be broad, covering all aspects of the journal from manuscript solicitation/submission through to final distribution and customer service, including marketing, sales, and operations. Input should be provided by all relevant staff, as well as the Editor-in-Chief and members of the Editorial Board. The focus should be both retrospective (how has the journal performed over the past few years?) and prospective (what can be expected for the next few years?), as well as aspirational (what do the respective parties want to change and why?).

In short, the purpose of the audit is to assess the overall health of a journal and to identify what needs to be done to make it better. A full internal audit should be conducted at least once every three years, with a brief review each year, timed in concert within the budget cycle so that any actions which impact the finances can be factored into the price-setting process and marketing plans.[27]

The following is a partial list of items to consider in an audit. Some are specific to individual journals, while others apply to the whole list. While this list is primarily geared to a subscription-based product, many of the items apply to OA or hybrid journals as well.

### *Copy flow*

- Are submissions rising, level, or declining? Are there any discernible patterns?[28]

---

[26] Note that this type of audit is separate and distinct from the accounting and management audits conducted by outside consultants and auditing firms. It is also distinct from an audit of the journal accounts that may be requested by the owner of a journal published under contract.

[27] In the case of a journal published for an outside proprietor, the timing and nature of any audit may be defined by contract.

[28] For example, do submissions spike some time before a major grant or assessment deadline, or after a major meeting? Since some assessment cycles and major

- What are the demographics of the author pool? Have they changed?
- Are the submissions in the desired subject areas? With the desired spread of coverage, or concentrated in one or a few areas?
- How many submissions are rejected before peer review? How many are rejected because of inappropriate subject matter and how many because of poor quality?
- Which countries are submissions coming from? Is this changing? (For example, an increase in papers from non-native English-speakers may have editorial time and cost implications.)

### Accepted papers

- What is the ratio of accepted to rejected papers?
- How many submissions are accepted on the first pass? With minor revision? With major revision?
- How long does it take to the first decision (reject/accept/revise)?
- How long does it take to final acceptance (i.e., forwarding accepted paper to production)?
- Is the flow of accepted papers appropriate for the page budget, too little or too much?

### Production

- Does the journal appear regularly and on schedule?
- What is the turnaround time from receipt of accepted manuscript to proofs being ready for review by authors?
- What is the time from receipt of accepted paper, after proof corrections, to initial mounting online?
- How long does it take from acceptance to publication in print and/or online? From submission?
- Is there a backlog of accepted papers in production?
- Are there any problematic editing or style issues?
- How are the third-party vendors performing in terms of quality, schedule, price?

international meetings only take place every two or three years, the analysis must encompass several years of data.

### Subscriber/user data

- How is the subscriber base divided among the various types of subscribers (institutions, individuals, etc.) and media (print, electronic, combination)?
- What is the geographic distribution of the subscriber base?
- What is the demographic mix of subscribers? How are the numbers changing? What are the renewal rates by category?
- Is circulation data available for the competition?
- Are there any new groups or societies to target for subscriptions?

### Online platform

- How user-friendly is the current online edition (navigation, readability, functionality)?
- Is it at the current state of the art or lagging behind the competition?
- Is system downtime (both for planned maintenance and for unplanned problems) held within acceptable limits?
- Are users requesting additional features?
- Can any trends be deduced from an analysis of customer-service queries?

### Print edition

- Is the current design still functional? Does it need to be adjusted for a change in content?
- Are there any possible economies in the printing/distribution process?[29]
- Is the print edition being delivered in a timely and cost-effective manner?
- Is a print edition still needed at all? Would an annual bound volume or print on demand suffice?

### Revenues

- Are financial targets being met?
- Does the added income from consortia sales offset any related decrease in traditional subscription income?

---

[29] For example, is the trim size optimal for the presses used and available paper stock?

- Are there changes in the nonsubscription revenue streams from the print and electronic versions?
- Are there additional income streams to pursue?

### Costs

- Are costs in line with projections? Are there any potential savings to be made?
- Are overheads increasing or decreasing?

### Positioning

- What are the main competitors to the journal? What differentiates this journal from the competition?
- How does this journal compare with its competitors in terms of price and amount of content?
- How do metrics such as usage data, impact factors, citation half-life compare with the competition?

### Marketing

- What is the goal of the marketing efforts: to increase submissions, to retain/add subscribers, to increase usage?
- How effective have recent marketing efforts been? Does any one approach work better than others in different market segments?

### Editorial scope and policy

- Does the journal meet the needs of the field (authors and readers), or does the scope need to be redefined?

Note that all of the above items need to be monitored on an ongoing basis by the relevant parties, and any issues brought to the attention of the responsible managers for action. The purpose of the formal audit is to bring all the information and participants together for a comprehensive review of all the data in context, in order to benefit from multiple perspectives in planning future action.

## Dealing with an ailing journal

The periodic audit of a journal is akin to a regular medical checkup: it looks for deviations from the norm and seeks to determine if these are transitory issues that can be handled easily, or chronic problems requiring further diagnosis and action. Once a problem has been identified, the next step is to determine the underlying cause(s) and then take appropriate action. The following is a list of some common problems, with some suggested causes and solutions.

### *Lack of content (or of content of acceptable quality)*

Insufficient content can result from a number of factors:

*Authors are not aware of the journal.* Target marketing to the perceived author pool. Add a Call for Papers to existing marketing efforts (direct mail, advertising).

*The scope of the journal (or its title) is too narrow.* Review the scope with the Editor-in-Chief to see if it really is too narrowly focused, and redefine as necessary. If the scope is not defined too narrowly, review the projections of the size of the author pool. A journal title that suggests too narrow a field is another problem. Renaming a journal is a serious undertaking: it requires a significant advance rebranding effort, usually forces a change in the ISSN (the primary identifier of the journal in many library, subscription agent, and bibliographic databases),[30] will negatively affect the impact factor for several years,[31] and confuse (and possibly lose) existing authors and customers. It may be better to consider adding a subtitle to expand the scope.

*The Editor-in-Chief and Editorial Board are not actively soliciting papers.* Ask the Editor-in-Chief and Editorial Board members to mention their affiliation with the journal when they present a paper at a meeting, and actively to invite presenters of worthy papers they hear to submit to the journal.

*The composition of the Editorial Board does not reflect the journal's scope or balance.* This can occur when a particular segment of the field dominates

---

[30] www.issn.org/2-22636-All-about-ISSN.php.
[31] As noted on the Thomson Reuters website (http://thomsonreuters.com/products_services/science/free/essays/impact_factor/).

the Board. Balance can be restored in the long term as members rotate off the Board, or in the short term by immediately adding Board members.

*The journal is perceived as not receptive to certain segments of the field, even though these areas are covered by the journal's scope.*[32] If this is due to the composition of the Editorial Board, the steps noted above should help. If a balance among the various segments is desired, active solicitation, by the Editor-in-Chief and Board, of papers in under-represented areas is essential. Appointing a Guest Editor to solicit papers for a special issue devoted to these topics is a useful tactic that also offers some marketing opportunities.

*The rejection rate is too high.* Review the Instructions to Reviewers (see Box 3.2 in Chapter 3, Editing) with the Editor-in-Chief to make sure reviewers are not interpreting them too harshly. Determine whether authors revise papers as requested, or simply withdraw and submit to another (less demanding) journal.

*There are financial barriers to authors (e.g., manuscript submission fees, color printing costs, OA publication fees).* It may be necessary to reduce or waive submission fees or color charges, particularly if other journals in the field do not impose such charges. Similarly, for an OA journal, it may be wise to discount or waive the publication fee until submissions pick up, especially if there is an existing wide-circulation subscription-based journal in the field.

*The journal is not covered in the relevant A&I services.* Despite the prevalence of online searching, this is still a concern for many authors. While this is primarily a problem for new journals, which need to deliver a certain amount of content for evaluation before an A&I service will decide to include them, it is also necessary to make sure that existing journals have been submitted for consideration in all the relevant indexes. An up-to-date listing of A&I coverage should appear in the front matter of every print issue of the journal, on its home page, and on all marketing pieces.

*The journal does not have a Thomson Reuters impact factor (or the ranking is not high enough).* No matter what one thinks of the accuracy or validity of the Thomson Reuters impact factor (see Chapter 5, Journal metrics) as a metric, it is essential to have one. The journal must be submitted for

---

[32] In some journals, articles are divided under subject headings in the Table of Contents. While this is useful to the reader, it does tend to highlight any imbalance in coverage.

evaluation and, if it is already listed, it is important to check that it is assigned to the most appropriate subject category or categories.[33] The simplest way to raise the impact factor is to publish more highly citable papers (e.g., comprehensive review articles). Other strategies abound, some of which are somewhat questionable (e.g., requesting, or even requiring, authors to cite prior relevant work in the journal; see Chapter 5, Journal metrics, and Chapter 12, Ethical issues).

*Authors feel the need to submit to the dominant or society-owned journal in the field*. When authors make a presentation at a meeting, they often feel obligated (or are sometimes even required) to submit papers derived from their presentations to the journal of the society sponsoring the meeting. Often, the volume of submissions from such meetings is so great that many worthy papers are declined simply because there is not enough room to publish them all in that journal. There is little one can do about this, other than waiting for authors to submit these papers on the second pass, or seeking an affiliation with that society.

It is important to coordinate with marketing to make sure that information about any relevant changes which may affect copy flow is communicated to the author community.

### Too much content

On the other hand, having more content than planned for can also be a problem. This can happen if the rejection rate is too low, if the scope of the journal is too broad, or if there has been an increase of work and/or researchers in the field covered. If the rejection rate is too low, the Editor-in-Chief will need to review the Instructions to Reviewers to ensure that appropriate quality is maintained, or indeed that the bar is raised (stressing the distinction between "worth publishing" and "worth recommending to the reader"). If the scope of the journal is too broad, it can be narrowed.

However, if the surfeit of worthy papers is due to an increase of work in the field, the size of the journal could be increased (content per issue and/or number of issues), with a concomitant increase in subscription rates. An alternative approach for a subscription-based journal might be

---

[33] The assignment to particular subject categories is important, because the relative ranking of a journal in its assigned field(s) says more about its value than the absolute value of the impact factor.

to launch a new OA journal to accommodate some of the surfeit of submissions. If the surge of papers is in a specific subfield, the launch of a more specialized journal to handle the papers in this particular growth area should be explored (using either the subscription or OA business model as appropriate for the field).

A surfeit of submissions may not be viewed as much of a problem for an OA journal, because an increase in accepted papers ties directly to the volume of author-side payments. However, review and production systems (and personnel) must be in place to handle the increase in work, if delays in publication are not to impact future submissions.

### Lack of subscribers

What is usually of greater concern, for journals that depend on subscription revenue, is the lack of institutional subscribers, although for a journal that sells advertising, lack of individual subscribers (albeit at a lower price) may also be an issue. There may be a number of reasons for these problems.

*The target number of institutional subscribers is unrealistically high.* Review the original projections for institutions and compare with available data for other related journals. Look at the breakdown between academic and commercial institutions. Have online consortia sales reduced the pool of potential traditional subscriptions? Reforecast as required.

*The journal's title does not accurately reflect its content.* Consider adding a subtitle and expanding marketing copy appropriately (but note comments earlier about the downsides of changing a journal's title).

*The journal's scope is too narrow, limiting the number of potential institutional subscribers.* Review the market data on researchers working within the scope of the journal. In new fields representing an intersection between two existing areas, be careful not to overestimate the overlap. Consider broadening the scope and marketing appropriately.

*The journal is perceived as offering poor value for money (e.g., the institutional subscription rate is seen as too high, and/or the journal is perceived as not publishing enough quality content).* Review the content in light of the competition. Does it suffer in comparison? Are the presentation or production standards an issue? Is there a problem with the way the Editor-in-Chief manages the submission and peer review? Is the price too high?

*Desired features are missing from the journal.* Are there features that the journal lacks which would make it more attractive to subscribers? Are these an issue of content (e.g., book reviews in some HSS journals, supplementary datasets in STM)? Or do they affect ease of use, navigability, and presentation (e.g., dynamic updating of reference links in the online edition, advanced search functions, automatic reflow of content, mobile device access, etc.)? Some of these can be addressed with minimal cost, but others may need a more detailed cost/benefit analysis.

*There are too many individual/member subscribers.* This can occur with a new journal launched with a society whose membership grows much faster than expected. There is little impetus for the institution to subscribe to the journal if faculty already have member subscriptions. In this case it will be necessary to recast projections for institutional subscriptions, and to review the allocation of costs over the various subscriber classes.

## Lack of sufficient income

Revenue problems related to a lack of circulation are addressed above. Other factors affecting income may include the following:

*The institutional subscription price is too low.* How does it compare with other journals in the field? Is the journal sufficiently distinctive that most existing subscribers would renew even if the price were increased?

*The online edition is underpriced.* In this scenario, if all print subscriptions were to convert to online only, projected margins would decrease precipitously. Does the online pricing strategy adequately integrate all relevant electronic platform and support costs?

*The price for member subscriptions is too low.* The member subscription rate should, at the very least, cover the incremental cost of servicing a member subscriber and, optimally, should be at or above the unit cost of production so that it contributes to the overall margin. If the journal is owned by the society (or there is a contractual arrangement with an affiliated society), the contract will likely stipulate the mechanism for setting member rates; if there is scope for increasing it in the next pricing round, raise the issue with the society in good time. If the member rate is a promotional rate offered at the publisher's own initiative to build the subscriber base, there is more flexibility to set the rate at the needed level.

*There may be a problem with late payments or bad debts.* While most journal subscriptions are prepaid, installment payments for member subscriptions may sometimes be arranged with societies to accommodate their cash flow; prompt billing and follow-through is essential, in order to avoid delays in payment. A problem with bad debts (i.e., those which are unlikely ever to be paid) is most likely to occur with those subsidiary income streams where invoices are issued. An efficient credit and collections staff is essential, and it is prudent to allow for a certain level of bad debt when setting prices for these areas.

*Advertising sales are low.* Is the journal attractive to advertisers (relevant scope and/or sufficient distribution among the desired demographic)? Not all journals attract advertisers. Those that do may suffer from the effects of consolidation/mergers within the relevant industry, shrinking the number of advertisers. There may also be fallow periods between product launches, or cuts in advertising expenditures due to a general economic downturn. Review whether journals in your field are suitable vehicles for advertising and, if so, what marketing and sales support is required.

*Subsidiary income streams are underperforming.* Review both the volume of activity and the pricing of all ancillary income streams (see Chapter 9, Subsidiary income). With the move to online publishing, some print-based income streams have dropped significantly (author reprints, print back-issue/volume sales), while newer ones have entered the mix (pay-per-view article downloads, access to back volumes online). Be sure to include an adequate allowance for the costs of invoicing and collection on all nonprepaid items.

### Costs are too high

*Invoices are running higher than the initial estimates.* Review the parameters involved: are the increases a result of more articles being published, or of a change in the nature of the material being processed (e.g., more artwork, tables, references to be linked)? Are too many copies being printed? Is the number of items to be mounted online increasing (e.g., more supplementary material)?

*Costs are allocated incorrectly.* Are the journal financials being hit with costs that really belong elsewhere in the enterprise? This can be an issue when shared direct costs have to be allocated between product lines (e.g., exhibiting at conferences). However, it can also be an issue when allocating overheads (see Chapter 8, Journal finances).

*Tasks done in-house could be handled more economically if outsourced (or vice versa).* A periodic review of the comparative costs for doing certain tasks in-house or outsourcing them (e.g., copy-editing), based on current and projected volumes, is sound business practice (and should include bids from multiple vendors to ensure an accurate cost comparison). Any decision to move work in or out of house should factor in the costs of the transition, and staffing implications (e.g., hiring or redundancies).

### Issues within the Editorial office

Some of the issues discussed above are directly tied to the operation of the journal's Editorial office. In evaluating them, one must consider whether the incumbent Editor-in-Chief is still the best man or woman for the job. Is he or she viewed as being at the forefront of the field, or part of the old guard? Is he or she open to new developments? Does he or she have time to manage the journal submissions?

Consider whether the current Editor-in-Chief would benefit from more office support, one or more Assistant or Section Editors, or a more active Editorial Board. Alternatively, it may be time to appoint a new Editor-in-Chief (see the section on "Replacing the Editor-in-Chief," above).

## In extremis

If all else fails to help a struggling journal, there are several other measures to consider:

- A complete relaunch and rebranding of the journal, with particular emphasis on the editorial coverage, backed by a full marketing campaign.
- A formal affiliation with a society, offering them a reduced member rate. This would increase both the subscriber base and the pool of authors, as well as offering joint marketing opportunities (for a society-owned journal, the affiliation could be with a society in another geographic area).
- A merger of the ailing journal with another title.
- A new publisher (in the case of a society-owned journal).
- A change of business model.
- Sale or closure of the journal.

## Pruning the list

Just as each individual journal should be subject to a regular audit, the composition of the publisher's whole list should also be reviewed periodically, not only to identify what areas might be expanded, but also to make sure that the existing titles are still appropriate for inclusion. The editorial direction of the list and the field covered by a given journal may diverge over time. The goals or editorial policies of a society-owned journal published under contract may change. The publisher's overall publication policy and/or strategy may change. Or the performance of an individual title may fall consistently (and irremediably) below the publisher's targets. In such cases, it is necessary to consider removing the journal from the list – either by selling it or by closing it down.

### *Selling a journal*

The process of selling a journal is the inverse of acquiring a journal from another publisher, discussed above. A prospectus for the journal must be prepared, potential purchasers identified, and their interest in the title solicited. The Editor-in-Chief should, of course, be apprised of the decision to sell at the earliest opportunity (bear in mind that he or she – or even the entire Editorial Board – may not wish to continue if the new owner is considered unacceptable). As noted in the section above regarding acquisitions, a nondisclosure agreement may be appropriate before sharing full details about the journal with potential buyers. The purchaser may require certain guarantees from the seller with regard to copy flow, transfer of subscription lists, and ability to assign the existing contracts (e.g., with the Editor-in-Chief or others) to the buyer.

As noted above, the valuation of a journal is usually based on a multiple of the annual revenue or the net profit/surplus with the specific multipliers given by rules of thumb based on the type of journal (e.g., "2 × revenue" or "8 × net profit/surplus"); the latter is generally more useful. The selling publisher may simply choose the highest bidder or, in some cases, the bidder who it believes would be the best partner for the journal, even if not the highest bidder.

While it is not rare, selling a journal is not a regular event for most publishers. When it does happen, serious consideration should be given to engaging the services of an experienced outside consultant/broker, both to manage the tendering process and to maintain a level of anonymity for the selling publisher in the early stages.

Once the sale has been agreed and contracts signed, it will be necessary to announce the transfer to customers (both authors and subscribers), and to schedule the transfer of subscription lists, work in progress, electronic files, etc., so that there is minimal disruption of service to customers. The transfer/conversion of the electronic edition from one platform to another may be particularly thorny; it is advisable for the seller to be allowed to service existing online customers for a set period after the sale, as the online data is migrated to the new platform (see the UKSG Transfer Code of Practice, 2008).

### Closing down a journal

While a journal, as an open-ended series of published items, has no predetermined end, there is nevertheless a life cycle that goes from birth (launch) through growth into maturity. A mature journal may stagnate, lose its focus, and fall by the wayside of its discipline, no longer attracting enough submissions or readers to justify its existence. The discipline it covers may itself shrink. Or it may be that the journal and its Editor-in-Chief have become so closely identified that one cannot exist without the other.

If, after a dispassionate and careful review (and if there are no potential buyers), it is decided to discontinue the title, there are a number of further decisions to be made and tasks to complete (see the checklist in Box 2.6).

Remember that the authors and readers of this title are still the publisher's customers; future relationships and obligations to them must be considered, particularly with regard to continuing access by subscribers to the online edition of the closed journal.[34] Independent of the closure of a journal, a general company strategy should already exist on the provision of continued access to the online editions of the publisher's journals in the event of a major disruption of service. While distributed initiatives such as LOCKSS and CLOCKSS, and the local loading requirements of some consortia agreements, provide partial solutions, it is best to make

---

[34] It has become the practice for many publishers' online licenses to include "perpetual access" to the volumes to which the customer has subscribed.

## Box 2.6  Checklist for closing a journal

- Advise the Editor-in-Chief and Editorial Board of decision and rationale for closing the journal.
- Stop accepting submissions.
- Determine what will be the final issue (preferably, the last issue of the volume with which current subscriptions expire).
- Estimate the amount of material needed to complete the volume.
- Review work in progress, from submission to production, to determine whether enough is in hand to complete the volume. If more than enough has been accepted, determine whether finances will allow publication of extra pages; if not, return accepted papers with apologies, noting why it is not possible for these papers to appear in the journal.
- Arrange for ongoing online access via third parties (e.g., OCLC, Portico, or CLOCKSS).
- Consider whether to offer institutional subscribers a copy of the electronic files for local loading.
- Announce the decision and rationale for closing the journal as early as practical.
- Send targeted announcements to current and recent subscribers and subscription agents; be sure to include information regarding continuing online access and handling of claims.
- Return any prepayments for subscriptions for future volumes, or work that will not now be completed (e.g., future supplements).
- Advise advertisers (both paid and exchange) of the decision to close the journal.
- Advise vendors for composition, printing, and third-party platforms.
- Publish an announcement in the journal (print and online) concerning the decision and rationale, thanking all those involved in the journal (authors, Editors, reviewers, subscribers, readers, advertisers, etc.) for their past support.
- Advise relevant bodies of the termination so that entries in databases can be amended (e.g., ISSN registries, CrossRef, Ulrich's, A&I services). It is particularly important to update the CrossRef data for all DOIs in the journal so that link resolvers will continue to point to the correct locations for the online edition.
- Establish a policy regarding the retention or transfer of copyright in the closed journal. If copyright is retained by the publisher, permission requests would continue to be handled internally. However, if copyright is transferred to a third party (e.g., whoever is hosting the online

**Box 2.6** (continued)

edition and providing future access), permission requests will need to be directed to the new copyright owner.

• Determine what is to happen to the remaining stock of printed issues. It is best to maintain sufficient stock to cover claims and potential back-issue sales for a specific period after termination; consider transferring the balance to a third-party back-issue jobber (although there is much less demand for print back issues these days).

• Maintain a web page for the journal on both your website and the online publishing platform, providing information about its closure, ongoing online access, availability of print issues (if any), and the procedure for permission requests.

• Prepare a stock of printed notices and email templates for use in responding to the inevitable future submissions and queries about the journal.

arrangements for a full "dark" archive to be maintained by a respected third party (e.g., OCLC, Portico, eDepot, CLOCKSS – see Appendix 2, Resources) for activation when needed.

## Training in journal publishing

Unfortunately, while there are a number of academic and continuing education programs in book and magazine publishing, there is a dearth of formal academic programs providing comprehensive training specifically in journals publishing. At the time of writing, we are aware of only two. One is the Certificate in Journals Publishing, a postgraduate course offered by the Oxford International Centre for Publishing Studies (OICPS) at Oxford Brookes University in collaboration with the Association of Learned and Professional Society Publishers. This program can be completed on campus or via distance learning. The other is the Master of Professional Studies in Publishing: Graduate Certificate in Journal Publishing, offered by George Washington University in Washington, DC.

One of the main organizations providing journals training is the Association of Learned and Professional Society Publishers (ALPSP), which offers a comprehensive series of one-day courses on all aspects of journals publishing; these are available in both the UK and the USA, and occasionally elsewhere, and an increasing number are also delivered online.

A rigorous three-day course on Journals Publishing[35] is offered in the USA in alternate years by the Association of American Publishers/ Professional and Scholarly Publishing Division (AAP/PSP). An intensive four-day course is offered by the International Association of Scientific, Technical & Medical Publishers (STM) in Europe and Asia; STM also organizes a Master Class, "Developing Leadership and Innovation," in the US and Europe, and numerous other seminars. In addition, the Council of Science Editors (CSE) organizes several intensive one-day short courses, geared to Editors-in-Chief, prior to its annual meeting.

In-house mentoring is also a major element of most people's training. In addition to formal courses and workshops, various professional publishing bodies, such as ALPSP, AAP/PSP, CSE, Publishers Association (PA), Society for Scholarly Publishing (SSP), and STM, also offer conferences, workshops, and topical seminars and webinars that are a good way to keep abreast of current issues.

For individuals at smaller publishing houses, attendance at these courses and seminars, and indeed at the annual meetings of these professional publishing groups (especially those allowing individual as well as corporate membership, such as SSP and CSE), also offers the opportunity to meet colleagues in similar positions at other publishers to network and learn from each other. The discussion lists and blogs provided by some of these organizations (e.g., ALPSP, SSP) also provide a useful channel for networking and obtaining information from more experienced colleagues (for example, "The Scholarly Kitchen," the publishing blog supported by SSP [http://scholarlykitchen.sspnet.org]).

## In conclusion

We have sought in this chapter to provide an overview of what needs to be addressed when managing a journal or a list of journals, without being too prescriptive in the details. Different publishers will have varying ways

---

[35] Long known colloquially as "Journals Boot Camp"; the 2011 incarnation was rebranded as "Journals Reboot."

of addressing these issues and many of the approaches arrive at the same goal. What is important to remember, as a manager, is the need to stay flexible and to recognize when what is "tried and true" has outlived its usefulness and alternative approaches must be adopted.

## REFERENCES

King, Donald W, Carol Tenopir, Carol Hansen Montgomery, and Sarah E Aerni, 2003, Patterns of journal use by faculty at three diverse universities, *D-Lib Magazine* 9(10) (http://dx.doi.org/10.1045/october2003-king)

Oxford University Press, 2010, *Open access uptake for OUP journals: five years on*, press release, June 10 (www.oxfordjournals.org/news/2010/06/10/open_access.html)

Tenopir, Carol, and Donald King, 2000, *Towards electronic journals*, Alexandria, VA, Special Libraries Association

UKSG, 2008, The Transfer Code of Practice, Version 2.0 (www.uksg.org/transfer)

## FURTHER READING

Adams, Scott, 1997, *The Dilbert Principle: a cubicle's-eye view of bosses, meetings, management fads & other workplace afflictions*, New York, Harper

Eades, Kenneth M, Timothy M Laseter, Ian Skurnik, Peter Rodriguez, Lynn A Isabell, and Paul J Simko, 2010, *The portable MBA*, 5th edn, Hoboken, NJ, Wiley

Parkinson, Cyril Northcote, 1957, *Parkinson's law, and other studies in administration*, New York, Houghton Mifflin

Peter, Laurence J, 1972, *The Peter Principle*, New York, Bantam

# Editing

## Introduction

Without editors, journals would not happen.

The *Oxford English dictionary* (*OED*) defines "editor" as "a person who is in charge of and determines the final content of a newspaper, magazine, or multi-author book."

However, in the field of scholarly journals, the terms "editing" and "editor" cover a particularly broad range of activities; to add to the confusion, the precise terminology used to describe the roles within this range varies widely among publishers, and elements of these roles may be combined in numerous different ways.

Broadly speaking, editorial roles fall into two distinct functional areas. On the one hand, there is the "content acquisition" role – generally carried out by a specialist in the journal's subject area. The journal Editor, in this sense of the word, will fit the *OED* definition: he or she will be responsible for deciding what does and does not appear in the publication. There may be a more complex team fulfilling aspects of this role – this is discussed in more detail below.

On the other hand, there is the "process and management" role – the preparation of the content for publication, as well as the overall business management of the journal. This type of editorial role is exercised within the publisher's offices (or under its control). Although it is often forgotten by those who assert that publishers are no longer a necessary part of the scholarly communication chain, Editors carry out a most valuable job, clarifying (and often correcting) the author's text and, vitally for online journals, checking the references to ensure that they can be linked wherever possible to the publications to which they refer. For online journals, they also prepare digital files for publication and make decisions about how the content will be presented.

## The Editorial team

### The Editor-in-Chief

The person who carries out the first type of editorial role may simply be called Editor[1] or Editor-in-Chief. The Editor will often be an active, or recently retired, specialist in the field, generally operating from his or her place of work (or, in some cases, from home) rather than in the publisher's office.

In the case of larger journals, there may be more than one Editor-in-Chief; sometimes the Editor(s)-in-Chief may be supported by one or more Editors/Associate Editors who are specialists in specific subfields covered by the journal, or who are responsible for handling articles from particular regions, or of particular types (such as book reviews, review articles, or other special types of content). These supporting Editors are sometimes drawn from the Editorial Board. One of them may be described as Assistant Editor or Deputy Editor, and may be seen to some extent as a trainee Editor-in-Chief, though this does not necessarily mean that he or she will automatically become the next Editor-in-Chief. (See discussion of Associate (or Section) Editors below.)

The Editor or Editor-in-Chief may have someone working within his or her office (but generally funded by the publisher), with a title such as Editorial Assistant. This person's job will entail dealing with correspondence, identifying and communicating with reviewers, and so forth; online submission and peer-review systems (covered in more detail in Chapter 4, The production process) streamline this job immensely. Alternatively, all or part of this role may be carried out in the publisher's office.

### Other members of the Editorial team

#### Associate (or Section) Editors

For those journals with a broad scope of coverage or a large number of submissions, one or more Associate (or Section) Editors may be named. These Associate Editors are responsible for overseeing the peer review of

---

[1] For clarity, we will indicate each of the various different editorial roles defined in this chapter with initial capitals throughout the book. We have used the generic term "journal Editor" to mean either the Editor-in-Chief or (in the case of larger journals) that member of the Editorial team to whom the function in question has been delegated.

submissions from specific disciplines within the scope of the journal (or papers from specific geographic areas, such as Japan). The Associate Editor then either makes the final recommendation to the Editor-in-Chief regarding acceptance, unless the authority to make the final decision on those papers is delegated to him or her.

## Guest Editor

This is an individual who is appointed to edit a special thematic section of an issue of a journal, and who is responsible for the solicitation and initial peer review of its content.[2] Guest Editors are not necessarily members of the Editorial Board; they are generally selected for their high profile in the relevant topic area.

## Reviews Editor

If a journal publishes reviews of relevant books, videos, software, online resources, hardware, etc., a Reviews Editor may need to be appointed to solicit both materials for review and qualified individuals to review this material. For book reviews, publishers sometimes agree to send each other their relevant books and other publications for review on a routine basis.

It is helpful to provide guidelines for the writing of such reviews – see the example in Box 3.1.

## Statistics Editor

In some scientific and social science disciplines where statistics are a significant aspect, an Editor with particular statistical expertise may be appointed to review the statistical aspects of accepted papers. In some journals one of the peer reviewers may be tasked with this role.

## Web Editor

Some journals have a very active website, with a variety of additional material adding value to the journal for its reader community; there may

---

[2] The term is also sometimes used to describe an Editor appointed specifically to handle the peer review of an article submitted by the Editor-in-Chief or another Editor, in order to avoid conflict of interest.

**Box 3.1** Extract from book review guidelines for *Learned Publishing*

Please focus on the content of the book, rather than your own views on the book's subject!

Your review should address the following questions:

- Context. Why was the book written?
- Authorship. Who is the author and what are his or her background and qualifications for writing this book?
- Readership. Who is the book written for? Does it work for that audience?
- Overview. What is the book about? (Summarize the main themes only – no need to list chapter headings, etc.)
- Comparison. Are there any other books on the topic, and if so how does it compare with them?
- Appraisal (the meat of the review). Please answer the following questions, giving support for your comments:
  - Does the publication do its job well?
  - Is it interesting?
  - Is it readable and useful?
  - Is it a worthwhile contribution to the literature on the subject?
  - What are the publication's strengths and weaknesses? How might its shortcomings (if any) have been addressed?
  - If the review covers more than one publication, please emphasize the strengths and weaknesses of each.
- Practicalities. As appropriate, please add specific comments on design, production, editing, index, value for money, etc.
- Conclusion.★ What is your overall assessment of the book – what are its best and worst features? Would you buy it, recommend it, use it, treasure it?

★Question courtesy of *ACM Computing Reviews*

be an Editor's blog or newsletter, newsfeeds on related topics, podcasts of relevant lectures or interviews, a Twitter feed, a Facebook page – the possibilities are endless (see Chapter 6, Marketing and sales, for some examples).

While the marketing department is likely to be actively involved in the creation and presentation of an effective and attractive website, editorial input will also be required in order either to create or to identify suitable content. This may be the responsibility of the Editor-in-Chief on a small journal, but on a larger one there is likely to be a member of the Editor's team with special responsibility for this area.

## The Editorial Board

The Editor-in-Chief is frequently, though not always, also the Chair of the Editorial Board (sometimes called Editorial Advisory Board, International Advisory Board, or various other names); it can, in fact, be helpful to have someone independent chairing the Board meetings. The role of Chairman also entails advising the publisher and/or society on the appointment of Board members.

If the journal is owned by the publisher, the Board members will be appointed by the publisher, after taking advice from the Editor, the Chairman of the Board, and other experts in the field. If it is owned by a society, the society may make the appointments, although it is helpful if there is consultation with the publisher. A representative of the publisher may be formally appointed as a member of the Board; alternatively, he or she may attend meetings in a purely informative/advisory capacity.

The Board needs to be large enough to cover all the main subject areas of importance in the journal, as well as reflecting the geographical spread of its authorship and readership. Typically, Editorial Boards tend to range between about twelve and twenty members, but may include as many as 100. Too small a Board will sometimes lack relevant expertise and will place a heavy burden on each of its members; too large a Board will be cumbersome and expensive.

When planning a journal launch, the composition of the Editorial Board is a very important element: eminent and internationally respected names add luster to the journal and help define its "brand" (as discussed in Chapter 6, Marketing and sales), but younger members who still need to make their name in the field may be more willing to put in the necessary work. A journal's intended national or international character is signaled by the geographical spread of the Editorial Board's membership – eminent and/or active Board members can help to attract articles from their own part of the world. The choice of Board members is also an indicator of the intended coverage of the journal; and it is a good idea to aim for appropriate gender and cultural diversity on the Board.

The Editorial Board usually meets at least once a year, at the publisher's (or society's) expense. If the Board is large and international, this can be costly; it therefore makes sense to hold the meeting in association with a major conference or other meeting which Board members may already plan to attend. The publisher is usually responsible for organizing the Board meeting and providing the secretariat for it. At other times of the year, the Editor may consult the Board informally (it may help the Editor if an email discussion list is set up for this purpose).

It is wise to clarify what the Board is and is not responsible for:

Members advise the editor on policy, strategy, and style, including directions in which a journal might develop, the balance of topics and approaches to them, series of articles, additional features, how to attract the best papers in the field and so on. They assist with refereeing, either doing it themselves or advising on suitable referees. In addition, they may encourage others to submit suitable papers to the journal, or advise the editor of people who might be approached. (Page et al., 1997)

As this makes clear, the primary focus of the Board's attention should be the content and editorial development of the journal, rather than its pricing, marketing, or other aspects of business management (which is the concern of the Managing Editor in the publishing house, in discussion with the journal's owner if it is not wholly owned). However, discussion may often stray into these areas and, indeed, the Board's expert knowledge of the market may be extremely helpful.

It is a good idea to provide Editorial Board members, when they are appointed, with a clear statement of what is expected of them. Some journals require a certain number of reviews from their Board members; some specify that Editorial Board members are expected to publish in the journal. Their term of office should also be clearly specified. Ideally, the terms of office of Board members should be staggered so that they do not all expire at once; there must also be a clear understanding with the Editor about rotation of Board members (covering both renewals and replacements).

## What the Editor-in-Chief does

The Editor-in-Chief is the public face of the journal; this is crucial for a new journal, where he or she has a vital ambassadorial role, but it continues to be important however long-established the journal may be. It is essential that the Editor-in-Chief is an internationally respected figure in the field, but also that he or she has the eye for detail, and the diplomatic skills, necessary for the role. His or her presence at key conferences and meetings around the world is good for the journal's visibility, as well as providing a valuable opportunity to solicit new contributions.

The Editor-in-Chief has overall responsibility for deciding what appears in the journal. (A list of the main types of article that appear in most journals is found in Table 3.1.) For the research articles that form most of the content of scholarly journals, this is generally done through the process of peer review (see below); the Editor often selects the most appropriate reviewers for each article, and once all the reviews are received and any suggested revisions have been made, he or she will make the final decision on acceptance for publication, as well as arbitrating in cases of difficulty or disagreement.

If the journal publishes review articles (articles summarizing the current state of knowledge in a particular area, with copious references), the Editor-in-Chief – or perhaps a designated Editor – is responsible for planning the intended coverage, identifying suitable authors, and commissioning the articles. Review articles are not always subjected to formal peer review; it may, however, be necessary for the Editor to ask for changes when the article is received. On occasion, it may even be

**Table 3.1** *The main types of article*

| Content type | Source | Peer reviewed? |
| --- | --- | --- |
| Editorial | Editor or invited contributor | Editorially reviewed |
| Research article | Unsolicited contributor | Yes |
| Methodology article | Unsolicited or invited contributor | Yes |
| Case study | Unsolicited contributor | Yes |
| Review article | Invited contributor | Yes, or editorially reviewed |
| Educational article | Invited contributor | Editorially reviewed |
| Republished article | Same or another publication | Selected by Editor(s) |
| Book (or other) review | Invited contributor | Editorially reviewed |
| Letter to the Editor | Unsolicited contributor (Editor may invite original author to respond) | Editorially reviewed |
| Obituary | Invited or unsolicited contributor | No |
| News item | Invited or unsolicited contributor | No |

necessary to reject a review article if it is unsatisfactory – this possibility should always be made clear to authors at the outset, to avoid undue embarrassment. Authors of review articles, at least in science journals, are sometimes paid a modest honorarium.[3]

If the journal carries editorials, the Editor-in-Chief either writes or commissions these; in some journals, they reflect the content of the particular issue, while in others they may address any topic of current interest.

In addition, the Editor-in-Chief (or a member of the Editorial team) is responsible for commissioning other types of content. These may include reviews of books (and other media), for which the items and/or the reviewers may sometimes have to be solicited. A standard checklist of information to be included can be helpful to authors of book reviews; see, for example, that provided by *Learned Publishing* in Box 3.1 above. The Editor-in-Chief or another team member may also commission educational material or other types of content, as well as processing Letters to the Editor and, if appropriate, requesting a response to such letters from the original author. If the journal has a lively and interactive website, the Editor (or a designated member of the Editorial team) will likely be involved in creating material for this (see discussion under Web Editor, earlier in this Chapter).

If the journal is sponsored by a society or similar organization, it may also carry news items from its sponsor, although some news content may appear only in the online edition.

On occasion, the Editor-in-Chief may also decide to reprint an article: a classic article from years ago, a translated article which originally appeared in another journal, or even an article in the same language but which was originally published for a completely different audience. This must, however, be done with care; duplicating articles risks confusing the record of citations (and thus citation analysis). It is important to make very clear that it is a republication, and to cite the original source prominently (see further discussion in Chapter 11, Copyright and other legal aspects). Sometimes, journals publish an article jointly (e.g., a clinical statement), especially if it was supported jointly by the sponsors of the journals.

---

[3] Review articles are popular with readers – as demonstrated by usage statistics – and are often cited more than research articles, which is good for the journal's impact factor (see Chapter 5, Journal metrics).

The Editor-in-Chief may decide to create/solicit one or more special issues or supplements, either within or additional to the normal range of issues. In some cases, this will be an issue around a particular theme, in which case the majority of articles will of course need to be commissioned; in some subject areas a "call for papers" on a specific topic is put out for the special issue. Unfortunately, authors do not always deliver on time – if one article is late, the publication of the whole issue may be delayed, which can be a problem if the issue is one of the regular series. Papers from a particular conference or other event may also be suitable for a special issue. In some disciplines, particularly medicine, advertisers may be willing to sponsor publication of a special issue or supplement, often by buying a substantial number of copies. In such cases, the request from the advertiser is likely to come via the publisher rather than direct to the Editor-in-Chief. (Note that special issues or supplements sponsored by third parties may raise conflicts of interest, which are addressed in Chapter 12, Ethical issues.) Unless the special issue or supplement is included in the budget for the journal[4] or is sponsored by a third party, the cost of including the extra pages will of course create a financial problem for the journal.

## Peer review

Peer review is sometimes referred to as the "Gold Standard" of scholarly journals; it is the system by which a research article is reviewed by independent experts (the author's peers) to help the Editor-in-Chief reach a decision on publication. Although the system has been much criticized for its potential to introduce bias and unfair behavior by reviewers, and to delay publication, no one has yet come up with a better system – rather like democracy, of which Winston Churchill famously remarked: "democracy is the worst form of government, except all those other forms that have been tried from time to time" (Hansard, 1947).

Traditionally, the identity of reviewers is not known to the author (single blind); in some cases the identity of the author is also withheld from the reviewers (double blind). There have been attempts to introduce open peer review where anyone is free to comment on an article which has

---

[4] It is sometimes the practice for journals owned or published by a scholarly society to include the proceedings of or abstracts from the annual meeting of the society as part of the journal's annual page budget.

been made available online and to engage in dialogue with the author. The comments may then be published alongside the article, which may itself have been revised. However, this has had only limited adoption so far; an experiment at *Nature* found that reviewers were reluctant to post public comments (*Nature*, 2006).[5]

For a thorough and detailed account of how peer review operates and the principles which should guide it, see Irene Hames' book *Peer review and manuscript management in scientific journals: guidelines for good practice* (Hames, 2007) – despite the title, much of what Hames says is equally applicable to journals in the social sciences and humanities.

There are many ways to perform peer review, but basically, the Editor-in-Chief (or a member of his or her staff) does a quick check of each submitted article to ensure that it lies within the scope of the journal and meets the basic mechanical requirements listed in the Instructions for Contributors. If the article passes these checks, the Editor-in-Chief, Associate Editor, or staff member identifies multiple reviewers (up to five – usually at least three) who have the relevant expertise to comment on the article's suitability for publication in that particular journal (a database of current and potential reviewers, indicating their fields of expertise, can aid selection). The potential reviewers are asked about their availability, and the submitted paper is then forwarded to some or all of the reviewers for comment. Their reviews should address issues not just of the quality of the study itself, but also of its relevance and interest to the journal's particular readership. They could also usefully be asked about the author's choice of title; does it make it unambiguously clear what the article is about? For example, humorous titles can be distinctly unhelpful to potential readers, and may actually be unintentionally misleading in web searches. It is useful to present reviewers with a standard printed or online checklist of questions, both to make their job easier and to ensure that the responses are comparable (see, for example, the guidelines of the Ecological Society of America, shown in Box 3.2). The reviewers are usually given a fairly short deadline by which to reply (automated systems make it much easier to keep them on schedule).

---

[5] *Behavioral and Brain Sciences* is an early example of a mixed system – the initial decision to publish was carried out through traditional peer review, but was then followed by a period of open peer commentary which was edited and published with the final paper. Forms of open peer review are discussed further in Chapter 13, The future of scholarly communication.

## Box 3.2 Reviewer guidelines of the Ecological Society of America

### Instructions to reviewers

*Quality peer reviews are essential for insuring the quality of scholarly journals. Your evaluation will play a major role in our decision as to whether to accept a manuscript for publication. We place a great deal of trust in you. We trust you to be prompt, fair, respectful of the rights of the authors, respectful of our obligations to the readership, and to evaluate the manuscript carefully and in depth. At the same time, on behalf of the ESA membership, we are very grateful for the time and effort you invest in the review process.*

### Confidentiality

This manuscript is a privileged communication. Please do not show it to anyone or discuss it, except to solicit assistance with a technical point. If you feel a colleague is more qualified than you to review the paper, do not pass the manuscript on to that person without first requesting permission to do so. Your review and your recommendation should also be considered confidential.

### Conflicts of Interest

If you feel you might have difficulty writing an objective review, please return the paper immediately, unreviewed. If your previous or present connection with the author(s) or an author's institution might be construed as creating a conflict of interest, but no actual conflict exists, please discuss this issue in your confidential comments to the editor. If in doubt, feel free to contact the Subject-matter Editor who requested your review.

### Comments for the Author

Identify the major contributions of the paper. What are its major strengths and weaknesses, and its suitability for publication? Please include both general and specific comments bearing on these questions, and **emphasize your most significant points**.

### *General Comments should address the following:*

- Importance and interest to this journal's readers
- Scientific soundness
- Originality
- Degree to which conclusions are supported

**Box 3.2** (continued)

- Organization and clarity
- Cohesiveness of argument
- Length relative to information content
- Whether material should be moved to the digital appendices
- Conciseness and writing style
- Appropriateness for the targeted journal and specific section of the journal

*Specific Comments:*

Support your general comments, positive or negative, with specific evidence. Remember that a review lacking substance will generally have less impact than a review that is well-reasoned and rich in content. You may write directly on the manuscript (or embed comments in a digital copy of the manuscript), but please summarize your remarks in "Comments for the Author(s)." Comment on any of the following matters that significantly affected your judgment of the paper:

1. *Presentation* – Does the paper tell a cohesive story? Is a tightly reasoned argument evident throughout the paper? Where does the paper wander from this argument? Do the title, abstract, key words, introduction, and conclusions accurately and consistently reflect the major point(s) of the paper? Is the writing concise, easy to follow, interesting?
2. *Length* – What portions of the paper should be expanded, condensed, combined, and deleted? (Please don't advise an overall shortening by X%. Be specific!)
3. *Methods* – Are they appropriate, current, and described clearly enough that the work could be repeated by someone else?
4. *Data presentation* – When results are stated in the text of the paper, can you easily verify them by examining tables and figures? Are any of the results counterintuitive? Are all tables and figures necessary, clearly labeled, well planned, and readily interpretable?
5. *Statistical design and analyses* – Are they appropriate and correct? Can the reader readily discern which measurements or observations are independent of which other measurements or observations? Are replicates correctly identified? Are significance statements justified? For further advice, consult our Guidelines for Statistical Analysis and Data Presentation.

## Box 3.2 (continued)

6. *Errors* – Point out any errors in technique, fact, calculation, interpretation, or style. (For style we follow the "CBE Style Manual, Fifth Edition," and the ASTM Standard E380 – 93, "Standard Practice for Use of the International System of Units." – An abbreviated version may be downloaded from the ASTM website.)
7. *Citations* – Are all (and only) pertinent references cited? Are they provided for all assertions of fact not supported by the data in this paper?
8. *Overlap* – Does this paper report data or conclusions already published or in press? If so, please provide details.

### Fairness and objectivity

If the research reported in this paper is flawed, criticize the science, not the scientist. Harsh words in a review will cause the reader to doubt your objectivity; as a result, your criticisms will be rejected, even if they are correct! Comments directed to the author should convince the author that (1) you have read the entire paper carefully, (2) your criticisms are objective and correct, are not merely differences of opinion, and are intended to help the author improve his or her paper, and (3) you are qualified to provide an expert opinion about the research reported in this paper. If you fail to win the author's respect and appreciation, much of your effort will have been wasted.

### Anonymity

You may sign your review if you wish. If you choose to remain anonymous, avoid comments to the authors that might serve as clues to your identity, and be careful about annotating the manuscript (see below). Unless you indicate otherwise (such as by signing your remarks for the authors), we will assume you wish to remain anonymous.

### Annotating the manuscript

IF YOU WISH TO REMAIN ANONYMOUS and want to make comments directly on the pdf with the Note tool, you will need to be sure you remove your identity from the properties BEFORE adding your comments.

IF YOU WISH TO REMAIN ANONYMOUS and use track changes in Word, you must first (before putting in the comments!) remove your identity by going to the Tools/Options/User Information. (In Word 2007

> **Box 3.2** (continued)
>
> go to Review/Track Changes/Change User Name.) You can restore it after saving and sending the document. (This is not necessary if you tell us that you choose to waive your anonymity.)
>
> If you wish to write comments on a printed copy of the manuscript, you could scan in the document and send it as an attachment with your review, or indicate that it is coming in your comments to the editor, and mail it to our office.
>
> Reprinted with the permission of the Ecological Society of America.

When the responses have all been received (or failing that, enough of them to make a decision) the reviewers' comments and recommendations are considered (note that reviewers should be asked to make a recommendation – not a decision – on publication). If all the reviewers agree, either for or against publication, it is unlikely that the Editor-in-Chief will go against this view; however, if there is a mixed response, the Editor-in-Chief's own view will determine the outcome.

In most cases, however, the reviewers do not make an immediate recommendation. They most commonly suggest changes which could improve the article. Depending on how fundamental these are, they may recommend acceptance if minor changes are satisfactorily made, or resubmission of a major revision, in which case the article will ideally go back to the same reviewers when the revised version is submitted.

For traditional journals, peer reviewers are asked to judge not only whether a study is sound, but also whether the work is sufficiently novel and interesting to warrant a place in the journal. However, since 2006, a number of Open Access "megajournals" have been launched (including *PLoS One*), where the criterion for publication is simply that the work is technically sound; the idea is that this lighter peer review will be supplemented by "community-based dialog" (as *PLoS* puts it). These journals often have very broad subject coverage. Because of their broad scope and light selection process, some of these journals have attracted very large numbers of authors; the correspondingly large number of publication fees has made these journals very remunerative for their publishers.

Peer reviewers may be drawn from the journal's own Editorial Board (see below), but this is unlikely to be large enough to cover all areas of the journal without unduly overloading its members; the Editor-in-Chief's (and the publisher's) knowledge of other experts in the field is key to expanding the list more widely. Reviewers are rarely paid for their help – indeed, it has even been argued that their independence would be compromised if they were, although some journals "reward" reviewers, financially or otherwise, if they respond within a very tight timetable. Often, however, publishers do thank their reviewers formally at the end of each year by publishing a list of their names in the journal, by hosting a reception for them at a major meeting, or even by presenting each of them with a small gift.

A number of online systems have been developed since about 2000 to expedite the tracking and processing of papers from submission through peer review to acceptance and forwarding to the publisher. These systems incorporate databases for both submissions and peer reviewers, standard forms, emails, reports, and prebuilt workflows that would meet the needs of most journals; they may be hosted either by a third-party vendor or on the publisher's site. For more information on selecting and configuring such a system, see Chapter 4, The production process.

## Who appoints the Editor-in-Chief?

In the case of wholly owned journals, the Editor-in-Chief will be appointed by the publisher, usually after consulting experts in the field to identify the most suitable person. If the journal is owned by a society or other organization, the appointment is generally made by the society's own governing body or a sub-committee thereof, ideally in consultation with the publisher.

The appointment is usually for a fixed term of three to five years, although there may be the possibility of renewal for one or more further terms. A one-year term is not really practical, as it takes most of that time for a new Editor-in-Chief to become fully familiar with the workings of the journal and the publisher, and to start to impose his or her personal stamp on the character of the publication; many of the articles will have started peer review, and some may even have been accepted, during the previous Editor's term, so that the articles accepted by the new Editor-in-Chief may not be published for some months after he or she takes up office.

Contractual provision for automatic renewal of the Editor-in-Chief's term has its advantages – it means that renewal is not simply forgotten – but, if the publisher does not intend to renew for any reason, it is important to pay careful attention to the notice date so that renewal does not happen by default.[6] The contract must specify the length of an automatic renewal term (unlike the original agreement, a renewal term of one year is acceptable).

### How the Editor-in-Chief is compensated

For the vast majority of journals, the position of Editor-in-Chief is a part-time (and in some cases, almost volunteer) one. The amount of work required varies with the number of manuscripts submitted (or solicited) and the level of peer review and revision. Editing a journal can be viewed as a service to one's profession, a way to advance one's career or shape the development of a field, or even as a labor of love.[7]

While some Editors-in-Chief are not paid at all, most do receive a fee (sometimes described as an "honorarium," though that makes no difference to its tax status) or even a royalty based on the journal's revenue. The fee may also be based on the number of manuscripts submitted, either including or excluding resubmissions of revised manuscripts. When a fee is paid, however, it is rarely comparable with the hourly rate for the Editor-in-Chief's work in his or her professional field. The fee or royalty is paid by the publisher or, if there is one involved, by the society that owns the journal.

There are exceptions – notably the *New England Journal of Medicine, The Lancet,* the *British Medical Journal,* and *Science* – where not only is the volume of material processed large, but advertising represents a significant proportion of the income. Here, the Editor-in-Chief or a group of Editors are full-time staff members of the publisher or the society that publishes the journal.[8]

In addition to any fee, the direct expenses of the Editor-in-Chief or the Editorial team will be paid for, generally by the publisher. This often includes the cost of office accommodation, staff support, and equipment

---

[6] The notice clause is generally bilateral – the Editor may also decline to renew. The contract should specify a notice period which gives time to identify a successor if necessary.

[7] This last applies primarily to the Editor who has carved out the niche for the title and generated the concept.

[8] Some other large journals – e.g., *Physical Review* – also employ the Editorial team in-house.

and supplies. If office space or clerical staff is provided within the Editor-in-Chief's place of work, such as a university, overheads may also be charged, perhaps as a percentage on top of the basic costs. The publisher also generally provides an online submission and peer-review system, and supplies the Editor-in-Chief with printed stationery for use when email is not possible.

The publisher may also pay the Editor-in-Chief to join and participate in professional groups such as the European Association of Science Editors and the Council of Science Editors, or discipline-specific organizations such as the World Association of Medical Editors. The Editor-in-Chief may also find it helpful to attend the panels held for Editors of subdiscipline journals at some major society meetings. Support for attendance at specific major meetings to solicit papers or to hold an annual meeting of the Editorial Board may also be provided.

A checklist of items which should be included in the Editor-in-Chief's contract is included in Chapter 11, Copyright and other legal aspects (Table 11.2).

### What if things go wrong?

Editors-in-Chief are busy people, and eminent experts in their field; they can therefore, with some justification, be demanding and high-maintenance – and a few of them are! But once in a while, an Editor-in-Chief may prove to be unsatisfactory – for example, not producing enough content for the publication (or too much), causing unwarranted delays in peer review and/or publication, or making decisions with which the publisher (or society) is unhappy. (While it is of course essential that the Editor-in-Chief retains editorial independence from the publisher or other owner of the journal, as well as from advertising interests, there are cases where the working relationship breaks down completely because of a major difference of opinion.) This is a very difficult situation and one which it is hard to resolve without some damage to the journal.

If members of the publisher's staff have serious worries about the performance of an Editor-in-Chief with whom they are working, they should discuss the matter with their own manager as soon as possible; it may be necessary to involve the publisher's lawyers. The situation can be extremely complicated if the Editor-in-Chief is appointed by a society which owns the journal. The Editor-in-Chief's contract (see above) should cover the circumstances in which his or her appointment will be terminated, but before that stage is reached, the publisher must of course discuss the problems with the Editor-in-Chief (and, if appropriate, the society) and try to resolve matters. If all else fails, the termination clause will have to be invoked; this can be unpleasant, and the Editor-in-Chief might even demand compensation. In the meantime, the publisher needs to be sure that someone else is lined up to take over immediately, to avoid further damage and delays.

## Editorial roles within the publishing house

### Commissioning or Acquisitions Editor

This is the person within the publisher's office who is responsible for researching, developing, and launching new journals, signing up their Editorial team, and setting up appropriate relationships with societies or associations – some publishers use the title Developmental Editor (see Chapter 2, Managing journals, for more details). As well as creating new, independent journals, the Commissioning Editor is likely to be involved in looking at other publishers' journals for possible takeover, and in putting together bids for the publication of society journals (see Chapter 10, Contract publishing). The commissioning role may be combined with that for commissioning books in the same subject area, which can maximize cross-fertilization of ideas and make use of the Commissioning Editor's contacts in the field; alternatively, it may involve responsibility for commissioning journals in several or indeed all areas, depending on the publisher's size.

The Commissioning Editor often also has continuing overall responsibility for the management of the journal (see below under Managing Editor). Obviously, the creation of new journals is much less frequent in the case of a specialized society publisher, where the subject area is defined by the society's mission. In these circumstances the commissioning role – if any – is much more likely to be combined with that of overall journals management.

### *What the Commissioning Editor does*

The Commissioning Editor may come up with an idea for a new journal, or it may be suggested by an outside advisor, a colleague, or the potential Editor-in-Chief; the topic may be a completely new one, an overlap of two different but related areas, or a subdivision of an existing field that warrants its own journal (sometimes known as "twigging"). An existing journal may have become unwieldy, and need splitting into two or more separate parts (often, the new offshoot may be distributed for the first year or so to all subscribers to the parent journal). Sometimes, there may be an existing journal which its publisher wishes to dispose of, or whose sponsoring society wants to examine offers from alternative publishers. For more on launching a new journal, see Chapter 2, Managing journals.

## Managing Editor or Publisher

In a publishing house with multiple journals, the Managing Editor (or Publisher or equivalent – this is a job with a confusing variety of titles) may be responsible for the overall management, editorial health, smooth running, and profitability of all (or a group of) journals. This also includes liaising with the journals' owners (if, for example, they are society journals published under contract), the Editors-in-Chief, and the Editorial Board members, as well as overseeing both freelance and in-house editorial and production staff. Chapter 2, Managing journals, discusses in detail what this role entails. There is also much good advice in Irene Hames' book, *Peer review and manuscript management in scientific journals*, mentioned above.

The Managing Editor must have a close working relationship with the sales and marketing department(s). The Managing Editor can offer detailed knowledge of the market for the journal, for input into the strategic marketing plans. He or she can add understanding to the analysis of market, sales, and usage statistics, and can use these to improve the journal's match to the needs of its authors and readers.

In some cases, an individual (major) journal may have a Managing Editor in the Editorial office, rather than in the publisher's office. He or she oversees the day-to-day running of the journal, taking the entire administrative load off the Editor-in-Chief and his or her team of Editors (if any). This leaves the Editor-in-Chief and team free to concentrate on the editorial content, while the Managing Editor is responsible for all editorial (though in this case not usually financial) management of the journal.

## *What the Managing Editor does*

The Managing Editor provides the crucial interface with the Editor-in-Chief or Editorial team, with societies if they are involved, possibly with authors, reviewers, and freelance editors, and with the internal functions of preproduction and production as well as marketing and sales. Hence, the management of relationships is all-important.

He or she also manages a busy flow of traffic, with articles for each journal at many different stages of processing; everything must run smoothly and efficiently, and any problems must be rapidly detected and resolved, so that articles can be published with the minimum of delay and issues can appear on schedule. For larger journals, this aspect may be managed by a separate Production Editor (see below).

An online submission system makes available a wealth of valuable data: the Managing Editor monitors (and reports to the Editor-in-Chief and the Editorial Board) the number, source, and increase or decrease in submissions; the rate at which they are passing through the system, identifying any external or internal bottlenecks or weak points (for example, a particularly slow reviewer); and any backlog of papers awaiting publication. If authors have to wait too long for publication, they may take their future papers elsewhere, so a backlog must be addressed (as soon as budgets permit) by increasing the size and/or frequency of journal issues.

The Managing Editor must bear in mind the legal responsibilities which go with the maintenance of personal information (about authors, reviewers, and others) in electronic form; Chapter 11, Copyright and other legal aspects, covers this in more detail under "Data protection."

At the same time, this is a business role; the Managing Editor is responsible for ensuring that his or her journals make money for the publisher and/or the society. Costs must be controlled, prices carefully managed, and subsidiary income maximized.

### Copy-Editor

Some publishers no longer have journal articles edited in detail to improve the clarity of the authors' expression, to ensure consistent and accurate use of technical terminology, etc. However, there has been a marked increase in the number of papers coming from countries where English is not the first language, such as China and India; for these, language editing is increasingly necessary and can be very time-consuming. Indeed, some publishers offer this as a service for which authors or their institutions pay. This type of editing is often carried out by freelance editors, who may be based in another country from that of the publisher (perhaps where the typesetting is carried out). It requires a degree of subject expertise as well as an excellent grasp of clear English.

Even when detailed language editing is no longer carried out, however, most publishers still have articles copy-edited (again, often by freelancers) to ensure consistency with house style. If technical/language editing is being carried out, copy-editing is generally done as part of the same process. Although authors are increasingly expected to prepare the electronic script which will be used for composition, it is unlikely that they will have read the publisher's "Instructions for Contributors"/ "Instructions to Authors," however carefully drafted! (The essential items which should be included in the "Instructions for Contributors" are listed in Box 2.2 of Chapter 2, Managing journals.)

## *What the Copy-Editor does*

Copy-editing is a matter of preparing the text so that it follows the journal's style – not just in terms of visual appearance, but more fundamentally in terms of article structure: different logical levels of headings and subheadings must be identified correctly, so that the appropriate typographical style can be applied, thus helping the reader to navigate the author's argument (this is particularly crucial for online journals, which may provide internal linking to sections and subsections within the journal). This used to be a separate task, but is now usually done on-screen as part of whatever level of editing is carried out.

Every author has his or her own distinctive style of writing, and the aim should never be to remove this and reduce every article to an identical, bland style. Clarity and comprehensibility are the aims, rather than literary elegance. The Copy-Editor[9] needs to consider the article from the point of view of the reader: will the reader (even if not a native English-speaker) understand immediately and unambiguously what the author is trying to convey? Words may need to be substituted, or sentences (or even whole

[9] Sometimes referred to as a Technical Editor (usually one with specialist knowledge of the journal's field) or Sub-Editor.

paragraphs or sections) reordered, to ensure understanding. It goes without saying that mistakes in usage, grammar, or punctuation should be corrected; however, many international journals will accept either US or British English spelling and usage, provided there is consistency within an article.

The journal should have a brief outline of key style and formatting points – the "Instructions for Contributors" mentioned above – which is made available online to prospective authors. However, as we noted, it is rare indeed for authors to consult this, even on such basic matters as reference style. Fortunately, authors today have software tools to manage the use of references, which usually make it relatively easy for them to change reference style on request. More complex journals (particularly those involving multiple Technical/Copy-Editors) may have a more detailed style manual for in-house use.

Authors do not always get their facts right, and reviewers do not always spot all their mistakes; that is why a Copy-Editor needs knowledge of the journal's field. He or she needs to have a nose for facts that may be wrong, and to be familiar with the sources in which they can be checked.

In any specialized field, journal articles are likely to use technical language which is particular to that field. The Copy-Editor must check that terminology, units of measurement, etc., are used correctly and consistently throughout the journal (such minutiae as punctuation points can matter very much!).

If the Copy-Editor encounters any material that raises questions of potential plagiarism, libel, or other legal problems, he or she should bring it to the attention of those who deal with ethical and legal issues at the Editor's or publisher's office. (See Chapter 12, Ethical issues, for detailed discussion of this area.)

Is the article's title too long? If so, and if it cannot be shortened, the Copy-Editor may need to create a shorter version for running heads in the print edition. Most journal articles include an abstract written by the author; however, authors are not always very good at this. The abstract is the "hook" which may – or may not – lead browsers, particularly online, to read the full article; it therefore needs to summarize both what the article is about, and what the findings are, and the Copy-Editor needs to be on the lookout for abstracts which do not adequately perform this function – authors may need help in rewriting them. A fixed length is often specified for abstracts, and it may be necessary to check that the author has kept within this limit.

Some journals also ask authors to supply keywords – terms which would help someone searching for the subject of the article. Keywords can also be helpful to indexers (if used)[10] and to abstracting and indexing (A&I) services (touched on in Chapter 6, Marketing and sales). Keywords are also valuable in identifying appropriate reviewers at the peer-review stage. If the author has supplied keywords, the Copy-Editor will need to examine these carefully, as authors are not always the best people to identify which words a potential searcher might use (offering drop-down menus within the submission system is one way of controlling this). However, the use of keywords in the published journal is increasingly uncommon, as search systems no longer require them since fulltext searching is so efficient.[11]

The list of references/citations at the end of the article can present a particular challenge. There are various citation styles, of which the most frequently used are Vancouver (numbered in text, listed numerically at the end of the article) for scientific journals and Harvard (author, date in text, listed alphabetically at the end) for humanities journals (see *Chicago manual of style online*, www.chicagomanualofstyle.org/tools_citationguide.html, for a quick summary of both styles). As mentioned above, the reference management software used by authors can generally change the reference style if necessary, to conform with the journal's requirements.

Whatever style is used, the key minimum information which should be included is as follows:

For a journal article – author(s), title, publication title, volume and/ or year, first (and usually last) page number.

For a book chapter – chapter author, chapter title, book title, editor, publisher, city, year of publication, edition.

It is usual to insist that all citations in a given journal follow the same style, and indeed apply it in exactly the same way in terms of italicization,

---

[10] A growing number of journals are abandoning the inclusion of an annual, or volume, index because they are so rarely used; readers tend to use searching tools instead. While it cannot be denied that a professionally prepared index is far superior, the cost may not be justified.

[11] However, good conceptual keywords can usefully be included in online metadata to improve users' search results; this is a task for a knowledgeable Technical or Copy-Editor, not the author.

punctuation, and use or otherwise of journal abbreviations. Any addition to or deletion from the references in Vancouver style will make it necessary to re-number all the rest; although reference management systems and most word-processing systems do this automatically, errors can creep in, and it is therefore important to cross-check between the references in the text and the list at the end of the article. Many preediting software packages (discussed in Chapter 4, The production process), or macros within word-processing systems, will do this for the Copy-Editor.

The accuracy of a reference will determine whether that article gets a citation "hit" in citation analysis programs. In addition, since so much of the cited material is likely to be available online, the value of the list of citations to the reader is greatly enhanced if each citation is directly linked to the item to which it refers, using the Digital Object Identifier (see Box 3.3; also see

---

**Box 3.3** The DOI system

- What is a DOI?
  A unique, actionable identifier for every piece of digital content on the web.★
- What is it for?
  Makes it possible for links to online content to be persistent, even if web location of the content changes (e.g., with a change of publisher, or change of platform).
- How does it work?
  The central DOI directory uses the "Handle" system to link the identifier of each digital object with its current web location and/or the location of information about it (metadata). The publisher (or other owner) is responsible for giving notice of any changes.
- What does a DOI consist of?
  A prefix, indicating the registrant (e.g., 10.1017 – Cambridge University Press), followed by a slash (/), followed by a suffix, which can be constructed by the registrant in any way it chooses – for instance, for journal articles some publishers use their own internal reference numbers, some use the journal ISSN plus a sequence number, some use a number indicating year, volume, issue, page.

★*Technically, it is the identifier that is digital, not the object – DOIs could equally well be used for physical objects, where they would resolve to information about the object, rather than to the object itself.*

www.doi.org for more information). However, for these links to work, the citations have to be absolutely accurate, and it has been shown that many are not (Meyer, 2008). The Copy-Editor may recognize that some are incomplete or incorrect, and may use automated tools to validate references against metadata databases such as the one at CrossRef (www.crossref.org – see Chapter 1, Introduction to journals, for more details about CrossRef). If validation fails, some online research may be necessary to complete the inaccurate references, before the details can successfully be submitted to CrossRef to obtain the relevant DOIs.

In addition to references/citations, some journals will include footnotes (usually presented at the bottom of the page in the print edition); these seem to be more common in humanities journals. Depending on the reference style used in the journal, these will be numbered either using Arabic numerals (with Harvard-style references) or using some other system such as symbols (with Vancouver-style references). Once again, any changes can introduce errors and a careful cross-check must be made.

When illustrative material is included, the Copy-Editor (or sometimes the Production Editor – see below) has to decide whether what the author has supplied is adequate for reproduction; if not, a new figure or file will need to be requested from the author, or failing that the figure will have to be redrawn. Tables of statistics or other data must be cross-checked with the text to make sure that they are consistent. If the author has converted a file originally produced in a different software package, the results may be gobbledygook! The preferred positioning of each illustration, table, or figure needs to be indicated in the text; captions must be checked for style, accuracy, completeness, and correct numbering.

It is also important to check that permissions have been granted for any copyright material, both textual and illustrative, and that the required acknowledgment has been included (for more information on permissions see Chapter 11, Copyright and other legal aspects). In some types of journal – particularly medical journals – pictures of recognizable individuals may be included; there are very strict guidelines[12] ensuring that the subjects have given their consent, and whenever practicable it may be

---

[12] See, for example, the *Uniform requirements for manuscripts submitted to biomedical journals* of the International Committee of Medical Journal Editors regarding patient privacy and protection of human subjects: www.icmje.org/.

preferable to conceal their identity by not showing the face, or at least blacking out the eyes.

With most authors providing their articles electronically, and Copy-Editors working on-screen with one of the standard word-processing packages, it is increasingly difficult to say where editing stops and composition begins. The edited file is likely to flow directly into whatever system is used for composition – the days are long gone when a compositor rekeyed the entire text. However, this does not mean that glitches cannot creep in,[13] so it is still important to check the proofs, particularly where late changes have been made, although many publishers no longer proof-read journal articles, relying (perhaps unwisely) solely on authors.

One of the "bibles" of copy-editing is Judith Butcher's *Copy-editing*, first published by Cambridge University Press in 1975 and now in its 4th edition (Butcher et al., 2006). In addition, a number of major societies produce their own style guides, some of which are widely used within their discipline; the key ones are listed under "Further reading" below.

### Production Editor

The Production Editing role is one of liaison and process management (and may often be subsumed with one or more of the other roles mentioned in this chapter, such as the Copy-Editor or Editorial Assistant roles). Much more detail is given in Chapter 4, The production process.

## What the Production Editor does

He or she passes articles to the typesetter, usually as soon as they are ready (sometimes known as a "copy flow" or "article-based workflow" system), but sometimes in a batch for each issue. Online systems make it much easier to keep track of what stage each article has reached. Once each article has been composed (and checked), the layout has to be finalized to make sure that tables and figures appear as close as possible to their ideal location in the text, and that any spacing problems caused by the

---

[13] A common problem occurs with special characters when an author uses a mixture of Windows and other operating systems to prepare a submission, or when an author is inconsistent in how special characters are encoded.

composition system are corrected, while making the most economical use of space.[14]

With the growth of online publication and the pressure from authors to make articles available as soon as possible, many publishers have begun to publish articles online as soon as all necessary corrections have been completed. This may not be practical for all papers (e.g., some articles may need to be published in sequence). This may mean that the paper is published online without final pagination, and a suitable unique identifier must therefore be provided for proper citation (e.g., DOI). In such instances, it is the usual practice to replace or amend the "publish when ready" version with the final "paginated" version when the paper is included in a traditional issue.

The Editor-in-Chief may choose which articles and other items appear in the next issue, and in what order; the journal may simply publish articles in order of acceptance, or they may be grouped together according to topic, article type, or for other reasons. Once the articles have been identified, it is the Production Editor's job to ensure that they all fit neatly in the number of pages allocated and make up a practical layout for printing (if there is a print version – if not, of course such concerns do not apply and, indeed, articles may be published as soon as they are ready, rather than waiting for the next issue date). If advertisements are included in the journal, their positioning also needs to be determined, possibly to make best use of partial color printing (e.g., on one side of the sheet in certain sections only), and ideally also to minimize the cost of including color illustrations where the authors need these, by including them in the same sections as color advertising (see Chapter 4, The production process). Some journals have a policy of grouping advertisements together at the beginning and/or end of the issue, while others are happy to intersperse them between or even within articles.

Once the contents and layout of the issue have been finalized, the Production Editor sends the files to the printer to produce the printed copies (if any), and to the online host for mounting the electronic version. He or she must check that both versions appear on schedule (some journals have a policy that the online version should appear first; in increasingly rare cases, it is the other way round).

---

[14] Obviously, if a journal is published only online in an HTML-based format, checking for these print-based niceties may be irrelevant.

## *Editorial Assistant*

Large journals, and large publishers, may have the luxury of one or more Editorial Assistants – in smaller setups, these duties may be subsumed in other jobs.

The Editorial Assistant provides clerical and general support for one or more journals. Most correspondence is electronic, but he or she is likely to deal with input into electronic systems such as the reviewer database, the submission/peer-review system, and the content management system (these may or may not be interconnected – for more information, see Chapter 4, The production process).[15] The Editorial Assistant may also check submitted material for completeness and adherence to the journal's Instructions for Contributors.

This job can often be the entry point for a new recruit; it provides an excellent introduction to all aspects of journal publishing, with the potential to lead to a career either in editorial management and/or commissioning, as outlined above, or in production.

### REFERENCES

Butcher, Judith, Caroline Drake, and Maureen Leach, 2006, *Butcher's copy-editing: the Cambridge handbook for editors, copy-editors and proofreaders*, 4th edn, Cambridge University Press

Hames, Irene, 2007, *Peer review and manuscript management in scientific journals: guidelines for good practice*, Oxford, Association of Learned and Professional Society Publishers/Wiley-Blackwell (http://onlinelibrary.wiley.com/book/10.1002/97804707)

*Hansard*, 1947, *House of Commons Debates*, November 11, 1947, UK Parliament, London (http://hansard.millbanksystems.com/commons/1947/nov/11/parliament-bill#column_206)

Meyer, Carol Anne, 2008, Reference accuracy: best practices for making the links, *Journal of Electronic Publishing* 11:2, Spring (http://dx.doi.org/10.3998/3336451.0011.206)

*Nature*, 2006, Overview: *Nature*'s peer review trial, *Nature* online debate, December (www.nature.com/nature/peerreview/debate/nature05535.html)

Page, Gillian, Robert Campbell, and Jack Meadows, 1997, *Journal publishing*, Cambridge University Press

---

[15] While these systems rely on authors to input their own personal and article details initially, they may need help or troubleshooting from the Editorial Assistant.

## FURTHER READING

ALPSP Advice Notes (available to all employees of member organizations) on: Managing the Editorial Office, CrossRef, and many other topics – see the ALPSP website (www.alpsp.org)

American Medical Association, 2007, *AMA manual of style: a guide for authors and editors*, 10th edn, Chicago, American Medical Association/Oxford University Press – also available in an online edition at www.amamanualofstyle.com/oso/

American Psychological Association, 2009, *Publication manual of the American Psychological Association*, 6th edn, Washington, DC, American Psychological Association – also available online at http://apastyle.org with corrections and updates

American Sociological Association, 2010, *ASA style guide*, 4th edn, Washington, DC, American Sociological Association

Brown, Diane, Elaine Stott, and Anthony Watkinson, 2003, *Serial publications: guidelines to good practice in publishing printed and electronic journals*, 2nd edn, Worthing, Association of Learned and Professional Society Publishers

*The Chicago manual of style: the essential guide for writers, editors, and publishers*, 2010, 16th edn, University of Chicago Press – also available in an online edition at www.chicagomanualofstyle.org

Coghill, Anne M, and Lorrin R Garson (eds.), 2006, *The ACS style guide: effective communication of scientific information*, Washington, DC, American Chemical Society

Council of Science Editors (www.councilscienceeditors.org) – site contains a number of useful models for editorial forms and correspondence

2006, *Scientific style and format: the CSE manual for authors, editors, and publishers*, 7th edn, Wheat Ridge, CO, Council of Science Editors

European Association of Science Editors, *Science editor's handbook*, European Association of Science Editors, ongoing – looseleaf (www.ease.org.uk/handbook)

Modern Language Association of America, 2008, *MLA style manual and guide to scholarly publishing*, 3rd edn, New York, Modern Language Association of America

Reynolds, Regina Romano, and Cindy Hepfer, 2009, In search of best practices for presentation of e-journals, *Information Standards Quarterly* 21: 20–4 (www.niso.org/publications/isq/free/FE_E-Journals_Presentation_isqv21no2.pdf)

Ritter, Robert M, 2003, *The Oxford style manual*, Oxford University Press

2005, *New Hart's rules: the handbook of style for writers and editors*, Oxford University Press

Warren, Thomas L, 1999, *Words into type*, 4th edn, Upper Saddle River, NJ, Prentice Hall

# 4 The production process

When manuscripts were submitted on paper, mailed in envelopes with postage, and edited with color pencils, production started after a manuscript was accepted for publication, and the term "production" is still used for that stage of manuscript processing. However, with the use of electronic files, the preparation of the manuscript and related figures, datasets, etc., for publication starts long before its acceptance, so that it makes sense to combine discussion of peer-review systems and production processes. As authors are asked to prepare their manuscripts for electronic submission in ways that will make the production process more efficient, we will start our discussion of production with an overview of electronic submission and peer-review systems.

## Electronic submission and peer-review systems

With the development of electronic technology for preparing manuscripts, authors went first from mailing typescripts to journal Editorial offices to mailing disks they had prepared using word-processing programs, and then to not using the mail at all when it became possible to attach article and figure files to emails or to send them using file transfer protocol (FTP).

In the late 1990s, web-based submission and peer-review systems were developed (Hames, 2007; Tananbaum and Holmes, 2008) that allowed everyone (journal Editors, reviewers, authors, assistants) involved in peer review to access, from anywhere in the world, a site on the web that allowed them to deal with a manuscript, rather than sending it to someone or waiting to receive it. This saved both time – especially time waiting for manuscripts and reviews to arrive in the mail – and money – specifically in copying, faxing, mailing, and telephone costs. In many cases, savings were realized in staff costs as well, as there was no longer a need for staff to open mail, log in paper submissions, count pages, make copies, mail manuscripts to journal Editors and reviewers, and so on. However, for many journal operations, one or more administrative staff members are still necessary, and they require a different, more technically proficient and customer-service oriented skill-set than those who counted manuscript pages and logged submissions on paper charts or spreadsheets.

Web-based submission and peer-review systems represent a vast improvement over paper-based systems, in that they are a one-stop, interactive shop for everything to do with the peer review and processing of any given manuscript. They function to:

- *Store manuscript files and related correspondence.* Text and figure files in all of their submitted and revised versions, and all correspondence about the manuscript, are stored and labeled in a way that keeps versions clear.
- *Record all peer-review steps.* The entire history of the peer-review process for that manuscript is logged and automatically time-stamped as each stage happens (submission of manuscript, assignment of reviewers, submission of reviews, Editor's decision).
- *Manage the process.* Each action performed by a user in the system (e.g., author, journal Editor, reviewer, staff) moves the manuscript through the process automatically and informs the appropriate user of the next step and its deadline, sending periodic reminders of those deadlines to the appropriate users.

There are many choices for web-based submission and peer-review systems, at a range of prices, including open-source software (e.g., the Public Knowledge Project's Open Journal Systems, http://pkp.sfu.ca/ojs) that can be downloaded from the Internet for free – see Appendix 3, Vendors, for a list of the main ones. Making a choice among systems and vendors involves the same elements that inform the decision-making process when contracting for any software tool: price, comfort with working with a vendor, product reputation, etc. But there are a few elements particular to these systems that should be considered:

- *Scalability.* Is the system able to handle a journal of your size (measured by number of submissions) and its growth? Can it handle multiple journals?
- *Features.* Does the system provide a range of features and a menu of choices to accommodate the needs of present and future journals, Editors, or staff?
- *Workflow.* Will the system accommodate the peer-review workflow used historically, especially if it is unusual or complicated? Or will the team have to change its way of working to fit the system? (This may not always be a bad thing if the system was not optimally efficient!)

- *Customizability.* Can the system be customized to accommodate users' needs if specific features or workflow choices are not already offered? Is the vendor skilled and flexible enough to customize the system in intelligent ways? However, experience with these systems has shown that a completely or heavily customized or home-built system is not necessarily the best way to go. Many authors, reviewers, and journal Editors submit to and review for multiple journals, and the fewer system idiosyncrasies they have to learn, the better the experience is for them, and the less time staff members need to spend helping them. Also, maintaining a heavily or completely customized system is much more difficult than contracting with a vendor who improves the system on a regular schedule according to what features are most often requested by all its customers.

### Staffing and author requirements

For some very small journals (e.g., fewer than fifty submissions per year), an Editor alone or with an assistant can manage the traffic of manuscripts and reviews very well via email, with a simple database or even a spreadsheet used for tracking. But even a web-based system that automates the process of peer review, sends automatic reminders, and tracks everything that happens does not remove the need for a staff person or people, sometimes called Editorial Assistants. Editorial Assistants check that manuscripts are moving through the system properly, troubleshoot software problems (sometimes with the help of the vendor's helpdesk), send reminders when the auto-reminders are exhausted, and – as experts in using the system – help authors, reviewers, and Editors when they get stuck.

Editorial Assistants also check that submitted manuscripts meet the requirements for the peer-review system and, ultimately, for production. Requirements for peer review include:

- All elements of the manuscript and associated information must be present (e.g., title, authors, affiliations, abstract, text of article, references, tables, figure files).
- The text and figure file types must permit concatenation into a single document (usually a PDF) for the convenience of reviewers.
- The authors must have correctly entered the "metadata" for the manuscript (e.g., title, author names, institutions, and email addresses) into the system.

- The authors must have answered questions that are nonoptional (e.g., prepublication or conflict-of-interest statements, Copyright Transfer statements, agreement to pay fees).

Requirements for the production of the manuscript after acceptance are also checked by a staff person (this may sometimes be the Editorial Assistant, sometimes a Copy-Editor, sometimes a Production Editor – see Chapter 3, Editing, for more details on the different roles). Although all requirements are clearly stated in the journal's Instructions for Contributors,[1] sometimes they are not enforced until the paper is accepted, the argument being that an author should not be troubled for these things until they are really needed. However, because the technology speeds up the processes of peer review (if not necessarily the reviewers themselves), production, and online publication to such an extent, many publishers try to get production-ready files from authors as early in the process as possible, sometimes even upon submission. Requirements for production may include:

- Text, and particularly figure, file types that will be optimal for both online and print publication.
- Formatted text files that can be used for peer review and immediate online publication (without further copy-editing or typesetting) upon acceptance, if the journal offers this.
- Signed Copyright Transfer form or License to Publish, as well as proof of permission to reuse previously published material, if applicable.

Authors have complained that the rigidity of what is acceptable for submission to a peer-review system and then for production has transferred to them much of the work previously carried out by the publisher (Ware, 2005). Not only do they have to provide manuscript and figure files in very specific software types and formats, but the elements of the manuscript need to be prepared according to strict guidelines to minimize any delays or errors in production.

Electronic figure files provide particular challenges both for authors and for editorial and production staff. Authors can prepare their figures using any number of different software packages; sometimes these packages permit the user to save a figure in a variety of other file types, but saving to the file type required by the journal does not always produce successful

---

[1] Also known as Instructions to/for Authors; see Box 2.2, Chapter 2, Managing journals, for more on author instructions.

results. Journal staff members have had to become quite knowledgeable about figure file types, in order to obtain from authors the files that will give the highest-quality images, both online and in print.

Once an article is accepted for publication, it moves into the traditional production phase, during which the manuscript is prepared for composition (i.e., formatting and laying out pages) and publishing online, as well as (in most cases, even now) in print.

## Print production

Much of the traditional work done in the prepress production phase of publication, such as copy-editing and composition, will apply to both the print and online versions of the journal, and so will be covered below in the section on online publication. In this section on print publications, we will limit ourselves to the aspects of production that are needed for print only.

### Paper

Depending on the size of a journal's printrun, and the bulk of the journal itself, paper can be a major portion of the expense of printing a journal (Page et al., 1997). Some larger publishers purchase paper themselves, usually through brokers, who try to balance the volatility of paper prices against storage costs. Other publishers contract for paper through their printers, thereby losing some of the control over the pricing, but allowing the printers to manage the risk and timing of buying paper and allowing for more flexibility in choosing paper stock for specific titles.

### Printing and binding

Scholarly journals are typically printed on web- or sheet-fed presses using computer-to-plate, or CTP, offset printing technology, in which a printing plate is created directly from an electronic file. Color matching and accuracy are also managed by an electronic system (called a closed-loop system) on the printing press – no longer with just the trained eye of an experienced pressman. Journals are printed in signatures – large sheets printed on both sides, containing four, eight, sixteen, or thirty-two pages, which are arranged ("imposed") in such a way that when folded, the pages fall into their correct sequence. Because it is more expensive to print in color, and this extra expense is the same whether one page or many pages on the same side of the printed sheet contain color, some publishers go to a good deal of trouble to make sure article pages with color fall into the same signatures with color advertising, to take advantage of the color paid for by advertisers. At the very least, these publishers try to get the color pages for the journal issue into the smallest number of signatures they can. This planning process is called creating a color imposition for the print journal.

The printed signatures are then sent to the bindery, where they are usually perfect bound. In perfect binding, the folded edges of the signatures are cut and roughened ("roughed-up") to improve adhesion, and glue and a heavier-stock paper cover are applied to the spine.

## Fulfillment

Some journals are then shipped to a fulfillment house for shipping to customers, but for many journals, the printer handles this, too. Fulfillment companies or in-house fulfillment departments follow all postal regulations closely to afford the publisher the best mailing rates. The customer mailing list is usually provided by the publisher, although fulfillment houses will manage the list for a publisher as well if required. (See Chapter 7, Fulfillment.)

## Reprints/offprints

With individual articles so readily available online, there is less call for printed copies of individual articles than there used to be. However, some publishers still give or sell reprints or offprints to authors and/or sell "commercial" reprints, usually to pharmaceutical or equipment companies, who use them as a sales tool.

*Offprints* are created by printing additional quantities of the journal pages as part of the initial printrun. These "extra" copies are then trimmed and stapled or saddle-stitched as individual articles. The articles will not, of course, necessarily start on a right-hand page or finish on a left-hand page unless the journal is laid out so that this is always the case; the end or beginning of the adjacent article may therefore sometimes be included (some publishers reverse the first page of the offprint if this is the case). Because they are printed at the same time as the issue, the creation of offprints requires that the publisher receives orders from authors at an early stage of production. A "reprint order form" is usually included with the author's page proofs, and due back from the author when the proofs are returned.

*Reprints* are printed separately from the main printing of the journal issue, from the same digital files used to print the journal signatures. When printed on an offset printing press, this is a much more expensive process than creating offprints because of the need to remake printing plates. But it allows for a better end-product, especially if journal articles include other elements (e.g., advertisements, or the first or last page of the adjacent article), because the printer is able to remove these elements before printing.

Reprints can also be printed digitally on a commercial-grade laser printer. This permits maximum flexibility, because changes (e.g., the removal of ads or other material) can be easily made to the pages, and the make-ready cost of creating new offset printing plates is eliminated. As the cost-per-page of printing digitally has come down, and the quality of digitally printed half-tones has gone up, this has become a more popular method of producing reprints.

### Digital printing and print on demand

Before the advent of digital printing technology, the minimum economical printrun for a journal was about 250 copies. However, the price of digital printing is continuing to fall, and its quality to rise. Although the unit cost (cost per copy) is still higher than with offset printing, it is now economically feasible to print journals with very low press runs (under 250) digitally. Because the fixed make-ready cost of preparing an offset press for each job is eliminated, the unit cost of a digitally printed journal issue varies little, whether 50 or 250 copies are printed, giving publishers the flexibility to print the number of copies that is really needed, rather than some minimum amount, the surplus of which must be either stored or discarded.

This level of flexibility has also allowed publishers to consider not printing at all unless a print copy of a journal issue or volume is ordered by a customer. This is often called "print on demand," or POD. Again, although the cost per unit is higher than with offset printing, the risk (and cost) of printing and storing copies that may not be required is eliminated, and the higher printing cost can often be recovered in the print price to the customer.

Some publishers have set up direct online ordering of print copies for customers, allowing the customer to "customize" his or her order, perhaps by personalizing the copy, or choosing different cover options. It also allows publishers to offer publisher- or customer-selected collections of articles. For instance, publishers can collect all the review articles from a journal volume and offer them to reviewers as a thank-you gift. An author can collect all of his or her publications from a journal into one bound anthology. A pharmaceutical company's sales force can give collections of articles that mention their drug – perhaps with their own designed cover, if the publisher allows it – to the medical professionals they call upon.

## Online journals

### History

The first electronic journals were distributed by email.[2] Other early examples of journal content delivered electronically were compilations of print journals loaded onto CD-ROMs, sometimes with the addition of large datasets and graphics that could not be included in print. In 1992, the *Online Journal of Current Clinical Trials* was launched by AAAS and OCLC on the Internet, but did not interest enough authors, who were wary of submitting articles to a journal that only appeared on the ethereal Internet (Page et al., 1997) and required special software to access. The introduction of the World Wide Web in the mid-1990s changed all that, however. Shortly thereafter, publishers began to make their journals available online to take advantage of the increased access and functionality afforded by the web, while maintaining print issues for their security and archivability. Some early web editions of journals were the *Journal of Biological Chemistry*, launched on the HighWire Press platform in 1995, *Protein Science*, launched by Cambridge University Press with the Protein Society in 1995, and the *NAR Online* (the online version of the very successful *Nucleic Acids Research* journal) launched by Oxford University Press in 1996 (Richardson, 1997). The increased access and functionality (e.g., rotatable protein structure models in *Protein Science*) afforded by these web-based journals were so popular that by 2008, 96.1% of publishers of science, technology, and medicine (STM) journals offered an

---

[2] For example, the *Bryn Mawr Classical Review* started in 1990 and its offshoot, the *Medieval Review* (formerly the *Bryn Mawr Classical Medieval Review*) in 1993.

online version, as did 86.5% of arts, humanities, and social science publishers (Cox and Cox, 2008).

## Backfiles or legacy content

Researchers took to finding journal content online so well and so quickly that by the late 1990s, journal Editors and publishers began to fear that anything from their journal's preonline content would no longer be cited or even found. Major scanning projects of back issues of journals, some going back to the first published issue of a journal, became popular. Often called the backfiles or "legacy content" of a journal, the articles were most often posted online as PDF files, made searchable by the use of an uncorrected or "dirty" optical character recognition (OCR) scanned text file hidden behind the PDF.[3]

A surprise for some publishers was that it was not just the research article content of these older issues that was of interest to present-day users. Science historians and others were very interested in the entire journal as it was published in print, with book reviews, meeting announcements, editorials, indexes, covers, and even advertising. Librarians, too, in their role as archivists, were not always willing to recover shelf space by discarding old print issues unless the entire content, cover to cover, was available in the online version.

### Online platforms

Online journals are placed on the web on a "platform," which provides the servers, operating system, and software to manage and organize the journal content in a way that makes it easy for users to find it and use it. The platform also provides a production-like structure or content management system so that publishers or compositors can provide content in a way that ensures it is efficiently posted online.

Some large commercial and society publishers have built their own online platforms (e.g., Elsevier's ScienceDirect, Cambridge University

---

[3] "Dirty" OCR content is created by scanning a printed page. The OCR software translates what it "sees" on the page to individual characters. In order to save many hours and dollars, the results of the scanning are not proofread by a person, and are therefore called "dirty." Although the OCR scanned text is imperfect, it is considered good enough for search engines and is never seen by "human" readers.

Press's Cambridge Journals Online, American Psychological Association's PsycNET). Other publishers contract with a hosting platform vendor – see Appendix 3, Vendors, for a list of the main players. Building a site allows a publisher complete control over functionality and features, and can make it easier to sell a package of all the publisher's journals and enhance the publisher's brand. Contracting with a hosting platform provider is the way to go for publishers who do not have the resources to build their own hosting platform. It also provides a proven template for designing an online journal, so that publishers without that expertise can benefit from the knowledge of the vendor. Third-party hosting platforms can also provide a community of like-minded publishers from which to learn best (or at least most common) practices.

When choosing a hosting platform vendor, many of the same considerations apply that were listed in the section about choosing a peer-review system vendor. If there is little expertise in-house at the publisher, a vendor with clear, useful templates for the journal interface, and one with helpful staff who will guide the publisher through the process, is a good choice. If the publisher wants to be extremely creative about the structure and elements of its online journal, a flexible, innovative vendor is a better choice. One aspect that can affect a publisher's choice is that the hosting platform sometimes takes on an identity, or branding, of its own. If a publisher wants its journals to be "seen" with the group of journals already on that platform, that can be a compelling argument to use that vendor; on the other hand, if it wants its own identity to be paramount, a highly visible platform "brand" may be less desirable.

## Search engines

Making content discoverable (see Chapter 6, Marketing and sales) is one of the most important functions of a well-designed hosting platform. In addition, it is essential to optimize the journal site itself so that those using web-wide search engines are driven to that journal's content. This involves making the content open to the search engine's "crawlers" (programs that index every word they find); this does not mean that the publisher has to make the content freely accessible to all comers.

The search engine on the journal site itself must be designed to make it easy for a searching or a browsing user to find what he or she is looking for. Most online platforms have fulltext searching capabilities, allowing users to search on any term, finding it anywhere in the text. These searches can also be structured by the metadata of an article, so that just the title, author, year of publication, abstract, or some combination of the above, is searched. Semantic searching (searching by related terms, which do not necessarily occur in the text) requires each article to be encoded using a taxonomy (prescribed and structured terminology, generally subject-specific). Creating a taxonomy and semantically encoding journal articles are highly technical and complex jobs, but vendors such as TEMIS (www.temis.com) and online platforms such as Silverchair (http://silverchair.com) provide this service.

### The elements of an online journal

While online journals can vary even more widely than print journals in the elements they contain and how these are organized (see "Building a journal issue," below), even the simplest online journal issues tend to have a table of contents or issue list, with articles listed in some kind of order, usually but not necessarily paginated through the whole issue, as they would be in print. A user browsing journal content should be able to navigate easily (whether in current articles or older content), and know where he or she is on the journal site, how to search for authors or topics, and where to look for useful information, such as how to purchase an article or subscription, how to request permission, or how to reference articles in the journal. Online platform vendors can offer templates for these elements, but publishers that heavily customize these templates or build their own sites are wise to conduct usability studies to learn how users will interact with their sites.

In general, the link for each article in the list of contents will open onto an HTML abstract page, which in many cases will offer the reader the option to view the full text of the article in HTML or as a PDF. The articles themselves may be presented in a number of ways, the most popular of which have been HTML and PDF.

The HTML file displays the article in a way that is easiest to read on a screen, with links to other sections of the article, references, figures, tables, and supplemental data. Figures and tables can be viewed in separate windows and enlarged. Overall, this gives readers a much more interactive experience with the article.

The PDF looks like the printed journal page, and is most popular with those who prefer to print an article to read offline. The typical two-column format of many printed journals can be awkward to read online. Therefore, as portable electronic readers of all kinds, including mobile phone devices, become more widely used, it is very likely that a "reflowable" format, optimized for the web (such as HTML and its derivatives), will become the more popular choice, and publishers will move away from the static PDF.

Some journals have had fulltext articles downloadable to popular portable devices, such as mobile phones and e-readers, for years. Ironically, one mobile phone application being used by publishers was developed for readers who prefer to read print. Readers who still prefer to print out a PDF on paper for reading away from their computers have no access to any related online-only information, such as supplemental data and links to other related content. Therefore, some publishers started embedding QR codes (a bit like compact bar codes) in the PDF of an article to allow the reader of the printed PDF to access online-only content. The QR code can be scanned by the ubiquitous mobile phone and contains the link to some piece of online-only content (sometimes an advertisement!) that is then viewed on the phone or other mobile device (Anderson, 2011).

### Immediate or preissue publication

Many science journals now publish articles online, individually or in daily or weekly batches, as soon as they are accepted; this may precede by some time the appearance of the final edited and formatted version in an online or print issue. These are sometimes called "Papers in Press," or "preprints," both misnomers, harking back to the days when any release of a paper, or data from a paper, before the issue was printed was considered a prepublication release. It is now acknowledged that the posting of an accepted paper on an online platform constitutes publication, even if the paper is not yet copy-edited or formatted; some of these unformatted papers are given more accurate names such as "Early View." Some publishers resolutely keep these papers in a manuscript format to make it absolutely clear that they do not represent the final publication, which will include the publisher's added value of copy-editing and layout. Others carry out basic formatting, or ask the authors to provide their manuscripts already formatted, in order to give the reader a better experience (for example, a reasonable typeface and two-column layout can prevent a reader from having to print forty pages of double-spaced typescript). Either way, these articles are still put through a more traditional production cycle before "final" publication. (See the discussion of the "Article version of record," below.)

## Production cycle

The creation of the HTML and PDF files for hosting online can follow a fairly traditional production cycle, which consists of the following steps:

- *Copy-editing*, which is done in a word-processing program.[4] The manuscript is often "preedited" first, using macros or a program such as eXtyles (www.inera.com/) to perform many routine copy-editing tasks such as regularizing punctuation and spelling, making changes to match house style, and styling reference lists. While some publishers still have their own copy-editing staff, most copy-editing functions are outsourced to freelancers or indeed to compositors. In addition, consistent word-processing style sheets can be applied (ideally during the preedit process, sometimes by the Copy-Editor) that expedite the conversion to XML or HTML.
- *XML encoding of the text*, which can be done before or after composition, and is sometimes part of the preediting programs run before copy-editing. By coding the elements of the text in a way that is both format- and medium-neutral, XML tags allow text to be reformatted to adapt to the presentational requirements of various rendering environments (e.g., print, online, mobile), or repurposed to enable the creation of derivative products. In addition, XML can provide valuable structural or semantic information about the content. In fact, many leading journal composition suppliers use XML as an inherent part of their workflow, whether or not the publisher requires XML as a deliverable from them. Those publishers that still only offer a PDF version of the content may feel they can skip this stage – however, we would argue that it is a false economy as it limits the ability to repurpose or "update" the content as the standards for online presentation evolve. (See Box 4.1 for a brief description of markup languages.)
- *File preparation for composition* involves not just copy-editing and coding the text, but preparing figure files and other files that will be linked to an online article as supplemental material (e.g., videos, large tables or datasets, software). These supplemental files in many cases cannot be published in print and are published only in the online format.

---

[4] Usually Microsoft Word, although articles on technical subjects that use a lot of math and symbols are sometimes submitted and copy-edited in TeX.

## Box 4.1 Markup languages

XML: Extensible Markup Language, now the most widely used markup language by scholarly publishers. XML may also use Document Type Definitions (DTDs) or other forms of schemas to define the markup and metadata for a given type of publication. Like SGML, it is actually a "metalanguage" used to create specific markup languages or vocabularies. The most common XML schema used by STM journal publishers is JATS, the Journal Archiving and Interchange Tag Suite, commonly known as "the NLM DTDs." Other common XML schemas are DocBook, TEI, MathML, and XHTML.

SGML: Standard Generalized Markup Language, the first markup language widely used by scholarly publishers to tag structural elements of a manuscript rather than tag for format, as was traditionally done by typesetters. SGML tags allow the manuscript to be repurposed in different media and formats without manually changing the tagging, but by running the SGML against a different style sheet. SGML uses a DTD to ensure that the elements of a manuscript are all present and consistent in placement.

HTML: Hypertext Markup Language, used to structure a document for presentation on the World Wide Web. XHTML is HTML expressed in conformance with XML requirements (see below). XHTML is also the format used for most content documents in EPUB, the standard for reflowable e-books.

HTML5: The fifth revision of the HTML standard, it is designed to provide a more strictly structure-focused model than previous versions of HTML (relying on Cascading Style Sheets to provide presentational information); to accommodate audio, video, scripting, and rendering of visual content; to provide more sophisticated typographic and layout capabilities; and to be expressed as either HTML or XHTML. It is currently a work-in-progress, although aspects of HTML5 are in common use.

- *Composition* takes the copy-edited word-processing file and lays it out in a format suitable for publication. Typesetting in the sense of rekeying the manuscript on typesetting equipment is no longer necessary, of course – computer programs can apply the selected typeface and style automatically. But although it is now primarily focused on rendering publisher-supplied data into properly formatted pages, composition is still sometimes referred to as typesetting, and the vendors who perform it as typesetters.

Most composition is outsourced to vendors. Many of these are or have offices overseas, where it is more economical to purchase electronic production services. More complex journals, with heavy design elements and a magazine-like layout, may employ in-house design and production staff who use desktop publishing software for all or part of their journal, rather than the industrial-strength enterprise systems used by most large-scale journal compositors to flow text in simply designed pages quickly and efficiently.

- *Page proofs or proofs* are often not physically sent to the authors; instead, the system generates an email containing a link to an FTP site or secure website which provides a PDF of the composed pages. Authors are expected to mark the proofs with their corrections and return them, generally between forty-eight hours and one week after the email is sent. The proofs may also be read by a proofreader, but since composition does not involve rekeying the text, reading the proofs against the manuscript is rarely done any longer. Typically, the publisher will review proofs for proper page makeup but will not do a word-for-word proofreading.

- *Handoff to printer and online platform.* In most cases, the compositor hands off the PDFs created from the composition files directly to the printer and the online platform vendor. In some cases, there is an intermediate vendor that converts composition files to XML and may also optimize the PDFs for the web. Files provided for the online platform may include:

  - Metadata containing bibliographic data, abstract, DOI, etc.
  - XML text files (if produced), for creating the HTML and as an archival file.
  - Figure files, in appropriate screen resolution for viewing online (may also include higher-resolution versions for more detailed viewing).
  - PDF of article that matches the print version.[5]
  - Manuscript file for "preissue" publication, if this is the way the preissue publication is presented online (or this may come directly from the

---

[5] The compositor will generally produce two versions of the PDF files: a high-resolution version suitable for input to the printer's direct-to-plate software, and a lower-resolution version suitable for screen display and downloading for output on a local printer.

Editorial office or peer-review system at a much earlier stage, often in the form of a PDF of the unedited word-processing document).

## Production tracking systems

Although not as popular as web-based peer-review systems, some production tracking systems based on similar principles are available, which automate the stages of production outlined above. These systems allow all relevant persons to view and work in the same environment, including staff in the Editorial offices and those at the vendor's (usually the compositor/printer that runs the system) premises. Such systems house all the files related to each manuscript in all of their versions, and push each piece of the manuscript to the appropriate next stage and person (e.g., Copy-Editor, typesetter, proofreader), while tracking where everything is so that supervisors and others can see at a glance the status of an article or issue. They are sometimes even linked directly with a submission and peer-review system, so that content flows all the way through from submission to publication.

Most publishers still use some in-house database or spreadsheets to track manuscripts through the production process, separate from the robust tracking systems at the vendors. If the publisher's tools are sophisticated enough, they can help to build the issues of the journal, based on the criteria for order of publication of accepted articles (e.g., order of acceptance, or as soon as ready for publication), just as a vendor's system would.

## Scheduling

One of the greatest frustrations felt by authors (Swan and Brown, 1999) is the time that can elapse between submission and acceptance, and between acceptance and publication. As mentioned above, online submission and peer-review systems have taken transmission delays out of the preacceptance stage. Reducing postacceptance delays was part of the reason publishers started publishing unformatted papers upon acceptance. At the same time, it is also possible to shorten the time frame for the regular production cycle. Eliminating batching of articles in the production workflow, outsourcing much of the production to vendors with twenty-four-hour shifts, and using composition systems that automate page layout and pagination can all help to shorten production time. Journals in some fields are increasingly able to compete for the best authors by their shorter "time to publication."

### Building a journal issue

Building an issue involves ordering the articles, which can be as simple as placing them in the order in which they were accepted, or became ready to be published. Or the process can be controlled by the journal Editor or publishing staff members, based on topic or article type (e.g., research, editorial, review). Articles in an issue may also need to be placed in an order that is most economical to print, for example placing color pages in the same signature (see "Printing and binding" above). Content such as editorials, book (or other media) reviews, or Letters to the Editor may also need to be positioned before or after peer-reviewed articles, as appropriate.

Building an issue also involves making sure that the masthead page (which gives the journal title, volume, issue, and date, the Editor and Editorial Board, among other things) and the table of contents are updated. While these updates can be automated for the online journal (using an algorithm to update the volume and issue numbers and the date, and pulling the article titles and author names from each article), they should be checked for accuracy for the print issue, where they are often still prepared manually. Descriptions of the elements of a simple journal issue, print or online, can be found in Table 4.1.

Of course, some journals are much more than a collection of articles posted or printed together with a journal masthead. Many include thematic sections, news, and other features, and carefully placed advertising. These issues are designed to be read or at least browsed in print by their readers, and are built with great care. Journals of this type, such as the *New England Journal of Medicine*, *Science*, and *Nature*, have correspondingly sophisticated and feature-rich websites, in which it is sometimes hard to recognize the traditional journal structure. They are browsing destinations in their own right, with, for example, stand-alone videos that *are* an article type, not just supplements to an article, and other interactive elements.

For those journals with complicated sections, such as news sections (often part of the front matter), and lots of advertising, building an issue is a much more demanding task. Advertising must be prominently placed to please advertisers, but may need to be separated from article content,

**Table 4.1**  *Elements of a journal issue*

| Print | Online |
|---|---|
| **Cover**. Journal title, volume, issue, publication date, publisher, ISSN must be clearly displayed. Librarians refer to these elements when receiving issues. The US Post Office has specifications regarding these elements if the journal is to qualify for a cheaper postal rate. Artwork, sometimes an illustration from the journal issue, is often included. | **Cover**. This seemingly unnecessary online item is often included as a thumbnail on the journal landing page, as many journals are recognized by some element on their covers, such as the color. Interestingly, authors still vie to have one of their illustrations used as the "cover image," even though most look at the journal online. |
| **Masthead**. Includes the journal title, Editor-in-Chief, Associate or other Editors, the Editorial Board, key staff members, disclaimers and copyright statement, ISSNs and ISSN-L (see Box 4.2), publisher name and address. | **Masthead**. Masthead information is linked to and archived with journal issues, so that a reader will know who was Editor when an article was published. Online versions of journals should have a separate ISSN and list the ISSN-L (see Box 4.2), especially if online and print are purchased separately. |
| **Table of contents**. Sometimes found on the front or back cover, but most often part of the journal front matter. Includes the journal title, volume, and issue number, and lists the articles and authors in the order the articles appear in the journal. Annotated tables of contents list a very brief description of the article, usually taken from the abstract. | **Table of contents**. Often auto-generated from the article metadata, it is used as a landing page from which to browse issues. The table of contents is also often sent to subscribers as an email or RSS or other feed when a new issue is published. |
| **Advertising**. Often appearing on the back cover and inside both covers, advertising can also be found within the pages of a journal, although ads interspersed within or between articles are usually avoided in scholarly journals. Placement on covers and within the front matter, especially facing the table of contents, is considered premium placement and commands a higher price. In biomedical journals, it is considered unethical to place an ad that is related to the content of an article near that article. With the rise in popularity of online job posting and networking websites, print classified ads have declined in many titles. House ads for the journal or its publisher are often used to fill in blank spaces or pages. | **Advertising**. Banner ads and side-bar ads are found on journal websites. If a journal is produced for print and online, print advertisers are often given an incentive to include some kind of online advertising. Some journals that had a strong classified advertising section, and are owned by a society or other academic community, have been able to move those ads to the society's website. |

**Table 4.1** (*cont.*)

| Print | Online |
|---|---|
| **Articles**. The bulk of journal content is the research, reports, or review articles published in each issue. | **Articles**. Scholarly articles appearing in an online issue may have been posted online by the publisher prior to the creation of the issue in order to get the research published as soon as possible. Any item of content listed in the table of contents should be tagged with a Digital Object Identifier (DOI), and the DOI should be used in references to the article. See Box 4.2. |
| | **Supplemental material**. Material that could not have been published in print can now be published as part of an article online, such as video, audio, huge datasets, or unwieldy tables. Some journals only publish a shortened version of an article, or parts of an article, in print, and publish the full article online. |
| **Other article types**. Other article types include editorials, commentaries, news, meeting announcements or summaries, and book and media reviews. | **Other article types**. Other article types include editorials, commentaries, news, meeting announcements or summaries, and book and media reviews. Letters, commentaries, or other articles related to research articles can be directly linked to the original article, their proximity to each other in the order of a bound journal no longer necessary or meaningful. |
| **Errata and retractions**. Corrections to articles published in previous issues are placed throughout or at the end of a subsequent print issue. They must be listed in the table of contents, so that indexing services can find them. | **Errata and retractions**. Corrections can be linked directly to the article being corrected or retracted. Some online journals append an automatically updated page to article PDFs that includes errata and information about where the article has been cited. |
| **Index**. These were usually prepared by professional indexers, and normally appeared at the end of a volume of journal issues. | **Index**. Most journals have abandoned having indexes even in the print versions, because it is so much easier and more powerful to search for content online. |

**Table 4.1** (*cont.*)

| Print | Online |
|---|---|
| **Supplements**. A journal supplement must be "supplement to" a journal issue and usually mails with that issue, even though it is bound separately with its own cover. These supplements can comprise the abstracts from an upcoming meeting or the proceedings of a recent meeting, and are sometimes sponsored by advertisers or the meeting sponsor. | **Supplements**. The supplement to a journal issue can be published online as well, and sometimes is published online only, even when the regular journal issues are printed. |

especially in the medical sciences, where advertising next to an article on a related topic is seen as unethical and makes a journal ineligible to grant Continuing Medical Education (CME) credit.[6]

### Journal of record

As traditional print journals went online, a debate began about whether print or online was the "journal of record" (Johnson and Luther, 2007). Because the systems of correction, retraction, primacy for patents, etc., had been used and accepted for so long, and print was still the only viable archival format, there was a fierce – but brief – claim to make the print journal the journal of record. However, publishers and librarians soon realized that elements were being added to journal articles online that could not be included in print, videos being the most obvious example. Since these "supplemental" elements were an intrinsic part of the article, there was no choice for most publishers but to make the online journal the journal of record.

### Article version of record

An article goes through many versions (e.g., as the manuscript is passed among co-authors before submission, in the stages of revision during peer review, and then in the copy-editing and production stages) before it is published in

---

[6] Some medical journals provide CME credit to physicians, who read specific journal articles and are then tested on their knowledge. There are strict guidelines that must be followed for a journal to be certified for CME, including that the materials be objective. This includes avoiding any advertisements near CME-related material in the journal.

its final version. Traditionally, "preprints" were manuscripts that researchers sent to a few colleagues for comment and critique before submitting them to journals for formal peer review. When journals started publishing peer-reviewed articles online upon acceptance but before they were published in issues, they were often called "preprints" because they had not yet been edited and formatted. The publisher wanted to make the distinction that they had not added those valuable elements, though the articles had already been revised by the author in response to the peer reviewers' comments. This led to confusion about which was the version of record. Today, the publisher's "final" online version – the copy-edited, formatted, proofed, and corrected version of an article, whether presented in an issue or not – is considered the version of record.

Being online also made the subsequent publication of errata (also called corrigenda or corrections) and retractions more obvious to the reader than they ever could be in print, thanks to the ability to link a post-publication note to the article itself. However, since it was now also possible to change anything in an article and post it back online without anyone realizing it, or even to remove the article altogether, questions arose as to how much *should* be changed in an already published article. After a few well-publicized cases in science journals of "disappearing" retracted articles,[7] the STM Association issued good practice guidelines on "Preservation of the objective record of science" (International Association of Scientific, Technical & Medical Publishers, 2006) and the traditional method of correcting the literature through the use of errata and retraction notices remains, although with variations on how it is done.[8] However, publishers will make important corrections after publication that do not affect the scientific record, such as fixing a spelling error in an author's name, or reloading a figure when the quality turns out to be unsatisfactory. This sometimes means that the online text will not match the printed journal exactly.

---

[7] For instance, between 1995 and 2003, Elsevier removed around thirty articles from its hosting platform, ScienceDirect; this was publicized when Elsevier removed a retracted *Human Immunology* article in 2002 (Plutchak, 2002).

[8] Sometimes the erratum linked to the published article describes the error and provides the corrected content (e.g., text or figure) – just as they did in print – and sometimes the article itself is corrected, and the linked erratum is a note pointing out that the change was made.

Many readers are not even aware that different versions of articles are available, although it seems that when they are aware they prefer to read (and cite) the final publisher's version (Thorn et al., 2009). In some disciplines, such as high-energy physics, they are comfortable to access, and even cite, unedited, prepublished versions. However, for publishers, as keepers of the scholarly record, it is crucially important that readers access, and authors cite, the definitive version of the article. In most cases, only the version on the publisher's site will have errata linked to an article, or will bear a retraction notice, so it is important that researchers know how to find the definitive version (Davis, 2011). In 2008, NISO (the US National Information Standards Organization) and ALPSP published a formal set of "Recommended Practices" (National Information Standards Organization, 2008). However, while publishers, and perhaps repositories, may be expected to follow these practices (although not all do), it seems unlikely that authors will ever do so. In another effort to make more obvious the definitive version, CrossRef created CrossMark (www.crossref.org/crossmark/index.html), a visual logo that is placed on an article's version of record. This mark can only be placed by the publisher of the work.

Establishing the version of record has become increasingly important as others (funding agencies, institutions and/or their libraries, and the authors themselves) post-published articles online. Publishers differ as to whether they allow authors and/or institutional repositories to post the version of record that was on the publisher's own website; many try to insist that at least a link be made from the article (in whichever version) on another website back to the journal itself. Whether they are happy about it or not, publishers have had to come to grips with the fact that the articles they have selected and prepared for publication can be found in many places other than the journal website, and are struggling with maintaining the recognition that the journal deserves for publishing a given article. (For more on this topic, see Chapter 1, Introduction to journals, and Chapter 11, Copyright and other legal aspects.)

Another aspect of versioning is that online articles on a journal's website can "change" from day to day, depending on the features that the publisher provides to users. As mentioned above, corrections can be made by the publisher through linked errata. Letters to the Editor, once the only form of post-publication commentary on an article by peers, usually separated by months in time and inches on a shelf of print journal issues, can be published months later but linked directly to the article, thereby becoming part of the article's updated record. Stretching the tradition further, some online journals allow post-publication comments to be made online either immediately or as soon as they have been vetted by an Editor. These are generally not part of a journal issue, as letters to the Editor are, but they do become part of the article record, even if they are posted long after the article issue is published. Some journals use "open peer review," and post the reviewers' (signed) comments made during peerreview. Indeed, some journals publish articles that are merely checked for sound methodology, and allow online post-publication comments to *be* the peer review. While some consider post-publication peer review to be the future of scholarly publishing, it has been slow to gain acceptance (Crotty, 2010).

### How production decisions can affect citations

*Building an issue, or not.* Even though articles can be published online as they are produced, one at a time or in batches, many publications still publish regular online issues on a monthly, bimonthly, quarterly, or weekly basis. But elements of the print issue, such as consecutively paginated articles in issues, are being broken down in the online versions. Some journals are published as individual articles online, and/or in online issues that are more frequent than print issues, and then finally in print "collections of issues" that are printed quarterly, or even once or twice a year, usually for those institutions, such as libraries, that desire a print copy for archiving. If the Editor chooses to group the articles thematically in the printed version, in order to ease browsing, the articles may not be paginated consecutively in print, as they were when they were first published online. Alternatively, some online-only journals have eschewed consecutive pagination; articles may be identified simply by article numbers instead (with each article starting on page 1). Issue numbers may not be used when articles are published one at a time as they are finalized; the calendar year may be the only bibliographic data that places the article in time.

However, issues and their tradition of consecutively numbered pages and neatly ordered tables of contents have remained important in an online world, and not only because of the print analog. Although online technology could immediately have made journal issues obsolete, customers – both libraries and abstracting and indexing (A&I) services – still expected to "receive" their journals in issue form, and all of their processing was (and still is to some extent) based on discrete issues. The American Physical Society and the American Geophysical Union eliminated page numbers when they declared their online journals the version of record in 1998 and 2001 respectively, identifying articles simply with article numbers. Both were correct in asserting that consecutive page numbers were no longer necessary, but customers had to catch up in their thinking about how journals, and the articles they contained, were used and referenced (Renner, 2002). Even now, while the A&I services can accommodate models not based on page numbering, these are still considered outside the "norm," partly because of the proliferation of approaches and lack of standards when creating article citations when the traditional volume/issue/page numbers are not used (National Federation of Advanced Information Services, 2009). When launching a new journal, it is wise to consult the most important A&I service(s) in the field to see how citations will be handled, especially if the journal's future reputation relies on measuring the number of citations. (See Chapter 5, Journal metrics, for more about the importance of citation metrics.)

*Nontraditional reference style.* Likewise, before creating a very complicated, or, conversely, bare-bones reference style for a new journal, it is a good idea to consult with someone at the *Journal Citation Reports* of Thomson Reuters, the publishers of the impact factor, to be sure that they think that citations to the new journal will be picked up consistently by their service; otherwise, valuable "hits" may be missing when the journal's impact factor is calculated.

*Early or preissue publication.* As was stated above, even though this preissue posting of an article by the publisher may not be copy-edited or formatted, it is considered "published" and citable by virtue of its online dissemination. It is important that a DOI also be assigned and displayed with this version, so that it will be picked up when the article is referenced. The same DOI should be used for the final version of the article that appears in an issue, so that citations to that article are not split or lost. (See Box 4.2 for a description of journal and article identifiers, such as the DOI.)

### Overlay and virtual journals

Some publishers have created overlay or virtual journals online. These journals contain no content unique to them, but link to content from

**Box 4.2** Article and journal identifiers and how to obtain them

**DOI:** The Digital Object Identifier (DOI) is the ISO standard that identifies content in the digital environment. For most journals, a DOI is assigned to each published article, but some journals identify smaller pieces of content (e.g., figures within an article) as well. The system is managed by the International DOI Foundation (www.doi.org/).

DOIs are obtained by registering as a publisher with a DOI System Registration Agency, such as CrossRef (www.crossref.org/). The DOI consists of a numeric string identifying the publisher, and an alphanumeric string identifying the journal and the content to be identified (e.g., the article). CrossRef provides the publisher's identifier (the prefix) and the publisher assigns the alphanumeric identifier (the suffix) to each piece of content.

**ISSN:** The International Standard Serial Number (ISSN) has been the ISO standard for identifying periodical publications, including scholarly journals, since the 1970s. It is used when purchasing journals, to avoid confusion between journals with similar or identical titles, so should be prominently displayed on the journal and its marketing pieces. A distinct ISSN should be obtained for each version (i.e., print, online) of a journal.

The ISSN is obtained, free of charge, from the ISSN International Centre (www.issn.org/).

**ISSN-L:** The linking ISSN (ISSN-L) enables mapping of different media versions of the same journal. In other words, the different ISSNs assigned to the print, online, or CD-ROM versions of a journal are all linked and discoverable through the ISSN-L.

The ISSN-L is designated by the ISSN International Centre, based on the journal's ISSN(s), and communicated to the publisher (www.issn.org/2-22637-What-is-an-ISSN-L.php).

other sources,[9] either articles published in other journals or a combination of published articles and other available material (e.g., gray literature: technical reports, white papers, Ph.D. theses). "Overlay" journals are meant to be built exclusively from open access (OA) sources: OA journals

---

[9] The American Institute of Physics and the American Physical Society publish a series of virtual journals (http://vjs.aip.org/vjs/about).

and institutional repositories, material in the public domain (e.g., US government reports), etc. "Virtual" journals make arrangements with publishers to include content from subscription-based journals; readers who link to one of these articles will either have access to the source material by virtue of an institutional subscription, or may access the article by pay per view. While overlay and virtual journals provide no new content, they conveniently gather and organize content around specific fields or topics and send alerts when new "issues" are released, helping researchers keep abreast of new articles in their disciplines.

Of course, it is now possible for any reader to construct his or her own "virtual journal" from articles of interest in one or more journals. Analogous to print-on-demand (POD) custom print journals, some online journal sites include features that allow both the publisher and the reader to make online collections of articles of interest. A publisher might create a link to a list of all the review articles published in the journal or all articles about a particular topic; a reader might be invited to create his or her own collection, or "favorites."

### Archiving/preservation of journal content

As the journal of record, the online journal has unique archiving challenges. Unlike print journals, which have historically been archived in libraries, and which remain readable and usable as long as they are not physically damaged or destroyed, electronic journals need to be preserved in such a way as to be readable using whatever software and hardware is in use at the time the journal is accessed. The expectation initially was that online journals would be preserved in this manner by their creators, the publishers. However, this has proven to be a complex and difficult task (Kelley, 2012), and there is always a risk of lacunae in the literature if journals – or even entire publishing imprints – should disappear.

Archiving initiatives have therefore sprung up (e.g., Portico [www. portico.org], LOCKSS [http://lockss.stanford.edu], and CLOCKSS [www.clockss.org]) with very different preservation and business models and different models for content migration as electronic archiving and accessing systems evolve. Reflecting the paradigm of sharing the responsibility for archiving, most of these vendors derive their revenue from publishers as the content creators and providers to the archiving system, as well as from libraries as the content users who see this as an insurance policy for accessing these electronic journals through the future.

Briefly, LOCKSS ("Lots of Copies Keep Stuff Safe") preserves content by distributing it to computers (LOCKSS boxes) at participating libraries. A web crawler compares the journal content on the web with that preserved in the LOCKSS boxes and continually corrects corrupted content. If access is lost to any journal content, even in the short term, it can be transparently replaced at the participating institution with LOCKSS content, because LOCKSS preserves the content in all of the publishers' formats. In this way, LOCKSS is more of a short-term backup system (and a way for libraries to have perpetual access to a journal they subscribed to but may want to cancel) than its sister system, CLOCKSS (or Controlled LOCKSS), or Portico, which are dark archives.

A dark archive is "a collection of materials preserved for future use but with no current access" (Pearce-Moses, 2005). Unlike LOCKSS, content preserved in a dark archive is not made available until a catastrophic trigger event occurs – for example, because the publisher ceases publication of the journal and does not pass on the publication rights to another publisher, or because the publisher ceases to exist or has a permanent failure in its delivery platform. After a trigger event, content that has been preserved in CLOCKSS is then made freely available in the publishers' formats, migrated to the currently readable file formats at the time of the trigger event. Content that has been preserved by Portico is made available (to those libraries that have subscribed to Portico) after a trigger event in a standard archival format – not the publishers' formats – which is continually migrated in the dark archive as formats change.

Issues of ensuring long-term preservation and access are also being addressed by a number of national libraries and other organizations, for example the British Library (see www.bl.uk/aboutus/stratpolprog/ccare/introduction/digital/preservplans/index.html).

## Conclusion

Thanks to electronic technology, the production of journals has probably changed more than any other aspect of journal publishing, but the basic goals of good journal production remain: to present and disseminate journal content as clearly and quickly as possible, in a way that is easiest to find, use, and preserve.

# REFERENCES

Anderson, Kent, 2011, QR codes in a journal – printing little computer programs for mobile integrations, *Scholarly Kitchen* Jan 31 (http://scholarlykitchen.sspnet.org/2011/01/31/qr-codes-in-a-journal-printing-little-computer-programs-for-mobile-integrations/)

Cox, John, and Laura Cox, 2008, *Scholarly publishing practice 3*, Worthing, Association of Learned and Professional Society Publishers (www.alpsp.org/ngen_public/default.asp?ID=200)

Crotty, David, 2010, David's pick for 2010: peer review may be old and imperfect, but it still works, *Scholarly Kitchen* December 23 (http://scholarlykitchen.sspnet.org/2010/12/23/davids-pick-for-2010-peer-review-may-be-old-and-imperfect-but-it-still-works/)

Davis, Phil, 2011, When bad science persists on the Internet, *Scholarly Kitchen* April 13 (http://scholarlykitchen.sspnet.org/2011/04/13/when-bad-science-persists-on-the-internet/)

Hames, Irene, 2007, *Peer-review and manuscript management in scientific journals: guidelines for good practice*, Oxford, Association of Learned and Professional Publishers/Wiley-Blackwell (http://onlinelibrary.wiley.com/book/10.1002/9780470750803)

International Association of Scientific, Technical & Medical Publishers (STM), 2006, *Preservation of the objective record of science* (www.stm-assoc.org/2006_04_19_Preserving_the_Record_of_Science.doc)

Johnson, Richard K, and Judy Luther, 2007, *The e-only tipping point for journals: what's ahead in the print-to-electronic transition zone*, Washington, DC, Association of Research Libraries (www.arl.org/bm~doc/Electronic_Transition.pdf)

Kelley, Michael, 2012, Potential crisis may be brewing in preservation of e-journals, *Library Journal* February 23 (www.thedigitalshift.com/2012/02/preservation/potential-crisis-may-be-brewing-in-preservation-of-e-journals/)

National Federation of Advanced Information Services (NFAIS), 2009, *Best practices for publishing journal articles*, Philadelphia, NFAIS (www.nfais.org/files/file/Best_Practices_Final_Public.pdf)

National Information Standards Organization (NISO), 2008, *Journal article versions (JAV): recommendations of the NISO/ALPSP JAV technical working group*, Baltimore, NISO (www.niso.org/publications/rp/RP-8-2008.pdf)

Page, Gillian, Robert Campbell, and Jack Meadows, 1997, *Journal publishing*, Cambridge University Press

Pearce-Moses, Richard, 2005, *A glossary of archival and records terminology*, Chicago, Society of American Archivists (www.archivists.org/glossary/index.asp)

Plutchak, T Scott, 2002, Sands shifting beneath our feet, *Journal of the Medical Library Association* 90: 161–3 (www.ncbi.nlm.nih.gov/pmc/articles/PMC100760/)

Renner, Rebecca, 2002, News focus: online pioneer winds up lost in cyberspace, *Science* 297: 1468–9 (http://dx.doi.org/10.1126/science.297.5586.1468)

Richardson, Martin J, 1997, A system for the publication of biomedical journals in multiple formats, *Learned Publishing* 10: 221–5 (http://dx.doi.org/10.1087/09531519750146923)

Swan, Alma, and Sheridan Brown, 1999, *What authors want*, Worthing, Association of Learned and Professional Society Publishers (www.alpsp.org/Ebusiness/ProductCatalog/Product.aspx?ID=49)

Tananbaum, Greg, and Lyndon Holmes, 2008, The evolution of web-based peer-review systems, *Learned Publishing* 21: 300–6 (http://dx.doi.org/10.1087/095315108X356734)

Thorn, Sue, Sally Morris, and Ron Fraser, 2009, Learned societies and Open Access: key results from surveys of bioscience societies and researchers, *Serials* 22: 39–48 (http://dx.doi.org/10.1629/2239)

Ware, Mark, 2005, Online submission and peer review systems, *Learned Publishing* 18: 245–50 (http://dx.doi.org/10.1087/095315105774648771)

## FURTHER READING

Brown, Diane, Elaine Stott, and Anthony Watkinson, 2003, *Serial publications: guidelines to good practice in publishing printed and electronic journals*, 2nd edn, Worthing, Association of Learned and Professional Society Publishers (www.alpsp.org/EBusiness/ProductCatalog/Product.aspx?ID=45)

Kasdorf, William E, 2003, *The Columbia guide to digital publishing*, New York, Columbia University Press (http://cup.columbia.edu/book/978-0-231-12498-0/the-columbia-guide-to-digital-publishing)

Ware, Mark, 2005, *Online submission and peer review systems: a review of currently available systems and the experiences of authors, referees, editors and publishers*, Worthing, Association of Learned and Professional Society Publishers (www.alpsp.org/EBusiness/ProductCatalog/Product.aspx?ID=40)

# 5 Journal metrics

## Why measure journals?

The measurement and ranking of journals has been an obsession of the scholarly communication community since at least the mid-1970s when Eugene Garfield, scientist and founder (in 1955) of the Institute for Scientific Information, first published the *Journal Citation Reports* (*JCR*), which ranked journals by the journal impact factor (JIF) (Thomson Reuters, n.d.; Adler et al., 2008). A variety of journal metrics have evolved since the release of the first *JCR*, purporting to measure a variety of journal aspects such as quality, usefulness, popularity, and influence.

But why the interest in measuring journals? Librarians want information that can inform their decisions on which journals to purchase or renew; authors want to know which are the most prestigious places to publish; and publishers want to know about the relative standing of the journals they publish and those they may try to acquire. Additionally, funding bodies and promotion committees have controversially used journal metrics as an indicator of the quality of individual authors' papers published in those journals. This in turn increases the pressure on authors to publish their work in the highest-ranked journals, and on publishers to get their journals ranked as highly as possible in order to attract the best authors.

## Journal citation metrics

Abstract notions such as prestige, influence, and quality cannot really be measured in a quantitative way, so proxy measures have become widely used. To date, the most widely used proxy for quality is citations – the system within scholarly publishing whereby authors reference (cite) earlier work that is relevant to their current research. These citations can be

With thanks to Jo Cross, who contributed most of this chapter. Parts of the content have previously been published in Cross, 2005, Cross, 2009a, Cross, 2009b, and Cross, 2010, and are reproduced with permission.

counted, and a range of "journal citation metrics" derived from these counts.[1] Since the first *JCR* was published, journal citation metrics have been widely adopted for use as proxy measures of journal quality, based on the premise that "the value of information is determined by those who use it" (Thomson Reuters, n.d.), the idea being that the value of a journal can be measured by the number of times it is acknowledged by other researchers.

### The original citation metrics

The *JCR* is published annually by Thomson Reuters, reporting metrics based on the citation activity that occurred in one year (referred to hereafter as the *JCR* year). Each edition tends to come out in June of the following year. For example, the 2011 *JCR*, which is based on citation activity in 2011, was released in June 2012.

## Total citations

The most basic metric published in the annual *JCR* is total citations. This gives the total number of citations received in the *JCR* year to articles published in the journal of interest, regardless of the publication year of those articles. So, for example, the total citations metric in the *JCR* for 2011 gives the total number of citations found in the reference lists of articles with a 2011 publication year, to articles from any publication year back to volume 1, for a given journal. When assessing the total citations metric in the *JCR*, it is important to bear in mind that older and larger journals will generally have received more citations, because they have larger bodies of previously published articles available to be cited.

## Two-year journal impact factor (JIF)

The traditional or two-year JIF is, for now at least, the most pervasive journal metric. At the simplest level, JIFs indicate the average number of

---

[1]  The ability to measure journals based on the citation system originates from the 1950s, when Eugene Garfield came up with the idea of creating an indexing service that used these article connections, the *Science Citation Index* (*SCI*). Articles were indexed along with all the citations that they made; as these articles were cited in turn, the citing articles and their citations were added to the index as well. Thus, from one article, users could follow a trail to both earlier and more recent related work.

times that articles in a journal are referenced by other articles. Creating an average, rather than just using total citations, eliminates the effects of the size and age of a journal.

Calculating a JIF requires a denominator (the total number of articles published) and a numerator (the total number of citations received by those articles). A time period, or "window," needs to be defined for both these variables. The publication window is the period during which the articles included in the calculation were published. The citation window is the period during which citations to these articles were counted.

The traditional JIFs use very specific publication and citation windows. The citation window here is the *JCR* year and the publication window refers to the two previous calendar years. Therefore, the JIFs for 2011 were calculated as follows:

$$\frac{\# \text{ citations received in 2011 to articles published in 2009 and 2010 in } Journal\ X}{\# \text{ articles published in 2009 and 2010 in } Journal\ X}$$

## Immediacy index

The immediacy index is essentially a type of one-year impact factor. It looks at citations received in the current *JCR* year to articles published in the same year. So the immediacy indexes for 2011 are calculated as follows:

$$\frac{\# \text{ citations received in 2011 to articles published in 2011 in } Journal\ X}{\# \text{ articles published in 2011 in } Journal\ X}$$

The immediacy index is generally considered to be a measure of how quickly a journal accrues citations, rather than a measure of journal impact or quality. Thomson Reuters, though, does suggest that the immediacy index can provide a useful perspective when comparing journals specializing in cutting-edge research.

Immediacy indexes can be strongly influenced by self-citations (citations to the same journal, discussed more fully in Chapter 12, Ethical issues), especially in journals that publish special or topical issues, as these often contain many citations to other articles in the same issue. They are also sensitive to publication timing: issues published late within a year will have very little time to be cited within the same year.[2]

## Cited half-life

The cited half-life of a journal is a measure of how long its articles continue to be cited. The figure is arrived at by taking every citation to the journal in the year in question, looking at the age of the articles being cited, and calculating the median figure; thus, half of the citations are to articles older than the citation half-life, and half to articles younger than the citation half-life. So, if a journal has a citation half-life of six in 2012, then half of all the articles cited that year were published in the six-year period 2007 to 2012.

The cited half-life is very subject-dependent (shorter in fast-moving subjects such as medicine and computer science, longer in areas such as mathematics or philosophy) and also varies significantly with journal type; for example, a standard research journal is likely to have a longer cited half-life than a rapid communication journal. They are not generally used as a value measure for comparing titles.

### Problems with the use of citation-based measures

Much has been written on the problems of using citation-based measures, and especially JIFs, for measuring the quality of journals. Some of the most important issues are as follows:

1. *What citations actually measure.* There is much discussion as to whether citations really are a good proxy measure for either quality or value. It is argued that a citation can mean many different things, including being a warning about flawed research (Adler et al., 2008).
2. *Human error.* Humans make errors, and errors in citations lead to errors in the citation count. The error rate for citations has been estimated to be around 7% (Moed, 2002).

---

[2] It is worth noting that publication delays also have a detrimental effect on JIFs, as late publication can mean that issues are not indexed in time for the *JCR*, and citations may miss the citation window.

3. *Limited range of journals.* All citation metrics are derived from a limited citation universe. In the case of the JIF and other *JCR* metrics, this universe is made up of the reference lists of the journals covered in the Thomson Reuters' *Science (SCI)*, *Social Sciences (SSCI)*, and *Arts and Humanities Citation Indexes (A&HCI)*, as well as the publications covered in Thomson Reuters' *Conference Proceedings Citation Indexes*. The main citation indexes currently cover approximately 11,500 journals, but according to *Ulrichs Periodicals Directory* the total number of academic, scholarly, refereed journals currently being published is over 27,500. Citations from journals not included in the citation indexes are not counted towards the JIF or other *JCR* metrics, and so these metrics give an incomplete picture. Furthermore, the coverage is not equal across subject areas; for example, as few as 15% of education journals are covered in the *SSCI*, so this problem is more severe in some subjects than others. Another criticism of the Thomson Reuters' citation indexes is that they are biased towards US and UK journals; however, they have recently expanded their coverage of journals from other countries, adding 1,600 regional journals to their indexes between 2007 and 2009.

4. *Variations between subjects.* Typical citation levels, and thus JIFs, vary widely between subject fields. There are many reasons for this, including subject differences in the lengths of reference lists; in the proportion of citations to and from nonjournal sources; in rates of coverage within the citation indexes; in the average number of authors on a paper (Davis, 2011); and in how quickly other authors cite new articles (Cross, 2009a). This means that raw citation figures and JIFs can only be used to compare journals within the same or closely related subject fields. In arts and humanities, the typical level of journal-to-journal citations is so low that citation-based journal metrics are generally not used in these fields.

5. *Variations between basic and applied fields.* Applied fields also differ from basic research fields in terms of the total number of citations received. Journals in applied fields are more likely to reference journals in related basic research fields than other applied journals. There are generally far fewer citations in the other direction, from basic research journals to applied or practitioner-focused titles.

6. *Variations by article type.* Some types of article tend to receive more citations that count towards the JIF. Review articles, i.e., articles that attempt to sum up the current state of research on a particular topic, are

generally cited more often than primary research articles. This is because authors will often cite one review article rather than the many primary research articles on which it is based. Therefore, review journals, or journals that publish a significant amount of review content along with their primary content, usually have higher impact factors than other journals in their field. (Amin and Mabe, 2000; Cross, 2009a). Rapid communication articles (known as letters in some journals) can also inflate the JIF, as these tend to be cited more rapidly than standard research articles. This means that a higher number of citations to these articles fall in the all-important JIF citation window (Amin and Mabe, 2000).

7. *Small journals.* JIFs are not very robust statistics for small journals. JIFs can be highly variable from year to year; however, it is important not to read too much into subtle changes in these figures, especially for smaller journals. A very small change in the total number of citations to a journal that publishes relatively few articles a year will lead to a high percentage change in the JIF between years. This is especially true when we look at journals that have relatively low JIFs to start with. These apparently large changes can cause celebration or consternation depending on the direction of change; however, these variations are often not significant (Amin and Mabe, 2000).

8. *What is counted.* There is a discrepancy in citation and article counts for the JIF. Many journals publish nonsubstantive items such as news articles, editorials, letters to the editor, and meeting abstracts, often referred to as "nonsource items." These items are almost never cited and, so that journals publishing this material are not unduly penalized, they are not counted in the article total (the JIF denominator) for JIF calculations. Although these "nonsource items" are rarely cited, there are exceptions, and interestingly these citations do count towards the citation total (the numerator of the calculation). The consequence of this discrepancy is that journals publishing a large number of "nonsource items" (which is more common in some fields, such as medicine), or journals publishing particularly interesting "nonsource items," can have artificially inflated JIFs. For these journals, citations to articles that are not counted in the denominator *are* counted in the numerator. These citations can be considered to be "free" citations (Cross, 2009a).

9. *Skewed distribution within the journal.* The distribution of citations to articles within a journal is generally highly skewed. JIFs are designed to be

"a measure of the frequency with which the 'average article' in a journal has been cited in a particular year" (Thomson Reuters, 1994). However, in most journals, a minority of articles receives the majority of citations (Seglen, 1997; *Nature*, 2005; Adler et al., 2008). This means that the JIF often does not actually give a good indication of the frequency with which the "average article" has been cited (Cross, 2009a).

10. *Potential for manipulation.* There is a feeling that citation metrics can be manipulated. The alleged manipulation methods include negotiating with Thomson Reuters about which items should and should not be included in the JIF denominator (Rossner et al., 2007). There is also some evidence of attempts by journal Editors to boost JIFs by publishing editorials which cite a large number of articles from the last three years of the journal, or by insisting that authors include more references to the journal before their articles will be accepted. Thomson Reuters has responded to this in recent years by suppressing JIFs for journals with a suspiciously high level of self-citation.

### Newer citation-based metrics

For many years, potential alternatives to the Thomson Reuters' two-year JIF have been put forward. Until recently, most languished in relative obscurity, but in the last few years a few have gained some traction.

Several of these are based on a different citation universe from that of the *JCR* measures. In 2004, Elsevier launched its own citation database, Scopus, as a direct competitor to the Web of Science (the online version of the Thomson Reuters' *SCI*, *SSCI*, and *A&HCI*). Scopus currently covers 18,000 journals and so has a larger pool of citations than the Web of Science (though this is still far short of comprehensive coverage of all the world's scholarly journals).

Most of the newer metrics are designed to address some of the shortcomings of the JIF, but all still have the general problems of using citations as a proxy for "quality."

### *Five-year impact factor*

One of the main criticisms faced by the traditional JIF is that it captures only a small percentage of the citations received by articles over their lifetime, and this percentage varies greatly by subject area (Cross, 2009b).

For many years, there were calls for the creation of a metric that would take into account a greater percentage of lifetime citations, and that would provide a more meaningful indicator in subject areas where research retains relevance for longer periods, such as the social sciences and mathematics. It has always been possible to calculate five-year JIFs manually from data available in the *JCR*, but without the stamp of an officially published metric these lacked authority.

In the 2009 *JCR* release (covering 2008 data), Thomson Reuters published five-year JIFs for the first time. These use the same one-year citation window as the traditional two-year JIFs, but extend the publication window back an additional three years. Thus the 2011 five-year JIFs are calculated as follows:

$$\frac{\text{\# citations received in 2011 to articles published in 2006–10 in } Journal\ X}{\text{\# articles published in 2006–10 in } Journal\ X}$$

In summary, the differences between the two-year JIF and the five-year JIF are as shown in Table 5.1.

Thus the impact factor window for the five-year JIF will cover a much larger percentage of lifetime citations. However, although this can be considered a more meaningful indicator than the standard two-year JIF in subjects where citations take longer to build, the five-year JIF does little to reduce subject differences in impact scores. The larger article population used in the denominator of the five-year JIF should, however, iron out some of the high year-on-year variation seen in the two-year JIF values, especially for very small journals.

**Table 5.1** *Differences between two-year and five-year journal impact factor*

| Two-year JIF | Five-year JIF |
| --- | --- |
| Each article published is included in the denominator for two *JCR* years (the two years after the year of publication). Thus, an article published in 2005 is included in both 2006 and 2007 impact factors. | Each article published is included in the denominator for five *JCR* years (the five years after the year of publication). Thus, an article published in 2005 is included in the five-year JIFs from 2006 to 2010. |
| Citations received in the year of publication, or in the third year after publication or later, will not count towards any JIF calculation. | An extra three years of citations will be counted towards the five-year metrics compared to the two-year metrics. |

## Eigenfactor

The Eigenfactor was developed as an academic research project in the Department of Biology at the University of Washington by Jevin West, Carl Bergstrom, Ben Althouse, Martin Rosvall, and Ted Bergstrom. Using the same set of journals indexed in the *JCR*, the Eigenfactor is designed to be a measure of the influence of a journal within the body of scholarly literature, using techniques from network theory to rank journals not only according to how often they are cited, but also taking into account the "influence" of the titles that cite them. Thus, not all citations are equal: citations from journals that receive a high number of citations themselves are given more weight than those from less-cited journals. This is similar to how Google's PageRank algorithm ranks the influence of web pages. Eigenfactor scores are scaled, so that the sum of the scores of all journals listed in the *JCR* is 100 (Bergstrom et al., 2008).

Eigenfactors attempt to adjust for subject differences in the number of citations available by using the weighted percentage of total citations to all journals in the dataset, rather than the absolute number. In addition, less weight is given to citations from review articles, which tend to have very long reference lists. Another difference between the citation data used to calculate Eigenfactors and JIFs is that Eigenfactor data automatically exclude self-citations, since Eigenfactors are designed to look at the interconnectivity of journals.

The Eigenfactor is designed to be a measure of the total influence of a journal, rather than the influence of the average article within it, and as such it is not adjusted for journal size. Thus, Eigenfactors are in some ways more comparable to the total citations metric, except that Eigenfactors only count citations received in the *JCR* year to articles published in the previous five years. Since the Eigenfactor does not account for journal size, larger journals will generally tend to have higher Eigenfactors. Furthermore, journals which are less than five years old will be at a disadvantage, as fewer publication years will be included in the metric.

## Article Influence Score

Another metric created by the developers of the Eigenfactor is the Article Influence Score (AI Score). This metric is designed to measure the influence of the average article within a journal, and as such is more comparable to the five-year JIF.

AI Scores are calculated by dividing the Eigenfactor by the percentage of all articles covered by the *JCR* in the previous five years that were published in that particular journal. AI Scores are normalized, so that the mean figure for the whole *JCR* is 1.00. Therefore, a score of 2.00 indicates that the "average" article in the journal has twice the "influence" of the average article within the *JCR* dataset, while a score of 0.50 indicates that it has half the "influence" of the average *JCR* article.

Further information on Eigenfactors and Article Influence Scores can be found at www.Eigenfactor.org/methods.htm. This site also includes Eigenfactor and Article Influence Score rankings from 1995 to 2006; however, the subject classification on this site is different from that in the *JCR*.

## SJR (SCImago Journal Rank) indicator

The SJR indicator is another metric which weights citations based on the impact of the citing journal, but using Scopus as its data source. This metric is similar to the Article Influence Score, as it also takes journal size into account. However, it is based on a three-year rather than a five-year publication window and the weightings are different, so the two measures are not comparable (González-Pereira et al., 2010).

The SCImago website (www.scimagojr.com), which is free to access, also gives Cites per Document figures similar to the JIF for journals covered in Scopus. Two-, three-, and four-year figures are available.

## SNIP (Source Normalized Impact per Paper)

The SNIP metric is another recent metric based on data from the Scopus citation database. The main aim of SNIPs is to attempt to adjust for subject differences in citation patterns, by normalizing raw impact (average citation) scores against the citation potential in a journal's subject field. The normalization process means that raw impact scores are increased for journals covering subjects where there are fewer citations, and decreased for journals in subjects with a higher frequency of citations. The idea is that SNIPs, unlike JIFs, give a measure that can be used to compare journals across fields as well as within fields. SNIPs also address one of the other commonly raised issues with JIFs – that references to all papers are included in the citation count, but not all types of paper are included in the article count (Cross, 2009b).

There is some evidence to suggest that SNIPs do adjust for subject difference to at least some degree (Moed, 2010). However, this is a relatively new metric and it has yet to face the years of scrutiny to which the JIF has been subjected. It will be interesting to see critiques of the metric as time goes on. It appears that SNIPs will not be easily comparable between years. Although the previous years' metrics will be recalculated at each release to account for changes in the database, each year of SNIPs appears to be normalized against the median journal for that year. This means that the normalization factor for a journal will vary from year to year, making differences between years difficult to interpret.

SNIPs are freely available at www.journalindicators.com, a website of the Centre for Science and Technology Studies at Leiden University, where they were developed; they are also available at the Elsevier site www.journalmetrics.com, as well as being integrated into the Elsevier's Scopus Journal Analyzer along with SJR indicators.

## h-*index*

Another metric that has gained a certain amount of attention is the *h*-index or Hirsch-index. This metric was initially suggested by Jorge E. Hirsch to look at the output of a single researcher rather than the output of a particular journal.

Hirsch defined the index as follows: "A scientist has index h if h of his or her $N_p$ papers have at least h citations each and the other $(N_p - h)$ papers have $\leq$h citations each" (Hirsch, 2005). Thus, a researcher with an *h*-index of 4 has published four articles that have received four or more citations (and any number of papers that have received fewer than four citations). This measure is designed to take into account both productivity (number of articles published) and impact (number of citations received), indicating the number of more highly cited articles and how highly these have been cited. Unlike the average number of citations per paper, the *h*-index is not skewed by one very highly cited article, nor does it disadvantage authors who have published a large number of papers. Since its inception, many variations on the metric have been proposed which attempt to do various things, such as giving more importance to the top-cited articles, or adjusting for subject differences (Alonso et al., 2009; SCI, 2010).

Although the *h*-index was designed to look at the output of a single researcher, it can be applied to any set of articles. Thus, although the *h*-index is not an official journal measure, it can be calculated for the output of a particular journal. Both Web of Science and Scopus will automatically calculate an *h*-index for a journal when a search of all articles published in that journal is selected. The figure will differ in the two databases, owing to the different citing population, and will also be affected by the number of publication years included in the search. Unlike the *JCR* metrics mentioned above, there is no strict definition of the publication window for an *h*-index. *h*-indexes based on Scopus data are also published for journals on the SCImago website – these appear to be based on all publication years covered in Scopus.

All these new journal metrics aim to tell us more than the simple JIF; but its simplicity is one of the reasons the JIF has remained so pervasive in the scholarly communication world. Unlike some of the newer metrics, it is easy to understand, and its calculation can be broken down into two simple components: the number of citations received and the number of articles published. Its value also has stand-alone meaning: a journal with a JIF of 2.000 receives on average two citations per paper in the specified time period. An Eigenfactor of 0.022, for example, is meaningless out of the context of the scores for all other journals.

### Ensuring that a journal is measured

For a journal to be given a JIF, or any of the other metrics published in the annual *JCR*, it must be indexed in the *Science Citation Index* or the *Social Science Citation Index*. To be covered in these indexes, a journal must undergo review by Thomson Reuters' editorial staff, who make a judgment call on the value of the journal to their indexes' core markets. Journals covered only in the *Arts and Humanities Citation Index* are not included in the annual *JCR*, as the level of journal-to-journal citations within these areas is not generally high enough to sustain any robust citation metrics.

Thomson Reuters states that "many factors are taken into account when evaluating journals for coverage, ranging from the qualitative to the quantitative." They go on to say that "no one factor is considered in isolation but, by combining and interrelating the data, the editor is able to determine the journal's overall strengths and weaknesses" (Testa, n.d.).

Thomson Reuters breaks down the factors that it looks at into four categories:

1. *Basic journal publishing standards.* These include publishing issues on time; evidence of peer review; informative journal titles; descriptive article titles and abstracts; complete bibliographic information for all cited references; full addresses for every author; and the inclusion of bibliographic information in English.
2. *Content.* The subjects and topics covered by the journal. If the editor feels that a journal's field is adequately covered by journals that are already indexed, then that journal may not be selected for inclusion. So it is important to emphasize the uniqueness of a journal in the publisher's submission.
3. *International diversity or unique regional perspective.* Where journals target an international audience, international diversity is looked for in the journal authors, editors, and Editorial Boards. Regional journals that the evaluating editors feel would enrich the "coverage of a particular subject or provide studies with a specific regional perspective" are also accepted (Testa, n.d.).
4. *Citation activity.* The evaluating editors study citation activity from journals already covered in the citation indexes to the journals they are evaluating. They look at total citations and rough JIFs, along with potential levels of journal self-citation (which must not be too high). For newer journals, they may also look at the citation profile of the journal authors, Editors, and Editorial Boards.

Getting a journal covered in Scopus as well as the *JCR* will ensure that it is included in the Scopus-based metrics: the SJR and SNIP. Scopus uses a Content Selection and Advisory Board comprising "an international and independent panel of experienced editors of peer-reviewed international journals, and other experts in the fields of publishing, bibliometrics and library science" (Scopus, n.d.) to review titles suggested for inclusion, and to define the quality standards for the journal content of Scopus.

According to the Scopus website (www.info.sciverse.com/scopus/scopus-in-detail/content-selection), titles must meet the following minimum criteria to be considered for coverage:

1. The title should have peer-reviewed content;
2. The title should be published on a regular basis (preferably have an ISSN);
3. The content should be relevant and readable for an international audience (for example, have English language abstracts and references in Roman script);
4. The title should have a publication ethics and publication malpractice statement.

Additionally, Scopus looks for qualitative indicators such as:

5. Conformity with established best publication industry practice in respect of ethics and formatting;
6. Originality of thought and content;
7. Credibility and trustworthiness of content;
8. Utility of content to a specialist or general readership. (Scopus, n.d.)

Like Thomson Reuters, Scopus also looks at citations – both to articles within the journal and to other articles by the journal authors and Editors.

It is generally considered easier to get a journal accepted for coverage in the Scopus database than in Thomson Reuters' citation indexes. Scopus seems more focused on breadth of coverage than Thomson Reuters, who use their more stringent selection process as a selling point for their databases, on the basis that their databases limit users' searches to the most important journals in a field, filtering out research in journals of a lower standing (Testa, n.d.).

## Journal usage metrics

In the print world, it was hard to measure how much journals were being read, though librarians tried through surveys, re-shelving studies, and even by examining the dust on the copies on the shelves! Now that almost all journals are available online, usage data showing fulltext downloads and other activities can be extracted from server logs recorded by the sites that host them (although of course this does not include any usage from the print version, if there is one). These rich online usage data are now available to publishers and libraries. How much a journal is read could be considered to be a good measure of its popularity or usefulness.

Unlike citation data, usage data tend to be produced by the publishers themselves or by their contracted platform providers. In order for usage to become a trusted source of data for the compilation of journal metrics, an independent organization was needed to create and implement industry standards. This role has been taken on by COUNTER (Counting Online Usage of NeTworked Electronic Resources), a not-for-profit company whose Board of Directors, Executive Committee, and International Advisory Board are made up of representatives from the publishing and library communities, along with other parties interested in the provision of usage data.

The COUNTER Code of Practice for Journals and Databases (currently on its fourth release) specifies the types of data that should be provided to journal subscribers, and the format in which this data should be provided; it also spells out guidelines on the exclusion of certain types of download from the data, such as those generated by Internet crawlers/robots, and those generated by user double-clicks. The full Code of Practice can be found on COUNTER's website (www.projectcounter.org). COUNTER also requires that compliant vendors are audited, to ensure they meet all the requirements of the Code.

The provision of standardized and reliable usage data from journal publishers has allowed librarians to look at metrics based on the usage of journals at their institutions. The most common metrics are total usage and cost per download (cost of the journal divided by number of downloads). These have both become extremely important metrics when making decisions on which journals to cancel, when budgetary pressures require the downsizing of collections. (See Chapter 6, Marketing and sales, n. 10).

Publishers, of course, have access to their own usage data, which they can use to create internal metrics with which to compare the popularity of their journals, and also to identify which ones may be at highest risk of cancellation due to low usage. (For more on this, see Chapter 6, Marketing and sales.) However, the overall usage data for journals currently tend not to be in the public domain, and as yet there are no universal usage metrics akin to the many available citation metrics.

COUNTER has been looking into the creation of such metrics for several years now, in what started as a joint project with UKSG (formerly the UK Serials Group). The latest report from their collaboration, the Journal Usage Factor project, concludes that the production of such a measure is feasible and would be widely, if not universally, welcomed by the scholarly communications community; it will be interesting to follow developments in the next few years (Shepherd, 2011).

Metrics based on usage data have some advantages over citation metrics. For example:

- Usage data are more immediate than citation data, which can take several years to accrue.
- Usage data are available for all subject areas, including those, such as arts and humanities, where lower citation levels mean that citation metrics are not useful.
- The usefulness of practitioner and applied journals may be better represented by usage data.

However, it is accepted that journal usage data suffer from some of the same problems as citation data, such as being skewed by a minority of highly used articles, being highly volatile and prone to statistical noise, following different patterns in different subject areas, and being affected by different document types. Usage metrics are also potentially much easier to "game" than citation metrics. The CIBER research group, based at University College London, which undertook the most recent phase of the Journal Usage Factor project, has therefore made the following recommendations as to what a Usage Factor metric should be and how it should be used:

- The Journal Usage Factor should be calculated using the median rather than the arithmetic mean . . .
- A range of usage factors should ideally be published for each journal: a comprehensive factor (all items, all versions) plus supplementary factors for selected items (e.g., article and final versions) . . .
- Journal Usage Factors should be published as integers with no decimal places . . .
- Journal Usage Factors should be published with appropriate confidence levels around the average to guide their interpretation . . .
- The Journal Usage Factor should be calculated initially on the basis of a maximum time window of 24 months. It might be helpful later on to consider a 12-month window as well (or possibly even a 6-month window) to provide further insights . . .
- The Journal Usage Factor is not directly comparable across subject groups and should therefore be published and interpreted only within appropriate subject groupings . . .
- Small journals and titles with less than 100 downloads per item are unsuitable candidates for Journal Usage Factors: these are likely to be inaccurate and easily gamed . . .
- Further work is needed on usage factor gaming and on developing robust forensic techniques for its detection. (Shepherd, 2011)

Usage data also have their own limitations. Downloaded doesn't necessarily mean read, and read doesn't necessarily mean "found useful." Thus,
usage metrics based on counts of fulltext downloads (FTDs) are still proxy,
rather than direct, measures of a journal's usefulness. Platform differences
may also greatly affect the number of downloads an article receives. Some
platforms direct entitled users straight to the full text (usually including the
abstract), while others take them to the abstract first (with the full text
requiring a further click). In either case, the user may decide that the
article is not relevant based on the abstract and read no further; on the first
platform this would count as a fulltext download, but on the second it
would not. Promotions that highlight papers or special issues can also
greatly affect the usage of a journal, especially if the content is made free
for a period of time. (See discussion of "The power of 'free'" in Chapter 6,
Marketing and sales.) It would seem harsh to consider this "gaming" of the
usage figures, but it is certainly likely to benefit larger publishers, with
larger marketing budgets, over smaller publishers. Accessibility is also
likely to affect usage data. Open access content tends to receive higher
usage than content behind subscription barriers (Davis, 2011). If an
element of usage metrics simply measures accessibility, this will reduce
the validity of these metrics as proxy measures of usefulness or quality.

## Peer-review-based journal classification systems

Many academics, especially those based in subjects where citation activity
tends to be lower, feel that the traditional citation-based ranking systems
do not serve the journals in their fields. They may feel that a usage-based
journal metric would be more suitable, but, as mentioned above, the
industry is still some way from actually producing a universal set of Journal
Usage Factors.

   This has led to the development of journal classification systems based
on qualitative judgments (i.e., a form of peer review) rather than quantifi-
able measures. Examples of these ranking systems are highlighted below,
though it should be noted that some do include an element of citation
analysis alongside peer evaluation:

- *ERIH (European Reference Index for the Humanities).* This ranking system
  developed by the European Science Foundation (ESF) classifies journals
  as NAT (National) or INT (International), and further splits the

international journals into INT1 and INT2 based on the panel's judgment of each journal's visibility and influence level (www. esf.org/research-areas/humanities/erih-european-reference-index-for -the-humanities.html).

- *The Journal Quality List.* This covers academic journals in Economics, Finance, Accounting, Management, and Marketing. The Journal Quality List does not itself rank journals, but rather pulls together rankings and scores from around twenty journal ranking lists in these fields. It is created by Anne-Wil Harzing, a professor in International Management (www.harzing.com/jql.htm).

Some countries (e.g., Australia, Norway, and South Africa) have also produced lists of approved journals, publication in which counts towards research evaluation. The Excellence in Research for Australia (ERA) list ranked journals A★ to C but after "evidence that the rankings were being deployed inappropriately within some quarters" (Carr, 2011), a decision was made to discontinue these rankings.


## The rise of nonjournal metrics

Journal metrics, especially the JIF, have been controversially used by funding bodies and promotion committees to measure the quality of an author's output. Authors could gain points, or even direct financial rewards, for publishing in journals with higher JIFs. However, as mentioned, JIFs can be highly skewed by a few highly cited articles, and may say little about the citation profile of the majority of articles in a journal. This has led to a move towards the use of article-level metrics, and the combination of these into metrics at the author, research group, institution, or even country level.

If one has access to either Web of Science or Scopus, the number of citations to an article published in a journal indexed by them can easily be found. Citation counts can also be found from Google Scholar, though there is some concern about the quality of citation matching, including problems with double counting where a citing article is available in more than one form on the Internet (e.g., preprint and final published version). The CrossRef system, which enables linking from the references in one publisher's journals to articles in other participating publishers' journals, can also be used to provide citation counts for individual articles (for more on CrossRef, see Chapter 1, Introduction to journals). It should be noted that the number of citations given by different sources will often vary, owing to their different coverage and citation-matching systems. Many publishers are now starting to publish citation counts next to the articles on their own platforms. The Public Library of Science (PLoS), for instance, provides citation counts from Web of Science, Scopus, and CrossRef for articles published in its journals. PLoS and other publishers also now publish the number of downloads received so far for each article.

One of the problems with usage data is that articles can be available in several forms in different places – for example, on the publisher's website, in an aggregator's fulltext database (e.g., EBSCOHost or JSTOR) and in institutional or subject repositories. COUNTER has been working with JISC (the body that funds IT-related projects for UK universities) on a project called PIRUS (Publisher and Institutional Repository Usage Statistics) to look at the feasibility of collating article-level usage metrics which incorporates usage from all the various article locations.

In 2009, the PIRUS project reported that it had demonstrated:

- The technical feasibility of creating, consolidating, and reporting usage at the individual article level, based on usage data from a range of different platforms.
- A practical technical/organizational model for a Central Clearing House (CCH) for the global consolidation of article usage statistics that can handle the large volumes of usage data and associated metadata involved.
- An economic model that provides a rational and cost-effective basis for allocating the costs of the CCH among the repositories, the participating publishers and other clients that would use it.

However, the report notes that "organizational, intellectual property and political issues have yet to be fully addressed and it should be noted that the surveys carried out in Phase 1 showed that not all publishers and not all repositories enthusiastically endorse the principle of reporting usage at the individual article level" (PIRUS, 2009). While some of these obstacles still exist at the end of the second phase of the project, the PIRUS2 project did develop a workable technical model and more practical goals targeted at organizations that are in a position to help overcome organizational or economic obstacles (PIRUS2, 2011).

As well as citations and usage, people are starting to look at other article-level metrics, often based on the social web. The altmetrics movement (http://altmetrics.org), for instance, is encouraging the development and testing of article metrics based on links and bookmarks to, and conversations about, articles on social media sites. Other sites such as Faculty of 1000 (http://f1000.com) publish reviews and rankings by other researchers for articles in particular biomedical subject areas.

Using article-level figures as the raw data, both citation metrics and – potentially – usage metrics can be calculated at various levels. The *h*-index, as mentioned earlier, was originally derived as an author-level metric. One problem with creating author-level metrics is disambiguating authors with the same name. To get round this, the main citation providers have started to produce unique identifiers for authors which allow the calculation of author citation metrics:

- Author ID (Scopus) provides search disambiguation and citation and publication metrics for authors on Scopus.
- Researcher ID (Thomson Reuters) provides publication and citation data for registered researchers via a freely accessible website (www.researcherid.com).

However, a multiplicity of different "unique identifiers" for authors is not ideal, and so another initiative, ORCID (Open Researcher and Contributor ID, http://orcid.org), has been set up with the stated mission "to solve the author/contributor name ambiguity problem in scholarly communications by creating a central registry of unique identifiers for individual researchers and an open and transparent linking mechanism between ORCID and other current author ID schemes." Authors can also gather data on their personal citation profiles using the *Publish or Perish* program (www.harzing.com/pop.htm), which uses data from Google Scholar.

Both Thomson Reuters, via its InCites brand, and Elsevier, via its SciVal brand, also sell custom research including citation profiles at the institutional or research group level. These profiles can contain a variety of relatively simple metrics such as total citations, average citations per paper, and percentage of uncited papers. They also often provide more complex analysis of collaboration and co-citation patterns (where articles cite one or more of the same papers), and of emerging research fronts. These custom reports are targeted at policy makers and administrators at government agencies, universities, and funding bodies, among others. It is intended that these types of tool will help such bodies move away from journal-level metrics to citation data specific to individual authors or groups.

A standard set of institutional-level citation metrics (based on Scopus data) for institutions publishing over 100 articles a year is also available from the SCImago research group on their Institution Rankings page (www.scimagoir.com). The main SCImago Journal and Country Rank page also contains a wealth of free citation information at the country level.

The growing importance of article-level metrics (and the combination of these into higher-level ones) may well have an interesting effect for journal metrics. It will no longer be enough simply to publish an article in a journal with a high JIF. There will be more pressure on authors to raise the citation profile of their own articles. However, this does not necessarily mean that authors will become less interested in publishing in journals with high JIFs; there is some evidence of a "Matthew Effect"[3] for journals (Larivière and Gingras, 2010). Occasionally, identical papers are published in multiple journals (sometimes under dubious circumstances – see Chapter 12, Ethical issues) and there is evidence that these duplicated articles tend to receive more citations when published in journals with higher JIFs. Thus, even if analysis of authors moves towards article-level metrics, it seems likely that publishing in a high-impact, high-profile journal will continue to be advantageous.

## Using citation and usage data for journal development

Publishers who have access to Web of Science or Scopus can easily see which papers from their journals have attracted the most citations. They can look for recurring authors and themes in these papers, and use this information to inform the future direction of the journal. Internal usage data can also be used in a similar way, and many publishers should have access to rich data in this area.

Journal publishers can also use the freely available data on Researcher ID.com to find out more about the citation profiles of potential editors

---

[3]  "For to all those who have, more will be given, and they will have an abundance; but from those who have nothing, even what they have will be taken away" (Matthew 25:29, the Bible, New Revised Standard Version).

and authors. In addition, the data on SCImago Journal and Country Rank can provide data on publication and citation trends by country for the subjects covered by the publisher's journals.

## REFERENCES

Adler, Robert, John Ewing, and Peter Taylor, 2008, *Citation statistics*, Berlin, International Mathematical Union (www.mathunion.org/fileadmin/IMU/ Report/CitationStatistics.pdf)

Alonso, S, F J Cabrerizo, E Herrera-Viedma, and F Herrera, 2009, *h*-index: a review focused in its variants, computation and normalization for different scientific fields, *Journal of Informetrics* 3: 273–89 (http://dx.doi.org/10.1016/j. joi.2009.04.001)

Amin, Mayur, and Michael Mabe, 2000, Impact factors: use and abuse, *Perspectives in Publishing* 1: 1–6 (www.elsevier.com/framework_editors/pdfs/Perspectives1.pdf)

Bergstrom, Carl T, Jevin D West, and Marc A Wiseman, 2008, The Eigenfactor metrics, *Journal of Neuroscience* 28: 11433–4 (http://octavia.zoology.washington. edu/people/jevin/Documents/Bergstrom_J_neurosci_2008.pdf)

Carr, Kim, 2011, *Improvements to Excellence in Research for Australia*, Australian Government website (http://minister.innovation.gov.au/carr/mediareleases/ pages/improvementstoexcellenceinresearchforaustralia.aspx)        (accessed September 12, 2011)

Cross, Jo, 2005, Impact factors – back to basics, *Editors' Bulletin* 1: 23–30 (http://dx. doi.org/10.1080/17521740701695897)

2009a, Impact factors – the basics, in Graham Stone (ed.), *The e-resources management handbook*, Newbury, UKSG (www.uksg.org/publications/ermh)

2009b, New journal metrics make an impact, *Editors' Bulletin* 5: 209 (http://dx.doi. org/10.1080/17521740902920037)

2010, Are impact factors facing the SNIP?, *Editors' Bulletin* 6: 43–50 (http://dx.doi. org/10.1080/17521742.2010.534874)

Davis, Philip M, 2011, Open Access, readership, citations: a randomized controlled trial of scientific journal publishing, *The FASEB Journal* 25: 2129–34 (http://dx. doi.org/10.1096/fj.11-183988)

González-Pereira, Borja, Vicente P Guerrero Bote, and Félix de Moya-Anegón, 2010, A new approach to the metric of journals' scientific prestige: the SJR indicator, *Journal of Informetrics* 4: 379–91 (http://dx.doi.org/10.1016/j. joi.2010.03.002)

Hirsch, Jorge E, 2005, An index to quantify an individual's scientific research output, *Proceedings of the National Academy of Science* 102: 16569–72 (http://dx.doi.org/ 10.1073/pnas.0507655102)

Larivière, Vincent, and Yves Gingras, 2010, The impact factor's Matthew Effect: a natural experiment in bibliometrics, *Journal of the American Society for Information*

*Science and Technology* 61: 424–7 (www.ost.uqam.ca/Portals/0/docs/articles/ 2009/MathhewsEffect.pdf)

Moed, Henk F, 2002 The impact-factors debate: the ISI's uses and limits, *Nature* 415: 731–2 (http://dx.doi.org/10.1038/415731a)

2010, Measuring contextual citation impact of scientific journals, *Journal of Informetrics* 4: 265–77 (http://dx.doi.org/10.1016/j.joi.2010.01.002)

*Nature*, 2005, Not-so-deep impact, *Nature* 435: 1003–4 (http://dx.doi.org/10.1038/ 4351003b)

PIRUS, 2009, Project team, Tim Brody, Richard Gedye, Ross MacIntyre, Paul Needham, Ed Pentz, Sally Rumsey, Peter Shepherd, Developing a global standard to enable the recording, reporting and consolidation of online usage statistics for individual journal articles hosted by institutional repositories, publishers and other entities, January (http://tinyurl.com/PIRUSreport1)

PIRUS2, 2011, Peter Shepherd and Paul Needham, Final Report, June (www. cranfieldlibrary.cranfield.ac.uk/pirus2/tiki-index.php)

Rossner, Mike, Heather Van Epps, and Emma Hill, 2007, Show me the data, *Journal of Cell Biology* 179: 1091–2 (http://dx.doi.org/10.1083/jcb.200711140)

SCI, 2010, *h-index and variants*, SCI Thematic Public Website (http://sci2s.ugr.es/ hindex/#basicnew)

Scopus, n.d., *Advice to journal editors and publishers: securing accession for a journal to Scopus*, Scopus website (www.info.sciverse.com/UserFiles/CSAB_statement_Advice_to_ journal_editors_and_publishers.pdf)

Seglen, Per O, 1997, Why the impact factor of journals should not be used for evaluating research, *BMJ* 314: 497 (www.bmj.com/content/314/7079/497.1.full/)

Shepherd, Peter, 2011, *The Journal Usage Factor project: results, recommendations and next steps*, London, Project COUNTER (www.projectcounter.org/documents/ Journal_Usage_Factor_extended_report_July.pdf)

Testa, James, n.d., *The Thomson Scientific journal selection process*, Thomson Reuters website (http://thomsonreuters.com/products_services/science/free/essays/ journal_selection_process)

Thomson Reuters, 1994, *The Thomson Scientific impact factor*, Thomson Reuters website (originally published in the *Current Contents* print edition June 20, 1994, when Thomson Scientific was known as the Institute for Scientific Information [ISI]) (http://thomsonreuters.com/business_units/scientific/free/ essays/impactfactor/)

n.d., *History of citation indexing*, Thomson Reuters website (http://thomsonreuters. com/products_services/science/free/essays/history_of_citation_indexing)

# 6 Marketing and sales

## Introduction

One might think that "everybody knows the important journals in their field," but marketing is an absolutely crucial function in journal publishing – not only for the publisher but for the author, reader, and buyer (the librarian) as well. "Marketing" entails a wide range of activities well beyond what the "marketing department" does, and requires support from editorial, fulfillment, production, technology, and accounting departments.

When a product manager emails authors about a new feature in an online journal; when an editor conducts a workshop for young scholars on how to get published in a journal; when a customer-service representative helps restore access to an IP range that had been shut off; when the IT group sends metadata to a library search engine; when an indexer lists keywords for the article abstract; when a programmer optimizes a web page for better search engine results – they are all helping to market the journal. This chapter discusses marketing in this broadest sense: an inter-related set of activities that promotes the brand (of the journal and the publisher) while maximizing the discoverability of each individual article.

"Brand" refers to the "identity" of a product, service, or company in the eyes of its customers – or the identity that the company would like the customer to perceive. In the journal world, the publisher's brand matters to the Editors-in-Chief who are recruited to manage a journal, but the brand known to authors is almost always that of the journal rather than the publishing company. The reputations of the Editor-in-Chief and Editorial Board are an integral part of that brand for most authors. Brand matters to readers, too; a 2010 study showed that readers "use a variety of criteria and quality clues to choose which articles to read," including the quality of the journal (and peer review is seen as a fundamental attribute of quality) (Tenopir et al., 2010).[1]

[1] The leading attributes of articles preferred by readers are "written by an author I recognize as a top scholar, in a top-tier peer reviewed journal, and available online at no (personal) cost."

Publishers naturally want to promote the journal's brand – and their own – as broadly as possible, and the multitude of marketing activities discussed in this chapter will help to define and reinforce such branding.

Most scholarly journals are supported by institutional subscriptions and license fees[2] and/or, increasingly, by author publication fees. However, there are many "markets," or audiences, for journal publishers that require a marketer's attention in one way or another. These include:

- *Librarians.* They are seldom the users of a journal, but they are the information gatekeepers responsible for knowing about it as an information resource, for purchasing it as an annual subscription or license, for promoting it to their patrons, and for making value decisions to justify its cost within the total serials budget of their institutions. Today, librarians are able to acquire many journals by licensing content, from a single journal to the entire corpus of one or more publishers, often in a buying consortium with other libraries. Faculty have a powerful voice in journal selection (which does need to support the teaching and research activities of the institution, after all), but librarians are likely to resist subscribing to journals whose prices seem excessively high, or whose demonstrated "cost per use" (see below) is well above the norm. Many marketing departments use library advisory boards that meet at least once a year to review pricing and product proposals and to give expert advice to the publisher.

- *Authors.* With several publication outlets from which to choose, why should an author consider submitting a manuscript to one journal over another? Publishers used to pay little attention to "author marketing," after an initial "call for papers" at the launch of a new title (discussed below). However, publishers recognize that the quality of their journals depends on contributions from the top people in the field (which is ultimately reflected in the journal's impact factor, as discussed in

---

[2] Traditional subscriptions, by which libraries obtain journals at the publisher's list prices, often through subscription agents, are increasingly complemented by license agreements negotiated directly between the publisher and the library. For example, a company with a single site might pay the published subscription rate for a journal but a multinational corporation might negotiate a worldwide license price based on the number of its sites or the total headcount of its employees (see Chapter 8, Journal finances). Whether they are regarded as "subscribers" or "licensees," all customers for electronic journals must agree to the terms and conditions in the publisher's standard user agreement, which is discussed more fully in Chapter 11, Copyright and other legal aspects.

Chapter 5, Journal metrics). Indeed, publishers now see authors as vital customers for their publication services – possibly the publisher's most important customers. Publishers are therefore increasingly providing online authoring tools and other services to attract authors and to keep them happy.

- *Readers.* How do professionals know where to go for the information they need? They once started with the primary print journal in their field – where they often found articles of interest simply by browsing the table of contents – or with one of the many subject-specific bibliographic databases purchased by their library. Today, they are more likely to conduct a simple Google search, or perhaps to set up a subject-level RSS feed (or another type of current-awareness service), bringing them to articles of interest – but bypassing the "journal" and the journal's "brand" – in the process.[3] New forms of marketing are required in this environment, focused on making articles "discoverable" to readers. Moreover, readers[4] – particularly if they are faculty – serve a powerful advocacy role for journals, whether they recommend a new subscription or resist library cancellation plans for a journal on which they depend.

- *Members.* Sometimes readers are members of a learned or professional society, for whom the journal is one of several benefits of membership. In some cases, society members get their society's journal as part of their dues payment, while in others they may be required to pay for the journal separately. Even for those who get the journal as part of membership, a degree of marketing may be required. For example, low usage may indicate a need to promote more traffic to the journal; or perhaps a newly introduced online feature requires additional marketing to get it noticed, and used.

- *Nonmember individuals.* Individuals, other than society members, represent a tiny fraction of journal subscribers for most publishers. This is less true in the humanities and social sciences (HSS) than it is for scientific, technical, and medical (STM) journals, but, overall, subscriptions to individuals have been shrinking over time. This is in large part because the widespread

---

[3]  For this reason, many publishers make sure that every article and every page in an online journal identify both the journal and the publisher, which was not always true for print journals.

[4]  In some disciplines, such as physics, authors and readers are the same people. In other more applied areas, such as clinical medicine and engineering, authors are a small subset of readers.

availability of online journals through campus-wide site licensing and Big Deal-type sales arrangements (discussed more fully below and in Chapter 1, Introduction to journals) has reduced the need for individuals to have a personal subscription. Open access (OA) advocates argue that subscription and license prices put journals beyond the reach of many readers, and yet more journals are more widely available and accessible to more readers today than ever before (Ware and Mabe, 2009).

- *Peer reviewers.* Peer review, though often seen as a thankless task, is essential to the functioning of the editorial process. Publishers are increasingly designing reward or recognition programs for their best reviewers, and to attract new reviewers.
- *The public, the media, and professionals in related fields.* These groups should be targeted for press releases (discussed in more detail below) about articles or findings that are especially noteworthy to a nonspecialist audience.
- *Editorial Boards, society executives, review committees, and governance bodies.* These groups constitute an internal market that also needs to understand, and feel positively about, the publisher's products and "brand."
- *Sales agents.* Whether these are the publisher's employees, freelance representatives, or employees of a third-party organization, the people selling journals "on the ground" need all the product information and market intelligence the marketing department can provide.
- *Subscription agents.* It is as important to communicate accurate product and price information to subscription agents as to a publisher's own sales agents; they are the major intermediaries between publishers and their library customers.

Of course, the audience for many journal publishers – especially in the fields of science, technology, and medicine (STM) – is not limited to the English-speaking world. There may be an international readership for English-language journals, but marketers should not assume they can effectively reach decision-makers among librarians, reviewers, and even authors by English-language promotions alone; marketing is therefore a multilingual challenge.

## Journal marketing and the "virtuous circle"

In the broadest sense, marketing is not just the way in which publishers promote a journal (or any product), but also the way the journal is conceived and positioned through, for example, the choice of title, the selection of the editor, the scope of the subject matter, decisions about format (print as well as online?), and policies with respect to long-term preservation and archiving. There is also the fundamental question of business model: will the journal be supported by "reader-side" subscriptions and licenses, or by "author-side" publication fees? Or will the journal rely on a combination of both, either by relying on library subscriptions/licenses and author page charges or by adopting a "hybrid" model, selling subscriptions/licenses to libraries but also allowing authors to pay publication fees to publish open access articles? In other words, there are many editorial and production decisions that have an impact on the marketing message. In the classic formulation, marketing is all about the "4 Ps": product, price, promotion, and place; note that "promotion" is only one element in this mix.

Once these kinds of basic product decision are made, it is up to the marketing staff to present the journal in the marketplace in the way best suited to produce more submissions, more readers, more usage, more citations, and more revenue. This has been referred to as the "virtuous circle" (see Figure 6.1): marketing attracts authors and readers to the journal, which increases usage, which leads to higher citations, which leads to more subscriptions (or author publication fees) and more profit or surplus.

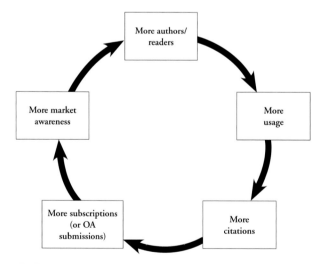

**Figure 6.1** The "virtuous circle"

Generating a profit or surplus is important, because even not-for-profit publishers need to reinvest in the publishing program and, especially today, to keep up with the latest technology.

## The evolving journal marketplace

For many years, academic institutions have been the primary market for professional and scholarly journals, at least in terms of revenue. When the journal is published by a learned or professional society, the society's members may constitute the biggest group of readers, but revenues from institutional subscriptions and license agreements, rather than whatever portion of member dues the society allocates to its journal, still usually make up the main source of revenue for the publisher. Some journals, especially primary research journals, will have many corporate and government (including military) institutional subscribers, and many biomedical titles will have substantial subscriptions in hospitals, laboratories, and pharmaceutical companies. But "the institutional market" largely means the "academic library market" for most publishers.

This market is often described as "broken" or "dysfunctional" by its critics. As discussed in Chapter 1, Introduction to journals, library budgets have simply not kept pace with the growth in actual research (and in the worldwide research community). Further weakening the market, many library budgets were substantially, and perhaps permanently, reduced in the global recession of 2008–9.[5]

As a result, publishers today cannot rely on the institutional subscription/ license market alone, and must find other sources of revenue to support their journals. These might include personal or member subscriptions (though both are declining), OA publication fees, author page and color charges, advertising, corporate sponsorship, royalty revenue from aggregators, and single article sales. (See Chapter 9, Subsidiary income.)

Many publishers in STM disciplines will also have nonacademic institutional subscribers, including industrial research firms, research institutes (such as the Max Planck Gesellschaft in Germany), federally funded laboratories, military research centers, and even public libraries, especially

---

[5] In addition, many research libraries have seen their budgets reduced as a proportion of total university expenditures, from a high of 3.7% in 1984 to less than 2% in 2009 (Association of Research Libraries, 2012).

in countries where major national libraries serve researchers as well as nonspecialists.

There are, of course, also "special" libraries with collections in law, music, art, sports, military history, and the like, as well as many in industry (all of them represented by the Special Libraries Association [www.sla.org]). However, even the commercial sector has seen a retrenchment in library resources. Fewer major companies support an in-house library, and the "information officers" who support the researchers increasingly rely on document delivery for all but the most heavily used journals. It is harder for journal marketers to reach the corporate library market than the academic market (outside of the pharmaceutical industry, which is well defined and well funded), because there are fewer associations, conferences, or publications aimed directly at corporate librarians. A sales force is therefore always a good idea for publishers selling into the corporate market.

## Pricing, usage, and value

In the days of print-only journals, the price was the same for every institutional subscriber, regardless of the amount of use the journal received. Indeed, publishers had almost no idea of how much, or how, their journals were used. If bigger institutions paid more for a title, it was only because they required multiple subscriptions to serve geographically distinct user groups – an applied physics title might be found in the main library and the physics and engineering libraries, for example, with perhaps a reading copy in the physics department as well. By the 1990s, however, library funding cuts had heavily eroded these multiple subscriptions.

When licenses for online journals began to allow for campus-wide use,[6] the income from any remaining multiple print subscriptions was immediately threatened. And yet a single online subscription provided the same "value" to the customer as the many print copies it might replace: multiple users could read the same journal issue – even the same article – simultaneously. While librarians initially expected to pay no more than the price of a single print subscription, usage data showed quickly that downloads at a large research university could be hundreds of times greater than

---

[6] Early pricing models that required institutions to pay according to the number of "concurrent users" or on a department-by-department basis, or even by the number of registered IP ranges, proved very unpopular and difficult to administer.

downloads from a regional college. Clearly, it made sense for the size of the institution – as a proxy for usage – to be taken into account in the price for that institution. As a result, by the late 2000s, a number of publishers had introduced tiered pricing – based on the type of institution or the size of the institution or both – for their online journals (Chesler and King, 2009).

Pricing became more differentiated for other reasons, too. Since the marginal cost of distribution[7] for an online journal is very low, the publisher could offer heavily discounted prices to attract new business. Some began to offer lower prices for high schools or two-year colleges. Some started to take national Gross Domestic Product into account, offering lower prices (or even free access – see below) in the developing world. Some offered steeply discounted access for a subscribing institution's remote campuses or labs.

In addition, as publishers digitized their older content, producing electronic backfiles (which might extend back to the nineteenth century or even earlier), some included these backfiles in the basic price of the journal (thus lowering the per-article price); others chose to market them under a separate subscription/license. (Others offered their backfiles as a separate archive for a one-time fee – see Chapter 9, Subsidiary income.)

The result has been a plethora of pricing models, and journal prices that are no longer transparent to the customer. (The range of models is discussed more fully in Chapter 8, Journal finances.) There are journals listed in subscription agents' catalogs today with more than eighty-five pricing options – for print only, online only, print plus online, online with and without backfiles, each format with different tiered pricing levels, plus choices of freight for print delivery, and sometimes with discounts based on the buyer's national economy.

As academic libraries increasingly began to purchase journal content through consortia arrangements with other university libraries (see "Selling to consortia," below), many publishers started to offer a "package deal" for their whole list, at a price often based on the FTE (full-time

---

[7] The "marginal cost of distribution" is the cost of servicing one additional customer; it is usually distinguished from the "first copy cost," the fixed investment in editorial and production costs necessary to deliver a product to the first customer. Print copies were expensive to print, bind, and mail whereas adding one additional online customer entails only a very small overhead cost.

equivalent) count of the institution's students, or for a surcharge on what the institution was already paying for its existing subscriptions. Such licensing arrangements, possibly involving hundreds of titles across dozens of disciplines, became known as "the Big Deal"[8] (see Chapter 1, Introduction to journals). The Big Deal was also popular with individual research universities that already subscribed widely to the publisher's journals.[9]

Whether applied to consortia or stand-alone institutions, Big Deal and other such license agreements allow the library to obtain additional content (whether current or archival) to which it did not previously subscribe, often at a very low price per article, and/or to provide access to additional (sometimes remote) user groups. The terms often include caps on annual price increases, pay-per-view options, permanent access to backfiles, and other benefits. The publisher, in return, receives a commitment that the library will not cancel any titles (or not without substituting others in their place), and can count on predictable price increases for the duration of the license.

In effect, every institution today essentially pays a customized price. This makes it virtually impossible for customers to compare what they are paying for online content. However, most publishers now provide institutional subscribers with COUNTER-compliant usage reports (see Chapter 5, Journal metrics), enabling them to see the actual usage of each title and to make comparisons between titles – at least, within the same disciplines (since usage will differ markedly with the size of the research community in any given discipline). The COUNTER data enable librarians to calculate the value of their various subscriptions/licenses in terms of "cost per use" (although this will mean something different when journals are purchased in a "Big Deal" package rather than as individual subscriptions). Prices in each discipline could start to cohere around a norm over time, as librarians begin aggressively using COUNTER data to push back on publisher prices

---

[8] While some librarians complained that the Big Deal eliminated the role of collection development and downgraded librarians from curators to mere "licensees," advocates pointed out that the curated collections of the member libraries were not meeting the research needs of the users; more than half the article downloads by OhioLINK users was from content that had not been previously accessible, while many previously subscribed journals went entirely unused (Sanville, 2001).

[9] Big Deals are still very common today, but face growing criticism in a time of shrinking library budgets because of the amount of money they tie up, often for what are perceived as "marginal" journals. However, they can still offer excellent value to the institution (Conyers and Dalton, 2008).

that result in a "price per use" much higher than the average for that discipline.[10]

It is crucial, therefore, that marketers systematically review the usage data for each institutional subscriber, title by title, since these are what librarians will use to calculate the value of their license. When similar institutions show wide variances in how a journal is used, there may be problems that the marketing department can address. Are faculty and students aware that the journal is available on the campus network? (Posters and other point-of-use promotions might help.) Are they accessing a journal's articles through an aggregated database rather than through the publisher's platform? (Speak to the librarians about "tuning up" their link resolvers.) Have research needs shifted? (Perhaps there's a related title to offer, maybe on a free trial?) In some cases, marketers might want to be highly proactive and offer a reduced price, before the journal hits that library's cancellation list. In any case, COUNTER data offer an unparalleled view of how each institutional customer is making use of the content, and allow the marketing team to identify at-risk subscriptions early enough to intervene.

## The power of "free"

Marketers know the power of "free" in consumer marketing: anything offered for free boosts response rates. In journal marketing, "free" is powerful in another way. By adding more backfile content to an online journal for the same price, publishers reduce the average cost per article and, potentially, the average cost per use.[11] This is a pricing strategy for the many publishers who include a complete archive – back to Vol. 1, No. 1 – with the price of a current subscription; it does not reduce the library's cost, but it does increase the journal's value by providing more content

---

[10] COUNTER reports show uses of the table of contents, searches performed, abstract pages viewed, and other metrics. However, there is an unfortunate tendency among librarians to reduce all of this to a simple count of article downloads. As publishers provide more and more tools to readers to filter the literature (such as previewing all of the article's charts and graphs from the abstract page), the reader may find less and less need to download the entire article – even though he or she has had plenty of "use" out of it. So if librarians do judge the value of a journal strictly on a "cost per download" basis, this may become a real problem for publishers.

[11] "Potentially," because unless the extra content is actually used, there is no change in value for the customer. But many publishers report quite heavy use of their backfile content.

for the price. Publishers achieve a similar effect when they give an institution access, for little or no additional cost, to all of those journals to which it did not previously subscribe – but which is likely to generate additional usage (and value).

Free content is deployed in many ways – it is all publicity for the journal, after all. When Nobel prizes are announced, scientific publishers often provide time-limited free access to the original research papers of the winners. In times of natural disaster, civil engineering publishers have released free collections of papers germane to the situation (earthquakes, hurricanes). Medical publishers made available for free a wealth of pertinent papers in response to the outbreak of H1N1 ("swine flu") in 2009. Papers about notable cultural and historical figures are often made free, temporarily, on the anniversaries of their births or deaths. Publishers who regularly publicize the "most downloaded papers of the month" sometimes make the full text of those papers free to access. Indeed, some publishers make all their research articles free, either for a short while (e.g., Institute of Physics makes its articles free for the first month after online publication) or even permanently (e.g., *BMJ*, whose free research articles attract traffic to other types of content in this otherwise subscription-based journal). "Free" builds traffic – remember the "virtuous circle."

It is important to understand that journal publishers generally do not have a monopoly on the content they publish. It is almost always possible for a librarian or user to find an "instance" of an article somewhere other than the publisher's online platform – from interlibrary loan, from a document delivery service, from a preprint server, from an author's website, from the university's institutional repository, from a mandated database,[12] or directly from an obliging author. Publishers are therefore competing on price and convenience to sell the content that they publish. It is very useful, and humbling, for marketers to remember that customers have some choice in how, and from whom, they acquire articles; this places an additional constraint on the publisher's pricing decisions. (Publishers should worry when an institution's cost per download for an article exceeds the cost of getting the article through interlibrary loan.)

The low marginal distribution cost of online journals has another benefit: publishers are able to offer free (or extremely low-cost) fulltext content to

---

[12] One such mandate comes from the US National Institutes of Health, which requires all NIH-funded research articles to be deposited in PubMed Central.

scholars and professionals in many of the world's poorest countries. Open access titles are free to such users, of course, but there are a couple of major programs through which publishers can also make their subscription-based journals available:

- INASP. The International Network for the Availability of Scientific Publications works with developing countries not only to provide access to research journals, but also to build the information networks and professional infrastructure necessary to support local scholars. More than fifty publishers and aggregators currently provide access to fulltext content through the INASP program, PERii (Programme for the Enhancement of Research Information). Details are available at www.inasp.info.
- Research4Life. This is the collective name for three subject-based collections of peer-reviewed literature that are made available under the auspices of a public–private collaboration of the United Nations, Yale and Cornell Universities, and the International Association of Scientific, Technical & Medical Publishers (STM), with Microsoft acting as the technology partner. The programs include HINARI, covering medicine, nursing, and related health and social sciences; AGORA, offering content in agriculture, fisheries, food, nutrition, and related veterinary, biological, environmental, and social sciences; and OARE, covering a very broad range of environmental disciplines. For more information, see www.research4life.org.

Providing free access to users in poor countries may not seem like much of a "marketing" initiative, but publishers might look at this as helping to establish a future market when these nations' economies rise. One need not be cynical about this, however; journal publishers have proven eager and willing to donate free content to struggling researchers working with minimal resources because it is the right thing to do – and because online distribution makes it eminently possible by removing any cost barrier.

Another significant initiative in this regard is *patient*INFORM, a web collaboration of voluntary health organizations, medical societies, and medical and scholarly publishers, supported by STM and PSP, the Professional and Scholarly Publishing division of the Association of American Publishers. The participating volunteer health organizations provide material to help patients and caregivers understand current medical research, with links to peer-reviewed content from the participating publishers. The publishers provide free access to their articles to anyone following a *patient*INFORM link. See www.patientinform.org.

## The role of subscription agents

Most academic libraries, and many other institutional libraries in the government, corporate, and healthcare sectors, use the services of a subscription agent to order, renew, and maintain journal subscriptions. Consider that a big university library could have tens of thousands of serials in its collection, produced by thousands of publishers. It is far simpler for the library to deal with one or a few subscription agents (many libraries use more than one) to order these titles than to cope with all of the individual publishers – especially those dealing in foreign currencies.

It is important that subscription agents have accurate information about the publisher's titles in their databases. If the publisher offers tiered pricing, it is important that the agents understand what institutions qualify for what tiers. The agents often host local "Open Days" in various countries where publishers can meet their library customers, and these can be invaluable for publishers who do not have their own local marketing presence. We will discuss subscription agents more below, in "The sales function," and in Chapter 7, Fulfillment.

Some publishers tend to neglect subscription agents, seeing them as little more than "order takers" for libraries. But marketers would be wise to talk to the bigger agents before any dramatic change in their journal policies, or before the launch of a new product or pricing scheme. Dealing with thousands of publishers and libraries, subscription agents have a big-picture view of the scholarly publishing world and can help marketers avoid mistakes made by other publishers. Do libraries require a local host for long-term archiving? Are libraries in certain regions buying digital archives? Which countries have been paying late, and why? Publishers will want to do some market research directly with librarians on questions such as these, but they should also include the agents.

Subscription agents have expressed worries that they are being squeezed out of their traditional intermediary role, as larger publishers negotiate licensing deals directly with consortia and individual universities. However, some have found new roles: they have worked with groups of publishers to put together and sell multipublisher journal packages, such as the ALPSP Learned Journals Collection (http://aljc.swets.com). The larger agents have also sought to work in a more direct sales role for publishers, especially in emerging markets such as India and China. Agents have also assisted consortia in procuring publisher packages, negotiating price terms, and managing payments. (Swets, for example, is the appointed managing agent for the HEAL-Link consortium in Greece.)

Subscription agents can offer publishers excellent market intelligence on local currency fluctuations, public funding for university libraries, and other issues that affect circulation. The bigger agents exhibit at the same library meetings where journal publishers exhibit – ALA, SLA, MLA, UKSG (see below, under "Exhibiting at conferences") – so it is easy to arrange meetings with them. They will also be found at the Frankfurt Book Fair, the London Book Fair, and similar venues. The Association of Subscription Agents and Intermediaries (ASA) also holds its own annual meeting in London, generally in February. ASA members are listed at www.subscription-agents.org.

There are also, unfortunately, a number of fraudulent subscription agents. These are blatantly criminal enterprises whose employees or family members enroll in various societies under fake names, and order the society journal at the member rates. They then resell these member-rate subscriptions to institutions at a discounted institutional rate. Since institutional prices can be more than ten times higher than member prices, there are enormous profits to be made. In most cases, the library – which is, after all, paying close to the full institutional list price of the journal – may not even realize it is working with an illegitimate supplier. The real size of this black market became apparent in the 2000s and there are now more aggressive efforts by publishers and legitimate subscription agents to curtail it, including police raids and legal prosecutions. For those who manage society journals, it is essential to check out the subscriptions held by the society members. A "member" who buys every single journal from a society with multiple publications should probably raise suspicions. Very high usage of an online "member" subscription should also raise warning flags. Misuse of an online member subscription is at least easier to detect than misuse of the print version, and some societies now offer members only the online version of the society journal.

There is also a "gray market" in journals. It is not uncommon for a professor or department head or chief scientist to have a personal membership in a society, and to share the society journal with his or her students or staff, or even to donate it to the library. Publishers often print a statement on the cover of member copies to indicate it is "For personal use only, not to be shared with others." Passwords for online member copies come with similar messages. While publishers are not fond of this kind of sharing (in a static library market, every lost institutional subscription increases the cost for the remaining subscribers), it is harder to fault the motives of the society member. Nonetheless, some societies restrict the number of personal subscriptions a member is allowed to receive.

## Emerging markets

The international market for journal literature, especially in STM, was once dominated by academic institutions in North America, Western Europe, and Japan, the world's largest economies. Given the tightening of this market as discussed earlier in this chapter, especially following the recession of 2008–9, the market outlook for journal publishers would seem to be bleak. However, rescue has come in the form of the fast-developing economies of China, India, and Brazil. (The so-called "BRIC" countries include Brazil, Russia, India, and China, but Russia is still lagging as a journal market.) Countries in the Middle East are also investing significant new resources in academic institutions.

When China began to observe intellectual property laws in order to gain admission to the World Intellectual Property Organization (WIPO) in the late 1990s, publishers suddenly found themselves with hundreds of "new" subscriptions from that country, often from institutions that had previously accessed a pirated or otherwise illegitimate copy of the journal. The importance of China and India can be seen in the number of Western publishers who have opened local offices in these countries, and in the rapidly growing number of manuscripts, especially from China, that are being submitted each year for publication in Western journals. Many publishers already have a "China strategy" and perhaps one for India as well. These are markets in which the use of local sales agents brings many benefits, as discussed later in this chapter. Besides the BRIC and Middle Eastern countries, publishers may find strong market interest in their journals in Turkey, South Africa, Argentina, Mexico, and other nations emerging from underdevelopment.

Without these new markets, often identified with a central national consortium, many journal publishers would have seen little real revenue growth in the last decade.

## What does the marketing department do?

With this background, we will now discuss some of what the marketing department actually does.[13] We will end with a look at the sales function in journal publishing, which has newfound importance even for small publishers.

### *Market research*

Whether a publisher is considering launching a new journal, acquiring an existing journal from another publisher, or seeking to improve sales of a mature journal, market research is a vital tool. Successful journals have been launched in the past with little or no market research, relying in some cases on the gut instincts of the publisher or the enthusiasm of a well-known researcher eager to be an editor. It is far more likely today, however, that some market research will need to be done, even for a very inexpensive journal, since there is no "extra" money in the library market for a new title (see Chapter 2, Managing journals, for more on researching a potential new journal). Publishers accept that it may now take a decade or more for a subscription-based journal to reach the point when not only do revenues cover annual operating costs, but initial development costs are also fully recovered (see Chapter 8, Journal finances). Even if the journal is to be supported by author-side payments for free access on the web (open access), the publisher will need to be assured that there is a real need for a new title in the field (and sufficient resources to support author publication fees).

Sometimes new areas of research produce a rapidly growing number of papers with no obvious "home" in the existing literature. The profusion of "nano"-related journals in science and engineering in the 1990s and 2000s is a good example, as nanotechnologies took root in disciplines

---

[13] While this handbook focuses on journals, much of the marketing and sales information could apply equally to online conference proceedings and e-books, and perhaps even to technical standards. While these are very different products in print, as online publications they can be sold by annual subscription or license just like a journal. An increasing number of publishers have combined their online journals, proceedings, books, and standards into a "digital library," the entirety of which is available for a single annual subscription rate, and which is marketed just like a journal or database.

ranging from chemistry to biomedical engineering. The sheer growth of papers in nanotechnology indicated that subfields were being born, and needed journals to represent the new communities of researchers.

Market research can be conducted in many ways, from the simple and inexpensive to the elaborate and costly.

## Quantitative analysis

In disciplines with standard classification schemes (or "controlled vocabularies"), one might simply analyze the growth in papers published in each category. Examples of classification schemes include Physics and Astronomy Classification (PACS) codes used in physics (published by the American Institute of Physics), Medical Subject Headings (MeSH) used in medicine (developed by the US National Library of Medicine), the American Psychological Association's *Thesaurus of psychological index terms*, used in psychology, and the Education Resources Information Center (ERIC) Thesaurus used in education and sponsored by the US Department of Education. Unfortunately, not all scholarly disciplines have such schemes. The *Journal Citation Reports* produced by Thomson Reuters divide the indexed journal literature into fairly broad categories, but these may still be helpful for analysis. Thomson Reuters can also provide some quantitative analysis (for a fee) by searching on keywords (e.g., how many papers have been published in "biophysics" over the last five years? How many authors contributed articles in the field of women's studies in 2010 versus 2000?).

## Market analysis

What do practitioners – especially the "thought leaders" – think is happening in their disciplines? A good place to start is by talking with Editors-in-Chief and Editorial Board members. Some of the questions to ask: are there new professional societies being organized around new areas of research? Are your competitors' journals introducing new topic sections? Are new journals or book series being launched to cover new fields? Are funding agencies changing their grant priorities? Journal review committees, used by many publishers to examine the direction and health of their key journals every few years, also contribute to this process.

## Author/Editor surveys

Every publisher has databases with email addresses of authors, Editors, Editorial Board members, and peer reviewers. It is very simple these days to invite any of them to participate in an online survey, assuming you have clear goals around which you can structure a short poll with pertinent questions.

## Expert panels

The experts may be the same types of "thought leaders," authors, and Editors mentioned above, but gathered in a group setting (requiring their physical presence or videoconferencing), where they can react not only to the publisher but also to each other, in a more conversational setting.

## Informal focus groups

Marketers may want to visit universities or research centers for an on-site session with small groups of users and/or librarians. These are "informal" in that they do not represent a statistically valid sample of the user (or author, or librarian) population, even if the exercise is repeated in several locations (as it should be). This is a good way to learn how researchers – including the younger researchers who are the next-generation authors – are using a journal, what other journals they read, how they keep up with the literature, how they conduct information searches, whether they are engaged with new social media, where they want to publish and why, and a host of related questions.

## Formal focus groups

Sometimes a publisher really does want a scientifically valid sample of opinion, which means getting a representative slice of the user or author population, inviting them to a central location, and asking a carefully controlled set of questions under the guidance of a moderator. It may even be appropriate in some cases to make this a "blind" focus group, in which the participants are not aware (until perhaps near the end of the session) which publisher is conducting the research.

## *User studies*

Sometimes, marketers need to understand what users do rather than what they say. For example, to improve navigation and utility of the online format, some publishers have studied user behavior by watching users work at their computers, electronically monitoring their key-strokes, or even following their eyes as they scan across a web page.

### Launching a new journal

The launch of a new journal is always a major marketing event, and needs careful planning. (See Chapter 2, Managing journals, for more on this topic.) For one thing, the publisher needs to introduce this new journal to the researchers and authors who it hopes will contribute papers. The publisher also needs to find a way to get the attention of librarians, who will likely be extremely unwilling to subscribe to a journal that has not yet proven itself useful to a specific academic audience. Bear in mind that (as mentioned in Chapter 5, Journal metrics) it can take a few years for Thomson Reuters to decide to index such a title in its *Journal Citation Reports*, a key marker of quality for librarians.

In a sense, one of the key marketing elements of a new journal is entirely out of the hands of the marketing department. The choice of an Editor-in-Chief – and, with his or her assistance, an Editorial Board – is enormously important to authors and readers (see Chapter 2, Managing journals, for more on this). It is also important to convey a simple message about what makes this new journal different or unique. Why is it being launched now? What makes it necessary, with so many other journals in the field?

Cross-marketing to both librarian and author communities is generally necessary, whether the goal is to get librarians to subscribe, or to get authors to get hold of funds to pay for open access publishing. Irrespective of business model, librarians can help to support a new journal and inform potential authors about it (acting in their subject-specialty role as a monitor of important information resources), and potential readers need to know about new subscription-based journals, so that they can encourage their institutional librarians to buy them.

Even if a publisher expects a new journal to be supported entirely by subscriptions and license fees, it is common, in this era of tight library budgets and information overload, to provide free online access to the journal for a year or two, in order to show potential subscribers a steady stream of published papers and user traffic. Free access in this period will build usage and traffic more quickly than restricting access to a few initial subscribers; marketers will thus create "value" for the journal before asking libraries to invest some of their highly prized budgets in a subscription. It is important, however, to make every effort to help librarians activate this access and market it actively to their users (for example, by providing posters and other promotional material, creating training videos, sending email notices to faculty, even arranging "meet the editor" receptions).

## Call for Papers

One of the first marketing efforts for any new journal is a Call for Papers directed at professionals in the field (see Chapter 2, Managing journals). Advertisements for the new journal can be placed in appropriate publications that reach the kind of authors the publisher wants, including society newsletters. Flyers can be displayed at professional conferences, or distributed in the registration package that each attendee receives. Emails with an HTML version of the flyer will reach a much broader audience, and there are generally three sources from which to derive a mailing list of potential authors:

- The publisher's own in-house lists of authors. If the company publishes other journals and/or books in the same or related fields, it will have a prime list of potential authors for the new journal – "prime" because this group already has a track record of publishing with the company. Individual and member subscribers to those publications are also valuable prospects.
- Third-party lists, such as society membership lists and individual subscribers to other publishers' journals and trade publications in the field. Since these societies or publications may be competing for authors, not all of them will agree to rent their lists. Others may be willing to provide physical mailing addresses but not email addresses.
- Authors of papers on similar topics indexed by Thomson Reuters. The *Journal Citation Reports* database captures not only the authors of each new paper in the indexed publications (and their email addresses, when given in the journal), but also all of the authors that are cited by those papers.

New journals need extra attention, but this is only one type of marketing challenge. Whether a journal has just received its first impact factor (a key stage in the life cycle of an academic title), or has reached the kind of "maturity" marked by stagnant subscription rates, or faces a competitor that is siphoning away good articles, each title has its own marketing needs.

### The strategic marketing plan

Ideally, each journal in the publisher's portfolio will have its own marketing plan, although it may be more practical for larger publishers to develop a joint marketing plan for a related list of titles. Thus, a publisher with several titles in structural engineering or allied health or business management will typically develop a single yearly marketing plan for all the titles in that area, since there will be considerable overlap in activities for the individual titles. (They are all appropriate for the same conference exhibitions, for example.)

Each title or group of titles should have a marketing profile or plan that, ideally, includes the data shown in Box 6.1.

---

**Box 6.1** Items to include in a marketing plan

- Title, subtitle, and all bibliographic data (ISSN[s], URL, DOI prefix, volume and issue number, frequency, format[s]).
- Editor-in-Chief, Editorial Board, sponsoring society if applicable – with an indication of any Editorial Board changes that have implications for marketing.
- Business model – i.e., subscription/license-based, open access, hybrid, or other.
- Unique selling proposition (USP) – what makes the journal different from others in the field? What is its main competitive advantage?
- Subscription/license revenue by market segment (academic, corporate, government, etc.), with five-year trends.
- Subscription/license revenue by region (and key countries within regions), with five-year trends.
- Impact factor, immediacy index, Eigenfactor, and other metrics (see Chapter 5, Journal metrics), with five-year trends.
- Price history.
- Audience and scope.

> **Box 6.1** (continued)
>
> - Related titles in the publisher's list.
> - Key editorial features, highlighting what's new.
> - Key online features, highlighting what's new.
> - Competitor journals and their key differentiators (including price).
> - Market trends, conditions – a qualitative view of what's impacting the field (e.g., grant support for hot new research areas, growth, or decline of new Ph.D.s, etc.).
> - Special marketing opportunities – for example, the International Association of Mathematical Physicists holds its general meeting only once every three years, a marketing opportunity for publishers in that field.
> - Key strategic objective – the key objective for a new journal may be to grow traffic and article submissions, while the key objective for a mature journal may be to retain existing subscriptions and to generate ancillary revenues by licensing the journal's backfile. Other objectives may be to improve a declining impact factor; to attract more papers in specific subfields; to generate publicity for special focus issues; to drive more online traffic to the Editor's blog; to sell specially priced high school editions; to achieve growth in developing countries; and so on.
> - Annual marketing activities (exhibitions, email campaigns, etc.), preferably with budgets and benchmarks for evaluating results.

## Marketing tools of the trade

There are a variety of methods, media, channels, and tactics to accomplish the overall marketing strategy.

## Publicity

A sustained publicity approach is important to call attention to the most interesting papers in a journal, especially a new one, and this will require serious support from the Editorial team. Peer reviewers, Editors, product managers, and in-house publicists can all help identify articles that have significance to a wider reading public, and which need a press release to get the word out. Publicity need not only be about the article. A press release might be warranted for a provocative editorial blog, or for a podcast with a well-known author. It is important to keep in mind that "press releases are not just for the press anymore," in the words of marketing consultant David Meerman Scott (Scott, 2006). Publicists want their press releases to reach the appropriate news media, including bloggers, but they need to reach individuals as well, including the publisher's authors and subscribers.

Online discussion lists will often repost such press releases (if the "news" seems worthy), including a link back to the publisher's website. Once the press release is online, it will be indexed by search engines, broadening its reach tremendously. For marketers just getting started in this area, online press release distribution services such as PRWeb (www.prweb.com) can be a big help.

The press release may need to be embargoed, so that a news story based on it does not precede the event announced in the release, e.g., before an article is released online, or a meeting takes place, or a prize is awarded. If the marketing group determines that an article is worth a press release, then it needs to ensure that the article is freely available online (for some determined amount of time) when the press release is sent – providing a link to an article that only subscribers can see sabotages the whole effort.

While librarians are not themselves the users of most journals, they need to be kept in the loop when press releases are distributed. Marketers need to become familiar with the main online discussion groups for librarians. For example, in physics, PAMnet, the online forum for the Physics-Astronomy-Mathematics division of the Special Library Association, is indispensable (http://pam.sla.org/manual/pamnet-information). Marketers of engineering content will likely want to follow ELDNET-L (http://depts.washington.edu/englib/eld/listserv/listservs.php), sponsored by the engineering libraries division of the American Society for Engineering Education. MEDLIB-L is the Medical Library Association's email list for medical librarians (www.mlanet.org/discussion/medlibl.html). ANSS-L is the American Library Association's email list for librarians in anthropology, sociology, and related fields (http://lists.ala.org/sympa/info/anss-l). It is important to subscribe to such lists not only so that marketers can post news of their own products (when the lists permit such postings – not all do), but also so that they can see what their competitors are doing and, most importantly, so that they can read the unfiltered comments of the librarians who need to recommend their products.

Other useful library discussion lists include:

- STS-L, a list focusing on science journals, sponsored by the Association of College and Research Libraries (http://lists.ala.org/wws/info/sts-l).
- SERIALST, a forum for serials librarians hosted by the University of Vermont (www.uvm.edu/~bmaclenn/serialst.html).
- LIS-E-RESOURCES, for publishers, librarians, and intermediaries, owned by UKSG (www.jiscmail.ac.uk/cgi-bin/webadmin?A0=LIS -E-RESOURCES).
- ERIL-L, for marketers who want to learn more about the practical issues of handling electronic resources in libraries (http://listserv.bing hamton.edu/archives/eril-l.html).

One important library discussion list for marketers to follow, though not tied to any one subject area, is LIBLICENSE-L, sponsored by Yale University and devoted to "Electronic Content Licensing for Academic and Research Libraries" (see www.library.yale.edu/~llicense). Discussions on LIBLICENSE-L focus on pricing, online licensing terms, and publisher policies, though the contributors also look at technology issues, future business models, and related topics. Other than pricing announcements, LIBLICENSE-L does not accept press releases.

## Social media

Think of social media as "interactive publicity." An Editor's or author's blog, Twitter, Facebook groups – they all have the same function of bringing attention to an article or a journal or an author or a publisher, with the added benefit of user interaction and feedback. Of course, the more the marketing department can get the journal's audience to engage with such media, the greater the impact. In some cases, a publisher may have a sufficient presence in a given field (by publishing important journals, by sponsoring conferences, by working closely with the dominant professional society, or some combination of these) to consider hosting an online "community website." Examples of these abound, but many are pure marketing exercises whose content is entirely pushed out by the publisher, with little "community" involvement. A robust online community, on the other hand, will generate actions by the user population, including comments, ratings, reviews, and clickthroughs to content. One leading example is the Nature

Network (http://network.nature.com), hosted by the life sciences publisher *Nature*. Another is Sermo (www.sermo.com), "the largest online physician community in the US."

Social media are exploding through all types of marketing activity today, and change so fast that the "next new thing" could come along at any moment. There are plenty of examples to observe today of publishers providing not only Twitter feeds, Facebook pages, YouTube videos, and even Second Life encounters, but also online polls, blogs, and contests served directly from their own websites. The goal, as with all publicity, is to drive more users to the publisher's content. Twitter feeds alone have been known to produce thousands of clickthroughs to content, often from journalists and science writers as well as researchers, librarians, and students. However, some publishers have found that what young people do to network in their personal lives has almost no parallel in their professional lives. For example, early career researchers may be reluctant to express their thoughts freely in blogs and tweets, as these can have negative repercussions with senior researchers and tenure committees (Crotty, 2008).

In any case, it is generally inexpensive to try out online media and results are quick to obtain, so marketers can feel free to experiment and "free to fail." At the same time, social media should be carefully integrated with other marketing channels and monitored to make sure objectives are being met.

## *The journal website*

The ultimate form of social media for a journal publisher may be the journal website itself, if it can be made into a hub of user activity.

A decade and a half after the debut of the first web-based journals, the online versions still tend to be little more than representations of the printed journal page, albeit with useful hyperlinks and text searching abilities. And the journal's home page still tends to be largely a mix of masthead data, catalog copy, and subscription information. But there are a growing number of instances where the journal website contains additional content that supplements the information in the peer-reviewed papers. A recent example is the *Journal of Renewable and Sustainable Energy* (http://jrse.aip.org). The journal's home page includes many pointers to the articles published in the most recent issue, but also includes a newsletter from the editors, a newsfeed on energy-related topics, a blog (called *Clean*, nicely enough), and links to several podcasts featuring interviews with authors. Each podcast is a marketable event in itself, and these elements as a whole contribute to the overall awareness of the journal by authors as well as readers. Similarly, readers of the online *New England Journal of Medicine* at www.nejm.org will find not only the latest research articles but also videos with practical treatment tips, a contest to diagnose a disease of the week, a place for doctors to post comments on featured articles, and an audio summary of each weekly issue.

Some publishers have adapted their online journals in response to user behavior. For example, many scholarly publishers note that the bulk of their traffic comes from Google searches, which typically take the researcher to the abstract page of an article. This means that the overwhelming majority of users who come to an online journal bypass entirely the "publisher's website" or the "journal home page" and go directly to the article abstract. When publishers began to understand that "the abstract page is the new home page," they loaded more features into the abstract page itself (e.g., previews of all the tables and figures). In true Web 2.0 fashion, they are trying to engage users to interact with the journal site itself.

## Exhibiting at conferences

Publishers complain about the cost of exhibiting at professional conferences, the low return on investment, slow traffic, and so on, but there is hardly a better way to connect with actual people who represent "the market" the publisher is trying to reach. It's also useful to see what the competitors are up to, since these are often the places where publishers announce new products, or new features for existing products. And journal Editors may expect to see that their publisher has a presence at such meetings – a sign of support both for the journal and for the author community.

The trick is to build traffic to the exhibition booth, which can be achieved by raffles, give-aways, product demonstrations, "meet the editor" opportunities, surveys, and the like. Librarians will come to the publisher's booth with plenty of questions and requests, and it is important that the people who staff the exhibit, or a local sales representative responsible for a given library, respond by email within a few days after the conference ends. Conferences are also an opportunity for editors and marketers to interact with the scholarly community in roundtable sessions and workshops; not all of the action, therefore, necessarily takes place on the exhibition floor.

Where a publisher has only a single journal in a given field, the cost of exhibiting may be prohibitive, although some publishers share the cost of booth space or use a cooperative exhibition service. But there are opportunities to capitalize on a conference or meeting even without one's own booth. One can arrange to advertise in the conference program, to insert a flyer into the delegate registration package, and even to have give-aways distributed to the delegates' rooms at the official conference hotel. With or without the backing of a booth, marketing staff might also arrange meetings outside of the exhibition hall, such as "How to Publish in *Journal X*" workshops for younger researchers. Each conference or meeting is worth its own marketing plan, outlining the goals of exhibiting, so that the marketing team stays focused on specific outcomes.

There are hundreds of professional conferences with exhibiting opportunities that need to be considered for a given list of titles. Editors and authors can help identify the important ones. There are also several major library organizations whose annual meetings may need to be on a publisher's exhibition schedule (month shown may vary):

- American Library Association (ALA), US (Midwinter Meeting, January).
- Association of College and Research Libraries (ACRL), US (meets biannually, in April).
- UKSG (formerly UK Serials Group), UK (April).
- Electronic Resources and Libraries (ER&L), US (April).
- Canadian Library Association (CLA), Canada (May).
- Medical Library Association (MLA), US (May).
- Special Libraries Association (SLA), US (June).
- North American Serials Interest Group (NASIG), US (June – limited vendor exhibition).
- American Library Association, US (Summer Meeting, July).
- Charleston Conference, US (November – preconference exhibition only).

There are also numerous state and regional library meetings where a publisher might consider sending a sales representative, if convenient. Worldwide, there are national library meetings in many countries, useful for those who have local sales representation and can communicate in the local language. In addition, some of the best coordinated library consortia have instituted their own annual meetings, such as ANKOS, the primary university consortium in Turkey (which meets in May). Universities, regional library groups, and subscription agents may also host "library days" or "open houses," where publishers may be invited to exhibit or speak. These can be valuable opportunities to strengthen relationships and to build awareness among customers. Some publishers may also be invited to make presentations (or be "grilled," as many publishers would put it) at meetings of ICOLC, the International Coalition of Library Consortia (www.library.yale.edu/consortia).

## Metadata

Discoverability – the efficiency with which any given article can be found by a searcher – is a vital issue in an era of information overload. Well-chosen titles, well-written abstracts, and (where present) relevant keywords all help researchers find the content they need. Today, the most important routes to a publisher's content are consumer search engines – notably, Google, Bing, and Yahoo! – which, when enabled by the publisher, will regularly crawl and index its site. (See www.google.com/webmasters/docs/search-engine -optimization-starter-guide.pdf for an example of how to do this.) However, the discoverability of content will be much enhanced by distributing metadata – literally, "data about data" and more commonly called "bibliographic records" in the print era – into all the indexes, directories, catalogs, and "knowledge bases" that constitute the journal ecosystem. And, bearing in mind that metadata is what helps to make content discoverable, it is well worth devoting expert time and attention to including appropriate keywords (terms on which readers might search, including synonyms for important terms in the article) in the metadata.

In addition to being exposed to search engine crawlers, the metadata needs to be proactively supplied to:

- Subscription agent databases. Librarians rely on subscription agents for correct information about title, format, frequency, and price. Every journal title needs to be in all the agents' databases.
- ERM (electronic resource management) systems. These are (usually proprietary) software systems that support the acquisition, licensing, discovery, and evaluation of e-serials and other electronic resources. Vendors include

such companies as Serials Solutions, ExLibris, Innovative Interfaces, and SirsiDynix, but there are also open-source software tools as well, such as reSearcher, developed at Simon Fraser University. Some of these now work with publishers to accept a metadata feed that keeps the data accurate and up to date.

- Abstracting and indexing (A&I) services. Researchers and librarians formerly relied on A&I services to keep up with the literature to a much greater degree than they do today, when so much of the information is accessible through an online search. Many A&I services have folded or have been absorbed by bigger databases, and for many users the simplicity of a Google search has replaced the need for subject-level databases. This trend seems likely to continue, but there are still specialist indexing services that may be important for a journal, such as Medline, Chemical Abstract Services, Inspec, Mathematical Reviews, PsychINFO, Astrophysics Data System (ADS), and Historical Abstracts.
- The Directory of Open Access Journals (www.doaj.org), if the publication follows a "Gold" OA business model.
- Local search engines. Many regional library networks, consortia, government agencies, and other entities provide search engines specific to the content held by the libraries they serve; examples include OhioLINK, the Ontario Council of University Libraries (OCUL), and NEIKON (Russia). Some publishers expect to be paid for what they see as high-value metadata, which would include the article abstract and/or certain semantically tagged fields, but most would probably agree that it is important to get their basic metadata distributed as far and wide as possible – basically, to any searchable database of scholarly content. Metadata is advertising.

NISO and UKSG have formed the KBART (Knowledge Base and Related Tools) working group to recommend a standard format for publishers' metadata (www.niso.org/workrooms/kbart). This will improve efficiencies for everyone in the supply chain.

## Annual price and product announcements

Most academic journals publish, and are purchased, on a calendar-year basis. Generally speaking, librarians – usually in consultation with faculty – are making preliminary decisions in the spring of the current year about cancellations and acquisitions for the following year, a process tied to the release of the library's annual serials budget. Publishers have learned the importance of announcing their next-year prices as early as possible (and some publishers now announce their prices as early as April), so that subscription agents can cost out the renewal/acquisition list for their library clients, and librarians can begin the process of selection of new titles and weeding of existing ones.

Much of a library's budget will be tied up with the products of a handful of large commercial publishers, so those publishers' pricing announcements receive acute attention. Some publishers have found themselves subject to highly negative publicity in recent years because librarians considered their price increases excessive, or inconsistent. If a publisher has to increase one of its products' prices at a higher rate than other titles (say, because of a dramatic increase in published papers), then the marketing team needs to explain carefully the reasons why, and to give as much notice as possible.

Spring to summer is also the time of year to announce new products, in order to get them into the "wish list" of faculty and librarians. It does no good to announce a new product (except for OA journals, which don't depend on library budgets) that will be available from January 1, if the announcement comes after the library has already made its acquisition decisions for the following year. Generally, such announcements must be made (and, most importantly of all, communicated to subscription agents) by August or September at the latest; key meetings which will affect pricing decisions (e.g., with societies or other journal sponsors) should be timed with this in mind.

Publishers expect libraries to pay in advance for print journals, given the substantial costs of distribution. This print-centric thinking has bled into the marketing of online journals, and many publishers still require prepayment for online access. But some publishers offer to turn on access as soon as they receive a new subscription order, in order to encourage early orders and build usage. In fact, this is fairly typical in licensing to consortia, since weeks or months of negotiations might conclude much earlier or later than the standard January 1 start date. It is to the publisher's advantage to turn on access as soon as possible (once a new customer is clearly committed to placing an order). It obligates the customer to finalize the order, it gives users more time to use the content and thus contributes to usage data, and it generates goodwill from the librarian.

In the online environment, many librarians feel they are paying for a period of access, and not for a set number of "issues." If they subscribe to an online journal for a year beginning January 1, but the publisher does not turn on access until February 1, they may very well seek a refund, or a credit, for the month of access they did not receive. (This is more true of consortia, which have considerably more bargaining power, than it is for individual libraries.) As with cable TV, many customers feel they are paying for access to the publisher's "channel," not for a specific set of "episodes."

## Catalogs

The medium by which publishers once announced their new prices and products was the annual catalog, which was mailed to librarians worldwide and used at conference exhibitions all year round. This may still be useful for smaller publishers with a limited list, but print catalogs are expensive to produce and mail and have been rapidly replaced by online versions for most of the bigger publishers. Librarians, like everyone else, expect to find the information they need on the web. A link to the catalog website should be prominently featured in announcements to online library bulletins and on postcards that can be mailed in lieu of a full catalog, to drive traffic to the site. Even so, with so many factors affecting the price that a publisher charges an individual library (as discussed above and in Chapter 8, Journal finances), it is harder and harder for a librarian simply to look at the publisher's website and find the correct price for his or her institution.

## Trials and turnaways

It is common to offer trial access to a journal as part of the marketing effort, allowing the publisher and librarian alike to gauge its utility to users. "Usage marketing" is now common during free trials, as marketers employ email, point-of-use displays, social media, and other devices to make sure readers know and use this new journal resource. And it is important that marketers follow up such trials – which might run from two weeks to two months or longer – by presenting usage data (in the context of other titles used, the size of the user population, and other relevant factors) to the librarian or purchasing agent. Such access is controlled by IP authentication, so the institution will have to register for such a trial. (Be aware that some librarians are wary of free trials, as they may not have the funds to buy more content no matter how "successful" the trial may be.)

Marketers may also want to make one issue of an online journal (often the January issue) available for free access to potential users. Unless the publisher requires individuals or institutions to register, however, it will not be possible to provide specific feedback on usage to the prospective subscriber. With individuals, free trial issues may also tend to reinforce the unfortunate perception that everything on the web is free.[14]

One of the most valuable marketing tools is "denial of access" data – that is, information about the visitor who tries to access an online article and is turned away because his or her institution does not have a license or subscription.[15] Presenting evidence about the number of users at a given institution (indicated by their IP addresses) that have tried unsuccessfully to obtain the publisher's content can be a powerful tool in persuading librarians to subscribe.

## *Advertising*

Editors like to see their journals advertised, but low response rates generally dampen any enthusiasm on the marketer's part. Advertisements are unlikely to generate subscriptions, but may be useful to promote awareness by authors and readers. Online ads are at least measurable in terms of impressions (views) or clickthroughs (actions), giving marketers a better sense of whether their ads are being seen or not.

Since librarians rather than users purchase journal subscriptions, they are an important part of the advertiser's universe. However, the readership for

---

[14] The Berkeley Electronic Press (www.bepress.com) has an interesting model in this regard. Its "Guest Access Policy" allows anyone to download and read an article for free; however, users are asked to fill out a form that allows bepress to contact their library. When there has been significant interest, BE Press gets in touch with the library to suggest a subscription for the entire campus (Perciali and Edlin, 2008).

[15] Publishers and librarians alike generally refer to such failed requests as "turnaways," and we often use the same commonly understood term in this book. However, COUNTER reports only cover the titles that a library has access to, and in COUNTER terminology a "turnaway" is technically someone at a subscribing institution who is denied access because of limits on the number of simultaneous users. Most publishers do not limit the number of simultaneous online users, so most of their COUNTER reports show zero turnaways.

*Library Journal* and *American Libraries* in the US, and *CILIP Update* in the UK, is heavily dominated by those, such as public and high school librarians, who do not, unfortunately, buy academic journals. *Against the Grain*, a publication associated with the Charleston Conference held every November in Charleston, South Carolina, is a better venue for scholarly journals; also recommended are the programs for the ALA, SLA, ACRL, and UKSG conferences.

Constant online interaction with readers and authors has opened up new opportunities for promoting a product or service. There are myriad "touch points" where a publisher might insert a discreet promotional message, perhaps as part of the signature block:

• Email alerts, such as table of contents or subject alerts, that users sign up for to stay current.
• Emails sent to authors throughout the peer-review and production process.
• Shopping-cart pages from which users buy articles directly from the publisher's online platform; especially useful if the platform can automatically present other articles of similar interest (because they are by the same author, or on the same topic, or have cited – or been cited by – the article just purchased).

It is always an interesting exercise to assemble editorial, fulfillment, production, and technology staff to consider all of the points of communication, and the frequency with which they occur, between the publisher and authors, customers, and readers, because a brief advertising message could be presented at each of these points, with a link to more information.

Budget-minded marketers might note that there is a tradition among some scholarly publishers of exchanging ads of similar size in specialized publications of similar circulation, providing some publicity at no cost.

## Search engine marketing

Search engine marketing (SEM) is contextual advertising: it allows marketers to present relevant content to users, in the form of a pop-up text box, when they enter search terms appropriate to the publisher, journal, or article. SEM programs are available through Google AdWords and similar programs from Microsoft and Yahoo! They allow marketers to manage the daily or weekly advertising budget, to change text when the clickthrough rate dips, and to get daily results, so they can take more control over outcomes.

## Telemarketing

Librarians say they dislike telemarketing calls, but publishers have found them remarkably effective, given the right approach. Telemarketing can be done in-house, but large-scale campaigns will likely require outsourcing. There are now some professional telemarketing agencies that specialize in the scholarly market and whose agents can speak with academic librarians – usually in their own native languages – with an understanding of their actual needs and problems, and certainly without any hard sell. Sometimes, a phone campaign is done for the purposes of "teleresearch," designed not to promote a new product but to learn more about the customer's situation. Many publishers use telemarketing to contact nonrenewing customers; see "Chasing renewals," below.

## Direct mail

Direct mail was once the primary means of promoting a new publication; however, it is now generally used in conjunction with web or email promotions to reinforce a marketing message. It is often in the form of a simple flyer or postcard featuring a URL where the recipient will find more information (and interactivity). The expense of postage pushes marketers away from print and in favor of email, but the two media will reinforce each other if used together. Indeed, direct mail is staging a slight comeback in scholarly marketing. Of course, a nicely designed flyer no longer needs to be printed in bulk to be useful. It can exist as a PDF linked to the product's website, where it can be referred to or printed as one-offs by the customer, or for use at exhibitions or on sales calls.

## Point-of-use displays and training materials

Librarians are often looking for ways to publicize their resources and to enliven the environment in which students work (to the degree that students work in the library at all). Posters are popular and should be made available as PDF files on the journal website (and proactively printed and mailed to key customers). Marketers may give away coffee mugs, note pads, pens, etc., at the exhibition stand, but these are unlikely to get out of the librarian's office. Training videos can also be offered through the journal website, and may even be used in the library's bibliographic instruction courses.

### Chasing renewals

The journal business depends on high library renewal numbers (unlike the magazine business, which needs to replace a significant number of nonrenewing individuals every year). Renewing an existing subscriber is much easier than finding a new subscriber, and journal publishers expect to see renewal rates of 90% and higher. But renewals cannot be taken for granted, and every effort should be expended to renew every existing subscriber.

Publishers (and/or subscription agents) will send a series of standard renewal notices in the autumn and typically begin to receive direct orders and orders placed through agents throughout the last quarter, with late orders coming in randomly over the early months of the New Year. The publisher's fortunes rely on this annual influx of revenue, so the renewal period can be tense, and renewals will be closely watched by management. The annual renewal rate (or, seen from the other side, the annual attrition rate) is one of the key numbers marketers track from year to year. For more on the renewal process, see Chapter 7, Fulfillment.

Publishers allow a "grace period" during which they will continue to ship print copies and provide online access while waiting for a customer's renewal. The grace period for print is generally until February 28 (a date endorsed by the Association of Subscription Agents and Intermediaries). Most publishers will suspend further print shipments after that date if they have not been paid. However, it is premature to cut off online access at this point, unless the customer has clearly stated its intention to cancel. The marketing department will typically conduct a renewal campaign in the early months of the year, to all institutions that have not yet renewed, attempting to reach each subscriber by email initially. (The publisher's license agreement will include an email address for someone in the library. However, this person may not be the serials librarian or other decision-maker, so it is good to develop a related database of email addresses for each institution, drawn from any customer-service or marketing contacts.) If a librarian says he or she intends to renew, but has not yet sent payment, the publisher should maintain online access in good faith.

After this initial email effort, there will be a number of customers whom the marketing staff haven't been able to reach, or who have not responded to any queries. A telemarketing campaign may be advisable at this point. This can be done internally or outsourced, but outsourcing will almost certainly be required if the marketing department is attempting to reach every overseas customer (unless the publisher has overseas sales staff in key countries).

These renewal campaigns will not always affect a customer's behavior, or change the publisher's overall renewal rate. However, publishers have had some success with customers who did not necessarily intend to cancel, but whose renewals were "lost" in the bureaucracy. In any case, given the business significance of annual journal renewals, these email and telemarketing efforts will at least provide advance warning with regard to the company's bottom line for the year; reasons for nonrenewal may also highlight some problem with the journal, which needs to be addressed.

Needless to say, renewing license agreements, for consortia or for individual institutions, requires a more hands-on approach by the publisher's sales team. However, many consortium arrangements still allow each institutional member to order its own subscriptions (which must be tracked to assure each member is adhering to the terms of the license), and these customers' renewals need to be "chased" like any other.

### Author marketing

Publishers want to attract the best authors, meaning authors of high repute doing groundbreaking work. Authors draw readers, increasing the likelihood of citations, which improve the journal's impact factor (again, the "virtuous circle"). "Author marketing," however – as a sustained, coordinated activity – is a relatively new idea. It has come about partly because there is so much competition for authors and partly because technology allows publishers to reach these authors in more direct and automated ways.

For existing authors, the publisher wants to make the publishing experience as pleasant and efficient as possible. This begins with online manuscript submission, as publishers can communicate with authors at each stage of the editorial and production process, keeping them informed of their paper's progress. Authors want speedy publication, and some publishers forgo detailed copy-editing and proofreading of the authors' manuscripts in order to publish more quickly (and save costs). Because the peer-review process is usually what delays publication the most, some publishers have designed reward (and sometimes even penalty) systems for their peer reviewers, to encourage faster turnaround.

Once an article is accepted for publication, there are new opportunities for communicating with the author. He or she can be informed by email if the article generates a press release. Automated systems can be put in place to notify the author each time the paper is cited by another paper (if the other paper is published on the same hosting platform, at any rate). And the author can be fed a regular report on the number of downloads his or her paper has received, highlighting the good news if the paper is in, say, the "Top 20" downloads for the month.

Author marketing is designed to attract new authors as well as to satisfy and retain those already published. New authors can be reached in many ways – see the "Call for Papers" section earlier in this chapter. Authors of older papers in the publisher's journals should not be overlooked, either – with the right message, they may be convinced to submit again.

Some publishers, eager to court papers from researchers in emerging countries such as China and India, even award prizes to the "best paper of the year by a Chinese author," or the "best paper of the year from the Indian Institutes of Technology," with a small ceremony in the author's institution to mark the occasion.

## The sales function

Having a sales team was once the prerogative of the big commercial publishers with global operations. Many society publishers (particularly in STM areas) flourished in the postwar years without a sales force because of the strength of their content, and because library budgets for scientific literature in the post-Sputnik, arms-race era were strong. Users and librarians understood the importance of the American Physical Society, Institute of Physics, American Chemical Society, Royal Society of Chemistry, Institute of Electrical and Electronics Engineers, and many other scientific and technical societies responsible for the "core" literature in their fields. Their products almost literally sold themselves.

That era is over, and publishers, even smaller publishers, have a renewed interest in sales for several reasons:

- *More competition in a tighter market.* While publishers in different disciplines do not compete on content, they certainly compete for a share of the library's (often static or shrinking) budget. So, a sales person making a face-to-face visit (or even a phone call) to the library can have a critical impact.
- *Complications of price and licensing.* Online journals come with all kinds of licensing terms, price variations, features and functionalities, and packaging possibilities. Well-briefed sales people can convey the essential product benefits and cut through any confusion in the mind of the librarian.
- *Consortia and the international market.* Consortium licensing needs to take into account the number of institutional members, the number of subscriptions to the publisher's products among the member institutions, the number of physical locations that want access, and the IP ranges that define them. Depending on the pricing model employed, the publisher might also need to know the size of the user population overall, or in given disciplines, and possibly the usage statistics from the prior year. Whether it is in-house staff or a sales person "on the ground" (who may be the local subscription agent), one or more dedicated sales people are necessary in this process. And the rise of consortia internationally, and especially in the BRIC countries, has made it increasingly necessary to have sales people who can speak the local language and, if possible, invoice in the local currency.
- *Demand for training.* Online journals are well understood by users, but librarians sometimes ask for end-user training to improve understanding of specialist databases. Some of the larger consortia expect "training" as a matter of course, even by small publishers ill-equipped to provide it. In some cases, a video or slide presentation can be prepared to satisfy the demand. However, for the publishers with the resources to provide it, delivering this training in person can be an excellent way of increasing users' familiarity with the publisher's content, while at the same time gaining more market intelligence about users, and possibly moving them "upstream" by promoting advanced features or new content (at higher prices). In any case, sales agents need to have enough solid product expertise to train librarians and users in the use of the content, and marketers have to train the trainers.

One of the problems for smaller publishers is that they not only lack the resources to employ their own sales people, but also have too few titles to put together an attractive pricing package – or, indeed, to gain the attention of librarians. A librarian faced with a licensing agreement for two or three titles from a small society publisher and an agreement from a big commercial publisher with two or three hundred titles is not likely to give the smaller publisher much consideration.

As a result, many publishers have found it necessary to join together to offer librarians a larger bundle of related content. Project MUSE, from the Johns Hopkins University Press, promotes university press publishers largely in the arts and humanities. The ALPSP Learned Journals Collection gives a vehicle to many of the (predominantly not-for-profit) member publishers of the Association of Learned and Professional Society Publishers. BioOne brings together a good amount of (mostly society) biological content in a single package. Subgroups of HighWire Press publishers have united to license their content. In short, publishers are aggregating themselves in packages to sell content (whether to single institutions or to library consortia) in a mirror image of the way libraries are aggregating themselves in consortia to buy content (whether from single publishers or as multipublisher packages).

Smaller publishers do have more options for sales agent services these days. Thanks largely to the rise of consortia, which can offer a bigger payoff to a sales representative working on commission than he or she would see from selling individual subscriptions to individual institutions, and thanks also to the growth in new emerging markets, there are a number of local and regional sales agents willing to offer their services. In many cases, they are former (or present) subscription agents or CD-ROM distributors trying to reinvent themselves in the online world. Our best advice for publishers is to see who is selling for the competition and for noncompetitive publishers in the same sector (e.g., STM, the arts and humanities, or the social sciences). One of the most convenient places to meet with potential sales agents is the Frankfurt Book Fair (www.buchmesse.de/en/fbf), still the largest gathering of publishing professionals, held annually (usually in October). But make appointments ahead of time – Frankfurt is incredibly busy.

There are countries where it will be nearly impossible to sell without a local agent, if for no other reason than that the publisher needs someone who can invoice customers in the local currency and remit payment to the publisher in its own currency. And there are a growing number of large, government-funded consortia that require the publisher to have a local presence simply to provide better customer service, available with a local phone call in the local language; for instance, the requirements of CAPES, the consortium of federally funded universities in Brazil, make life very difficult for publishers who cannot offer such a local presence.

The two biggest international subscription agents, EBSCO and Swets, now offer dedicated sales services to journal publishers for specific regions of the world. Each company has a division – EMpact for EBSCO and Accucoms for Swets – that is meant to be completely separate from their library subscription services. Publishers looking for sales agents might also consult the web pages of other publishers in their fields, which sometimes list their international sales representatives.

Sales people need to be armed with appropriate data when visiting a potential new institutional customer, such as how many of the publisher's authors have come from that institution, what Editors-in-Chief or Editorial Board members work there, the number of downloads from that institution, whether or not there are personal subscriptions among the faculty, and so on.

The best data tools for journal sales today are those deriving from free trials and "denials of access," or "turnaways," as described earlier. COUNTER reports take away the guesswork in free trials: both publisher and librarian can count the uses of the title or titles available during the free trial, and a sales discussion about price and value can take place from there. The sales person might offer an "introductory price," so that the librarian feels the value of the journal is in line with his or her other holdings. The marketing department should support these trials by proactively encouraging as much use as possible among the user population. (See earlier discussions about publicity, social media, author marketing, etc.)

Turnaway data is persuasive because in theory it is based on unmediated user behavior. It is evidence that real people have a real need for the content. Turnaways of a few individuals may not be impressive, but aggregate turnaway data can be very powerful. Of course, much of the demand by these users will be driven by ongoing marketing activities.

Good, old-fashioned sales still involve face-to-face visits with subject-specialist librarians and faculty department heads, with longer-term strategies for growing the revenue from each library customer. But sales today often operate on a grander scale, to which we turn our attention next.

## Selling to consortia

One of the first questions to ask of a new consortium customer is, "Who's paying?" (Followed closely by, "Can I issue one invoice?") Some consortia (such as OhioLINK) have their own budgets, directly funded by the state or the national government, and can therefore purchase content independently of the member libraries; this is the "centrally funded, centrally administered" consortium model. Other consortia are "centrally administered, but individually funded." In this more common model, a central committee negotiates for the best licensing terms, but the content is purchased out of individual library budgets.

Many "centrally administered" types are examples of "closed" consortia, where each member participates in the deal. More common, however, is the "open" consortium, where the licensing agreement may be negotiated centrally on behalf of the members as a whole, but each individual library is free to opt in or out of the deal. In a "closed" consortium, when the license agreement is signed the publisher knows everything about the deal: what content is being licensed, how many sites will have access, and what revenue is to come over the term of the agreement (typically, three years). In an "open" consortium, when the license agreement is signed the publisher knows almost nothing – until the individual members of the consortium begin to opt in. Often, in the case of open consortia, the publisher needs to sign a licensing agreement with each institutional member, as the consortium as an entity may not be able to sign a contract for all.

Some consortia are simply "buying clubs." They negotiate the lowest possible price they can get from the publisher, then leave it up to individual libraries to decide to purchase that publisher's package or not. Some open consortia, such as JISC Collections in the UK and BIBSAM in Sweden, have close contact with the individual library members, and respond to their collective concerns and demands; on the other hand, a "buying club" such as KESLI in South Korea has relatively little interaction with its institutional members at a policy level.

There are also *ad hoc* consortia, when a few librarians form a committee to acquire some publishers' content that they could not afford individually, but the committee does not otherwise have any central administration or legal existence at all. And there are plenty of examples of publisher-driven consortia, in which the "consortium" consists simply of whichever institutions respond to a publisher's offer. These cases require legwork by a local sales agent who can visit each library individually, and sell the consortium offer. This can lead to some confusing terminology. The main university consortium in China is the Digital Resources Acquisition Alliance (DRAA, formerly known as CALIS, for China Academic Library and Information Services); but, because it is an open consortium, the members themselves will refer to the "RSC consortium" or the "SAGE consortium," consisting of the subset of all DRAA members who take those publishers' offers.

For a list of consortia worldwide, see the International Coalition of Library Consortia (ICOLC) website at www.library.yale.edu/consortia/. An excellent commercial (fee-based) resource is the Consortium Directory Online (www.ringgold.com/pages/cdo.html).

When the customer is a consortium – or, indeed, a large institution with multiple sites or user groups – prices must be negotiated to fit the specific circumstances (taking account of such factors as the number of institutions or sites, the size of the user groups, the level of usage, and the publisher's existing subscriptions). Negotiations may go on for weeks or months. And the terms governing issues such as interlibrary loan, archival rights, and cancellations are also subject to negotiation. All of this adds substantially both to the publisher's selling costs and to the library's purchasing costs. As a result, various organizations have attempted to simplify the licensing process, either by adopting "model licenses," or by reducing or doing away with licenses altogether (see Chapter 7, Fulfillment, and Chapter 11, Copyright and other legal aspects, for more details).

## Conclusion

This overview of the marketing function – and even briefer review of sales – necessarily leaves out a great deal of detail. It does not provide a primer on the basics of copywriting, for example, or the intricacies of social media. But we hope that it gives readers a picture of what "marketing and sales" mean in the broadest sense for journal publishers, and shows how pervasive the need for marketing really is throughout the publishing organization. Anything that contributes to the "virtuous circle" for a journal improves its chances for success, whether the activity takes place in the marketing department or not. For today's journal publisher, the serials landscape is an ecosystem involving authors, readers, librarians, subscription agents, and other intermediaries, all of whom contribute to a publisher's success, and all of whom need marketing attention.

## REFERENCES

Association of Research Libraries, 2012, *Library expenditures as a percent of total university expenditures, 1982–2009*, Washington, DC, Association of Research Libraries (www.arl.org/bm~doc/library-expenditures-as-a-percent-of-total-university -expenditures-1982-2009-40-universities.pdf)

Chesler, Adam, and Susan King, 2009, Tier-based pricing for institutions: a new, e-based pricing model, *Learned Publishing* 22: 42–9 (http://dx.doi.org/10.1087/ 095315108X378768)

Conyers, Angela, and Pete Dalton, 2008, *Assessing the value of the NESLi2 deals*, Birmingham, Evidence Base (http://issuu.com/carenmilloy/docs/assessing_the_ value_of_nesli2_deals)

Crotty, David, 2008, *Web 2.0 for biologists – are any of the current tools worth using?*, Posting on Bench Marks blog (http://cshbenchmarks.wordpress.com/2008/ 04/03/web-20-for-biologists-are-any-of-the-current-tools-worth-using)

Perciali, Irene, and Aaron Edlin, 2008, Journals at bepress: new twists on an old model, *Learned Publishing* 21: 116–22 (http://dx.doi.org/10.1087/095315108X 288929)

Sanville, Tom, 2001, A method out of the madness: OhioLINK's collaborative response to the serials crisis: four years later – progress report, *Serials* 14: 163–77 (http://uksg. metapress.com/index/n1mbcw2rugk8pkj2.pdf)

Scott, David Meerman, 2006, Marketing your content in a micro-segmented online world, Presentation at Society for Scholarly Publishing Annual Conference (www.sspnet.org/documents/192_SSPP02Scott.pdf)

Tenopir, Carol, Suzie Allard, Ben Bates, Kenneth J Levine, Donald W King, Ben Birch, Regina Mays, and Chris Caldwell, 2010, *Research publication characteristics and their relative values*, London, Publishing Research Consortium (www.publishingresearch. net/PRCTenopiretalWord2010ResearchPublicationCharacteristics_000.docx)

Ware, Mark, and Michael Mabe, 2009, *The STM report*, London, International Association of Scientific, Technical & Medical Publishers (www.stm-assoc. org/2009_10_13_MWC_STM_Report.pdf)

## FURTHER READING

Rapple, Charlie, 2011, Researching and implementing a new tiered pricing model, *Learned Publishing* 24: 9–13 (http://dx.doi.org/10.1087/20110103)

Scott, David Meerman, 2011, *The new rules of marketing and PR*, 3rd edn, Hoboken, NJ, John Wiley & Sons

# 7 Fulfillment

## Introduction

The fulfillment function (also referred to as circulation, distribution, and/ or subscription management) is the backbone of the publishing operation, connecting customers to content. The fulfillment operation is responsible for invoicing customers, generating renewals, receiving and tracking payments, and delivering the goods purchased. This includes physical distribution involving printers, warehousing, and postal regulations as well as electronic delivery with its own issues of technical support, user authentication, and access rights.

Regardless of whether the "deliverable" is print or electronic, the fulfillment team needs to work closely with subscription agents, online hosting services, printers, the marketing and editorial departments, and the company's own accounting systems. As with the discussion of marketing in the previous chapter, we will discuss "fulfillment" in the broadest sense, regardless of which department is responsible for the various activities that constitute it.

Online publishing has turned fulfillment into a 24/7 operation, very different from what was necessary to distribute print journals. With print, institutional "subscribers" were essentially shipping addresses, often with multiple mail drops within a single institution – but seldom related to each other in the publisher's database at an institutional or "customer" level. Indeed, many of the publisher's institutional customers were completely unknown to the publisher, buried in bulk-copy orders from subscription agents, who then redelivered the copy to the final recipient. Publishers and agents sometimes argued over who "owned" such customers, and agents were not always willing to identify them to the publisher.

Personal contact with customers of print journals was rather rare, except when issues did not arrive and librarians issued claims for nondelivery, a messy process for all concerned. What we now think of as a "knowledge industry" was very much a business of buying and selling physical goods, as well: the publisher delivered a physical product and, once a mailing label was affixed to an issue and it was dropped in the mail, "fulfillment" was done for all practical purposes (the subscription usually having been prepaid). The publisher did not need to know the size of the user population, the setup of the institution's computer network, whether the library was an independent customer or part of a larger institution with multiple libraries and overlapping IP addresses, and so on.

But online publishing brought deeper changes than this. Libraries, now asked to sign license agreements that specified prohibited and permitted uses of the electronic content, began talking to publishers about these terms and conditions, and a much richer dialogue began to take place over academic practices such as interlibrary loan and reuse of content in course packs, over the customer's rights regarding long-term ownership and access, and even over price, once a take-it-or-leave-it prerogative of the publisher.[1]

These are not all strictly fulfillment issues, of course. License agreements, for example, are not created by fulfillment departments and any negotiations over the wording of these agreements usually take place with editorial, rights and permissions, or sales and marketing staff – or the legal department, in larger publishing houses. License agreements are discussed in detail in Chapter 11, Copyright and other legal aspects. But we note that the license agreement itself is now an integral part of the fulfillment process, one of two requirements – the other being payment – necessary for the customer to receive the online content he or she wants. It is a fulfillment issue no matter which functional department is responsible for distributing, collecting, and negotiating the licenses.

While much of this chapter is more relevant to subscription-based than to open access journals (which by definition have no "subscribers"), even "Gold" open access journals have some fulfillment issues. If the publisher wants to see how much use an OA title is receiving at a given institution, or the customer itself wants COUNTER-compliant usage reports (see Chapter 5, Journal metrics) for the title (which is of interest even if the

---

[1] Almost all publishers of subscription-based online journals require customers to sign a standard license agreement, or "user agreement," specifying terms and conditions of use. In that sense, all customers are "licensees." However, as in Chapter 6, Marketing and sales, we will use "licensees" to refer more specifically to customers who have negotiated special license prices for access to a publisher's content, as opposed to "subscribers" who pay the publisher's normal list prices.

institution is paying nothing for the content), then the OA journal needs to be added to the customer's fulfillment record and integrated with the standard COUNTER reports.

Customer service is integral to the fulfillment function, even if the publisher has a "24/7" technical helpdesk distinct from a customer-service team handling all other fulfillment issues, including invoices, payments, order entry, licensing agreements, and print delivery. Print was slow, and speed was not always the first priority of customer service in resolving print delivery issues. But publishing is an Internet business today and customers expect the same sort of quick response they are used to getting from any other online service. Publishers have needed bigger customer-service teams, and a higher level of training for them. The customer-service reps may even be enlisted in telemarketing campaigns, promoting additional content or trying to recover lapsed subscriptions. (This will depend on how well integrated the marketing, sales, and fulfillment functions are.) In some cases, where publishers have the resources, each customer may fall under a single account manager and/or a customer support representative.

Fulfillment and marketing should work hand in hand. The fulfillment database is the primary source of customer information that marketers need for analysis and promotion, obviously. But real "business intelligence" comes from integrating subscriber information (including parent–child relationships),[2] usage statistics, author affiliations, and other data (peer-review and Editorial Board affiliations, for example) for a 360-degree view of each customer. (Off-the-shelf customer relationship management [CRM] software, such as SalesForce [www.salesforce.com] or SalesLogix [www.sagesaleslogix.com], and more industry-specific solutions, such as MasterVision from Data Salon [www.datasalon.com], may satisfy this need.) Since the key customer database has always been managed by fulfillment personnel, this new kind of "total customer view" might be managed by the same people. However, in some companies, this

---

[2] In print, each subscriber record was essentially a mailing address, and it made little difference to the publisher whether a single institution had multiple subscriptions or not, since each one served a distinct geographical audience. Since one online subscription can be shared across the entire institutional network, it becomes important to understand which "parent" institution owns the departments, institutes, labs, and libraries that are its "children" in order to define accurately the community of authorized users to be covered by the license.

database might find a home in the sales, marketing, or business-systems departments – another illustration of how porous the walls are between publishing functions in an online world.

## Outsource, or manage in-house?

Publishers may have their own in-house fulfillment system or may outsource this function in whole or in part. Publishers that outsource fulfillment may manage their own subscriber lists in-house and handle their own renewals and billings, only sending labels to the fulfillment service for the delivery of print copies; or they may rely on the fulfillment house for every aspect of the fulfillment process. The fulfillment house might also warehouse the publisher's print inventory and handle all delivery to customers, or the publisher might have current issues shipped directly from the printer, with the fulfillment house handling only delivery of back issues.

There are today relatively inexpensive off-the-shelf software products for managing a subscription database, but managing fulfillment in the modern, online sense may present a challenge to smaller publishing houses, which will need to invest in staff, software, and hardware to keep up with postal regulations, international database privacy standards, CRM systems, circulation auditing requirements, electronic order processing, and the like. Publishers thinking about outsourcing fulfillment will need to consider carefully their needs for customer service and for integration with the online hosting service, which may be outsourced as well. Who, for example, will be responsible for validating Internet Protocol addresses for institutional customers? Some online services allow librarians to enter their own IP ranges; however, when publishers verify the legitimacy of each IP address themselves, they often find contentious issues. Is a teaching hospital a legitimate part of a university's user population or an entirely separate organization requiring its own license? Is a multinational company a single customer that should pay for only one subscription because all of its users are behind a single proxy IP address? May a federally funded research laboratory managed under contract by a university share the university's online subscriptions? These are important questions with serious revenue implications – in that they often result in converting the subscriber to a multisite licensee with additional fees – so publishers need to make sure they have policies regarding authorized users and multiple sites, and that they can either enforce these policies directly or rely on their hosting service to do so.

Similar issues will occur with an outside fulfillment service. In Box 7.1, we itemize some of the questions that publishers looking to outsource distribution should ask.

Publishers with in-house systems usually purchase subscription-management software rather than building their own, and will need to

---

**Box 7.1 Thinking of outsourcing your fulfillment operation?**

Some questions to ask:

- Will the publisher have direct access to its customer database? Can it generate custom reports? (For instance, the publisher would probably like daily cash-flow reports during renewal season.) Or does the fulfillment house offer a specific, standard set of reports to the publisher? With what frequency?
- What currencies can the fulfillment house accept? How quickly will the publisher receive cash (or a reconciliation of accounts) after the fulfillment house receives payment? What is the frequency of disbursements after the initial payment? Does the vendor deduct its charges from these payments or invoice for these separately? Will it build an interface to the publisher's financial system? Is it compliant with the PCI (Payment Card Industry) Data Security Standard for handling credit card data?
- Can it process EDI (electronic data interchange) orders from subscription agents? Can it handle random expiry (also known as "anytime starts" or "rolling renewals," i.e., subscriptions that may begin at any time of the year) as well as calendar-year subscriptions?
- Can the fulfillment house accept data from third parties (e.g., member subscriber data from societies)?
- Is it compliant with privacy and data protection standards?
- How often does the fulfillment agent back up its files? Does it have a disaster-recovery plan?
- How does the fulfillment agency charge the publisher? Is the charge based on units, revenue, or transactions? Are there unexpected fees (e.g., for excess print inventory, if the agency provides warehousing)? What are the picking and packing charges when the publisher wants a few sample copies shipped to an exhibit?
- To what degree can the publisher preserve and promote its brand? Do invoices include the publisher's name or only the name of the fulfillment house? Is there a dedicated toll-free customer-service telephone number for the publisher at the fulfillment house?

**Box 7.1** (continued)

- Does the agency offer a 24/7 customer helpdesk? How good is their customer service? How well do they process orders by phone? Do they have multilingual capabilities?
- Does the agent have a warehouse? How clean and efficient is it? Does the agent provide monthly stock reports? How quickly does it process claims? Does it fulfill single-issue and back-volume sales?
- How familiar is the agency's staff with the library market and scholarly publishing in general? (Get references from other publishers.) What are the tone, timing, and frequency of renewal reminders, for instance?
- Does the fulfillment service support circulation auditing requirements for advertisers?
- How fast can a new online account be established and the details passed over to the online hosting service?
- What email message is sent to the customer to confirm that access has been established?

answer many of the same questions about the features and flexibility they want from these third-party systems, including how scalable they are to meet future needs and how well they accommodate customized product packages. They also need to consider whether they own or license the product, how much it can be customized for specific needs, and – in the event that the provider goes out of business – who owns the source code.

## Subscriptions and renewals

Academic journals are usually sold on a calendar-year basis. Sometime in the spring, the librarian, acting in consultation with faculty and with some preliminary idea of how much her acquisition budget will grow (or shrink), will prepare an order list (or work with the renewal list supplied by her subscription agent) for the next year's subscriptions. (Some of her holdings will come from consortia and other licensing deals, which are renewed differently and are discussed below.) Most publishers will not have announced their following-year prices at this point, so some assumptions will be made about price increases. The bigger subscription agents try to arm their customers with some idea, based on publisher surveys, of what to expect in the way of price increases, along with whatever information they can pass on about expected currency conversion rates. (Inflation and devaluation of currencies relative to the dollar, pound, or euro can make a huge difference in price for overseas customers.) As mentioned in Chapter 6, Marketing and sales, most publishers try to announce their prices for the next year as early in the current year as possible; it is not uncommon to see publishers announcing their next-year prices as early as March and April, with August now considered late.

Since as much as 80–90% of the publisher's subscription revenues may come through subscription agents, there is no need to invoice these subscribers directly. However, publishers will typically send renewal reminders to libraries throughout the renewal period. For customers that order directly from the publisher, the fulfillment department will send its own series of invoices, beginning in July or August. As publisher prices, and the librarian's budget, are finalized, so is the final acquisition decision. Some journals may be added or cut at this point.

Libraries that cancel subscriptions rarely inform the publisher; they simply do not renew. So there will be many "lapsed" subscriptions the publisher will chase until they can be either renewed or canceled. Publishers often recognize a subscription as "canceled" only when a library declares it so or a subscription agent sends in a list of confirmed cancellations. Otherwise, lapsed subscriptions remain in an indeterminate state for the rest of the calendar year, or unless the publisher declares the subscription "terminated" after a specified period of time. An email or telemarketing campaign is vital to help classify lapsed subscriptions and resolve the status of nonrenewed subscriptions.

Licensing agreements with academic consortia and with individual companies, government agencies, and universities are generally renewed directly by the publisher and librarian, bypassing the subscription agencies. (Subscription agents, however, do play a role in many of these deals, often helping to reconcile subscription orders at individual sites while the publisher negotiates the surcharge or "top-off fee" or "consortium access fee" for the new content shared by all. And some agents manage the purchasing process for the licensee institutions, and in rare cases even help to market and license a publisher package – as Swets does for the ALPSP Learned Journals Collection.) Many of these licensing agreements involve an agreed price cap, so the renewal might seem fairly straightforward – but new institutions (e.g., members of a consortium) might opt in or opt out of the deal each year, and the terms might include a "cancellation allowance" for members with drastically reduced budgets – so some degree of adjustment in the licensing fee is usually required even within the term of a multiyear license.

## Gracing

While a publisher might expect to get 65–80% of its institutional subscription orders by December 31, there will always be orders arriving well after January 1 of the actual subscription year. When most orders were for print, publishers commonly continued to ship a few issues of the print journal while waiting for payment, a process known as "gracing." This allows the library to continue service to users in spite of sometimes unavoidably late payments and to avoid wasting time on unnecessary claims. The Association of Subscription Agents and Intermediaries, the international trade association for subscription agents, says that gracing at least through February 28 is the "consensus" among publishers (Association of Subscription Agents and Intermediaries, 2009).

With online, gracing is even more important for many publications. It is one thing not to receive one or two printed issues of a journal. It is quite another to lose access to previously published online issues that the library has bought and paid for – even the publishers that promise "perpetual access" to previously subscribed material are not all able to provide ongoing online access on their own servers.[3] Disabling access when the customer's payment is somewhere in the pipeline is a practice that generates enormous ill will from librarians and users. We will return to this point when we discuss the problem of "abuse" later in this chapter.

However, the threat of lost access due to nonpayment will also help to spur tardy renewals. Publishers should repeatedly notify online subscribers that their access will be disabled by a given date – presumably around March 1, following the normal gracing period. (See Chapter 6, Marketing and sales, for a fuller discussion in "Chasing renewals.") Customers with licensing agreements rather than standard subscriptions are seldom cut off, since the publisher is aware of the renewal negotiations taking place, however long these may take.

---

[3] Some publishers guarantee "perpetual access" by sending the customer PDF files of the licensed content; others provide "post-cancellation" access – sometimes through a third-party service such as Portico – that does not cover the backfile to a title awaiting renewal.

## When is a subscription "new"?

A new subscription may not be what it appears. The industry has long been vexed with the problem of distinguishing a completely new order from a renewal order that has simply been switched from one subscription agent to another, or that has a change of address (or even a change in the institutional name). Thus, a "lapsed" subscription handled by one agent in the previous year and a "new" subscription received from another agent for the current year may very well be the same subscription. Publishers now commonly require agents to identify the ultimate recipient for every subscription order (in the past many were hidden in bulk print orders, which the publisher delivered to a central processing facility where the agent remailed or reshipped the journals to their ultimate recipients). However, different agents use different account numbers, and may provide slightly different customer names or addresses for the same client. Fulfillment folks are very familiar with the difficulties of disambiguating an institutional customer that might alternatively be denoted as University of Birmingham, U of Birmingham, Univ. of Birmingham, Birmingham University – or might even use the name of a main library, a departmental library, or a building as the name on the account. As a result, NISO, the US standards organization for information exchange (www.niso.org/home), has formed a committee to investigate a standard way of attaching a unique institutional identifier to "parent" institutions and to each of its "children." (See www.niso.org/workrooms/i2.) There are also a couple of private initiatives working towards similar objectives, including Ringgold (www.ringgold.com) and Publisher Solutions International (www.linkedin.com/company/publisher-solutions-international).

While ambiguity about institutional identities is a problem for online as well as for print fulfillment, the publisher at least has more clues to work with, in the form of IP addresses that the institution registers on its license agreement. Unfortunately, IP ranges can also change, or be hidden entirely behind a proxy IP address. What's more, IP addresses in the developing world and elsewhere may be owned by a telecommunications utility or a state agency with no apparent connection to the university or research institute served by the publisher; in some cases, such IP addresses can be dynamically reassigned by the owner. To a large degree, the publishing world operates on trust, and this is one of those areas where the publisher may just have to trust the customer – although a local sales agent can provide invaluable advice.

## Licensing "deals"

The standard license agreement required by publishers for online access usually requires only the customer's signature (or assent, if a "click-through" agreement is involved), indicating that the institution understands and agrees to the terms and conditions. But this basic license is also frequently adapted to cover special pricing circumstances, used for institutions with multiple sites or for consortia deals, or for single-site or multisite institutions purchasing a "Big Deal" bundle or even a multi-publisher package of content. Such deals involve negotiations between the publisher and the customer and almost always require a formal license agreement, signed by both (or all) parties. These agreements cover a variety of situations, even for single institutions:

- A university that wants to extend access to its subscribed titles to users at remote sites, such as a marine biology lab or an astronomical observatory (for which many publishers will not require extra fees).
- A university that wants to extend access to its subscribed titles to other campuses (in which case the publisher will almost certainly require extra fees, if not completely separate subscriptions).
- A university that wants to extend access to a teaching hospital in a separate location (policies may be different for medical and nonmedical publishers).
- A university that wants access to all of the publisher's content and not just to the titles it had subscribed to in print – the Big Deal, in other words.

Licensing agreements used for multisite or consortium deals are equally varied – for more on the different types of consortia, see Chapter 6, Marketing and sales. In particular, there are some unique issues in consortia deals that will need to be clarified:

- Is the consortium "closed" or "open"? That is, are all members of the consortium bound by the deal, or is each one allowed to opt in or opt out? How is the pricing affected by the number of members who opt in? Is each member bound for the term of the licensing agreement, typically three years, or may it opt out before the end of the term? Under what conditions may it opt out?

- Pricing model? Pricing schemes vary widely. In some deals, institutions with existing subscriptions pay a different rate for those journals than do nonsubscribing institutions. Sometimes, a single fee is charged for the consortium as a whole (even though the consortium may allocate this expense differently among its different members) and sometimes per-site fees are charged according to full-time equivalent (FTE) faculty and students or other measures of size. In all cases, the publisher hopes that it can issue a single invoice and let the consortium collect payment from its members, but it also happens that, even with a single fixed annual price, the publisher may have to invoice each member separately, and sometimes at different rates. (Collecting payment from a few recalcitrant holdouts, who are essentially threatening the deal for all the rest, is often a problem with this type of open consortium.)
- Whose license? Publishers are used to dealing with their own agreements, but in many cases they will be required to agree to the consortium's license terms, which can vary greatly. For example, the national consortium in Brazil, CAPES (the Coordenação de Aperfeiçoamento de Pessoal de Nível Superior, www.capes.gov.br), which is a department of the Ministry of Education, requires a Portuguese-language contract, and, at least for some publishers, a bank guarantee on the invoice amount (which is insurance against the possibility of loss of access). There are other consortia that – at least nominally – extract penalties from the publisher in the event online service is down for any length of time.

## What do fulfillment reports measure?

Licensing deals have made it more difficult to track sales success relative to the publisher's traditional circulation reports, which were based on subscription counts. Circulation was simple when one subscription had one (domestic) price, and we all understood what a "subscription" meant. A publisher's success could be measured in subscription units, which could be tracked with great precision. (Revenue is always an important measure, but it is somewhat abstract for those who want to quantify sales growth from year to year in terms of customers.) "Distribution" could be counted exactly because it referred to physical copies of the journal.[4] With the online version, however, "distribution" means access by some unspecified number of users. What unit does the fulfillment department count when some customers pay full price for a journal and many others get access at discounted rates via a bundled license or consortium deal? (Indeed, "full price" is becoming less and less meaningful, to the extent that the American Library Association has stopped measuring "price per journal," and fewer and fewer prices are listed in *Ulrich's Periodicals Directory*.) A journal might see a decline in "subscriptions" compared to the previous year but experience a significant rise in revenue – and in the number of users who have access to it.

For publishers with a mature business (i.e., one with a strong legacy of historical subscriptions in addition to newer license agreements), there are a number of institutional revenue channels that it may be necessary to track in order to measure year-on-year growth:

1. Subscriptions – i.e., traditional subscriptions paid at standard rates by individual institutions. Most publishers have plenty of "subscribers" by this definition, even in this age of licensing deals. Such subscriptions could be for individual titles or for discounted packages of related journals typically offered by smaller publishers (a mini-version of the Big Deal associated with the big commercial publishers).
2. Subscriptions within consortia agreements. Many licensing deals provide additional online content to consortia members partly on the condition that the subscribing institutions renew their individual subscriptions. In some cases, these subscriptions are protected by a price cap over the term of the agreement, so the prices will vary over time from those paid by other subscribing institutions.
3. "Nonsubscriber accounts" within consortia – each account being a distinct institution or geographical site, with an associated range of IP addresses, holding no subscriptions of its own but gaining the publisher's content through a consortium licensing fee.
4. "Licensees" – institutions (usually with multiple sites) or consortia that pay a single negotiated license fee. These may be entirely new customers whose fee is based on FTE or some other measure of size, or a

---

[4] Of course, unauthorized copying (piracy), fraudulent "member" copies sold to institutions, and real member copies "shared" with the member's institution (see Chapter 6, Marketing and sales) all distorted the publisher's view of its distribution.

mix of subscribing and nonsubscribing institutions whose fee is determined in part by the collective price of all the subscriptions held.

To further complicate things, a subscribing institution might have multiple "accounts" representing different journal subscriptions and/or different departments – the engineering library at Harvard might have one subscription account and the business library might have another. But an "account" in consortia licensing deals usually means an "institution" – one that gets all of the publisher's licensed titles and not individual "subscriptions." As with "subscribers," the publisher needs to be sure it is distinguishing between apples and oranges, and not equating all "accounts." The design of the publisher's fulfillment reports needs collaboration among fulfillment, sales, marketing, and accounting personnel to ensure that everyone in the organization understands what the reports say about the business – and also to ensure that clear and consistent information is being presented to owners of journals under contract to the publisher. (Good fulfillment reports are able to sort customers by country, by region, by size [if the publisher has tiered prices], and by market sector, i.e., academic, government, corporate, medical, and so on. A good system should be able to tell the marketing team the degree to which corporate subscriptions among top-tier subscribers in Japan are up or down, for example.)

## Working with subscription agents

We mentioned earlier that as much as 80–90% of a publisher's subscription revenues may come through subscription agents, although this is less true for larger publishers with many licensing deals in place, as these are renewed directly by the publisher and the customer. Agents are a huge convenience for libraries, which would otherwise have to place orders with thousands of separate publishers. Equally, they are a convenience for publishers, who would otherwise have to deal with thousands of separate customers speaking different languages and operating under different legal/financial regimes. Moreover, agents take payments in local currencies and convert them to currencies accepted by the publisher, which generally means dollars, euros, pounds sterling, and perhaps yen; they may even pay the publisher before they have actually received payment from the customer (although this is less common in today's economic climate).

Traditionally, subscription agents were paid through a combination of discounts from publishers and service fees from libraries.[5] (It is well to remember, however, that the agent works for its customers, the libraries, rather than for the publishers.) The 1990s witnessed a big upheaval among subscription agents, as budget retrenchments by publishers and libraries reduced these margins exactly at the moment when the agents needed to invest heavily in technology to remain competitive in a newly online world. Dozens of major subscription agents succumbed to bankruptcy, mergers, and buyouts in this period, leaving just a few truly international players, including Swets, headquartered in the Netherlands; EBSCO, located in Birmingham, Alabama; and, to a lesser degree, Harrassowitz, based in Germany. (However, there remain many national-level agents of importance. In Japan, for example, many publishers still appoint an exclusive agent to distribute their content, which was a virtual requirement in the print era, given the language barrier and the country's nearly impenetrable postal system.) For a list of subscription agents, see Appendix 3, Vendors.

The largest agents have sought greater efficiencies in the ordering process, in part through the application of standards. ICEDIS, the International Committee on Electronic Data Interchange Standards (www.icedis.org/index.html), is an industry body working towards standard guidelines for a machine-readable exchange of data across the supply chain. However, the plethora of small agents (and small publishers) worldwide limits the application of these standards, since they are most efficient with large order volumes. ONIX for Serials is another set of standards for communicating machine-readable information about journals, developed by NISO and by EDItEUR, an international committee representing various sectors of the knowledge industry (www.editeur.org/).

The Association of Subscription Agents and Intermediaries (ASA) is involved in these standards initiatives and also posts its own "Supply Chain Guidelines" at www.subscription-agents.org/resources/supply-chain -guidelines. These are best-practice guidelines for handling claims, tenders, grace periods, and so on, rather than formal software standards such as those developed by ICEDIS and ONIX.

---

[5] Many nonprofit society publishers have never offered discounts to subscription agents, a longstanding controversy within the industry. This has changed somewhat in recent years as societies have seen more tangible benefits, such as electronic data exchange, from agreements with the agents.

EDI standards have lessened the workload on publishers' fulfillment operations, which need to process a large number of renewals and new orders for journal subscriptions in a relatively short time frame, near the end of the year. As more subscriptions become wrapped in bundles or consortia licensing deals, some renewals will be delayed during negotiations between the publisher and the customer or consortium, stretching out the renewal period – and also the payment period. Journal subscriptions typically require prepayment before the start of service. But the renewal process for many licensees (whether consortia or individual institutions) may drag on for weeks or months, so the payment for any subscriptions within the overall deal may be delayed as well. (See Chapter 6, Marketing and sales, for more on renewals.) On the other hand, consortia renewals are usually guaranteed by contract (i.e., by the licensing agreement), so these can be treated by the finance people as receivables, reducing the number of nonrenewed subscriptions that are truly at risk for the publisher.

Subscription agents are a somewhat endangered species, especially because some of the larger commercial publishers are keen to have direct billing and renewal relationships with their major library customers, governed by licensing agreements. This threatens agents' revenues from both publishers and libraries. Many agents, seeking new lines of business, are marketing themselves to publishers as exclusive sales representatives, particularly if there is new money in the market from government-supported consortia activity. In any case, the larger agents understand the need for greater cooperation with publishers to earn their fees or discounts, and EBSCO and Swets, at least, each have a suite of services to improve the flow of information to publishers (or their fulfillment agents) with respect to subscriptions, licensing deals, payments, and claims. (More on claims below.)

## The customer database

As fulfillment has become more tied to online distribution, the nature of the fulfillment database has changed, too. It is no longer sufficient to record the subscriber, its ship-to and bill-to addresses, the titles bought, the formats involved (including e.g., CDs), the price, payment date, agent used, and the like. The subscriber's records must also include the range of IP addresses for which access will be authenticated and a technical contact person reachable by email. It is very helpful to record as well any telephone or email contact with other librarians associated with the account, not to mention the response to any promotional offers that have been accepted or rejected. And all of this must be done in accordance with privacy-protection rules (more fully discussed in Chapter 11, Copyright and other legal aspects).

In short, the fulfillment database is also a customer-service tool, and should record all transactions with the library staff, and the resolution of any complaints. Indeed, a large fulfillment service will be running a 24/7 call center operation and will need to consider modern customer-service software of the kind that Internet consumers are used to.

## Claims

Inevitably, some print copies will go astray before reaching the customer, and the customer will submit a claim for a replacement copy. Reasons for nondelivery could be anything from physical damage to the mailing envelope to faulty labels to misdirection in the local mail or common pilferage. Occasionally, an issue is so damaged the librarian wants a new one. Sometimes, the customer may not have renewed or paid, but assumes he or she has. Sometimes, the library's own check-in procedures are at fault. The problem might even be with a freight consolidator rather than the publisher. (Several subscription agencies offer consolidation services, which allows them to receive publishers' journals at a single drop-ship point and to repackage them for overseas delivery, saving on the publisher's own postage charges.) Since some customers on the other side of the world elect to get surface-mail delivery, the chances for delayed delivery or even nondelivery are compounded.

Claims are a major headache for publishers, unless they decide it is less expensive to fulfill claims automatically than it is to investigate them. (Some publishers take the opposite approach: they discard all first claims and wait to see if the situation resolves itself before a second claim is received, knowing that the problem may simply be a mail delay.) Otherwise, they need to make sure the issue was printed, the customer's ship-to address is correct, the subscription is paid, and the issue entered the mail stream. Some customers and agents are notorious for over-claiming, and the publisher will want to check this, too. Publishers usually put time limits on claims, for example, six months (with, perhaps, nine months for

Asia because of the longer delivery times). Publishers can count claims among the many reasons why they would like to see print eliminated.

With the online format, a "claim" is usually a complaint about lost access for one or more IP ranges. These can be resolved quickly for the most part, and it is important to do so, since, as mentioned above, the customer may have lost not one or two issues of a journal but an entire online archive.

## Resolving "abuse" problems

Most publisher license agreements prohibit "systematic" (or "programmatic") downloading and enforce this prohibition by cutting off access for any IP range where it is detected. Systematic downloading results from the use of software programs ("spiders," "bots," or "web crawlers") which are used to download a large amount of material in a short period of time – usually faster than any human being would be capable of. Publishers worry about theft of their intellectual property in this manner, although this kind of activity is often "innocent" – a graduate student may be trying to load a collection of reference material onto a CD-ROM or thumb drive, for example. There is also the concern that wholesale downloading will affect the performance of the online hosting system, slowing service to other users.

Publishers usually establish a threshold, or trigger, for the amount of downloading they find acceptable, one well within normal usage patterns of regular users. "Abuse" occurs when a user exceeds the threshold, which will cause access for that IP address to be disabled automatically. That means that no user in that IP address or range can get to the publisher's content – not even "perpetual access" content guaranteed by the publisher's license agreement (unless such content is fulfilled by a third-party service such as Portico); it is therefore imperative that the publisher work quickly with the library staff to resolve the problem. An email is typically dispatched to the library's technical contact immediately, and usually the library needs only to confirm that it will investigate the problem before the publisher will restore access. (Any subsequent abuse will be met with an equally prompt loss of access, of course.)

The procedures for resolving this kind of abuse situation are generally spelled out in the license agreement. One typical publisher's agreement states that the publisher "will use reasonable efforts to notify the Licensee as soon as possible, usually within three (3) days of any such suspension of service" – but this is a weak standard and hardly good customer service. Publishers, or their online providers, should strive to do better.

## Individual and member subscriptions

The fulfillment department will also manage subscriptions to individuals, including those that come with one's membership in a professional society. With society journals, there is often a nonmember individual rate as well as the membership rate; and the nonmember rate is sometimes limited to specific groups, such as students or members of other, sister societies. The publisher will need to establish rules about how to qualify such groups. The most accurate course is to require an ID number of some kind, and to validate it with the organization that issued it. In many cases, an ID is required but not always validated, a procedure known as "soft credentialing" (basically, the publisher takes the individual's word for it).

Societies generally renew their own members' subscriptions in tandem with their annual dues renewals, and feed the current subscriber data to the fulfillment house. (See Chapter 6, Marketing and sales, for more on society policies with respect to member publications.) Some additionally handle all of the customer service associated with the members' subscriptions (at least on the "front end"), while others depend on the fulfillment group to manage this responsibility. It is, in any case, essential for the fulfillment staff to hold a current email address for society members, as with other individual subscribers, for any customer-service notices required (e.g., to announce a planned downtime of service).

The mode of online access for society members will also depend on the society, which might feed the members' password and user ID information to the publisher's fulfillment system so that members can log in directly, or which might require all members to access the content through a gateway on the society website.

Subscriptions for individuals have traditionally been sold on a calendar-year basis. However, they can also be offered to start at any time ("random expiry" or "anytime start"), just like a popular magazine subscription. Society member subscriptions will correspond to the term of membership itself, which may not start at the beginning of the calendar year.

Individual subscriptions can be problematic for publishers. There have been many instances where subscribers sent their copy to the library, despite the prohibition against doing so that is often printed directly on the cover of the individual's copy, or to which the individual agrees (tacitly or otherwise) as a condition of subscription. There are also many cases where the subscriber, if a faculty member, shares his or her copy with students, sometimes placing it in a departmental reading room or library. In either case, the individual copy is substituting for a much higher-priced subscription that the library would have to maintain. (Librarians sometimes profess to be shocked by the price difference of institutional and individual subscriptions. But of course it is the institutional rates that pay for the publishing operation and allow the publisher to offer discounted individual rates in the first place. Put more properly, both revenue sources support the publishing operation, but the publisher could never survive on the individual rates alone. In the same way, because paying customers support a journal financially, the publisher is able to offer free or low-cost access to the developing world.) Society publishers try to educate their members against this practice but other publishers may not have the same moral weight with their individual readers.

Individual subscriptions to scholarly journals have been shrinking for years, as a result of two parallel phenomena: (a) individual subscription prices have risen steadily, to the point where a decision to subscribe is not made casually;[6] and (b) access to the online version of many journals, thanks to library and consortia licensing agreements – and to remote authentication for off-campus use – is ubiquitous enough to make a personal copy unnecessary. This is particularly true for STM titles with a large international market, as these new licensing deals expanded their reach to a greater degree than they did for many HSS titles. If anything, these factors only put a brighter spotlight on the remaining individual subscriptions. Worried about how these copies might be used, some societies that publish multiple titles limit the number of subscriptions that a member can have. Other societies and nonsociety publishers have ceased to offer print as an option for individual subscriptions at all. Even where this is not an explicit strategy to limit individual copies, the relatively high distribution cost of print compared to online has made the online rate more attractive for individual subscribers. Even when a publisher maintains the same domestic price for print and online, the fees

---

[6] Even some societies that used to offer their journal as a benefit of membership have decided, as this cost has eaten up more and more of the member's dues, to make the journal an optional choice that the member must pay for separately.

for overseas freight – not to mention the longer delivery times – can certainly bias overseas readers towards the online format.

Of course, online licensing for individuals has not eliminated the kind of sharing described above that threatens the publisher's institutional revenues. Indeed, it is much easier sharing a password than sharing a single physical copy. On the other hand, the publisher can directly measure usage of the online journal and will sometimes be able to detect usage that is abnormally high for a single person. Investigating that kind of "personal" use will require some tact and delicacy, though the publisher has a legitimate interest in making sure that no person other than the subscriber is using the content.

There are also illegitimate member subscriptions, another threat to the publisher's institutional revenues. This type of fraud is discussed in Chapter 6, Marketing and sales, in the section on "The role of subscription agents."

While the number of individual subscriptions is shrinking, the fact that a journal has individual as well as institutional subscribers may be of interest to advertisers. If the publisher is selling advertisements on the basis of circulation, then the fulfillment staff will have to cooperate with the auditing requirements of Business Publications Audit (BPA) or Audit Bureau of Circulations (ABC) or similar not-for-profit organizations, which are generally run by magazine and newspaper publishers and advertising agencies. These organizations assure advertisers that the publisher's stated circulation numbers are correct.

## When journals change hands

Scholarly journals are regularly bought and sold – acquisition is a strong business strategy for many publishers – which sometimes leaves a subscriber uncertain about where and how to renew (if they order direct rather than through a subscription agent). The complications for subscribers are compounded when the journal is online, since the new owner will have to establish IP access for each customer, honor any perpetual-access rights guaranteed by the previous owner, and fulfill specific contractual terms (in consortium agreements, for example) – ideally without any interruption in service. Libraries, for their part, will have to ensure that their ERM systems contain the new links to the content. Rather than rehearse here the many issues involved when a journal changes hands, we refer readers to the Transfer Code of Practice (www.uksg.org/transfer). The Transfer Code was developed by a Working Group of the UKSG and is endorsed by many scholarly publishers. It spells out the roles and responsibilities of both the "transferring publisher" and the "receiving publisher" to ensure seamless and uninterrupted access for the customer. (The Transfer Code is also discussed in Chapter 2, Managing journals, Chapter 8, Journal finances, and Chapter 10, Contract publishing.)

## Conclusion

A good fulfillment service is crucial for journal publishers and is often the most tangible part of the publisher's "brand" in the minds of customers. What was once one of the "quieter" aspects of journal publishing is now one of the most dynamic, with 24/7 customer service for a worldwide market, the absolute need for rapid resolution of access issues, and high-level interaction with the production, marketing, sales, and accounting functions, which all depend to some degree on the customer and financial data generated by the fulfillment database. In short, fulfillment is at the operational heart of journal publishing and must not be neglected: perceptions of how "good" or "bad" a publisher is may rest entirely on its interactions with the librarians it serves.

### REFERENCES

Association of Subscription Agents and Intermediaries, 2009, *Grace periods for electronic journals subscription renewals*, ASA website (www.subscription-agents.org/nord/90)

# 8 Journal finances

"My other piece of advice, Copperfield", said Mr Micawber, "you know. Annual income twenty pounds, annual expenditure nineteen pounds nineteen and six, result happiness. Annual income twenty pounds, annual expenditure twenty pounds ought and six, result misery." (Dickens, 1849)

## Introduction

No matter how well edited a journal is, how many subscribers/readers it has, or how high its impact, a journal cannot continue to exist unless the income it derives covers all of its expenses. Not only that, but a sufficient surplus of income over expenses must be generated if a journal (or a list of journals) is to survive in the long run. A surplus is needed to cover the inevitable discrepancies between financial projections and actual results, to provide seed money for future projects, and to build a reserve to weather downturns. In addition, learned society publishers need surpluses to fund their other activities, and university presses to support loss-making but nevertheless worthwhile publications; commercial publishers need to generate a sufficient return on investment to keep investors happy. In the current online environment, a surplus is even more necessary in order to cover both continuous product development and the need to convert content as new standards of online presentation and delivery develop. With a surplus of just one eighth of 1%, Mr Micawber was operating on a very thin margin.[1]

    The purpose of this chapter is to give the reader a working knowledge of the primary income streams and expenses that need to be considered in determining the financial health of an individual journal,[2] the importance

---

[1] Prior to decimalization in 1971, the pound sterling was divided into twenty shillings, each of which comprised twelve pence, making a total of 240 pence per pound. "Nineteen, nineteen six" means nineteen pounds, nineteen shillings, and six pence – six pence less than twenty pounds.

[2] Secondary revenue streams are covered in Chapter 9, Subsidiary income.

of informed projections and active monitoring, and how these interact in a list of titles and the annual price-setting exercises. This is not a chapter on standard accounting practices or general financial management; these are subjects that the reader can find covered in various other texts.[3]

## Know thyself

First of all, it is important to know the nature of the publishing house and what is expected from the journal(s) it publishes.

### *What type of publisher is it?*

If it is a commercial (sometimes known as for-profit) enterprise, is it independent or part of a group of related (or nonrelated) companies? If it is a not-for-profit enterprise,[4] is it a University Press or the publishing arm of an institute or a scholarly society (or even maybe a library)? Does the publisher publish both books and journals (and, if so, which predominates and has better access to internal resources)?

### *What are the goals of the publisher?*

Is the aim of the publisher simply to provide a return to investors? Or is it to provide a cash flow to support other parts of the business? For example, the proceeds of many society publishing programs help to pay for a range of member benefits, outreach programs, educational initiatives, public advocacy, etc. Some publishers may be risk-averse, concentrating on the existing cash flow, letting others take the lead (and risk) in developing new features/products which they will eventually adopt. However, as the Red Queen said to Alice, "Now, here, you see, it takes all the running you can do, to keep in the same place. If you want to get somewhere else, you

---

[3] A number of texts provide a general overview of finance and accounting (e.g., Grossman and Livingstone, 2009).

[4] A few words about the terms "for-profit" and "not-for-profit" are in order. A for-profit enterprise is created with the primary goal of distributing a profit to its owners/shareholders. A not-for-profit/nonprofit enterprise is created for a specific charitable, educational, or other legislatively defined purpose. Any surplus (the term used rather than profit) derived from the operation of a not-for-profit enterprise must be retained by the enterprise and used for self-preservation and furtherance of its purpose.

must run at least twice as fast as that!" (Carroll, 1871). The research community continues to generate an ever-increasing number of scholarly papers to publish (see Chapter 1, Introduction to journals). Just to maintain the publisher's current share of the market, it is necessary to increase the content published and attendant revenues. Growth often requires investing profits into developing enhancements to existing products in order to attract more customers (both authors and readers). In some cases, journal acquisitions and/or launches may also be part of the publisher's plan for growth.

### How are these goals expressed in financial terms?

Are there targets set for revenues, or for gross or net profits? Are these targets a percentage of revenues or a specific dollar/pound/euro figure? For example, while a low-circulation, low-priced journal may offer a higher profit as a percentage of revenue, a high-circulation, higher-priced journal may have a lower percentage profit margin but yield a higher cash return.

### Do these goals vary depending on whether the journal is publisher-owned or not?

A publisher may have to accept a lower return on journals it publishes but does not own. While it must share profit with the owner, the publisher generally acquires publishing rights to an existing title, thereby avoiding the heavy initial investment of a start-up. (See Chapter 10, Contract publishing.)

### Do the goals vary by product line?

Many humanities and social science (HSS) titles are relatively inexpensive to produce (they often lack complex typesetting and illustration requirements) and are thus fairly modestly priced. By contrast, most science, technology, and medicine (STM) titles tend to be more expensive to produce and are thus higher priced. Journals dealing with "applied" subjects (e.g., clinical medicine, engineering, professional practice, etc.) usually have a small author base but wide circulation; this means that they can yield a higher cash return, even though the net profit as a percentage of revenue may be less than that of more research-oriented titles with smaller circulation.

*Do the goals vary between a new journal start-up and an acquisition of an already established journal – and how soon do these targets need to be met?*

A new journal start-up requires a heavy investment, not just in creating a title and filling it with content (see Chapter 2, Managing journals) but also in reaching its target audience and building up its institutional and individual customer base until annual revenues can cover annual expenses. Even a completely open access (OA) journal will need an up-front investment as it builds up its author and support base to become self-sustaining. Twenty years ago one could target to reach a break-even point for a subscription-based title by year three or four, and then to recoup the losses carried forward from the early years by year seven or so. Today, with even more journals competing for limited institutional budgets and alternative OA titles often being available to authors, the break-even point can take much longer to achieve.

In the case of an acquisition, the purchase price is not the limit of the initial investment. There is also the need to alert the market to the change of publisher, to ensure that payments come to the right place; to rebrand or relaunch as needed; and to convert and integrate the current and legacy content into the new publisher's online publishing platform, an ever more complex task.

Note that asking these questions may yield different answers in different publishing houses.[5] It is also wise to be on the lookout for unstated relationships (e.g., continuing support for a weak journal in order to maintain greater coverage in a given subject area or to complement a profitable book series).

*How do the goals compare with those of other publishers?*

Unfortunately, the financial data that are made publicly available from individual publishers or industry trade groups are of limited use for determining how the finances of a particular journal compare with

---

[5] And, of course, company policy may not always have reflected by past reality.

those of other journals in its field. Publishers mostly provide consolidated data – merging data from both large and small journals, perhaps over a variety of disciplines, or even combining data from all publishing operations.

## Basic terms

This section is a brief overview of some basic terms:

- GROSS PROFIT[6] equals NET REVENUE minus DIRECT EXPENSES. When shown as a percentage (Gross Profit divided by Net Revenue), it is referred to as the GROSS MARGIN.
- NET PROFIT equals GROSS PROFIT minus OVERHEAD COSTS. When expressed as a percentage (Net Profit divided by Net Revenue), it is referred to as the NET MARGIN.
- NET REVENUE (or Net Income) is the total revenue attributed to a journal (including subscription/license revenues, advertising space sales, permission fees, grants, OA article fees, allocations from consortia sales, etc.), less ("net") any discounts, commissions, bad debts (money owed that the publisher does not realistically expect to receive), or currency conversion fees taken before the money gets into the publisher's hands.
- DIRECT EXPENSES are the costs of goods and services directly related to a particular product. These can be further divided into FIXED COSTS, which do not vary with the volume of sales, and VARIABLE COSTS, which do. In traditional print publishing, the Fixed Costs were sometimes referred to as the FIRST COPY COST because these were the costs incurred to produce the first copy of a journal (e.g., Editorial office support, copy-editing, typesetting, printer make-ready, etc.). The "incremental" cost of printing extra issues and servicing one more subscriber is referred to as the MARGINAL COST. For an online journal, the First Copy Cost represents the Fixed Costs needed to acquire, process, and mount the content online, and the Marginal Cost represents the Variable Costs of adding access and customer support for one more subscriber. Publishers differ as to their

---

[6]  In the world of not-for-profit publishing, the term "surplus" is generally used in place of "profit."

treatment of direct marketing and sales expenses in Direct Expenses. Some will exclude these costs when calculating Gross Profit and then calculate a separate figure for "Profit after Marketing," while others may include these costs in Direct Expenses.

- UNIT COSTS for print publishing were traditionally considered in two ways: UNIT COST OF PRODUCTION – the total fixed and variable cost of production[7] divided by the number of copies actually produced (although they may not all be sold) – and UNIT COST OF SALES – the total cost of production divided by the actual number of subscriptions sold. In an online environment, the Unit Cost of Production loses its meaning as only one online "copy" is produced (making this equivalent to the First Copy Cost). The Unit Cost of Sales retains its meaning for subscription-based online journals, but needs to be redefined for both fully OA journals (which have no paying subscribers) and hybrid journals (where subscribers only cover part of the costs) (see below for more on open access).

- OVERHEAD COSTS (also known as Indirect Costs) are those costs which cannot be allocated directly (or easily) to a particular product (e.g., staff salaries and benefits, marketing and sales staff, rent, lighting, heating/cooling, support departments such as personnel, finance, IT, customer service, etc.). These represent the cost of doing business. What is included in Overheads can vary from publisher to publisher, based on the way the operation is structured. Consider copy-editing: if it is done by freelance editors, it can be easily allocated to a particular journal as a direct cost. However, if copy-editing is done by in-house staff for a number of titles, it may be less easy to allocate and thus may be seen as part of the Overhead.

- CASH FLOW refers to the timing and flow of money into and out of the enterprise. For traditional subscription-based journals, a large portion of the subscription revenue for an established journal was in hand before the first issue of the volume was mailed and the production bills came due. In an author-pays OA environment, fees are usually invoiced on acceptance, and inward cash flow may thus vary significantly throughout the year, depending on the flow of submissions.

---

[7] The cost of production includes the direct costs of content acquisition, preparation, and distribution but excludes any direct costs related to marketing, sales, and payment of royalties/profit share to third parties.

- CALENDARIZATION is tied in to the concept of cash flow; it refers to the process of breaking down individual line items in the annual budget into the amounts forecast to be received or spent in a given period (e.g., monthly). Reviewing actual monthly (and year-to-date) revenues and expenses against a calendarized budget is a good way to spot problems early on. An established subscription-based journal might have 75% of the institutional subscription revenue in hand by the end of January, while publication in quarterly or bimonthly issues would result in composition, printing, and mailing costs and/or online issue mounting costs hitting in some months and not others. Continuous online publication article by article spreads costs more evenly over the year.
- DEFERRED REVENUE, sometimes referred to as Unearned Revenue, refers to revenue received for goods or services that have not yet been delivered, and represents a liability until delivery is made to the customer. For a traditional subscription-based journal, a pro rata fraction of the subscription revenue is "earned" as each discrete component is delivered (complete issue or article by article online) during the term of the subscription. In an OA context, the author publication fee can be considered "earned" upon publication.
- BREAK-EVEN POINT describes that point when the net income covers all costs – direct and indirect. Targets to reach the break-even point were sometimes simplified to a number of subscribers at a specific price for a subscription-based journal or a number of accepted papers at a specific publication fee for an OA-based journal. As mentioned above, a new journal may take several years to reach a break-even point for the current volume, and then several more to recover the initial investment and to reach a cumulative break even.

## Business models

A business model is simply the method of doing business by which an enterprise can sustain itself – that is, the way an enterprise expects to generate enough income to cover costs and ongoing obligations and stay in business. Business models come in a variety of forms. Some of the more common ones are product-based, advertising-based, subscription-based, utility-based, or subsidy-based.[8]

---

[8] Some of these models may be combined, as in a hybrid journal (or a telephone service).

- In a product-based business model, a product is created/manufactured, marketed to a particular audience, sold through a distribution network, and payment eventually arrives after delivery. Printed books and most consumer goods follow this model. However, it is important to note that the product need not be a physical object but can also be a service – such as testing and validation (e.g., the peer review and publication of a paper).

- In the advertising-based business model, the goal is not necessarily to make money selling a product, but rather to develop a product that appeals to a specific targeted audience. The major source of income comes from selling advertising space to companies seeking to reach that audience. The product itself is priced to "sell," not so much to cover costs (indeed, some examples are given away free of charge) but to build its target audience. Again, the bulk of the cash arrives after delivery. Examples of this model include newspapers, trade magazines, controlled circulation magazines, broadcast radio, and television, etc. It is a viable model to supplement (or even, occasionally, replace) journal subscription revenue in specific subject areas (e.g., clinical medicine, which attracts drug advertising from pharmaceutical companies).

- For the subscription-based model, the goal is also to develop a product with a targeted audience and content niche. However, the product is perceived to be of sufficient value to the target market for customers (end-users or their institutional librarians) to be willing to pay ahead of time to assure delivery as soon as the content is available for distribution. Thus, the cash flows in before delivery. Traditional scholarly journals have followed this model – as does the local cable television franchise.

- In the utility-based model, the product is generally something which is easily measured and for which customers pay by the amount actually used over a set time period. Payment is primarily at or after delivery. Gas utilities and pay-per-view articles are examples of this model.

- The subsidy-based model presupposes that some third party will cover the cost of producing a product and delivering it to the ultimate user. In subscription-based journal publishing this model was exemplified by supplements to medical journals sponsored by pharmaceutical companies. Many OA journals seek institutional sponsors and grants to help cover their publication costs (and their author-side publication fees are often subsidized by grant funding).

## The journal business model

### The subscription-based model

The traditional business model for an academic print journal was fairly simple: deliver validated intellectual content (peer-reviewed journal articles) to readers in a series of discrete bundles (journal issues) over a defined time period (annual volume) in exchange for an up-front payment (subscription). Given the specialized nature of the content and the fact that the audience for many journals lay entirely within academia, the primary sources for subscription income were academic and research libraries. This was a remarkably stable customer base for established journals, with well over 90% of these institutions renewing from year to year, providing a predictable income stream to publishers.[9]

For more than 300 years publishers appointed Editors to acquire content; oversaw the editing, typesetting, printing, and mailing of paper journal issues; and set subscription rates they hoped would recover costs and provide a return on their investment. Once the journal issues were delivered, the obligation of the publisher to the reader was essentially finished.

The nature of print enforced certain constraints: Editors had to work within a set annual page budget; the composition, proofing, printing, and mailing cycles took time; articles were bundled into issues which appeared at regular intervals and had a set size. After submitting a paper an author might wait three to six months to learn if the paper would be accepted or rejected. If accepted without revision, the paper might then spend a further three to six months in production waiting to appear in an issue (more if the paper just missed the copy deadline, if the author was late with corrected proofs, if the journal was published bimonthly or quarterly, or if there was a backlog of accepted papers).

With the expanded capabilities of the Internet offered in the 1990s by the development of the World Wide Web, browsers, HTML and PDF standards, and higher-speed access, customers began to expect journal publishers to provide:

---

[9] Periodicals heavily dependent on individual subscribers experienced a much lower number of returning customers and had to expend significant marketing efforts to attract new subscribers in order to maintain the same circulation level from year to year.

- A fulltext online edition.
- Publication of individual articles online before print ("as soon as publishable").
- Online reference linking.
- Inclusion of online-only supplemental materials.
- Conversion of legacy print volumes to online.
- "Perpetual" access to the online edition (i.e., continuing access to purchased material in future years, even if the subscription came to an end).
- Regular format updates as standards evolve.
- Discounted rates for online-only access.

Even with this change in medium and mode of delivery and the obligations for the publisher to provide continuous online access after "delivery," the subscription model could still apply, even though the online edition was now "licensed to" the customer, and not "owned by" the customer as was the tangible printed edition.

## The advertising-based model

Supporting a peer-reviewed scholarly journal purely by advertising sales is not a common business model, but it does exist. In many cases, periodicals that deliver a highly targeted audience to advertisers will rely on in-house generated or non-peer-reviewed content, athough there are some peer-reviewed journals that are totally supported by advertising.[10]

For most peer-reviewed journals, however, advertising forms a subsidiary income stream, whether the primary model is subscription-based ("reader-side") or OA ("author-side"). While many journals have little or no advertising, there is a significant number of journals that attract sufficient advertising sales to generate a substantial proportion of their total revenue. These titles tend to be in subject areas with a large practitioner base of readers who can approve, specify, or recommend the purchase of the products advertised. General medical journals such as *The Lancet*, the *New England Journal of Medicine*, the *Journal of the American Medical Association* (*JAMA*), and the *BMJ* (formerly *British Medical Journal*) are prime examples, but there are also large specialty journals (such as *Neurology*), as well as a number of subspecialty titles in hardware-intensive

---

[10] See, for example, the Wiley-Blackwell UK medical controlled circulation journals listed at www.escriber.com/view/0/index.html.

fields, that attract significant advertising income. On the HSS side of the spectrum, advertisements for books and journals predominate.

The *BMJ* presents an interesting example. It receives revenue from subscriptions, classified and display advertising, rights and royalties, and sponsorship. The research articles are freely available online, but access to other content requires a subscription. The OA publication fee, of £2,500 per accepted research article, is applied only "when the funder of the research that is reported in the article has already pledged to pay for open access publication and when authors can claim the *BMJ* fee, in full, from their funder for that specific piece of research" (http://resources.bmj. com/bmj/authors/peer-review-process).

## *Mixed model – open access and related initiatives*

The perceived economies of online distribution indirectly gave rise to an alternative business model, open access, in the 1990s (see Chapter 1, Introduction to journals, for more on open access). The Open Access movement grew out of the Open Archives movement of the 1980s, which initially sought to make preprint versions of journal articles (i.e., the version as submitted to the journal, before peer review, editing, or formatting) freely available at the author's website or in institutional or subject-based repositories (the classic example of the latter is the ArXiv repository for high-energy physics and related areas, http://arxiv.org). More recently, advocates of open access have campaigned for the final, accepted version to be made freely available despite the costs incurred up to that point by publishers in providing the peer-review and editorial infrastructure through which the article is selected and, usually, improved.

It has further been argued that journal articles derived from government-supported research should always be made available "toll-free," since the "public" has already paid for the research once and should not have to pay again to read it. A number of grant-awarding bodies (e.g., the National Institutes of Health in the US and the [private] Wellcome Trust in the UK) now mandate that the published version of grant-subsidized articles be made openly accessible after an embargo period. Efforts continue to expand these mandates to nonbiomedical disciplines and to shorten the embargo periods, further limiting the time in which a publisher can monetize access to a journal and recover costs, which poses a serious challenge to publishers.

The question of how to provide toll-free access to the reader, as advocated by OA proponents, and still cover the costs involved in acquiring/processing journal articles for online publication and providing continued access, called for a different business model. In place of traditional "reader-side" payments (e.g., subscriptions or licenses), publishers sought to cover their costs from "author-side" payments (e.g., submission and/or publication fees) – a product-based business model where the "product" is the evaluation (peer review) and certification (publication) of the submitted article. In a number of instances this income is supplemented by grants and solicitation of institutional "memberships" – adding the subsidy-based model into the mix. See Friend (2011) for an overview of OA business models. The business model(s) for OA journals will no doubt continue to evolve.[11]

A considerable number of online-only OA journals have been launched; recently, many of these have been launched by "traditional" journal publishers.[12] A half-way course adopted by some publishers is to offer authors the option to make their accepted articles OA by paying a fee, creating "hybrid" journals containing some articles freely available online and others restricted to subscribers.[13]

## The issue of "perpetual" online access

Whichever business model is chosen for an online journal, there is an expectation that the content will continue to be available online in

---

[11] For example, the Sponsoring Consortium for Open Access Publishing in Particle Physics (SCOAP³, http://scoap3.org) is seeking to transition from the subscription model to OA by forming a consortium of funding agencies and libraries to support a central peer-review service for high-energy physics papers. It was launched in October 2012 and is expected to be operational in 2014.

[12] A regularly updated listing is available at www.doaj.org, although even this may not be complete.

[13] Setting subscription rates for these hybrid journals poses some interesting questions: Are the rates to be set on a fixed "page budget" of non-OA articles with the OA articles to be considered a bonus to the subscriber? If the OA articles are to be considered in the same mix as the non-OA submissions, how should subscription rates be adjusted to account for the OA fees? (Some publishers have explicitly stated that they will reduce future subscription rates based on the number of OA articles published.) And for a journal that appears in both print and online versions, should the OA articles be online only or also appear in print (with fees adjusted for the added costs of print distribution)?

perpetuity.[14] Institutional subscribers expect continuing online access to the material for which they have paid a subscription, even if they were to cancel their current subscription. Similarly, authors who have paid a publication fee to an OA journal expect their articles to remain available in perpetuity. Publishers have generally accepted this as a new obligation which comes with online journals (long-term preservation of print journals was, of course, carried out by the libraries that subscribed to them). Many publishers now contract with third parties (such as Portico) or participate in distributed archives (such as CLOCKSS) in order to create an archive outside the enterprise that can be accessed if the publisher's own platform is seriously disrupted or, in extremis, if the publisher ceases to exist. See Chapter 4, The production process, for more on archiving initiatives.

## Profit and loss – an overview

Whatever the business model adopted, the profit/loss statement (p/l, P&L) is a summary of all the money coming in and going out of an enterprise or a particular part thereof. Properly prepared and evaluated, it is an important tool for monitoring the health of a journal. While the numbers in the formal p/l reflect the actual revenues and costs over a given period, various preliminary versions of the p/l (sometimes referred to as budgets or projections) are created when evaluating an acquisition/start-up, setting prices, or establishing a budget for the coming year. The general format for a journal p/l is fairly simple: a subtotaled listing of incomes; a subtotaled listing of direct expenses; the gross profit; an overhead allocation; and the net profit. The actual layout of the p/l and how individual costs are assigned varies from publisher to publisher. (Note also that, in addition to the above internal p/ls, there may also be a contractually defined p/l format for a journal which is not owned by the publisher but by another party. In such cases the format, items to be included, and overhead formula are stipulated in the contract and this p/l format is used to determine the profit share due to the owner.)

While the overall financial data for a publisher are prepared on a fiscal/financial year basis, the usual practice for journals is to look at a p/l based

---

[14] No one, of course, can literally guarantee access "in perpetuity" – for ever! The foreseeable future is the most anyone can promise.

on the calendar-year volume, as this is the usual "unit of sale." This means that the revenues and costs included are tied to the volume, even though much of the actual revenue may come in before the first issue appears, and some invoices may arrive after the last issue is distributed.

### Revenues

Table 8.1 lists a number of income streams associated with print journals and both subscription-based and OA online journals. In the "Pricing policy" section of this chapter we will discuss income from subscriptions/licenses

**Table 8.1** *Income streams for journals*

| Income derived from | Print | Online | |
|---|---|---|---|
| | | Subscription/ license | Open access |
| Subscriptions/licenses | x | x | |
| Allocation of revenue from consortia and package sales | | x | |
| Advertising | x | x | x |
| Reprint sales | x | | |
| Single-issue sales | x | | |
| Back-volume sales | x | | |
| Pay-per-view article downloads | | x | |
| Back-volume online access | | x | |
| Document delivery fees | x | x | |
| Rights and permissions fees | x | x | |
| Subscriber list rental | x | x | |
| Special sales (e.g., supported supplements) | x | x | |
| Author submission fees | x | x | x |
| Author page charges | x | x | |
| Author support for color printing | x | | |
| Author publication fees (OA) | | | x |
| Institutional memberships | | | x |
| Grants or other subventions | x | x | x |

and allocation of revenue from bundle and consortia sales, and also delve into the revenues needed to support OA journals. Advertising and other revenue streams are addressed in Chapter 9, Subsidiary income.

### Expenses

### Direct expenses

Table 8.2 lists various direct expenses associated with print journals, online subscription/license journals, and OA journals. These encompass the costs of obtaining content, preparing it for publication, "manufacture" of print issues or mounting content online, distribution and storage, and selling the product. Costs associated with subsidiary income streams, as well as payments to owners, also fall in this category. As noted above, these are the costs that can be directly linked to a particular journal, usually because the work is outsourced and directly invoiced (traditionally, typesetting, paper, printing, and mailing). Note that some of the payments may be defined by contract (e.g., support for the journal Editorial office).

### Direct and/or indirect

Some functions split into both direct and indirect components. A prime example of this is marketing: it is possible to track expenses related to efforts devoted to a single title (direct mail, email campaigns, etc.) as a direct marketing expense. However, items covering multiple publications (such as catalogs and conference exhibitions) and marketing staff costs would fall into an overhead allocation. Another example is the copy-editing function: if freelanced, it is a direct expense but if done in-house for a number of titles, it may be indirect.

The situation can be further complicated by the mix of in-house and outsourced systems for online submission and peer review, fulfillment, and online publishing. Depending on the publisher's size and in-house philosophy, these systems may be provided by third-party vendors, purchased as custom software, or developed internally. Aside from any initial outlay for purchase, the costs for these systems can be broken down into initial system/journal setup/configuration, annual maintenance, transactions (per submission, per subscriber, per item mounted online, etc.), customer/technical support, and the inevitable upgrades (both software

**Table 8.2** *Direct expense lines which may appear in a profit/loss report*

| Direct expenses associated with | Print | Online Subscription/ license | Open access |
|---|---|---|---|
| **Costs of obtaining content** | | | |
| Honorarium/royalty to Editor | x | x | x |
| Editorial office staff | x | x | x |
| Office running expenses (e.g., postage, phone, fax) | x | x | x |
| Overheads and rent for Editor's office to host institution | x | x | x |
| Dedicated office equipment and software (e.g., computers) | x | x | x |
| Online submission and peer-review system costs | x | x | x |
| Other expenses (e.g., travel to meetings, Editorial Board dinners, etc.) | x | x | x |
| **Costs of preparing content for publication** | | | |
| Copy-editing/tagging for SGML/XML | x | x | x |
| Coding for online reference linking | | x | x |
| Art handling and sizing | x | x | x |
| Camera work/image scanning | x | x | x |
| Composition/creating PDF files | x | x | x |
| Proofreading | x | x | x |
| Corrections and author alterations (AAs) | x | x | x |
| Design | x | x | x |
| **Costs of "manufacturing"** | | | |
| Prepress (preparation of printing plates) | x | | |
| Press setup and running | x | | |
| Paper (text and cover stock) | x | | |
| Binding | x | | |
| **Costs of fulfillment, distribution, and storage** | | | |
| List maintenance system | x | x | |
| Mailing line at printer | x | | |
| Packaging for mail | x | | |
| Domestic and foreign mailing (surface, bulk airfreight, airmail) | x | | |
| Freight and warehousing costs (including distribution of replacement copies, etc.) | x | | |

**Table 8.2** (*cont.*)

| Direct expenses associated with | Print | Online | |
|---|---|---|---|
| | | Subscription/ license | Open access |
| **Costs of online publication** | | | |
| "Preissue" mounting online (if applicable) | | x | x |
| Final mounting online | | x | x |
| Online access control system | | x | |
| Server rental and support | | x | x |
| Customer technical support 24/7 | | x | x |
| **Costs of selling** | | | |
| Direct mail marketing | x | x | x |
| Space advertising | x | x | x |
| Exhibits | x | x | x |
| Telemarketing | x | x | x |
| Internet marketing efforts | x | x | x |
| Sample copies/trial online access | x | x | |
| Premiums | x | x | x |
| Renewal efforts | x | x | |
| Direct sales expenses | x | x | |
| Commissions on sales | x | x | |
| **Costs related to other income** | | | |
| Reprints (production, shipping and handling, billing, replacements) | x | | |
| Advertising costs – both production costs and commissions | x | x | x |
| Conversion costs of legacy print issues | | x | |
| Fulfillment costs for single-issue/back-volume sales | x | | |
| Costs related to special sales (supplements, etc.) | x | x | |
| Payment systems for online pay per view | | x | |
| **Payments to proprietors** | | | |
| Royalties on revenues | x | x | x |
| Share of profit | x | x | x |

*Note:* Depending on mix of in-house and outsourced functions, some of these lines may be covered in overheads.

and hardware). The transactional and title-specific costs fall easily into the direct expense category while the more general ones (system setup, upgrades, technical support) go into overhead.

Where these systems are owned or developed by the publisher, it is important to define the transactional and per-title allocations so that they realistically reflect the costs involved. As a matter of good business practice, the publisher should periodically review the features and the costs (direct and indirect, as well as maintenance and development) of an in-house system against those of outside vendors, to ensure that maintaining the in-house system is still a viable position.

## Indirect expenses

As noted above, indirect expenses are those which cannot easily be tied to a specific product. Among these are the general publishing-specific costs (editorial, production, and marketing staff) that cannot easily be split up as well as the myriad other costs associated with running a modern business (information technology infrastructure and Internet access, customer service and technical support, upper management and administrative staff, office and warehouse space, utilities – the so-called general and administrative expenses [G&A]).

It is relatively simple to total the various indirect expenses and arrive at an aggregate overhead cost for an enterprise. This overhead figure is often expressed as a percentage of total revenue. However, unless only journals are being published, complications can arise when determining how much of the various components of this aggregate overhead to allocate to the journal program (for example, what proportion of IT support, finance, or human resource management should be charged to journals). And given the variety of titles which may be present in a multijournal list, it is even more difficult to allocate overheads to individual journals. Using the same percentage across the board is tempting in its simplicity – but it has the disadvantage of artificially benefiting weak titles and penalizing strong ones.

A more granular approach is preferable, in order realistically to gauge the health of each title. While some general overhead components are best left as a percentage of total sales (e.g., "G&A"), many categories can be logically allocated based on the particular attributes of each title – number of printed page equivalents/issues, items mounted online, number of

**Table 8.3** *Sample basis for allocation of indirect costs by title*

| Departments | Allocated as function of |
| --- | --- |
| Editorial and acquisitions | Number of titles in list |
| Production (content preparation) | "Page equivalents" |
| Manufacturing (paper, print, and bind) | Printed pages/issues |
| Online publishing | Items mounted |
| Fulfillment and customer/technical service | Number of subscribers |
| Marketing and promotion | Direct marketing costs |
| Sales (advertising and consortia) | Respective sales volume |

subscribers, etc. Table 8.3 lists a sample set of parameters used by one publisher to allocate the indirect costs by department. Whatever method is used to allocate overheads to individual journals, it is important to make sure that the sum of the individual overheads is equal to the overall overhead figure.

## Sample p/ls

It is time to take a look at some numbers. While based on actual data, please note that the financial data presented in this chapter are purely for illustrative purposes and should not be construed as representative of any particular journal or publisher.

Consider the three bimonthly subscription-based medical journals in Table 8.4. Each journal has both a print and online edition, with the majority of subscribers receiving both (sold as a bundled package). Editorial color illustrations are fairly common, but vary in number from journal to journal; this publisher has therefore chosen to break out the cost of color separations as a separate expense line (normally color separations are included in the content preparation line).

The overall overhead for this publisher's list is 30% of sales (of which 7% is G&A and the remaining 23% is allocated over various departments). However, the actual overhead allocated to an individual title varies based on a number of factors (pages published, number of subscribers, advertising sales, etc.).

**Table 8.4** *Sample profit/loss statements for three medical journals with both print and online editions*

| | Journal A | | Journal B | | Journal C | |
|---|---|---|---|---|---|---|
| | Surgery | | Pathology | | Oncology | |
| | Established | | Established | | Recent launch | |
| | Society owned | | Publisher owned | | Society owned | |
| **Revenue** | $ | | $ | | $ | |
| Subscriptions and bundles/ consortia | 994,950 | | 265,000 | | 175,000 | |
| Advertising | 238,650 | | – | | 30,650 | |
| Other income | 20,750 | | 9,300 | | 8,600 | |
| **Subtotal revenues** | **1,254,350** | | **274,300** | | **214,250** | |
| **Direct expenses** | | | | | | |
| Editorial office support | 70,000 | | 8,600 | | 30,500 | |
| Content preparation | 23,328 | | 15,552 | | 15,552 | |
| Color separations | 18,000 | | – | | 4,500 | |
| Paper, print, and bind | 135,000 | | 23,855 | | 59,250 | |
| Print distribution | 50,250 | | 8,500 | | 9,150 | |
| Online mounting | 3,000 | | 2,000 | | 2,000 | |
| Direct marketing | 20,000 | | 15,000 | | 40,000 | |
| Royalties/surplus share | 357,000 | 28% | 12,500 | 5% | 20,000 | 9% |
| **Subtotal direct expenses** | **676,578** | 54% | **86,007** | 31% | **180,952** | 84% |
| **Gross profit** | **577,772** | 46% | **188,293** | 69% | **33,298** | 16% |
| **Overhead allocations** | | | | | | |
| Flat per title allocation (acquisitions, manufacture, IT) | 18,000 | | 18,000 | | 18,000 | |
| Editorial and production (per page) | 21,600 | | 14,400 | | 14,400 | |
| Fulfillment (per name maintained) | 32,100 | | 9,000 | | 9,000 | |
| Marketing and sales (% of subs revenue) | 59,697 | | 15,900 | | 10,500 | |

**Table 8.4** (*cont.*)

|  | Journal A | | Journal B | | Journal C | |
|---|---|---|---|---|---|---|
| Advertising (% of ad revenue) | 42,957 | | – | | 5,517 | |
| General and administrative (% of total revenue) | 87,804 | | 19,201 | | 14,997 | |
| **Subtotal overheads** | **262,158** | 21% | **76,501** | 28% | **72,414** | 34% |
| **Net profit** | **315,614** | 25% | **111,792** | 41% | **(39,116)** | –18% |
| **Institutional subscribers** | 1,000 | | 1,000 | | 300 | |
| **Total paid subscribers** | 5,350 | | 1,500 | | 1,500 | |
| **Average printrun** | 5,900 | | 1,750 | | 1,750 | |
| **Annual page budget** | 864 | | 576 | | 576 | |
| **Frequency** | Bimonthly | | Bimonthly | | Bimonthly | |
| **Unit cost of production** | $50.78 | | $33.43 | | $69.12 | |
| **Unit cost of sales** | $56.00 | | $39.00 | | $80.63 | |

Journal A is an established society-owned journal with a large member subscriber base that is very attractive to advertisers. The advertisers' heavy use of color helps to subsidize the inclusion of a large number of editorial color illustrations in the print edition, without the need to charge the authors for support of color printing; this makes the journal attractive to authors in a field where color illustrations are important. However, this does drive up printing costs. But even with the costs of color printing and a large return to the society, this journal returns a healthy gross profit of 46%. The overhead allocated to this title, while numerically much higher than that of the other two titles, is 21% of total revenue, less than the overall figure of 30%, This results in a net profit of 25% to the publisher.

Journal B, an established publisher-owned title, has the same institutional subscriber base as Journal A, but a much smaller individual subscriber base and no advertising income. It has much lower unit costs of production and sales than Journal A, owing to its smaller printrun and lack of color. Even with a small royalty to the journal Editor, it yields a gross profit of 69%. With an allocated overhead of 28% of revenue (much closer to the overall 30% figure), the publisher obtains a net profit of 41%.

Journal C is a recently launched society-owned journal, now in its second year. It is still in the process of establishing itself, and requires added marketing resources to build up the institutional subscriber base. The member subscriber base is attractive to advertisers, but not to the extent of Journal A. Journals A and C are both heavily illustrated in color. However, the print edition of Journal A benefits from the economies inherent in its large print subscriber base, which result in a lower unit cost of production even though more pages are printed; in addition, its larger institutional subscriber base results in a lower unit cost of sales. Journal B, similar in extent, circulation, and frequency to Journal C but without color printing, has much lower unit costs of production and sales. Given the costs of color printing and the high marketing costs, the gross profit for Journal C is only 16%. However, while the allocated overhead is numerically less than that of Journal B, it forms a larger percentage (34%) of the lower revenue of Journal C. The result is that Journal C produces a net loss of 18%. This journal needs to grow the institutional subscriber base and/or improve advertising sales to be viable.

As noted above, the overhead allocated to each of these journals differs from the overall overhead figure of 30% for the entire list (see Table 8.4 to show how various components of the overhead were allocated). Had a flat 30% overhead been applied to all three titles, the net profit for Journals A and B would have been deflated by 9% and 2%, respectively, while the loss of Journal C would have been artificially reduced by 4%.

Table 8.5 illustrates several quarterly titles of varying circulation from a hypothetical HSS publisher. Direct costs for content preparation vary with the trim size, the number of pages, and the complexity of the content.[15] Printing costs are primarily a function of circulation, although Journal F, with about a third fewer pages than the other three, is lowest. Print distribution costs, while tied to the number of copies distributed, are also a function of geographic distribution (one of the reasons that Journal F, with more overseas subscribers, costs more to distribute than Journal E, which has more subscribers in total). The return on Journal E is

---

[15] Note that for this list, editorial color illustrations are rare and so the costs associated with them are subsumed in the content preparation expense line instead of being broken out separately as in Table 8.4.

**Table 8.5** *Sample profit/loss statements for four HSS journals (bundled print and online)*

| | Journal D Economics Society owned | | Journal E Psychology Wholly owned | | Journal F Linguistics Wholly owned | | Journal G Political science Society owned | |
|---|---|---|---|---|---|---|---|---|
| | $ | | $ | | $ | | $ | |
| **Revenue** | | | | | | | | |
| Subscriptions and bundles/consortia | 285,000 | | 160,500 | | 200,250 | | 555,000 | |
| Advertising | 8,000 | | – | | – | | 60,000 | |
| Other | 10,000 | | 4,000 | | – | | – | |
| **Subtotal revenues** | **303,000** | | **164,500** | | **200,250** | | **615,000** | |
| **Direct expenses** | | | | | | | | |
| Editorial office support | 25,500 | | 20,000 | | 11,500 | | 100,000 | |
| Content preparation | 36,000 | | 32,000 | | 18,000 | | 30,000 | |
| Paper, print, and bind | 53,700 | | 25,600 | | 18,800 | | 109,000 | |
| Print distribution | 25,250 | | 2,550 | | 4,450 | | 41,000 | |
| Online mounting | 4,000 | | 3,300 | | 2,500 | | 4,000 | |
| Direct marketing | 6,000 | | 4,500 | | 5,000 | | 35,000 | |
| Royalties/surplus share | 79,287 | 26% | 9,800 | 6% | 4,000 | 2% | 168,750 | 27% |
| **Subtotal direct expenses** | **229,737** | 76% | **97,750** | 59% | **64,250** | 32% | **487,750** | 79% |
| **Gross profit** | **73,263** | 24% | **66,750** | 41% | **136,000** | 68% | **127,250** | 21% |

**Overhead allocations**

| | | | | | | | | |
|---|---|---|---|---|---|---|---|---|
| Flat per title allocation (acquisitions, manufacture, IT) | 10,000 | | 10,000 | | 10,000 | | 10,000 | |
| Editorial and production (per page) | 10,800 | | 9,000 | | 5,616 | | 9,792 | |
| Fulfillment (per name maintained) | 6,000 | | 1,500 | | 3,300 | | 6,000 | |
| Marketing and sales (% of subs revenue) | 8,550 | | 4,815 | | 6,007 | | 16,650 | |
| Advertising (% of advert revenue) | 400 | | – | | – | | 3,000 | |
| General and administrative (% of total revenue) | 12,120 | | 6,580 | | 8,010 | | 24,600 | |
| **Subtotal overheads** | **47,870** | 16% | **31,895** | 19% | **32,933** | 16% | **70,042** | 11% |
| **Net profit** | **25,393** | 8% | **34,855** | 21% | **103,067** | 51% | **57,208** | 9% |
| **Institutional subscribers** | 2,000 | | 500 | | 1,100 | | 2,000 | |
| **Total paid subscribers** | 2,900 | | 1,100 | | 1,600 | | 14,500 | |
| **Average printrun** | 3,400 | | 1,300 | | 1,900 | | 15,500 | |
| **Annual page budget** | 1,200 | | 1,000 | | 624 | | 1,088 | |
| **Frequency** | 4 | | 4 | | 4 | | 4 | |
| **Unit cost of production** | $42.49 | | $64.19 | | $29.08 | | $18.32 | |
| **Unit cost of sales** | $49.81 | | $75.86 | | $34.53 | | $19.59 | |

on the low side for a publisher-owned title, and this title would benefit from more institutional subscribers. While just over a quarter of the revenue for Journals D and G goes to their owners, and the net margin to the publisher in each case hovers around 10%, the publisher does benefit in other ways: both owners are high-profile societies in their fields, and association with them through their journals helps the publisher to maintain its high profile in those areas.[16]

In this example the overall journal program overhead is 20%, of which 4% is G&A. Of the rest, after a flat allocation per title for acquisitions, IT, etc., production overhead is allocated based on "pages" published, the fulfillment overhead allocation is tied to the number of subscriber names "maintained" by the publisher, and marketing and advertising sales are a percentage of subscription and advertising revenue, respectively. In the case of Journals D and G, member subscriber data is maintained by the societies and provided to the publisher when needed for mailing (i.e., not maintained in the publisher's fulfillment system), so the overall overhead allocation is lower for both these titles.

## Contractual p/ls and expenses

As noted earlier, in some publishing agreements with outside journal owners, the payment to the owner is defined as a percentage of the profit, based on a profit/loss calculation defined by contract – with an overhead formula which may or may not mirror the publisher's own internal accounting system. (Table 10.2 in Chapter 10, Contract publishing, shows an example of a contractual p/l format for the society-owned Journal D in Table 8.5.) While the direct costs are relatively easy to identify when drafting such an agreement, owners have been wary of publisher overheads and have sometimes stipulated, in their requests for proposals, specific limits on overheads which may fall well below the actual overheads incurred by the publisher. In these instances, publishers may contractually define some of the departmental costs in internal

---

[16] An interesting philosophical difference should be noted between Journal A and Journal G. The member rate for Journal A was set close to the unit cost of sales of that journal. However, the member rate for Journal G was set at the marginal cost of printing and mailing, ignoring any allocation of the costs of acquiring or preparing the content. This was a deliberate strategy by the Acquisitions Editor to make a more attractive offer to the owner.

overheads as a direct expense allocation (e.g., production staff at a flat per page rate, list maintenance at a flat rate per subscriber) in order to recover some of those indirect costs.

## Working with the profit and loss statement

The p/l in its various incarnations is an important tool for evaluating potential projects, establishing budgets, setting prices, and monitoring income, expense, and performance. Comparison of actual data to projections also provides an essential tool for improving the next cycle of budgeting and price setting.

### *A cautionary word about projections*

It is essential to be realistic in making projections. While a conservative approach – understating income and overstating expenses – may appear to be a prudent course, it will tend to discourage investment in potentially worthwhile projects. And the temptation to be over-optimistic should, of course, be resisted.

Modern spreadsheet programs make it easy to evaluate multiple scenarios, sometimes burying the user in a bewildering array of alternatives. Spreadsheets used for projections should be designed in consultation with the relevant internal groups (editorial, production, marketing and sales, manufacture, IT, finance, fulfillment, etc.) to make sure that relevant variables can be input, that any formulae used are appropriate,[17] and that inflation adjustments are suitably granular.[18] However, as with any mathematical model, spreadsheets are built on a specific set of assumptions and the user must be aware of their limitations: a model built for a print journal with between 5,000 and 10,000 subscribers will not be accurate for one with 30,000 subscribers – or 500.

---

[17] While copy preparation costs scale linearly with the number of accepted papers, print manufacture costs require a more complex calculation based on the number of pages and issues, amount of color, and printrun.

[18] While it may be tempting to simply apply a generic inflation index across the board, not all of the expense lines in publishing increase at the same annual rate – some increase at a higher rate, others at a lower rate or not at all.

### *The initial projections*

When considering a potential start-up, acquisition, or relationship with a society or other third-party owner, one of the first steps in the evaluation process is a projection of income and expenses for the first three to five years, based on the known and projected parameters of the project (business model, amount of content, medium [print and/or online], penetration of target market, support/return required by the Editor and/or owner, etc.). For an acquisition, the process is somewhat eased by the existence of historical data for circulation, copy flow, pricing history, advertising sales, and subsidiary income streams, and by the availability of physical samples to evaluate and send out for quotations. However, for a start-up, none of this exists, and sufficient research must be undertaken to determine whether there is a need for the title, whether the author pool exists to provide the desired level of content, and whether the publisher can market that content to the target audience and attract enough paid subscribers or OA support to break even in the near future.[19] (See Chapter 2, Managing journals, and Chapter 6, Marketing and sales, for more on the research required before deciding to launch a new journal.)

As an example, consider a proposal to launch a journal at the growing intersection of two fields. There appears to be a sufficient number of papers to support a quarterly journal of ninety-six pages per issue. The publisher in this case contracts out both the submission/peer-review platform and the online publishing platform (first-year costs for these platforms include configuration fees for the journal). Assume that this publisher's overhead allocation consists of a flat sum of $10,000 per title, a per-page figure for editorial production, a per-name figure for fulfillment services, a percentage of sales for marketing and the advertising sales groups, and 5% of revenue for G&A. Let us start with a subscription-based model. To help attract new subscribers, the subscription rates are held constant for the first three years. (For the sake of simplicity, we have ignored consortia sales and nonsubscription revenues in these "first-pass" examples. A more comprehensive analysis would project these streams based on experience with other similar titles.)

---

[19] When partnering with a new society to launch a journal, special care must be taken to project growth realistically in both institutional and member subscriptions. Faster-than-expected growth of society membership may negatively impact potential institutional sales.

Table 8.6 shows a revenue and cost projection for a publisher-owned start-up with both print and online editions. The projection assumes that the market is receptive to the journal at the proposed subscription rates and, optimistically, achieves a positive net margin in the fourth year (although it will need several more years to recoup the initial investment).[20] The publisher could achieve the same relative position with half the subscription rate, but only if this resulted in more than doubling the subscriber base (to cover the increased costs). However, the total revenue

**Table 8.6** *Sample projection for launch of a subscription-based quarterly journal with print and online editions*

|  | Year 1 | Year 2 | Year 3 | Year 4 | Year 5 |
|---|---|---|---|---|---|
| **Revenue estimates** | $ | $ | $ | $ | $ |
| Subscriptions | 24,467 | 50,885 | 63,702 | 85,205 | 106,020 |
| Advertising | – | – | – | – | – |
| Other income | – | – | – | – | – |
| **Subtotal revenues** | **24,467** | **50,885** | **63,702** | **85,205** | **106,020** |
| **Direct costs** | | | | | |
| Editorial office support | 20,000 | 15,500 | 16,025 | 16,576 | 17,154 |
| Online peer-review support | 5,480 | 2,376 | 2,970 | 2,970 | 2,970 |
| Content preparation | 15,417 | 15,508 | 15,603 | 15,699 | 15,796 |
| Paper, print, and bind | 9,786 | 9,841 | 9,898 | 10,041 | 10,341 |
| Print distribution | 674 | 1,623 | 2,026 | 2,464 | 2,950 |
| Online mounting | 5,240 | 3,240 | 3,240 | 3,240 | 3,240 |
| Direct marketing | 13,000 | 7,500 | 7,875 | 8,269 | 8,682 |
| Royalties/surplus share | – | – | – | – | – |
| **Subtotal direct expenses** | **69,597** | **55,588** | **57,637** | **59,259** | **61,133** |
| **Gross profit** | **(45,130)** | **(4,703)** | **6,065** | **25,946** | **44,887** |
|  | –184% | –9% | 10% | 30% | 42% |
| **Overhead allocation** | | | | | |
| Flat per title allocation (acquisitions, manufacture, IT) | 10,000 | 10,000 | 10,000 | 10,000 | 10,000 |

[20] If paid circulation on this title does not increase beyond year 5 levels and significant subsidiary income is not developed, the initial investment would not be recouped until year 10.

**Table 8.6**  (*cont.*)

|  | Year 1 | Year 2 | Year 3 | Year 4 | Year 5 |
|---|---|---|---|---|---|
| Editorial and production (per page) | 4,800 | 4,800 | 4,800 | 4,800 | 4,800 |
| Fulfillment (per name maintained) | 725 | 1,500 | 1,875 | 2,400 | 2,850 |
| Marketing and sales (% of subs revenue) | 734 | 1,526 | 1,911 | 2,556 | 3,180 |
| Advertising (% of advert revenue) | – | – | – | – | – |
| General and administrative (% of total revenue) | 1,223 | 2,544 | 3,185 | 4,260 | 5,301 |
| **Subtotal overheads** | **17,482** | **20,370** | **21,771** | **24,016** | **26,131** |
|  | 71% | 40% | 34% | 28% | 25% |
| **Net profit** | **(62,612)** | **(25,073)** | **(15,706)** | **1,930** | **18,756** |
|  | –256% | –49% | –25% | 2% | 18% |
| **Cumulative net** | **(62,612)** | **(87,685)** | **(103,391)** | **(101,461)** | **(82,705)** |
|  | –256% | –116% | –74% | –45% | –25% |
| **Assumptions** |  |  |  |  |  |
| *Circulation* |  |  |  |  |  |
| Institutional – print + online | 65 | 140 | 185 | 230 | 275 |
| Institutional – online only | 60 | 120 | 130 | 170 | 195 |
| Individual – print + online | 20 | 40 | 60 | 80 | 100 |
| Individual – online only | – | – | – | – | – |
| Member – print + online | – | – | – | – | – |
| Total paid subscribers | 145 | 300 | 375 | 480 | 570 |
| *Subscription rates ($)* |  |  |  |  |  |
| Institutional rate – print + online | 195 | 195 | 195 | 205 | 215 |
| Institutional rate – online only | 155 | 155 | 155 | 163 | 171 |
| Individual rate – print + online | 125 | 125 | 125 | 130 | 135 |
| Individual – online only | 100 | 100 | 100 | 104 | 108 |
| Member – print + online | 65 | 65 | 65 | 65 | 65 |
| *Average printrun* | 400 | 400 | 400 | 425 | 493 |
| *Annual page budget* | 384 | 384 | 384 | 384 | 384 |
| *Frequency* | Quarterly | Quarterly | Quarterly | Quarterly | Quarterly |

on this particular proposal is relatively low and as such does not make it very attractive as a subscription-based product unless there is a very compelling nonfinancial reason to launch it

Table 8.7 assumes that the same journal is launched with a society, whose members would receive the journal in print and online as part of their dues (replacing the projected individual subscribers in Table 8.6). In this case, with a 10% royalty on nonmember revenue to the society, the journal returns a 7% margin in year 4 compared to the 2% margin in Table 8.6. In addition, the cumulative loss is lower both in absolute terms and as a percentage of revenue.

**Table 8.7**  *Sample projection for launch of a subscription-based quarterly journal with print and online editions in conjunction with a society*

|  | Year 1 | Year 2 | Year 3 | Year 4 | Year 5 |
|---|---|---|---|---|---|
| **Revenue estimates** | $ | $ | $ | $ | $ |
| Subscriptions | 51,925 | 75,850 | 86,175 | 104,775 | 122,483 |
| Advertising | – | – | – | – | – |
| Other income | – | – | – | – | – |
| **Subtotal revenues** | **51,925** | **75,850** | **86,175** | **104,775** | **122,483** |
| **Direct costs** | | | | | |
| Editorial office support | 20,000 | 15,500 | 16,025 | 16,576 | 17,154 |
| Online peer-review support | 5,480 | 2,376 | 2,970 | 2,970 | 2,970 |
| Content preparation | 15,417 | 15,508 | 15,603 | 15,699 | 15,796 |
| Paper, print, and bind | 10,726 | 11,061 | 11,301 | 11,552 | 11,811 |
| Print distribution | 2,671 | 3,585 | 3,933 | 4,295 | 4,672 |
| Online mounting | 5,240 | 3,240 | 3,240 | 3,240 | 3,240 |
| Direct marketing | 13,000 | 7,500 | 7,875 | 8,269 | 8,682 |
| Royalties/surplus share (10% of nonmember revenue) | 2,193 | 4,585 | 5,618 | 7,477 | 9,248 |
| **Subtotal direct expenses** | **74,727** | **63,355** | **66,565** | **70,078** | **73,573** |
| **Gross profit** | **(22,802)** | **12,495** | **19,610** | **34,697** | **48,910** |
|  | –44% | 16% | 23% | 33% | 40% |
| **Overhead allocation** | | | | | |
| Flat per title allocation (acquisitions, manufacture, IT) | 10,000 | 10,000 | 10,000 | 10,000 | 10,000 |

**Table 8.7**  (*cont.*)

|  | Year 1 | Year 2 | Year 3 | Year 4 | Year 5 |
|---|---|---|---|---|---|
| Editorial and production (per page) | 4,800 | 4,800 | 4,800 | 4,800 | 4,800 |
| Fulfillment (per name maintained) | 3,125 | 3,800 | 4,075 | 4,500 | 4,850 |
| Marketing and sales (% of subs revenue) | 1,557 | 2,275 | 2,585 | 3,143 | 3,674 |
| Advertising (% of advert revenue) | – | – | – | – | – |
| General and administrative (% of total revenue) | 2,596 | 3,792 | 4,308 | 5,238 | 6,124 |
| **Subtotal overheads** | **22,078** | **24,667** | **25,768** | **27,681** | **29,448** |
|  | 43% | 33% | 30% | 26% | 24% |
| **Net profit** | **(44,880)** | **(12,172)** | **(6,158)** | **7,016** | **19,462** |
|  | –86% | –16% | –7% | 7% | 16% |
| **Cumulative net** | **(44,880)** | **(57,052)** | **(63,210)** | **(56,194)** | **(36,732)** |
|  | –86% | –45% | –30% | –18% | –8% |
| **Assumptions** |  |  |  |  |  |
| *Circulation* |  |  |  |  |  |
| Institutional – print + online | 65 | 140 | 185 | 230 | 275 |
| Institutional – online only | 60 | 120 | 130 | 170 | 195 |
| Individual – print + online | – | – | – | – | – |
| Individual – online only | – | – | – | – | – |
| Member – print + online | 500 | 500 | 500 | 500 | 500 |
| Total paid subscribers | 625 | 760 | 815 | 900 | 970 |
| *Subscription rates ($)* |  |  |  |  |  |
| Institutional rate – print + online | 195 | 195 | 195 | 205 | 215 |
| Institutional rate – online only | 155 | 155 | 155 | 163 | 171 |
| Individual rate – print + online | 125 | 125 | 125 | 130 | 135 |
| Individual – online only | 100 | 100 | 100 | 104 | 108 |
| Member – print + online | 60 | 60 | 60 | 60 | 60 |
| *Average printrun* | 693 | 772 | 819 | 866 | 913 |
| *Annual page budget* | 384 | 384 | 384 | 384 | 384 |
| *Frequency* | Quarterly | Quarterly | Quarterly | Quarterly | Quarterly |

Table 8.8 presents the option of launching the journal online only, with no print edition, with the same online-only subscription rates and total circulation numbers as in Table 8.6. As above, this configuration breaks even in year 4, but the total revenue is still relatively low and may fall below acceptable targets for this publisher.

**Table 8.8** *Sample projection for launch of an online-only subscription-based journal*

|  | Year 1 | Year 2 | Year 3 | Year 4 | Year 5 |
|---|---|---|---|---|---|
| **Revenue estimates** | $ | $ | $ | $ | $ |
| Subscriptions | 21,375 | 44,300 | 54,825 | 73,520 | 91,170 |
| Advertising | – | – | – | – | – |
| Other income | – | – | – | – | – |
| **Subtotal revenues** | **21,375** | **44,300** | **54,825** | **73,520** | **91,170** |
| **Direct costs** |  |  |  |  |  |
| Editorial office support | 20,000 | 15,500 | 16,025 | 16,576 | 17,154 |
| Online peer-review support | 5,480 | 2,376 | 2,970 | 2,970 | 2,970 |
| Content preparation | 15,417 | 15,508 | 15,603 | 15,699 | 15,796 |
| Paper, print, and bind | – | – | – | – | – |
| Print distribution | – | – | – | – | – |
| Online mounting | 5,240 | 3,240 | 3,240 | 3,240 | 3,240 |
| Direct marketing | 13,000 | 7,500 | 7,875 | 8,269 | 8,682 |
| Royalties/surplus share | – | – | – | – | – |
| **Subtotal direct expenses** | **59,137** | **44,124** | **45,713** | **46,754** | **47,842** |
| **Gross profit** | **(37,762)** | **176** | **9,112** | **26,766** | **43,328** |
|  | −177% | 0% | 17% | 36% | 48% |
| **Overhead allocation** |  |  |  |  |  |
| Flat per title allocation (acquisitions, manufacture, IT) | 10,000 | 10,000 | 10,000 | 10,000 | 10,000 |
| Editorial and production (per page) | 4,800 | 4,800 | 4,800 | 4,800 | 4,800 |
| Fulfillment (per name maintained) | 725 | 1,500 | 1,875 | 2,400 | 2,850 |
| Marketing and sales (% of subs revenue) | 641 | 1,329 | 1,644 | 2,205 | 2,735 |
| Advertising (% of ad revenue) | – | – | – | – | – |

**Table 8.8** (*cont.*)

|  | Year 1 | Year 2 | Year 3 | Year 4 | Year 5 |
|---|---|---|---|---|---|
| General and administrative (% of total revenue) | 1,068 | 2,215 | 2,741 | 3,676 | 4,558 |
| **Subtotal overheads** | **17,234** | **19,844** | **21,060** | **23,081** | **24,943** |
|  | 81% | 45% | 38% | 31% | 27% |
| **Net profit** | **(54,996)** | **(19,668)** | **(11,948)** | **3,685** | **18,385** |
|  | −257% | −44% | −22% | 5% | 20% |
| **Cumulative net** | **(54,996)** | **(74,664)** | **(86,612)** | **(82,927)** | **(64,542)** |
|  | −257% | −114% | −72% | −43% | −23% |
| **Assumptions** |  |  |  |  |  |
| *Circulation* |  |  |  |  |  |
| Institution – online only | 125 | 260 | 315 | 400 | 470 |
| Individual – online only | 20 | 40 | 60 | 80 | 100 |
| Total paid subscribers | 145 | 300 | 375 | 480 | 570 |
| *Subscription rates ($)* |  |  |  |  |  |
| Institutional rate – online only | 155 | 155 | 155 | 163 | 171 |
| Individual – online only | 100 | 100 | 100 | 104 | 108 |
| *Annual "page equivalent" budget* | 384 | 384 | 384 | 384 | 384 |

An alternative is to consider launching this journal under an OA model, shown in Table 8.9. Since it is already assumed that there are enough manuscripts to support a journal in this field, the question to determine is how many of the authors have adequate funding available to pay OA publication fees. A discounted publication fee is assumed in the first two years to encourage submissions, building to the same number of articles by year 5. This presents a more promising financial picture, returning a net profit in year 3 and a positive cumulative return in year 4.

However, all these scenarios are based on a variety of assumptions derived from experience and from editorial and marketing research, as discussed in Chapter 6, Marketing and sales, and in Chapter 2, Managing journals. The projections in Tables 8.6 through 8.9 would likely lead to refining the assumptions, including projections for subsidiary income

**Table 8.9** *Sample projection for launch of an online-only open access journal*

| | Year 1 | Year 2 | Year 3 | Year 4 | Year 5 |
|---|---|---|---|---|---|
| **Revenue estimates** | $ | $ | $ | $ | $ |
| OA publication fees | 15,000 | 45,000 | 80,000 | 100,000 | 110,000 |
| Advertising | – | – | – | – | – |
| Other income | – | – | – | – | – |
| **Subtotal revenues** | **15,000** | **45,000** | **80,000** | **100,000** | **110,000** |
| **Direct costs** | | | | | |
| Editorial office support | 20,000 | 15,500 | 16,025 | 16,576 | 17,154 |
| Online peer-review support | 4,050 | 1,100 | 1,452 | 1,826 | 2,002 |
| Content preparation | 7,015 | 11,337 | 14,290 | 17,279 | 18,867 |
| Paper, print, and bind | – | – | – | – | – |
| Print distribution | – | – | – | – | – |
| Online mounting | 2,900 | 1,800 | 2,400 | 3,000 | 3,300 |
| Direct marketing | 13,000 | 7,500 | 7,875 | 8,269 | 8,682 |
| Royalties/surplus share | – | – | – | – | – |
| **Subtotal direct expenses** | **46,965** | **37,237** | **42,042** | **46,950** | **50,005** |
| **Gross profit** | **(31,965)** | **7,763** | **37,958** | **53,050** | **59,995** |
| | –213% | 17% | 47% | 53% | 55% |
| **Overhead allocation** | | | | | |
| Flat per title allocation (acquisitions, manufacture, IT) | 10,000 | 10,000 | 10,000 | 10,000 | 10,000 |
| Editorial and production (per page) | 1,312 | 2,625 | 3,500 | 4,375 | 4,812 |
| Fulfillment (per name maintained) | – | – | – | – | – |
| Marketing and sales (% of OA fees) | 450 | 1,350 | 2,400 | 3,000 | 3,300 |
| Advertising (% of ad revenue) | – | – | – | – | – |
| General and administrative (% of total revenue) | 750 | 2,250 | 4,000 | 5,000 | 5,500 |
| **Subtotal overheads** | **12,512** | **16,225** | **19,900** | **22,375** | **23,612** |
| | 83% | 36% | 25% | 22% | 21% |
| **Net profit** | **(44,477)** | **(8,462)** | **18,058** | **30,675** | **36,383** |
| | –297% | –19% | 23% | 31% | 33% |
| **Cumulative net** | **(44,477)** | **(52,939)** | **(34,881)** | **(4,206)** | **32,177** |
| | –297% | –88% | –25% | –2% | 9% |

**Table 8.9** (*cont.*)

|  | Year 1 | Year 2 | Year 3 | Year 4 | Year 5 |
|---|---|---|---|---|---|
| **Assumptions** | | | | | |
| *OA fee ($)* | 2,000 | 2,000 | 2,000 | 2,000 | 2,000 |
| Introductory discount | 50% | 25% | 0% | 0% | 0% |
| Items published | 15 | 30 | 40 | 50 | 55 |
| *"Page equivalents" per annum* | 105 | 210 | 280 | 350 | 385 |

streams and their associated costs, and/or modifying the parameters of the journal (price, circulation, OA support, pages) in hopes of improving the revenues or return. It is a recursive process.

Examination of the overhead allocations in these examples also points out inequities in allocation formulae for indirect expenses. While allocating various overhead categories as a percentage of sales or as a flat sum may work well for established titles, invariably such formulae understate the actual amount of time staff spend on a new project, particularly in the areas of editorial acquisition and marketing and sales. A separate flat sum per new title is one way of accounting for this.

### Budgets

A budget sets out the financial plan for an existing (as opposed to potential) project for a given period: a clear listing of projected income and expense, broken down into individual line items, based on an agreed set of parameters and assumptions. As before, a journal budget is usually tied to a calendar-year volume or volumes (which may or may not correspond with the publisher's fiscal/financial year); and it includes specification of the nonfinancial parameters that drive some of the financial elements (e.g., circulation numbers, pages/issues per volume, number of submissions, etc.).

The journal budget process begins in the spring with a review of how the journal performed in the prior year compared with budget, and how well it is doing against budget in the current year to date. The journal is reviewed with the Editor-in-Chief to determine whether any changes in extent, content, or format are warranted/desirable based on copy flow, acceptance rates, and the mix of submissions (both in terms of subject matter and geographically). The marketing department is consulted, to project subscription/license (and advertising) sales based on previous years' trends. For OA and hybrid journals, the number and rate of increase of OA articles is reviewed. Other relevant departments are consulted to provide expense estimates for the upcoming year, adjusted in line with any changes (e.g., more content published, either print or online; a significant increase in circulation from a society adoption). With a firm estimate of costs, the next step is to calculate prices that will yield sufficient revenue to attain the targeted returns.

A very simple spreadsheet format for budgeting and subscription price setting is shown in Figure 8.1. In this example, the publisher offers a single worldwide price in one currency, and provides both print and online editions. The level of detail is much more granular than in the previous examples as budgets need to be set for the individual expense lines. The cells with "xxx" are data elements/projections that come from various departments while the cells with "0" are calculated from the "xxx" data within the spreadsheet. Circulation, expense, and subsidiary income projections are entered, along with a first pass at subscription rates. The financial returns are calculated, and then rates and other projections are revised as needed to arrive at the desired targets. A simple pricing spreadsheet for an OA journal is shown in Figure 8.2. Pricing policy and philosophy are discussed below in greater detail.

Once budgets have been agreed, income and expense lines need to be calendarized to provide a picture of the cash flow over time. Where there is a large institutional subscriber base, two-thirds of the subscription income may be in hand by the start of the year. The expenses, on the other hand, will fluctuate month to month based on frequency of publication, contractual obligations (such as timing of editorial payments), and other factors. Table 8.10 shows the calendarized revenue for a regional branch of an international publisher.

### *Monitoring performance*

Sound business practice calls for active monitoring not just of income and expenses, but also of copy flow, page budgets, publication dates – all factors that influence the finances. Monthly reports for units, revenues, and expenses need to be reviewed, as well as adherence to publication

| | RATES | UNITS | | | SUBS REVENUE |
|---|---|---|---|---|---|
| Journal name xxx   Issues/volume xxx | | | | | |
| Volume year xxx   Pages/volume xxx | | | | | |
| | | Domestic | Foreign | Total | |
| Institution print+online | xxx | xxx | xxx | 0 | 0 |
| Institution online only | xxx | xxx | xxx | 0 | 0 |
| Individual print+online | xxx | xxx | xxx | 0 | 0 |
| Individual online only | xxx | xxx | xxx | 0 | 0 |
| Member print+online | xxx | xxx | xxx | 0 | 0 |
| Member online only | xxx | xxx | xxx | 0 | 0 |
| Student print+online | xxx | xxx | xxx | 0 | 0 |
| Student online only | xxx | xxx | xxx | 0 | 0 |
| Other | xxx | xxx | xxx | 0 | 0 |

| | Domestic | Foreign | Total |
|---|---|---|---|
| Subtotal paid | 0 | 0 | 0 |
| Gratis print | xxx | xxx | 0 |
| Total distribution | 0 | 0 | 0 |
| Total print distribution | 0 | 0 | 0 |

**REVENUE**

| | | | |
|---|---|---|---|
| Subscription revenue | | | 0 |
| Consortia allocation | | | xxx |
| Advertising | | | xxx |
| Offprints/reprints | | | xxx |
| Pay per view | | | xxx |
| Other: rights & permissions, back volumes/single issues, bulk sales, etc. | | | xxx |
| | | **TOTAL REVENUE** | **0** |

**DIRECT EXPENSES**

| | | | |
|---|---|---|---|
| Editorial office support | | | xxx |
| Online peer review | | | xxx |
| Copy-editing/proofing | xxx | average per page | 0 |
| Composition | xxx | average per page | 0 |
| Paper, printing, and binding | | | xxx |
| Online mounting | | | xxx |
| Offprints/reprints | | | xxx |
| Domestic postage | xxx | average per issue | 0 |
| Foreign postage | xxx | average per issue | 0 |
| Direct marketing costs | | | xxx |
| Royalties/surplus share | | (enter formula based on contract terms) | xxx |
| Other direct expenses: | | | xxx |
| | | **TOTAL DIRECT EXPENSES** | **0** |
| | | **GROSS SURPLUS/(LOSS)** | **0** |
| | | **(% of Total Revenue)** | **%** |

**INDIRECT EXPENSES**

| | | | |
|---|---|---|---|
| Flat departmental allocations | | | xxx |
| Editorial production | xxx | per page | 0 |
| Fulfillment | xxx | per name maintained | 0 |
| Marketing | xxx | % of non-ad revenue | 0 |
| Advertising | xxx | % of advertising sales | 0 |
| G&A | xxx | % of total revenue | 0 |
| | | **TOTAL INDIRECT EXPENSES** | **0** |
| | | **NET SURPLUS/(LOSS)** | **0** |
| | | **(% of Total Revenue)** | **%** |

**Figure 8.1** A very simple sample of a spreadsheet format for price setting of a subscription-based journal

| Journal name | xxx | Submissions/year | xxx | |
|---|---|---|---|---|
| Volume year | xxx | Articles published/year | xxx | |
| | | | | OA fees |
| Full OA publication fee | xxx | articles at | xxx | 0 |
| Discounted OA publication fee | xxx | articles at | xxx | 0 |
| Gratis OA items | xxx | articles | | |
| | | | | |
| Institution membership – level 1 | xxx | at | xxx | 0 |
| Institution membership – level 2 | xxx | at | xxx | 0 |
| Institution membership – level 3 | xxx | at | xxx | 0 |
| **REVENUE** | | | | |
| OA fees | | | | 0 |
| Institutional memberships | | | | 0 |
| Grant support | | | | xxx |
| Advertising | | | | xxx |
| Other: rights & permissions, etc. | | | | xxx |
| | | **TOTAL REVENUE** | | **0** |
| **DIRECT EXPENSES** | | | | |
| Editorial office support | | | | xxx |
| Online peer review | | per submission | | xxx |
| Copy-editing/proofing | xxx | average per article | | 0 |
| Composition | xxx | average per article | | 0 |
| Online mounting | | | | xxx |
| Online platform annual cost | | | | xxx |
| Direct marketing costs | | | | xxx |
| Royalties/surplus share | (enter formula based on contract) | | | xxx |
| Other direct expenses: | | | | xxx |
| | | **TOTAL DIRECT EXPENSES** | | **0** |
| | | **GROSS SURPLUS/(LOSS)** | | **0** |
| | | **(% of Total Revenue)** | | **%** |
| **INDIRECT EXPENSES** | | | | |
| Flat departmental allocations | | | | xxx |
| Editorial production | xxx | per article | | 0 |
| Marketing | xxx | % of non-ad revenue | | 0 |
| Advertising | xxx | % of advertising sales | | 0 |
| G&A | xxx | % of total revenue | | 0 |
| | | **TOTAL INDIRECT EXPENSES** | | **0** |
| | | | | |
| | | **NET SURPLUS/(LOSS)** | | **0** |
| | | **(% of Total Revenue)** | | **%** |

**Figure 8.2** A very simple sample of a spreadsheet format for OA journal price setting

schedules (and amount of material published). Both monthly and year-to-date data should be reviewed, to compensate for the inevitable timing offsets that occur (e.g., a scheduled payment that is booked a month early, or invoices for an issue published late). Any significant variances should be discussed with the relevant departments to identify the source of the difference and to determine whether corrective action is needed (or if an error was made in the original forecast). Sometimes the source of the variance may be beyond anyone's control (e.g., the collapse of a major subscription agent, as happened several years ago).

**Table 8.10** *Sample revenue calendarization for a journal program ($000)*

| Revenue | Jan | Feb | Mar | Apr | May | June | July | Aug | Sept | Oct | Nov | Dec | Total |
|---|---|---|---|---|---|---|---|---|---|---|---|---|---|
| Nonmember subscriptions | 7,200 | 950 | 450 | 350 | 275 | 175 | 25 | 20 | 20 | 15 | 10 | 10 | 9,500 |
| Member subscriptions | 25 | 100 | 50 | 70 | 75 | 15 | 30 | 25 | 30 | 10 | 60 | 10 | 500 |
| Consortia sales | 2,000 | – | 250 | – | – | 250 | – | – | 250 | – | – | 250 | 3,000 |
| **Subtotal subscriptions** | 9,225 | 1,050 | 750 | 420 | 350 | 440 | 55 | 45 | 300 | 25 | 70 | 270 | 13,000 |
| Monthly % of annual budget | 71.0% | 8.1% | 5.8% | 3.2% | 2.7% | 3.4% | 0.4% | 0.3% | 2.3% | 0.2% | 0.5% | 2.1% | |
| Advertising sales | 10 | 30 | 40 | 35 | 15 | 60 | 45 | 35 | 40 | 35 | 20 | 60 | 425 |
| Other income | 22 | 22 | 22 | 17 | 14 | 12 | 12 | 13 | 14 | 13 | 12 | 12 | 185 |
| **Total revenue** | 9,257 | 1,102 | 812 | 472 | 379 | 512 | 112 | 93 | 354 | 73 | 102 | 342 | 13,610 |
| Monthly % of annual budget | 68.0% | 8.1% | 6.0% | 3.5% | 2.8% | 3.8% | 0.8% | 0.7% | 2.6% | 0.5% | 0.7% | 2.5% | |
| Cumulative % of annual budget | 68.0% | 76.1% | 82.1% | 85.5% | 88.3% | 92.1% | 92.9% | 93.6% | 96.2% | 96.7% | 97.5% | 100.0% | |

## Accounts for journals

While the projections, budgets, and cash-flow estimates provide informed forecasts of what should happen in the future, the year-end journal accounts show what has happened in the past and how profitable (or unprofitable) the journal actually was. Most businesses are required to keep accurate general accounts for tax purposes. Publishers will also keep accounts for each individual journal. Accounts are important for identifying trends and reviewing how well (or poorly) various aspects of the enterprise are performing. The format of the accounts must be consistent over time, to allow for comparisons from year to year, with any extraordinary factors clearly noted. If costs and revenues are properly monitored during the year, there will be no surprises.

The accounts must include all income and expenses, itemized to a reasonable level of detail. Care must be taken to exclude any revenues for content not yet published (unearned income).[21] Similarly, there may be a need to allow for accrued expenses (the liability for invoices relating to published material, which have not yet arrived or been paid at fiscal year-end).

Accounts sent to outside parties for royalty or surplus share statements must be clear, accurate, and as simple as possible, as well as consistent in format from year to year (the format is often stipulated by contract). Note that in many cases a society will include a clause in its contract permitting it to audit the publisher's accounts for the journal if questions arise.

If the format for internal or external accounts needs to be changed, the prior year's accounts should be recast in the new format to provide a proper basis for comparison.

## Pricing policy

A policy is necessary to guide the progression from analysis of cost and market research data to setting prices that will result in the desired returns. Who will be footing the bill – reader-side (i.e., libraries) or author-side (i.e., the author's funders, for the most part) – is determined by the

---

[21] For example, prorated subscription revenue for an issue delayed beyond the end of the accounting period, or OA publication fees received within the accounting period for articles which were published after the end of that period.

business model. Given a projected number of subscribers (or accepted OA authors), one can calculate a minimum subscription rate (or author publication fee) to balance income and expenses. How much more to charge above this minimum in order to cover future development and to produce an acceptable return on investment is the purpose of the pricing policy. This is particularly important in the present environment, where continuing investment is required in online platforms and support systems.

## Subscriptions/licenses

Subscriptions have been the primary income stream for academic journals since their inception in the 1660s. The primary market for scholarly journals is the libraries that provide information access to the academic and research community. While the total universe of such libraries is large, the actual number requiring in-depth coverage of any specific area is limited to those that have faculty or researchers working in that area.

The "institutional" subscription rate tends to be seen as the "list price," and the base fee from which all other rates are derived. Any other rates offered – to individuals, society members, or students – are in effect special "discounted" rates based on the variable cost, and are only made possible by the core revenue from institutions. (In some cases in the past, the individual rate was available only to individuals affiliated with an institution that had a full-price subscription. And individual or member copies were sometimes printed with the statement "not for library use" on the cover to preclude them from being used as lower-priced substitutes for library copies.)

For many journals (particularly those dealing with basic research), institutional subscriptions/licenses form the bulk of both the subscriber base and the subscription income. However, a significant number of journals cover material of a more applied nature (e.g., engineering, clinical medicine), and are of interest to individual practitioners not necessarily affiliated with a subscribing institution, who may take personal subscriptions. Many journals owned by or affiliated with a professional or scholarly society will offer a reduced-rate subscription as a member benefit.

As many academic libraries operate on a fiscal/financial year tied to the academic year, they have pressed publishers to announce upcoming subscription rates as early as possible in the calendar year. As a result, many publishers now start the pricing process in the early spring – just after the prior year's accounts have been completed, and with barely a quarter of the current year's results in hand. As a first step in the process, the publisher's management will generally target a percentage increase in revenue for the overall program. It is up to the individuals working on price setting to figure how to tweak each rate category in each journal to achieve this goal, while at the same time moving underperforming titles closer to the target margins.

For existing journals, subscription prices are set based on a careful analysis of the existing subscriber base by type of subscriber, actual renewal rates,[22] market research to determine whether the field is growing or shrinking and how the journal compares to its competitors, any needed changes to the format or extent of the title, and any other income it generates, in addition to the cost projections.

If the journal has a stable, primarily institutional subscriber base with few or no individual subscriptions and/or little other income, the price will need to be adjusted (1) to maintain the margin against any cost increases and (2) to contribute to the desired target increase in revenue.

If the journal has a not-insignificant individual subscriber base in addition to institutions, the practice has been to increase individual subscription rates at a lower percentage than institutional rates, owing to the greater price sensitivity of individual subscribers. However, this does have the disadvantage that, over time, the individual rate becomes a smaller and smaller percentage of the institutional rate; an alternative approach is to maintain a pro rata relationship between the two. A further variable is the relationship between the print-only and online-only individual rates. Differential price increases may need to be applied to reflect the actual costs involved;[23] and the publisher may wish to change the balance between the two, for example in order to shift individual subscribers towards online only.

---

[22] That is, the percentage of prior-year subscribers who renew for the current volume. Non-renewals need to be replaced by new subscribers. If the renewal rate is low, a greater marketing effort will be required to maintain the number of subscribers from year to year. Renewal rates tend to be highest for institutions and lower for members and individuals. Calculation of a renewal rate is further complicated if the journal is available as part of a consortium package and existing institutional customers shift from being "direct" subscribers to gaining access via a consortium.

[23] For example, the individual print-only subscription price may need to increase at a higher rate if the number of print subscribers decreases, causing the unit cost of print production to increase.

There are a number of ways in which member subscription rates may be set. If a society owns the journal, then the contract generally sets the initial member rate and how it may be adjusted annually.[24] If the publisher owns the journal, it may negotiate a formal relationship with a society, offering a reduced member rate in exchange for the society's endorsement.[25] Or, in the absence of any formal agreement, the publisher may simply offer a discount off the individual rate to members of relevant societies.

## *Print, online, or both*

The relationship between print, online, and combined print + online subscriptions/licenses requires some comment. With the advent of viable online publishing platforms in the 1990s, many publishers added fulltext online editions that replicated the print journal (i.e., PDF files). In many cases, these were initially offered "free"[26] with the institutional print subscription, as an incentive for the libraries to activate online access and thus drive patron usage. As the number of online titles increased, publishers adopted various differential price strategies: some set the price of the online edition equal to that of print, while others made the online price lower or higher than print. The combined package of print and online was usually provided at a surcharge above the print rate.

Given that an online institutional subscription can be accessed by anyone at the institution, many publishers have tried to arrive at more rational ways of pricing online subscriptions and licenses, rather than simply having one online rate for all institutions, regardless of size. Some base their institutional license prices on the number of faculty (or students, depending on the market for the journal); some offer tiered rates based on other criteria such as prior-year usage and/or the Carnegie classification (http://classifications.carnegiefoundation.org) (see, for example, Chesler

---

[24] This is discussed further in Chapter 10, Contract publishing.

[25] Aside from the additional income from a bulk order for society member subscriptions, the publisher will also realize savings in handling costs and renewal expenses.

[26] Not quite – in the EU online publications are subject to a higher VAT rate than print. Even when the online component is nominally "free," the tax authorities sometimes insist on allocating a proportion of the total price to it, and charging tax accordingly. The allocation of a combined print + electronic price between print and online can still be an issue. In addition, the library has the expense of integrating the "free" online journal into its catalog and access systems.

and King, 2009).[27] Each publisher will have established its preferred relationship between the print, online, and print + online rates to implement in price setting. (See also the section "Pricing, usage, and value" in Chapter 6, Marketing and sales.)

While online journal publishing has evolved beyond simple PDF files to become more feature-rich than print could ever be, online subscriptions have not so far displaced print. There has been some erosion of print subscriptions, which varies with the subject area of the journal; this has the effect of raising the average cost per print copy as the printrun falls. However, a surprising number of institutions still maintain a print subscription in addition to their online access for a variety of reasons – such as the preferences of older faculty, concerns about reliable Internet connectivity, doubts about the long-term stability of online archives, and the fact that many libraries are evaluated on their "holdings" rather than their "access."

## Domestic and nondomestic subscription rates and currencies

The cost of delivering a print journal to a nondomestic subscriber can be significant. While "surface" postage costs may be low, overseas delivery times are long and often result in claims for missing issues. Resolving such claims can be an expensive process – see Chapter 7, Fulfillment. To provide a better service to nondomestic subscribers, many publishers opt to use freight forwarding companies to airfreight the overseas subscriber copies to various countries and "drop" them into the local postal system for delivery to the final recipient. As this is significantly more expensive than domestic postal costs, many publishers include an average of the nondomestic distribution costs in determining the nondomestic "rest of world" (ROW) print subscription rates. (Postal surcharges are obviously not relevant for online publications.)

Small and medium-sized publishers usually set their subscription rates in their domestic currency (the currency in which they pay their bills) for both domestic and ROW subscribers, leaving the ROW subscribers to cope with currency exchange rate fluctuations. Larger international publishers offer regional prices in major currencies (dollars for North America, sterling

---

[27] The Carnegie Classifications of Institutions of Higher Education apply only to the US and Canada. Other comparable criteria are used for non-North American and other institutions, as well as for commercial entities.

for the UK, euros for continental Europe).[28] However, fluctuating currency exchange rates can lead to difficulties during the annual price-setting exercise: euro or sterling rates set at the equivalent of a given dollar rate one year are very likely to be out of sync the next year. Simply increasing prices at the prevailing exchange rate may result in steep price increases in one currency with little or no increase in another, while applying the same percentage increase to all currencies may have a negative impact on the publisher's actual revenue. The policy for the annual adjustment of multi-currency prices in response to exchange rate fluctuations will be set by upper management.[29] The issue of exchange rate gains/losses does have implications for the financial accounts (budget converted at one exchange rate, actual results at another), particularly when reporting financial results to a sponsoring society.

## Journal bundles

Publishers with a large enough list in a given subject area may offer online access to bundles of journals – their entire list, or one or more subsets thereof – to individual institutions. The price for a license to the bundle can be calculated as a discount off the total of the institutional list prices for the journals in the bundle. The amount of the discount may vary with the size of the institution, and whether there are multiple campuses or affiliated institutions (e.g., a hospital attached to the medical school). For institutions with existing subscriptions, the price may be calculated as a surcharge on top of the library's payments for journals already subscribed to in the bundle.

## Library consortia

With mounting pressure on their budgets, many libraries have formed consortia to negotiate for online access to journals – usually the publisher's

---

[28] If they have publishing operations in multiple countries, the branch responsible for producing a journal may set subscription rates in its domestic currency; these form the basis for setting the rates in other currencies for customers elsewhere. In some cases, production of a journal is assigned to the branch with the largest number of subscribers to that title, or the printrun is split between two or more geographic areas in order to minimize distribution costs.

[29] For a large enterprise, the financial department may engage in forward buying/selling of currency to lessen the effect of exchange rate fluctuations.

entire list of journals, or a subset thereof – through volume agreements with publishers.[30]

Publishers with a large list, or with a "critical mass" of journals in a given subject, can negotiate directly with these consortia.[31] The goal for publishers in negotiating agreements with consortia is not just to preserve their existing business, but also to increase it incrementally. A large number of the existing subscriptions from consortium members would be replaced by access through the consortium agreement, shifting revenue out of the subscription line and into the consortia line. (See also Chapter 7, Fulfillment.) In addition, the consortium members would gain access to journals to which they currently do not subscribe, and some revenues must accrue to these titles (especially important if the publisher has to account for these sales to the journal's owner, e.g., a society). Initially, many publishers based their consortial license pricing on the value of existing business from those libraries, plus an increment for the additional access to nonsubscribed titles (often at a steep discount off their list price) and for any new user population (e.g., users at an institution with no prior subscription access). How the price was to be adjusted in future years for inflation and the addition or deletion of titles was subject to contract negotiation. Difficulties arise with this particular model if the consortium has little or no current business with the publisher. This model also decreases in usefulness as the time from the "existing business" base year increases. Newer models incorporating measures such as community size and/or usage are being developed (see Chapter 6, Marketing and sales).

It is important that the allocation of revenues back to the individual journals, from both multijournal bundles and consortia agreements, accurately reflects each journal's contribution to the deal and does not negatively impact its income. The allocation formula must be both logical and transparent; this is particularly important for journals published on behalf of societies.

---

[30] Some individual journals may be large and expensive enough that a consortium will seek to negotiate a deal for its members.

[31] Some publishers with smaller lists have been able to join initiatives such as Project MUSE (http://muse.jhu.edu) or the ALPSP Learned Journals Collection (http://aljc.swets.com) to take advantage of these opportunities.

### Open access pricing

Open access journals – whether fully OA or hybrid (see below) – may be supported by a number of different author-side revenue sources: publication (and occasionally submission) fees, institutional memberships, and grants.

The publication fee must be sufficient to cover the average cost of peer review of both accepted and rejected papers, as well as the actual costs of production in the online environment, provision of "perpetual" future access, and all the related overheads (including ongoing development of the platform). Fees at the time of writing (February 2012) vary widely:[32] $695 (Sage Open), $730–$2,505 (BioMed Central), $1,350–$2,900 (PLoS), $3,000 (Wiley Open Access), $1,350–$5,000 (*Nature*). Some start-up OA titles offer free or highly discounted fees to encourage submissions.

Note that revenue from author-side publication fees is tied to the flow of submissions and may not flow evenly throughout the year; submissions in turn can be affected by the vagaries of funding levels in the discipline covered. To generate a more consistent cash flow some OA journals offer "institutional memberships" which offset the publication fees, providing discounts or waivers (sometimes up to a given level) to authors affiliated with the member institution. These fees are sometimes based on the historical volume of submissions coming from the institution.

### *Hybrid journals*

For a traditional subscription/license-based print and online journal that offers OA as an option to authors, the pricing model needs to consider the costs of printing the OA articles as well as mounting them online. (Printing costs do not, of course, apply if the journal is online only.) In determining what the author publication fee for a hybrid journal should be, some publishers have simply divided current revenue[33] by the

---

[32] See, for example, the listing of fees for both OA and hybrid journals posted by the library at the University of California at Berkeley – www.lib.berkeley.edu/scholarly communication/oa_fees.html (updated August 2011) – or the Sherpa listing – www. sherpa.ac.uk/romeo/PaidOA.html (updated January 2012).

[33] "Current revenue" in this context should not be limited to subscription income, but should include all revenue streams that may be affected by the OA model. Various subsidiary income streams are reduced or eliminated in an OA context and should be considered in the calculation (e.g., reprints, permissions, single article sales, archive sales, etc.).

number of articles published, to determine a baseline figure that would result in the same revenue, were all authors to choose the OA option. As with the fees for fully OA journals, these fees also vary significantly ($950 to $3,900 on the UC Berkeley listing, www.lib.berkeley.edu/scholarlycommunication/oa_fees.html [last updated August 2011]) and discounts or fee waivers are sometimes available.

Librarians have expressed concern about institutional subscription rates for hybrid journals – specifically, they want to be reassured that the rates will be adjusted downward to reflect an increase in authors taking the OA option (some publishers guarantee this). However, most publishers have seen only a small uptake of the OA option by authors in these hybrid journals (Oxford University Press, 2010; Poynder, 2011), so the effect on subscription prices has been insignificant.

## Other income

As with subscriptions, the primary criterion in setting prices for subsidiary income streams is that the price must cover the costs. Some of these streams have been decreasing steadily for years (e.g., author offprints/reprints, and single-issue and back-volume sales), and the decrease has been accelerated by online publishing; at the same time, other streams have been created (e.g., pay-per-view article downloads).[34] A fuller discussion of these streams appears in Chapter 9, Subsidiary income.

As the majority of these revenue streams are invoiced, rather than prepaid, care must be taken to include a suitable figure in the price to cover the costs of raising invoices as well as credit and collections activities (and an allowance for bad debt). Where credit card payments are accepted, bank fees must also be considered.

The pricing for some of these subsidiary income streams often has a relationship to the institutional "list price" subscription rate. It was customary with the print edition to set the single-issue price by dividing the full institutional subscription rate by the number of issues supplied in the volume and adding a bit as an incentive to buy a subscription rather than purchase individual copies (as well as to cover the postage and handling). The analog in the online environment is the single article "pay-per-view" (PPV) price. Long before

---

[34] Of course, a number of these income streams are not applicable in an OA context.

online editions existed, many publishers had set a single article price in the form of the transactional fee stipulated in some Reproduction Rights Organizations (RRO) licenses. Some publishers charge the same rate for PPV as their existing RRO transaction fee, while others may discount it.[35] Many publishers arrive at the fee by simply dividing the institutional subscription rate by the number of articles published per volume and adding an appropriate markup. Publishers with a number of journals often standardize these fees over their list of titles; some differentiate by subject area, setting a lower fee for HSS titles, a higher fee for STM titles, and the highest fee of all for the lengthy articles in review journals.

## Conclusion

In working with journal finances, it is important to bear in mind that good financial management alone will not make a bad journal into a good one – but poor financial management can certainly speed the demise of a good journal. Every aspect of journal publishing has financial implications and everyone involved should be aware of how his or her own individual actions impact the financial picture.

### REFERENCES

Carroll, Lewis, 1871, *Through the looking glass*, London, Macmillan

Chesler, Adam, and Susan King, 2009, Tier-based pricing for institutions: a new, e-based pricing model, *Learned Publishing* 22: 42–9 (http://dx.doi.org/10.1087/095315108X378767)

Dickens, Charles, 1849, *David Copperfield*, London, Bradbury and Evans

Friend, Frederick, 2011, *Open access business models for research funders and universities*, Knowledge Exchange Briefing Paper (www.knowledge-exchange.info/Default.aspx?ID=459)

Grossman, Theodore, and John Leslie Livingstone, 2009, *Portable MBA in finance and accounting*, 4th edn, New York, Wiley

Oxford University Press, 2010, *Open access uptake for OUP journals: five years on*, press release, June 10 (www.oxfordjournals.org/news/2010/06/10/open_access.html)

---

[35] Some document delivery services charge their customers a fee comprising a processing fee, which the service retains, plus the publisher's own fee (or, in some cases, a standard copyright fee), which is remitted to the publisher.

Poynder, Richard, 2011, Open access by the numbers, blog post to *Open and Shut*, June 19 (http://poynder.blogspot.com/2011/06/open-access-by-numbers. html)

## FURTHER READING

King, Donald W, 2007, The cost of journal publishing: a literature review and commentary, *Learned Publishing* 20: 85–106 (http://dx.doi.org/10.1087/ 174148507X183551)

King, Donald W, and Frances M Alvarado-Albertorio, 2008, Pricing and other means of charging for scholarly journals: a literature review and commentary, *Learned Publishing* 21: 248–72 (http://dx.doi.org/10.1087/095315108X356680)

Page, Gillian, Robert Campbell, and Jack Meadows, 1997, Financial aspects, in *Journal publishing*, Cambridge University Press, 270–300

Tenopir, Carol, Suzie Allard, Benjamin J Bates, Kenneth J Levine, Donald W King, Ben Birch, Regina Mays, and Chris Caldwell, 2011, Perceived value of scholarly articles, *Learned Publishing* 24: 123–32 (http://dx.doi.org/10.1087/20110207)

Ware, Mark, and Michael Mabe, 2009, *The STM report: an overview of scientific and scholarly journal publishing*, Oxford, International Association of Scientific, Technical & Medical Publishers, 33–6 (www.stm-assoc.org/industry-statistics/ the-stm-report)

# 9 Subsidiary income

## Introduction

We noted in the marketing chapter that journal publishers who rely primarily on institutional subscriptions and license fees need to develop other sources of revenue. This chapter will briefly survey some of these other revenue channels. Since consortia licensing arrangements draw on the same institutional serials budgets that pay for subscriptions, we will not dwell on them here. (Consortia licensing is covered in Chapter 6, Marketing and sales.) Some of these items do depend on the institutional market, but not, generally, on the library's serials budget.

We make no attempt to rank these revenue channels by size or return on investment. Different publishers will have different results, depending on subject matter, the national or international character of the journal, real-world events, and the effectiveness of the publisher's own marketing and publicity efforts. Suffice it to say that, for most journals, subscription and license revenue and/or OA publication fees will still probably constitute the major part of the publisher's income.

## Alternative modes of access

Subscriptions and license fees are not the only way to gain access to a publisher's content, especially for those institutions or individuals who only need an occasional article, or who want to tap into a publisher's content for a brief period of time (as a student doing a thesis might).

### Online article sales (pay per view)

Sales of single articles are nothing new – see the discussion of document delivery services below. Such third-party sales involved making a photocopy from the printed page and faxing or mailing the copy to the user or library – a mechanical process which was sometimes slow, often produced hard-to-read images, and occasionally failed to deliver the desired article altogether. (And third parties were required, because very few publishers even maintained a print library of their own journals.)

However, online publishing "unbundled" individual articles from their journal "wrappers," essentially making the article, not the journal, the new unit of information (as noted in Chapter 1, Introduction to journals). With online production, each publisher has a database of articles that is complete and easily searched, and e-commerce makes the ordering process easy for any credit card holder. Delivery, of course, is instantaneous. But what really makes online article sales successful are the major web search engines, and Google in particular. (Many scholarly publishers report that Google delivers far more referrals to their websites than any other search engine, including Google's own dedicated service, Google Scholar.) Researchers could always find an article through one of the specialized abstracting and indexing services, such as Web of Knowledge, Chemical Abstracts Service, CSA Illumina (formerly Cambridge Scientific Abstracts), Medline, and so on – assuming (with the exception of Medline, which is free) that their institution subscribed to the service. But no scholarly abstracts database was ever truly comprehensive. Since Google, Bing, Yahoo!, and other search engines index the entire web, and since their sheer ubiquity makes them available to everyone with a computer, they have fueled "discoverability" of the scholarly literature to a greater degree than ever before. One scientific publisher reported that its online article sales doubled after Google first indexed its site (LaFrenier, 2009–10). Much of this traffic, of course, will come from users at institutions that subscribe to the publisher's journals; they will be recognized by their IP addresses as authorized users and passed directly into the content. Users from nonsubscribing institutions and other individuals will be asked for their credit card information.

Publishers should not take pay-per-view sales for granted. Small tweaks to the ordering and shopping-cart pages can make a real difference in sales for consumers used to one-click ordering. It is especially useful to offer the buyer "more like this" options before checkout – more articles on the same topic, more articles by the same author, and so on. It is also possible to experiment with different price points to encourage more sales, although anecdotal evidence suggests that buyers are more driven by their need for the material than by the price. (For more on how publishers establish their single-article prices, see Chapter 8, Journal finances.)

### *Article bundles (deposit accounts)*

We noted in Chapter 6, Marketing and sales, that Google and other search engines deliver searchers to specific articles of interest, not to the home pages of the journals in which they appear. Publishers can now combine articles on related subjects to deliver anthologies or new "virtual" journals, which are topical collections of articles with links to the source journal in which they were originally published. (For an example of a multipublisher virtual journal, see the *Virtual Journal of Biological Physics* [www.vjbio.org/bio]. For an example of a single-publisher product, see *Virtual Maney – Spinal Cord Injury* [www.ingentaconnect.com/content/virtual/maney/vm12].)

Related to this has been the realization that many articles within a prestigious journal may receive very little usage at all. Certainly, they are not all cited by other researchers.[1] One can imagine that a library would like to pay only for articles that will be used, if it were possible to determine this in advance. Enter the *prepaid article bundle.* In this model, the library creates a deposit account with the publisher by prepaying for a set number of articles, and the deposit account is debited each time an article is downloaded. While the institution could simply buy each article that a user wants one by one, it generally receives a substantial discount from the publisher by paying in advance. The advantage to the publisher, compared to single-article sales, is that it has a renewable business relationship with the customer. Librarians receive a web-based management tool that allows them to track the articles that are used, to monitor the debit account, and to replenish it when necessary. Also, publishers typically guarantee that the institution will never have to pay for the same article twice – once downloaded, it remains available to other users without further charge, as long as the account is paid and current. (Not all library deposit accounts have the same purpose. Ingenta, one of the largest online journal hosting platforms, offers this kind of payment model for the convenience of libraries with pay-per-view budgets, but does not offer discounts on its publishers' article fees. See www.ingentaconnect.com/about/librarians/purchasing_articles.)

---

[1]  The percentage of papers that go uncited is a subject of controversy and depends heavily, in any case, on the discipline, with more uncited articles in HSS than in STM fields. See, for example, Hamilton, 1991; Pendlebury, 1991; and Larivière et al., 2009.

However, prepaid deposit accounts that offer substantial discounts on article fees may represent a grave danger to publishers with mature journals and a well-established subscription business in academia. Since the initial cost of the article bundle is substantially less than the subscription prices for the associated journals, the publishers could take a real financial loss if substantial numbers of academic subscribers were suddenly to switch from subscriptions to deposit accounts – even though they might find themselves having to "top up," or replenish, their accounts more than once in the course of the year. And the temptation to switch could be a problem for the library as well. The "savings" sound terrific – but in fact it is always cheaper to subscribe to a very well-used journal than it would be to pay for each article download by download, even at a discount. Publishers are concerned that libraries will make the mistake of buying the less expensive product, even if the eventual expense exceeds the subscription costs over the course of the year. Logic suggests the library will just re-subscribe the next year, but publishers fear that once a subscription is canceled, it's over for good. To avoid such problems, the publisher of one leading article-bundle product, *IEEE Enterprise* (www.ieee.org/portal/innovate/products/research/articles/ieee_enterprise.html), makes the product available only to the corporate market.

In the current era of diminished library budgets, journal publishers face a growing interest among librarians in canceling low-use journals and converting to a pay-per-view model, so publishers face a tricky choice between preserving subscriptions for near-term revenue needs and offering new access options for long-term customer satisfaction.

There are variations on this model. Wiley-Blackwell, for example, offers librarians licensing plans that include an option to buy a set number of "tokens" that researchers can use to acquire individual articles from those Wiley-Blackwell journals to which the institution does not subscribe. Often in models such as this, if the value of the articles purchased from a given journal exceeds its subscription price, the publisher may invoice the library for a regular subscription or add the title to the license fee at the next license renewal.[2]

---

[2] This is one form of "patron-driven acquisition," whereby the behavior of users, rather than the curatorial expertise of the librarian, determines the need for a subscription.

### Time-based access

In a related model, a publisher might provide individual users with access to its database through time-based pricing. For example, a user (if he or she is willing to use a credit card) might be charged $5.95 for one hour, $19.95 for four hours, $49.95 for twelve hours, or $99.95 for 24 hours. There would need to be appropriate limits on how much material the user could download and print in whatever period of time he or she has purchased. This model has been much discussed as publishers look to other industries (newspapers, databases, music), but has not yet been put into practice by scholarly publishers (to our knowledge) – so this remains entirely hypothetical at the moment.

### Mobile apps

Many users would like to access journal content through a personal handheld device rather than their desktop or laptop computers. The problem is that most of the journals they want are paid for by their institutions. Mobile applications that expose journal content to iPhone, iPad, Blackberry, and Android users (and users of future, as-yet-unknown devices) therefore need to deal with the issue of authentication: how do we check that a user has access rights to content because of an institutional subscription? Without such authentication, the app is likely to deliver only the same search functionality the user experiences on the open web, and will not get the user past the firewall separating free (the abstract) and paid (the fulltext article) content. Thus, the American Institute of Physics advertises its iResearch app (http://scitation.aip.org/iphone) as an "offline reader" – one can download articles to the app for later reading, but cannot use the app to access articles directly. The American Academy for the Advancement of Science invites readers to browse content on the phone via its *Science* mobile app (http://content.aaas.org/mobile) and to email themselves links to fulltext articles for later reading at an "authorized user" computer (i.e., one whose IP address is part of the institution's license agreement with the publisher). *Annual Reviews* and its online hosting service, Atypon, were the first to announce a mobile app (www.annualreviews.org/page/about/mobile) that lets users retrieve fulltext articles on their phones away from their campus or company; however, the user still needs to log into www.annualreviews.org "while on an authenticated institutional wi-fi network"; the mobile device is then "automatically paired" with the institution's access rights.

Of course, access by phone is not a problem for users with personal subscriptions, who can enter their user ID and password just as they would on a desktop computer – and this may be a new reason for publishers to offer password access to users affiliated with an institutional subscriber/licensee. In any case, researchers and scholars will find plenty of uses for mobile devices besides reading the fulltext, peer-reviewed literature. They can receive alerts of new papers in their fields, search content, browse abstracts, see news and announcements, access job postings, receive blogs and podcasts, email links to colleagues, and so on.

Most scholarly journal apps that provide mobile access to users are free to install at this point, but this remains a potential future source of revenue for journal publishers, even at the very low prices typically charged for consumer apps.

## Royalties, rights, and permissions

This category of potential revenue for journal publishers is well established and serves individuals and organizations who want to reuse pieces of the publisher's intellectual property.

### Permissions

Authors and publishers will often seek permission to reprint or reuse an article, image, illustration, chart, or table from a scholarly journal – and, increasingly, material from blogs, podcasts, and electronic newsletters – and the journal publisher usually has a permissions person, or rights manager, to handle such requests. They are aided by new online tools, such as RightsLink (see next section), that can automate the permission process.

Fees for the reuse of the intellectual property of a publisher should scale to the size and purpose of the request, and whether the reuse is for commercial or noncommercial purposes. A glossy, high-circulation magazine with an international distribution that wants to put an image on its front cover and in its advertising materials might be expected to pay a substantial fee. The same is true of a pharmaceutical company that wants to reproduce an article mentioning one of its patented drugs in its marketing materials. In practice, most scholarly publishers tend to waive their fees when the request comes from another scholarly publisher, as long as the material is properly attributed. (See, for example, the STM Permissions Guidelines at www.stm-assoc.org/document-library.) Teachers who want to photocopy an article or provide a link to its online version for the classroom use of students are seldom charged, either, as long as the material is not sold to the students or the activity is not large-scale and systematic. However, when faculty use a commercial copy shop to produce an anthology of readings that is sold to students, or when they systematically mount large amounts of content online for students' use, the publisher has a right to expect compensation. Publishers have sued copy shops, or the universities that employ them, over this issue. (In the most notable recent case, three publishers sued Georgia State University for systematically posting substantial amounts of copyrighted material online as electronic reserves for classroom use, without the publishers' permission. A May 2012 court decision largely ruled in favour of GSU on fair use grounds, but with some limits imposed on the amount of copying allowed.) For more information on the handling of permission requests, see Chapter 11, Copyright and other legal aspects.

### *Reproduction Rights Organizations (RROs)*

RROs exist to streamline and institutionalize the process of obtaining permissions from publishers and other rightsholders by offering blanket annual licenses (sometimes called repertory licenses) to corporations, academic and cultural institutions, and governments, and by collecting and remitting fees to the rightsholders (authors, illustrators, and publishers). The Copyright Clearance Center (CCC) in the US (www.copyright.com), the Copyright Licensing Agency (CLA) in the UK (www.cla.co.uk), and Access Copyright, the Canadian Copyright Licensing Agency (www.accesscopyright.ca) are examples of such RROs. They are all not-for-profit organizations that issue collective licenses which allow copying from a licensed repertory that includes both print and digital editions of books, journals, and magazines, within limits and subject to some exclusions. Each licensee organization pays an annual fee, which eliminates the need for individuals in the organization to seek permission every time they want to copy. The allocation of these fees to the rightsholders (who must be registered with a national RRO) is based on surveys of a sample of academic and corporate licensee organizations. CCC also offers users a transactional, or pay-per-use, license for both academic and commercial uses, including course packs and document delivery. In recent years, CCC has developed an online licensing solution, RightsLink, which allows users to request permissions directly at the point of use, and at the article or chapter level. CCC reported that it distributed more than $179.4 million to rightsholders in 2012; CLA disbursed more than £65.9 million in 2010–11.

Some RROs (such as CCC) rely on publishers to forward authors' and illustrators' share in line with their existing agreements; others make these payments via those parties' collecting societies. CLA, for example, is owned and directed by the Authors' Licensing and Collecting Society (ALCS) and the Publishers Licensing Society (PLS), in association with the Design and Artists Copyright Society (DACS), and licensing revenues are distributed to rightsholders via these organizations. This removes the need for publishers to manage royalty payments to individual authors and visual creators.

## Document delivery services

Even among the great universities, few institutions have all the information resources their users need, no matter how many journals they may subscribe to or license, and they need to augment their holdings with articles from other sources. Academic and public libraries can obtain articles through "interlibrary loan," usually without fee or for a low handling charge (and with no copyright fee paid to the publisher, as this falls under "fair use"). Articles shared in this way are governed by the fair use (US) and fair dealing (UK) provisions in copyright law (see Chapter 11, Copyright and other legal aspects). But even academic libraries often need to augment interlibrary loan with the services of a fee-based document delivery vendor; in fact, most libraries use more than one such vendor.

In the corporate world, the use of document delivery services is key to satisfying R&D needs. Companies, on average, use three different vendors to meet user demand, and this tends to be the most outsourced information-management function in the firm (Outsell Briefing Report, 2008). The trend, overall, is to move away from "mediated" document supply, in which a librarian or information officer directs a user's request to the document vendor (after first checking the organization's own holdings) and returns the article to the user, to more reliance on "self-serve" models, in which the user directly submits the article request (using the online systems of whichever vendor the company has chosen). Self-serve document retrieval may save some overhead costs for companies, but mediated retrieval (handled by an information professional) may save time. Many companies provide a mix of mediated and self-serve services to their users.[3]

It is obviously less expensive to buy individual articles directly from the publisher (since there is no third-party handling fee), but corporations, universities, and other institutions want a comprehensive, consistent, convenient service (and one that does not require a credit card for every transaction). They also rely on such services to clear copyright and manage payment of appropriate fees to the rightsholders, either by direct arrangement or more commonly through a transactional service partnership with an RRO.

Publishers have often had a contentious relationship with document delivery services, particularly those in the not-for-profit sphere, which is dominated by large libraries such as the British Library, Canada Institute for Scientific and Technical Information (CISTI), and Linda Hall Library. Unlike commercial document suppliers, these institutions tend to fulfill article requests (often from other document delivery companies) from within their own collections – the British Library has more than 240,000 serials and millions of other documents, from which it fulfills 85% of the article orders it receives; see www.bl.uk/reshelp/atyourdesk/docsupply.

The problem for publishers is that some large national libraries and institutions of higher education operate "docdel" services that are clearly mass-scale, revenue-generating operations that contribute significantly to the bottom line of the parent organizations – without always paying, or even accepting the need to pay, the copyright fees that the publishers deem appropriate. Liberal interpretations of fair use or fair dealing, belief in the historical library mission to disseminate knowledge, local intellectual property laws (or lack thereof), arguments that, as nonprofits, the

---

[3] Survey data from Outsell (www.outsellinc.com) show that, between November 2005 and April 2007, the time required for a user to gather and analyze information increased by more than an hour (two hours in healthcare settings) – and most of the extra time was spent gathering the information (Outsell Briefing Report, 2008).

institutions are seeking "cost recovery" rather than "profit," and even political treaties among some nations have all contributed to disagreement and confusion between publishers and libraries over document delivery as practiced in academe. Publishers have identified many instances in which a library- or university-run document supply center has sold articles to employees of commercial organizations (who clearly fall outside of fair use/fair dealing provisions) without paying royalties, for example. Publishing trade associations such as STM, AAP/PSP, and PA have been working directly with these library organizations for several years to ensure that publishers receive proper compensation for the resale of their content.[4] (For more on publishers' dealings with document delivery suppliers, see Chapter 11, Copyright and other legal aspects.)

### *Translation rights*

Most science journals (and many humanities and social science journals) today are published in English, and authors and readers for whom English is not their native language are expected to develop sufficient fluency to read and write in English in order to communicate with their worldwide community of peers. Thus, one might expect that the possibilities for selling translation rights in journals would be limited.

However, this does not necessarily mean that it is easy for non-native English-speakers everywhere to read complex journal articles. Thus, publishers will sometimes receive requests for permission to translate an article, a collection of articles, or even an entire journal for use in another country (by an author, a society, a website, a local publisher, etc.). Such requests are particularly common for articles aimed at a practitioner audience, or for articles from HSS journals, whose readers abroad may be less likely to read English.

Translation requests may range from single articles to whole journals. An individual article might be translated for inclusion in a local journal, or for separate distribution (for example, by a pharmaceutical company). A collection of translated articles might be published in book form. Or all or most of the content of a journal might be translated and locally published

---

[4] For example, STM and the British Library (BL) have announced their agreement on a "framework license" between publishers and BL that will govern the supply of BL documents to certain noncommercial users outside the UK.

on a regular basis, with or without additional local material – for instance, the Japanese physics publication *Parity* regularly reprints translated articles from the US publication *Physics Today*.

When considering whether or not to license translation rights, and how much to charge, the publisher needs to consider whether existing subscriptions are likely to be adversely affected. The licensee should only be permitted to use the name of the original journal (either in English or translated) if the content is the same; if local material is to be added, or any other changes made (such as the order of articles), the publisher and the Editor or Editorial Board (and, if appropriate, the sponsoring society) might require the right of approval; it is wise to stipulate that any added material should be clearly identified. Full acknowledgment should be given to the original publication and publisher, including full bibliographic details in the case of an article, and including the names of the journal Editor and Editorial Board when all or most of the journal is translated.

If the agreement is for translation of all or most of a journal's content on an ongoing basis, the translating publisher will need to receive edited copy as rapidly as possible, to avoid publication delays – this is especially important in fields such as the biological sciences, where speed of publication is crucial.

In the case of the translation of a whole journal, or of a collection of articles in book form, the usual form of payment is a royalty (typically 5–10%, possibly rising after a certain number of sales, or for any reprint) based on the translating publisher's price multiplied by the printrun. A higher percentage royalty would apply if the royalty were based on the translating publisher's actual receipts. In some cases, the original publisher might seek an advance payment. In the case of single articles, however, a one-off fee is the only practicable method of payment.

## Digital archives

One of the major benefits of online journals is that readers are not limited to just the current issue or volume. Publishers typically include the recent electronic backfile in a current year's subscription or license – for example, Wiley-Blackwell provides a five-year backfile; the Institute of Physics provides a ten-year backfile. These are referred to as "rolling backfiles" since the previous year's content is added to the backfile each year as the oldest year of the backfile content drops away. Other publishers adopt a different model, providing subscribers with a backfile that extends back to the journal's first year of online publication; thus, access to the *Journal of the American Chemical Society* includes all published content back to 1996. Backfiles, even at an extra fee, have proven popular with libraries and researchers, and are well used, especially in STM fields with a long cited half-life.[5] Most leading publishers have now retrodigitized their older print volumes, usually back to the first issue. This newly digitized content is sometimes included in the price of the current year's subscription or license fee (for example, the *Journal of the Acoustical Society of America* provides subscribers with the full electronic archive for that journal back to 1929). Some publishers, however, offer access to these older online volumes for an additional fee; the earliest example is the *Physical Review Online Archive* (PROLA), which may be subscribed to with or without any other *Physical Review* journal and which provides access to physics research published by the American Physical Society since 1893. Another physics publisher, the American Institute of Physics, offers subscribers the choice of a "regular" subscription with a backfile to 1999, or an "extended backfile" subscription, with access back to Volume 1, Issue 1.

There is another nonsubscription revenue model for these digital archives,[6] namely, outright purchase. Many publishers sell their archives for a single, one-time payment (or for a one-time fee paid in installments) under a "perpetual rights" license agreement. (Publishers often charge an annual "maintenance fee" as well, to cover the costs of hosting, customer service, file upgrades, and so on.) A few librarians objected early on that this

---

[5] The cited half-life of a journal, another metric available from the *Journal Citation Reports* (see Chapter 5, Journal metrics), is the number of years extending back from the current year that accounts for half of the total citations received in the current year. So, if a journal has a citation half-life of six in 2012, then half of all the articles cited that year were published in the six-year period 2007–12; half were published before 2007. Journals about history or literary criticism will have long citation half-lives since their content remains relevant for many years; technical journals covering fields of rapid innovation will have shorter half-lives.

[6] While the terms "backfile" and "archive" are often used interchangeably, a "backfile" generally means any volume of content older than the current subscription year. "Archive" usually implies a more complete historical record, i.e., a backfile that goes back to Volume 1, Number 1, of a journal – or to the oldest available year of digitized content. Archives can often be purchased independently of a current subscription to the journal.

meant they had to buy the content twice, first in print and now online. But publishers rightly pointed out that the libraries' subscriptions over the decades bought them the print volumes, which they still own and which still sit on their shelves. None of this subscription revenue contributed to the cost of digitizing the older content, so that is a new expense the publisher must recover. If the library wants to own this historical content in digital form – and one reason to do so is simply to free up shelf space taken up by decades of physical volumes – then a new purchase is required. (Many, though not all, publishers accept that library subscriptions to material that was "born digital" should include "perpetual rights" to the electronic content, just as libraries owned the print volumes to which they subscribed.)

Examples of these "buy once, access forever" archives include:

- ACS Legacy Archives – American Chemical Society, 1879–1995
  http://pubs.acs.org/page/4librarians/products/archives/index.html.
- APS Journal Legacy Content – American Physiological Society, 1898–1998
  www.the-aps.org/publications/legacy/index.htm.
- *NEJM* Archive – *New England Journal of Medicine*, 1812–1989
  www.nejm.org/page/institution/pricing-and-ordering#Archive.
- IOP Journal Archive – Institute of Physics, 1874–2000
  www.iopjournalscatalogue-digital.com.
- Oxford Journals Archive – Oxford University Press, 1849–1995
  www.oxfordjournals.org/access_purchase/archive_pricing.html.

We include digital archives in this chapter on subsidiary revenue sources not only because archive sales are not subscriptions per se, but also because the payment is often made from "end-of-year" funds that the library has not expended on budgeted items. This "extra" money may come from the book budget or the general operating budget rather than the serials budget.

Although digitizing older print issues represents a substantial additional cost for publishers, unlike the digital files created in the course of online publication, they are no different in the eyes of the librarian and the reader. Thus, the publisher needs to consider carefully how its access policies for the retrodigitized archive (often called the "legacy archive") and backfiles that are "born digital" will mesh, both technically and financially. Let us assume, for example, that a library has been subscribing to *Journal X* since 2001, and that *Journal X* provides a three-year "rolling backfile" with current subscriptions. The library is also interested in access

**Table 9.1** *Archive with fixed date range*

| Current year subscription | Rolling backfile with subscription | First year subscribed | Archive date range in 2013 (fixed) |
|---|---|---|---|
| 2013 | 2010–12 | 2001 | 1900–97 |

**Table 9.2** *Archive that grows by annual increments*

| Current year subscription | Backfile with subscription | First year subscribed | Archive date range in 2013 (rolling) |
|---|---|---|---|
| 2013 | 2010–12 | 2001 | 1900–2009 |

to the complete archive of *Journal X*. Two scenarios, and various questions, present themselves.

In the first scenario (Table 9.1), the publisher offers an archive with a fixed date range (usually from the first published issue to the last year of print-only production).

In this scenario the publisher needs to answer the following questions:

- Does the subscriber have "perpetual rights" to the material back to 2001?
- If so, is the publisher able to provide continuing online access to this content, or can it only offer the material to the subscriber on CD-ROMs or DVDs?
- Is access to this content free as long as the customer renews its current subscription, or does the publisher charge a "maintenance fee" of some kind?
- How is the maintenance fee priced?
- Can the subscriber buy the years 1998–2000 (the gap years between the first year of subscription and the last year of the official archive) as a supplement to the 1900–97 archive?

In the second scenario (Table 9.2), the publisher's archive expands each year, adding the new year of content that has "rolled out" of the backfile included with the current-year subscription.

Here, the questions for the publisher are slightly different:

- Again, does the subscriber have "perpetual rights" to the material back to 2001?

- If the subscriber wants to buy the archive, will the publisher adjust the price in order not to charge for the 2001–9 material, which the customer has already paid for by subscription?
- Must the subscriber pay a maintenance fee for the archive, even if it renews its annual subscription?
- Will the "maintenance fee" increase for each new year of content that rolls into the archive (i.e., 2010 content that will become part of the archive in 2014)?

Careful consideration of such questions in advance will help publishers avoid several problems related to access and payment, which can (and do) arise when publishers' policies are informal or haphazard.

Some publishers offer "perpetual" rights to subscribed or licensed content, but do not yet have the technical capability to provide ongoing online access on their own servers. In such cases, libraries have accepted the content in a "physical" format such as CD-ROM or DVD. While this allows the publisher to honor its commitment to perpetual access, unless the recipient library has its own e-journal system, there is little the library can do to integrate this content with other online material accessible to its patrons. It is not a satisfying solution for the publisher, either, because it will be unable to track usage of this content.

Some, but not all, publishers allow libraries to mount the archive files on their own servers. This is the preferred model for OhioLINK, the Ontario Council of University Libraries (OCUL), and a few other academic networks. However, as noted above, the customer needs its own journal hosting system to make this work – that is, to mount the content, index it in a local search engine, and manage access controls for authorized users. Needless to say, there are not many individual university (or government) libraries with this capacity. In addition, such locally mounted archives will not have the same functionality that the publisher's platform provides.


## Aggregators

Aggregators can represent a major subsidiary income opportunity for journal publishers. Aggregators license content from a wide variety of journals to provide convenient collections for special markets. The benefit for the content producer is threefold: (a) the superior marketing power of the aggregator in reaching a specific group of customers; (b) the prestige (or promotional value) of being part of a focused, curated academic or business resource; and (c) the licensing fees paid by the aggregator. These products are intended to reach customers outside the publisher's traditional markets, but each publisher must decide if the licensing fees are worth the potential forgone revenue from direct sales or subscriptions, as no one wants to compete with their own content. There are roughly three categories of aggregator.

### Subject-level collections

One of the best-known and earliest online aggregators is Ovid, a unit of Wolters Kluwer Health (www.ovid.com/site/index.jsp). Ovid has licensed some 1,200 journals for its collections in medicine, nursing, healthcare, and science. Another leading aggregator is ProQuest (and its various divisions, such as Chadwyck-Healey), which combines scholarly journals and other information resources in its various databases covering business, history, arts and humanities, social sciences, healthcare, and other subjects (www.proquest.com). EBSCOhost offers libraries dozens of specialty databases, e.g., *Art & Architecture Complete*, *African-American Archives*, *Middle Eastern & Central Asian Studies*, and *Religion and Philosophy Collection* (www.ebscohost.com). Fulltext scholarly journals are also included in a number of aggregated databases designed to serve the secondary school market, such as EBSCOhost's *Political Science Complete* and ProQuest's *AP Science*.

### Mini-library collections

Some aggregations offer content across several disciplines and are intended to supplement the subscription holdings of smaller libraries, especially in the developing world, that cannot afford the extensive (and expensive) collections of academic research libraries. Perhaps the best-known examples are offered by EBSCOhost. Two of the most popular of these are *Academic Search Premier*, providing access to 16,000 abstracts and 8,500 fulltext journals, and *Academic Search Complete*, with 22,500 abstracts and 14,800 fulltext journals. In order to protect their own subscriptions, some publishers choose to make their fulltext content available in these products only after an embargo period, which typically ranges from six to twenty-four months.

### Business-solution aggregators

Some aggregators offer workflow productivity tools:

- DeepDyve (www.deepdyve.com), the "largest online rental service for professional and scholarly research articles," aims its service at what it claims is a large world of underserved professionals with no significant library resources. For a very low price, DeepDyve "rents" articles that readers can view but not download or print. Publishers have to forgo their own pricing and agree to DeepDyve's (very low) per-article prices. The company also offers various flat-fee subscription plans to institutional customers. While there are not many other services of this nature currently, it would not be surprising to see similar models in the future from new-media companies such as Google, Amazon, and Apple.
- AcademicPub, a product of SharedBook (www.sharedbook.com), targets faculty and administrators who want to create custom course packs for students, including book and journal content, without having to get permission from each individual publisher.
- UpToDate (www.uptodate.com/index) is a point-of-care resource designed to help clinicians provide better outcomes for patients. Available on the web and as a mobile app, this service is partly based on a continual review of 460 leading medical journals.

## Author-side payments

### Open access fees

Throughout this book, we have discussed the open access business model as the main alternative to the subscription-based journal. Typically, OA journals are supported by author-side publication fees, often paid by the organization that funded the research, as with the Wellcome Trust in the UK. Open access as a business model is discussed in Chapter 8, Journal finances. However, one need not be a "Gold" OA publisher to have author-side payments. Many scholarly journals are "hybrid" journals, offering authors (once their manuscript has been accepted for publication) the choice of paying to make their articles free on the web, or publishing "traditionally," i.e., with access restricted to subscribers. The uptake by authors has been modest (see Chapter 1, Introduction to journals), which is surprising since some hybrid journals would seem to offer the best of both worlds – allowing authors to reach any reader on the web while being identified with an established, high-impact journal. (With few exceptions, notably the PLoS family of journals, few "Gold" open access titles have yet achieved the same prestige as their subscription-based older siblings.)

### Other author fees

There are a variety of additional potential payments from authors:

### Offprints or reprints

Many publishers offer authors, for a fee, multiple offprints or reprints of their articles (it used to be common to supply a small quantity – say ten to twenty-five – free of charge, and to require payment for any extra). A minimum quantity of 100 reprints was once required to make this economical, but digital printing has made much lower quantities realistic. Interest in offprints is certainly diminishing with the ubiquity of the online article, which can be sent with a click, but some authors still like to have physical copies to distribute. An online alternative is to offer the author access to his or her article via a special URL, which can be passed on to the author's friends and contacts (in some cases, the number of downloads from this URL is restricted).

### Page and color charges

Page charges – per-page publishing fees paid by authors – were once a common revenue source for not-for-profit publishers (particularly those from the US), which helped keep prices low for libraries. Commercial journals helped to build their businesses in the postwar era, in competition with established not-for-profit journals, by not requiring page charges, and some society publishers were forced to drop author page charges to compete. However, page charges are still an important source of revenue for some publishers (mainly US society publishers). Publishers that do not impose standard author page charges may still require authors to pay for "excess" pages that exceed a standard article length.

The publisher may also require payment if an author wants color reproductions of his or her graphs, charts, or illustrations in the print edition of the journal, as this entails an extra printing cost.

## *Manuscript submission fees*

A few publishers require authors to pay a fee for submitting a paper. This is not unreasonable, since every manuscript that is rejected for publication – often after weeks spent in the peer-review process – entails a significant overhead. And some journals have very high rejection rates. *Physical Review Letters*, for example, rejects 75% of the papers it receives (American Physical Society, 2011); *Nature* rejects about 92% (*Nature*, 2012). Submission fees recover part of those overhead costs. They may also serve to discourage casual submissions from researchers who think they might just "get lucky" with a favored journal.

## Institutional memberships

Some society publishers have long offered membership to institutions to help support the work of the society. The Society for Industrial and Applied Mathematics (SIAM), for example, offers both Academic Memberships and Corporate Memberships (www.siam.org/membership). Societies such as the American Association of Physics Teachers (AAPT) and the Human Factors and Ergonomics Society (HFES) offer "Sustaining Memberships" to corporations. Benefits for the member institutions might include discounts on subscriptions, books, advertising rates, conference registration fees, conference exhibition fees, and the society's mailing list; free student memberships; and public recognition that the institution contributes to the research associated with the society.

Some open access publishers offer institutional memberships of another kind. In these arrangements, universities pay a yearly fee so that any author from that institution can pay a discounted fee – or nothing at all – to publish (if accepted) in an OA journal. University librarians see this as a way to support the OA movement, but it has been argued that a research-intensive institution could spend considerably more of its serials budget on these OA contributions than it currently spends on subscriptions from the same journals/publishers (Davis et al., 2004). Nonetheless, OA publishers such as the Public Library of Science and BioMed Central manage active institutional membership programs – see www.plos.org/support/instmembership.php and www.biomedcentral. com/info/libraries/membership.

## Advertising

Academic journals offer a focused, niche audience that may attract advertisers with similarly targeted products (such as book publishers, conference organizers, software developers, drug developers, and device manufacturers). Advertising is often sold as a print-plus-online combination; display ads in the print journal have the advantage of showing readers a fuller text message and compelling visuals, but the value of advertising in the print journal will vary from discipline to discipline. In some STM fields (where searching is more dominant than browsing and the online version is widely available) the print journal may see little use. Since search engine users generally arrive at the article abstract page when they click on a search result, that is where advertisers want to be seen. However, there are many ways the publisher can create advertising opportunities online. For example, a banner ad on an article abstract might be offered to advertisers in combination with a text message accompanying the table of contents email alert for that issue. Online ads can be offered for special places such as "Top 20 Downloads of the Month" or "Editor's Top Picks," or perhaps placed contextually near product names mentioned in an article. (Some societies that partner with commercial publishers reserve the right to approve advertisements, and many publishers do not allow advertisements to be placed in or near editorial content.)

Pricing for print advertisements is based on circulation, frequency, placement (inside front or back cover, outside back cover, facing table of contents, etc.), use of color, and size (quarter-page, half-page, etc.), while pricing for online advertisements is typically based on results. The advertiser may pay for a certain number of impressions (views), or click-throughs (links to the advertiser's website), or "actions" (i.e., because the reader did something after clicking on the ad, such as calling a toll-free number or placing an order). However, advertisers might also pay to have their ad exposed to viewers for a given period of time. In this case, the advertisement will appear in rotation with other advertisements across the publisher's site for a month or a quarter, for a fixed fee. Different publishers will have different pricing models. In general, though, advertisements sold by a scholarly publisher will represent a fairly modest source of income. The picture is quite different for journals in clinical medicine and related areas of healthcare, where there is a wide readership of practitioners that pharmaceutical companies want to reach. The same is true in some hardware-intensive disciplines (e.g., microscopy) whose readership is attractive to equipment manufacturers.

Small publishers with few staff to manage an advertising department can benefit from outsourcing the sales function. Commissioned advertising sales representatives have long been contracted to handle print advertising solicitation. In the online environment, small publishers might find benefit in the Google AdSense (www.google.com/intl/en/ads) or Microsoft pubCenter (http://pubcenter.microsoft.com/Login) programs. Both companies index publishers' sites to create the same sort of contextual advertising possibilities that they offer on their own sites, and then manage the ad sales to third parties; the publisher is paid on a cost-per-click or cost-per-impressions basis. The upside is that there is essentially no overhead for the publisher; the downside is that the publisher has no control over the ads that appear on its site, which, for a scholarly publisher, may raise issues of taste and appropriateness.

Classified advertisements (e.g., job postings, grant announcements, calls for papers) are very important to a handful of frequently published journals with magazine-like features, such as *Nature*, *Science*, *Physics Today*, and *Chemical and Engineering News*; many others, however, have found that the rise of online job sites has taken away this market. Given the time-sensitive nature of such advertisements, the real action, for advertisers and users alike, seems destined to move entirely online in the not too distant future; but, for now, some of these periodicals report that print classified ads remain strong.

## Sponsorship

Publishers may, in some instances, find organizations that have a sufficient interest in certain areas of research to be willing to support a publication financially, as a sponsor. One example is the American Physical Society journal *Physical Review Special Topics – Accelerators and Beams*, which is "funded by contributions from national and international laboratories."

In other cases, the publisher might find a sponsor for a single issue of a journal covering a special topic related to the sponsor's products or services. Or a sponsor might want to be associated with a specific community website. It may be a matter of semantics, but for some publishers what distinguishes a "sponsor" from an "advertiser" is that the sponsor is associated with the whole endeavor (a conference, a journal, even a particular research topic) rather than just paying to display an advertisement. Sponsorships also tend to promote the sponsor's brand rather than a specific product line.

"Special issues" of a journal are another potential source of sponsorship revenue. These may be assembled by a Guest Editor invited to focus on a specific topic for which the publisher might attract an appropriate sponsor (who will often wish to purchase bulk copies for promotional use). The special issue may be produced either as a regular issue or as a supplemental issue (e.g., a thirteenth issue in a monthly publication), in which case a sponsor will be needed to cover the additional paper, printing, and binding costs. It is important that the publisher maintain complete editorial independence and avoid any real or perceived conflicts of interest.

As discussed in Chapter 12, Ethical issues, as long as it is clear to the reader that a journal or journal issue is sponsored, there should not be any ethical problem, because the reader is able to bear in mind the possibility of bias. However, if the sponsorship is hidden, the reader cannot judge whether the content is presented objectively or subtly shaded to favor the sponsor's products or views. In a recent case, a major commercial publisher distributed a series of medical journals that were discovered to have been little more than a set of reprints and reviews with favorable coverage of the large pharmaceutical company that sponsored the titles (Grant, 2009). Aside from the ethical issues involved, such hidden sponsorships have the potential to impact the publisher's brand in a very negative way.

## Conference proceedings

Publishing the presentations made at a scientific or technical conference (formally known as "proceedings") on behalf of a society or other conference organizer can be another valuable market opportunity. Many journals have an ongoing relationship with particular conferences and publish their proceedings annually as a regular issue; in other cases (as with some sponsored issues), the proceedings may be published as an extra issue outside the normal run of the journal, in which case the sponsor covers the entire extra cost (plus an appropriate markup) of producing and distributing the issue, to subscribers as well as conference delegates. Speed of publication is obviously crucial – it is important to liaise closely with the conference organizer in order to obtain the final manuscripts of all the papers as soon as possible.

Another option is to publish the conference program and abstracts, which can then be distributed to delegates at the conference. While this is a slimmer publication and revenues will therefore be more modest, offering this type of service to conference organizers may help the publisher win the rights to publish the full conference proceedings in the future. Such programs also give the publisher a prime opportunity to sell advertising space to exhibitors at the conference.

With online journals, the publisher has other options to offer conference organizers, such as a password-protected site where papers are posted as preprints upon acceptance by the conference organizers; the attendees can thus see some papers just prior to the start of the conference (so as not to deter attendance) and all or most of the rest immediately after the conclusion of the conference.

### Bulk sales (special sales) of articles

A drug company whose product is favorably mentioned in an article, or an equipment manufacturer whose new product is lauded by an author, may be interested in buying the article in bulk, perhaps with a customized cover, so that their sales representatives can distribute the article to potential customers. Bulk sales, also called special sales or commercial reprints, are more prevalent in biomedical titles. However, there may be many occasions when a publisher might find a company interested in a special sale – for an article on clean energy or automotive engineering or a major urban cultural festival, for example. Nevertheless, unless the publisher has a dedicated person pursuing such opportunities, there is rarely the staff or time to exploit this revenue channel.

## Grants

Grant money is sometimes available from foundations, national academies, government agencies, or multinational companies for special publishing projects that add to our cultural or scientific heritage but are not likely to pay the publisher back for its efforts (in some cases only not-for-profit publishers may be eligible). The project might involve digitizing historical images from a private collection, or preserving the raw data behind a researcher's results, or mapping the history of an idea. Some projects might emerge in future from the growing interest among publishers and researchers to data-mine and text-mine their databases for new insights. The mission-driven Public Library of Science, devoted to publishing research that is freely accessible on the web, was launched with grants from the Gordon and Betty Moore Foundation and the Sandler Foundation totaling 13 million dollars; JSTOR, one of the first not-for-profit organizations to digitize and aggregate scholarly journal content, was originally funded by the Andrew W. Mellon Foundation.

## Back issues

With the continuing shift from print to online as the preferred medium for accessing journal content, sales of printed back issues/volumes have declined significantly. However, there is still a demand for back issues in fields where print remains dominant (e.g., the humanities); review journals may also fall into this category. However, the publisher must balance the ongoing costs of warehousing print inventory against the potential sales, to determine if this is still a worthwhile revenue stream to pursue. If not, it may be best to sell excess back stock to a third-party jobber who specializes in back-issue sales (another diminishing business). (Note that when disposing of back stock the publisher should retain several copies of each issue for an in-house archive, both for reference and to use for digital conversion if not already digitized.) Of course, print-on-demand technology has reduced the size of journal printruns, while also providing a way to fulfill orders for back issues without the need for much physical inventory (see Chapter 4, The production process).

## List rentals

Some publishers make a decent amount of income from renting their subscriber lists (or membership lists, in the case of a society publisher). Publishers who have traditionally rented their mailing lists may be more reluctant to rent their email lists, as this is sometimes perceived to be too invasive. Professional list brokers can advise publishers about this, as they will take the burden of promoting the value of the publisher's list, establishing pricing, and handling all the logistics of the rental. Publishers may want to establish some rules about who may rent their lists, excluding direct competitors or, in some cases, commercial organizations.

Lists of subscribers or members can be attractive, because these individuals have paid money to acquire something related to their field – the very action that the list buyer wants for its own product. But publishers have many other records at their disposal: authors, editors, inquirers, buyers of single (or multiple) articles, registrants for table of contents or subject alerts, registrants for community websites, and the like. Even when these people have not exhibited buying behavior, they may still be desirable to a third party because of their interest in a certain field. The list broker can advise about this.

The reuse of names gathered by publishers – including subscribers and authors – is subject to privacy/data protection rules, which differ in the US and the EU. The European Union has fairly stringent privacy-protection policies – for example, an EU company is not allowed to send personal data outside of the region without guarantees that the recipient will abide by the principles of the EU Data Protection Directive (Directive 95/46/EC). Organizations that collect personal data must ask each subject to opt in or opt out before his or her personal details can be used for any purpose unconnected with the customer's original contact. (See http://europa.eu/legislation_summaries/information_society/data_protection/l14012_en.htm.) Companies in the US need to follow the seven Safe Harbor principles (http://export.gov/safeharbor) developed by the US Department of Commerce. Virtually every US publisher has a privacy policy posted prominently on its website (which is one of the seven Safe Harbor principles). (Data protection issues are discussed more fully in Chapter 11, Copyright and other legal aspects.)

## Metadata

Metadata is the term often used for the kind of information found in library card catalogs and online databases – that is, structured data that helps users identify, find, describe, and retrieve information resources. There are many varieties of metadata (Brand et al., 2003); our interest here is in descriptive, or bibliographic, metadata – data that identifies journal articles.

Can metadata be a revenue source for journal publishers? Most publishers are happy to give metadata away – they accept the fact that a certain level of metadata (namely, records that include title, author, publication date, etc., but not necessarily including the article abstract or the linked references) must be distributed (or made available for "harvesting")[7] in order to make each article discoverable through search engines, abstracting and indexing databases, web portals, and so on. As stated in Chapter 6, Marketing and sales, "metadata is advertising." Most publishers will provide standard bibliographic records freely to any service, commercial or not, that helps users find the publishers' content. However, if the recipient of the publisher's metadata is building a commercial, value-added service, the publisher is likely to ask for payment, perhaps a percentage of sales; and higher payments might be expected for metadata that includes abstracts and references. See Chapter 7, Fulfillment, for more on metadata standards used in electronic data exchange. For more on the marketing uses of metadata, see Chapter 6, Marketing and sales.

## Conclusion

There are undoubtedly other potential revenue streams for journal publishers – the Public Library of Science even sells T-shirts and coffee mugs! And publishers are still finding new business models, depending on the community of authors and readers they serve. As one example, *BMJ Case Reports* allows healthcare professionals and researchers to pay an annual "fellowship fee," in return for which they can submit as many clinical case studies as they like, access all the published reports, and reuse any published material for personal use and teaching without further permission (see http://casereports.bmj.com).

However, while there may be many potential sources of subsidiary income for journal publishers, most of them also carry overhead costs. Even imposing a permissions fee requires someone to generate an invoice and follow up on payment. Similarly, article reprint sales will require full-time staff looking for every possible opportunity. So, aside from licensing agreements with RROs, aggregators, and other third parties, which need

---

[7] The Open Archives Initiative Protocol for Metadata Harvesting (OAI-PMH) (www. openarchives.org) is a tool that allows publishers to expose their metadata so that it can be easily collected for use by other service providers.

only be negotiated once (and renewed thereafter), each publisher will need to assess the value of its own intellectual property and decide whether, and how much, it is able to optimize such revenue channels.

## REFERENCES

American Physical Society, 2011, press release, *APS to adopt Creative Commons licensing and publish open access articles and journals*, Ridge, NY, American Physical Society (http://publish.aps.org/edannounce/CC-launch-press-release)

Brand, Amy, Frank Daly, and Barbara Myers, 2003, *Metadata demystified: a guide for publishers*, Hanover, PA and Baltimore, MD, The Sheridan Press and NISO Press (www.niso.org/publications/press/Metadata_Demystified.pdf)

Davis, Philip M, 2004, *Calculating the cost per article in the current subscription model*, Ithaca, NY, Cornell University (http://hdl.handle.net/1813/236) (this report supplements the CUL Task Force article referenced below)

Davis, Philip M, Terry Ehling, Oliver Habicht, Sarah How, John M Saylor, and Kizer Walker, 2004, *Report of the CUL task force on open access publishing*, Ithaca, NY, Cornell University (http://ecommons.library.cornell.edu/handle/1813/193)

Grant, Bob, 2009, Elsevier published 6 fake journals, *The Scientist*, May (http://classic.the-scientist.com/blog/display/55679/)

Hamilton, David P, 1991, Research papers: who's uncited now?, *Science*, 251:25 (http://dx.doi.org/10.1126/science.1986409)

LaFrenier, Douglas, 2009–10, Pay-per-view at the American Institute of Physics: one scholarly publisher's experience with the article economy, *Against the Grain* 21: 26–31, December 2009–January 2010

Larivière, Vincent, Yves Gingras, and Éric Archambault, 2009, The decline in the concentration of citations, 1900–2007, *Journal of the American Society for Information Science and Technology* 60: 858–62 (http://dx.doi.org/10.1002/asi.21011)

*Nature*, 2012, website, "For Authors" (www.nature.com/nature/authors/get_published/index.html#a2)

Outsell Briefing Report, 2008, *Document delivery – best practices and vendor scorecard*, Burlingame, CA, Outsell, Inc. (www2.reprintsdesk.com/downloads/Outsell_DocumentDelivery.pdf)

Pendlebury, David A, 1991, Science, citation, and funding (letter), *Science* 251: 1410–11 (http://dx.doi.org/10.1126/science.251.5000.1410-b)

## FURTHER READING

Owen, Lynette, 2010, *Selling rights*, 6th edn, Abingdon, Routledge

# 10 Contract publishing

## Introduction

It has been said that as soon as the number of scholars in a given subject area reaches 500, two events generally occur: a society is formed and a new journal is launched. Although many societies publish their own journals, the majority of society journals are published under contract.[1] Many new and smaller societies (and indeed some large ones) prefer to partner with a publisher to launch a new journal. The partner could be a commercial publisher, a non-profit University Press, or a related larger society with its own publishing program. (See discussion of societies' role in journal publishing in Chapter 1, Introduction to journals.)

While this chapter addresses contract publishing for societies, a journal may equally be owned by other bodies such as an academic department at a university or an independent institute. In addition, the "publisher" may also be a society that publishes its own journal and offers publishing services to other societies. The same procedures generally apply.

Partnering with a publisher to launch a new journal offers a society a number of advantages:

- It allows the society to concentrate on its mission to serve its members and advance the field.
- It allows the society to retain ownership of the journal without the financial risk of self-publishing.
- It provides a reduced-rate publication to members, again without the financial risk of self-publishing.
- It provides access to a depth of publishing and marketing expertise which would be difficult to match for a single title.

---

[1] In 2007, Ulrichs listed 23,277 active, peer-reviewed, scholarly journals; of these, 11,578 (54.71%) were published by, or on behalf of, universities, societies, and similar organizations (Morris, 2007).

- It offers economies of scale given the publisher's greater purchasing volume for publishing services, both for print and online.
- It provides access to an established online publishing platform with support for ongoing development.
- It offers greater opportunities for marketing and promotion when included with the publisher's list in the subject area, including relationships with a number of abstracting and indexing services.
- It has the potential for added income from inclusion in packages with "critical mass" for sale to library consortia.
- It offers affiliation with the publisher's brand, which can enhance the acceptance of a new journal.
- It brings deeper pockets: the publisher has the funds to invest in the new title until it is self-supporting.

Once the journal is well established, it is still a viable strategy for the society to continue to partner with a publisher.

For the publisher, publishing a journal on behalf of a society also has a number of advantages:

- It provides a preexisting pool of authors and member subscribers when launching a new journal.
- It adds content to the publisher's list without significant start-up and development cost when partnering on an existing title.
- It enhances the reputation of the title through affiliation with a respected group of scholars (it may find a better reception among libraries, for example).
- It provides the publisher with access to the expertise of the society in developing further products in the subject.
- It provides the publisher with expanded marketing opportunities for its related products.

For the partnership to work, both sides must gain some financial or other benefit from the partnership, recognize each other's areas of expertise, and be willing to cede control of some areas to each other.

Many of the points covered in this chapter will apply equally to a partnership to launch a new journal or to publish an existing one (and for that matter, irrespective of the business model). To simplify the discussion, we will focus primarily on a partnership to publish an existing, subscription-based journal (details specific to a journal launch are covered in Chapter 2, Managing journals); however, the journal could equally be published under the open access model (see discussion in Chapter 8, Journal finances). If the journal is a new launch, the steps outlined in Chapter 2, Managing journals, will apply.

## Identifying a partner

The first step in establishing a relationship is to identify potential partners.

For the publisher, the process starts with identifying areas of interest, where it already has a program in the general subject area (either books or journals) and has established a visible presence by exhibiting at relevant society meetings. The next step is to research societies with existing journals in those fields (or, for a launch, societies without an existing journal affiliation). It is important to develop contacts with society officers, journal Editors, and Editorial Board members and to express interest in their publishing program. It is invaluable for the publisher to establish a reputation for working well with the societies for which it publishes (and to establish relationships with the publishing consultants whom societies often engage to handle the bidding process).

For a society with an existing journal, the process usually starts with the appointment of a committee for a periodic evaluation of its existing publishing arrangements (whether self-publishing or partnering with a publisher). Many societies that had self-published a print journal chose to work with a publisher when moving to an online edition, rather than have to develop their own online platform, while others partnered with third parties such as HighWire Press or Project MUSE in order to migrate to online. Those currently partnered with a publisher periodically evaluate their relationship and, even if the arrangement is working well, may decide to put the journal out to tender as a matter of standard business practice. In that event, the Search Committee will identify those publishers that cover their subject area and related fields and then, based on their own personal experiences with these publishers as authors, Editors, and subscribers, create a list of potential partners. Recognizing the need for expert advice, many societies choose to engage the services of a publishing consultant to create a Request for Proposal (RFP), analyze the responses, and help the society through the evaluation and decision process.

## The RFP process

### Content of an RFP from a society

The RFP should provide an overview of the society and its journal(s) in sufficient detail to allow an in-depth evaluation by the publishers invited to bid. The following lists the information a publisher would like to see included in an RFP. While the list addresses subscription-based titles, most of the items are relevant to open access journals as well.

### *Sponsoring society*

- Name.
- Description of society, its history and purpose.
- Composition of membership (number of members in each category over last three years; projections for coming years).

### *Journal*

- Full title and ISSNs.
- Aims and scope.
- Names of Editor and Editorial Board with affiliations; note the role of the Board.
- Description of management of journal; definition of Editor, Editorial Board, Publications Committee, society staff roles.
- Description of the Editorial office operation, noting type of peer review (single or double blind or open) and whether submissions and peer review are handled online (if so, note software platform used).
- Parameters of the journal: frequency of issue and page budget for current and past three volumes; include projection for coming years.
- Print edition specifications – e.g., trim size, paper stock, current printer, methods of distribution (with sample copies provided).
- Online edition specifications – platform used, HTML/SGML/XML and/or PDF, feature set (e.g., incremental publication, reference linking, supplemental data) (with guest access provided to the publisher for evaluation purposes).
- Note whether legacy material (i.e., back volumes) is available online (and how access is provided and sold); if not, is conversion desired?

- Note any special supplements or related publications included with the journal.
- Copy flow – number of submissions in recent years, with data on acceptance rate and projections for copy flow; note whether there is a backlog of accepted copy.
- Data on average time from submission to decision and whether this needs to be improved.
- Data on average time from acceptance to publication and whether this needs to be improved.
- Metrics: Thomson Reuters impact factor and related metrics; also data (preferably COUNTER-compliant) for online usage if available from the current publisher.
- Circulation data broken down by type (institution, individual, member), medium (print, electronic, or both), and geographic area for current and last three years.
- Subscription rates broken down by type (institution, individual, member), medium (print, electronic, or both), and geographic area for current and last three years; note if there are any restrictions on future rates.
- Information about any consortium packages or bundles in which the journal is included.

## Financial data

- Subscription revenue for current and three prior years.
- Revenue allocated from consortia sales for current and prior three years.
- Advertising sales revenues for current and prior three years with advertising page counts; note if advertisements are sold in-house or by a commission sales representative (specify if figures are gross or net).
- Information on other revenue streams attributed to the journal by type (e.g., reprints, pay per view, rights) for current and prior three years.
- If journal is hybrid or fully OA, percentage of OA fees waived or discounted.
- Data on production costs (note that these data may not be available if the arrangement with the current publisher provides for a royalty as opposed to a surplus/profit share).

## *What is desired*

- Desired publishing services (full spectrum or only a limited subset).
- Desired service requirements (e.g., 24/7/52 technical support, allowable server downtime).
- Desired changes for the journal (e.g., more content, specific online features, customized website, etc.).
- Desired improvements in circulation or return.
- Desired/required level of financial support for the Editorial office.
- Requisite minimum financial return to the society.
- Preferred financial arrangement (e.g., royalty or surplus/profit share).
- The length of the agreement and when it is to start.
- Any other requirements (e.g., sample draft contract) or restrictions (e.g., limitations on overhead costs in a surplus/profit share).

## *Contact data*

- Contact person for questions about the RFP or further data.
- Whom the Commissioning/Acquisitions Editor may contact in the society or the journal Editorial office (or whether all contact must go through the designated contact person).

## *Proposal format and delivery*

- Desired format for the proposal, what points must be covered and in what order.
- Number of copies needed, what medium is acceptable.
- Due date for the proposal and where it must be delivered.

## *Decision timetable*

- When those submitting proposals will be advised if they have made the short list.
- Schedule for the remainder of the decision process (e.g., submission of revised proposals, in-person presentations, assignment to a publisher, negotiation, and signing of a contract).

Societies should take care, when specifying the submission, evaluation, and decision timeline, to allow adequate time for the publisher's staff to prepare a proposal for submission, and for an orderly transition after the contract is signed.[2] Several RFPs may arrive in the publisher's office at the same time, or the relevant Commissioning or Acquisitions Editor (see discussion of these roles in Chapter 3, Editing) may be out of the office for an extended period; if the society does not allow enough time for responses, it may miss out on some potentially attractive offers.

## Evaluation and review

After acknowledging receipt of the RFP, the Commissioning/ Acquisitions Editor will review the information supplied, to determine how well the journal fits within the editorial plan of the publisher, and will prepare a preliminary rough financial projection to determine whether the journal is financially attractive.[3] The RFP will also be reviewed to see if there are any up-front deal-breakers.[4] If the journal fails the tests of both editorial "fit" and financial attractiveness, the RFP will be politely declined. If the finances are extremely attractive but the journal is outside the current editorial scope of the publisher, an internal discussion will ensue as to whether the financial return would warrant expansion of the list. If the financials are weak but the journal fits the list, the internal discussion will focus on whether this journal complements or competes with existing titles.[5]

Once a decision is made to go forward, the Commissioning/ Acquisitions Editor will gather a team together to evaluate all aspects of

[2]  Ideally, the agreement should be signed in time to allow timely marketing of the change in publisher and upcoming subscription prices in the summer, prior to the first renewal efforts. Some RFPs have been declined because the time from contract signing to publication of the first issue was deemed too short.

[3]  See Table 8.7 and the related discussion of financial projections in Chapter 8, Journal finances.

[4]  What is a deal-breaker for one publisher may not be for another. Some publishing houses may decline RFPs requesting only selected publishing services which the publisher itself outsources (e.g., composition, printing, online hosting, etc.) and for which the publisher may not want to act simply as a broker. In other instances, the RFP may require the publisher to guarantee unrealistic growth projections, or the society may require an unacceptably low overhead figure for profit share arrangements.

[5]  Of particular concern is whether the competing titles in the current list are being published for another society, which may consider the journal under review as a significant rival for authors and/or subscribers (and which may even have included a "non-compete" clause in its contract with the publisher).

the RFP, to do independent research on the title (including obtaining outside reviews), to identify and request any further information needed from the society,[6] and to develop better estimates of direct and indirect costs. The goal is ultimately to craft an offer that is attractive to the society (both editorially and financially) as well as acceptable to the publisher, and which addresses all the requirements in the RFP. Larger publishers will have their own internal protocols for formation of this team and what needs to appear in the proposal (and possibly even basic blocks of copy to insert as needed), as well as a formal review and approval process for the proposed offer to the society.

Several points need to be considered and potentially included in the proposal when crafting an offer to a society:

- *Model for financial return to the society*. In the past, both surplus/profit share and royalty models (discussed in Chapter 8, Journal finances) were equally acceptable options. However, in recent years, societies have looked for a more stable and easily forecast return and there appears to be a preference for the royalty model. A guaranteed minimum return to the society can be included with either option (although it may be more risky to the publisher in the surplus/profit share model).
- *Timing of payments to the society*. If the financial return to a society is large, it may be desirable to provide an advance payment during the year; this, of course, reduces some of the cash-flow benefits of the journal to the publisher.
- *Member subscription rates*. While societies like low member rates, the publisher would want these rates to cover at a minimum the incremental cost of servicing the member subscriber, and preferably also to cover the costs of production. How much more financial return needs to be derived from member subscriptions depends on the return derived from other classes of subscriptions as well as from subsidiary income. If the expense of member subscriptions outweighs the society's revenue from the journal (so that the society ends up paying the publisher), the publisher may need to remind the society officers about the value of these subscriptions as a member benefit.

---

[6] Even with the most comprehensive RFP prepared by an experienced consultant, publishers will have further questions and some data may be missing or unavailable. To ensure a level playing field, many Search Committees will consolidate questions from the various publishers and provide a common response to all the potential bidders.

- *What a member subscription entails.* Ideally, a publisher would want all members of the society to receive a subscription as part of their dues, in order to improve revenue and provide a larger circulation base to advertisers. However, some societies, in an effort to keep dues low, will provide online access to all members but make the print subscription an optional add-on to membership dues.
- *Member access to the online edition.* While the society can provide regular updates of member data to authenticate members' online access on the publisher's platform, it may be advisable for the publisher to offer the society direct access to the online edition via a gateway from the members-only area of the society website. This helps reinforce the society's brand with its members and gives immediate online access to new members, without having to wait while their details are input into the publisher's access control system.
- *Timing of member subscription payments.* Full payment to the publisher at the start of the year may be difficult for the society, particularly if the "membership year" is not in sync with the "journal volume" year (or if the society allows members to join/renew at any time). The publisher may offer an installment plan (for example, invoicing the society for a pro rata percentage of member subscriptions on publication of each issue); while such deferred payments are less attractive from the point of view of the publisher's cash flow, they do benefit that of the society. If the projected royalty or surplus share due to the society is larger than the member subscription payment due from the society, the publisher may even offer to deduct the member subscriptions from the royalty or surplus share payment when this becomes payable.
- *Additional services for the society.* The publisher may offer support services to the society such as creation/maintenance of a society website, creation of an online subject portal, publication of conference proceedings, or dues collection and renewal services. Such offers may be attractive to societies that rely heavily on volunteers to manage the society. However, when tendering to a society with paid professional management staff, care should be taken in making such offers, so as not to be viewed as a threat by existing staff – bear in mind that they may have a voice in the decision process.
- *Length of initial contract.* An initial term of four or more years is desirable. An initial term of three years or less would make it difficult for the society properly to evaluate the publisher's performance before any

notice would need to be given if an alternative publisher were to be sought.

- *Transition expenses and signing bonus.* Competition for some society-owned titles can be fierce; some publishers will offer an up-front payment on contract signing to sweeten the deal. In the commercial sector, this is referred to as a "signing bonus"; in the not-for-profit sector it may be referred to as a one-time payment to cover transition expenses.
- *Transition strategy.* It is often useful to include a transition strategy and timeline in the proposal, both to convey a positive approach and to impress on the society the need to pay attention to this part of the process.
- *The RFP process as a negotiating strategy.* Be aware that in some cases a society will engage in an RFP process with no intent to shift the journal, but simply as a negotiating strategy to improve the terms with its current publishing partner.

### Preparing the proposal

While many departments will submit copy for the proposal, the Commissioning/Acquisitions Editor is responsible for consolidating all the material into one cohesive whole, arranging the material in the order and format specified in the RFP, and incorporating those elements required by the publisher.

A common proposal structure is to start with a one-page "Executive Summary" highlighting the salient points of the proposal, to follow it with the body of the proposal (twenty to thirty pages) containing an in-depth analysis of the offer and why the publisher is the best partner for the society, and to close with a series of appendices providing more detail on various aspects (e.g., detailed marketing plans, online feature sets, transition timetable, etc.). A title page and table of contents should also be included to help the reader navigate the proposal. Sample print issues and marketing pieces are often included with the proposal, as well as guest access passwords to the publisher's online platform and any related products.

How and in what order to present the information in the proposal may be stipulated in the RFP. It is important to identify what points are most important to the society (financial return, state-of-the-art online platform, marketing) and to tailor the text of the presentation to emphasize those points.

Once drafted, the various sections should be reviewed by staff in the respective departments and the proposal should also be given to someone other than the Commissioning/Acquisitions Editor both for a thorough proofreading and to check that all issues stipulated in the RFP have been addressed and the requested format followed.[7] If possible, the Commissioning/Acquisitions Editor should plan to deliver the finished proposal a few days ahead of the deadline (and confirm that it has been received).

### After the proposal has been submitted

The RFP should include a date by which the publisher will be advised if it has made the short list. In some instances, the society may ask for clarification or revision of certain points before this date (this sometimes becomes a process of matching points from the other bidders); in others, these requests will only be made of those on the short list.

Those on the short list will be asked to make a formal presentation to the Search Committee. How many people may join the Commissioning/Acquisitions Editor at the presentation, how much time will be allotted for the presentation and questions, and the order of presentations by the various publishers are determined by the Committee. Opinions vary as to whether it is better to be first up or last (but it is agreed that the slot right after lunch is not optimal).

## Negotiating a contract and managing the transition

Once the society has made its decision and final terms are agreed, these terms must be put into the precise language of a formal contract. For the partnership to be effective, the contract must be clear, specific, and strike a proper balance between the parties' obligations and responsibilities. A number of publishers have developed internal contract templates with preferred wording for a variety of options. Table 10.1 offers an annotated checklist of terms appropriate for a contract to publish a

---

[7] Given the propensity to recycle text from one proposal to another, this final proofreading should take particular care to ensure that the journal and society name are correct throughout the proposal and that any references (e.g., to the name of the discipline) are appropriate.

**Table 10.1** *Terms that should be included in a publishing contract between a publisher and a society for a subscription-based journal*

| | |
|---|---|
| **Names of the parties** | |
| **Name of publication** | |
| **Ownership of the publication** | title, copyright, mailing lists, electronic files, etc. |
| **Editorial scope of publication** | |
| **Publishing rights granted** | all – print, electronic, and any medium yet to be discovered |
| **Effective date of agreement** | first issue to be published by new publisher |
| **End date of agreement** | calendar date or final issue (volume and number) |
| **Practical aspects of publication** | number of volumes per year<br>number of pages/articles per volume<br>number of issues per volume<br>what counts as a page/article (include front matter and indexes, exclude advertising)<br>format of print edition<br>format of online edition<br>whether supplements are planned<br>schedule for discussing changes<br>who has final say on changes<br>inclusion in publisher's online platform |
| **Subscription rate setting** | when rates must be agreed |
| **Member copies/ subscription rate setting** | mechanism for proposal and approval; usually society has ultimate say<br>what a member subscription entails (print, online, or both) and whether it is compulsory or optional |
| **Nonmember subscription rate setting** | mechanism for proposal and approval; final approval of nonmember rates may rest with either publisher or society |
| **Payment of member copies/subscriptions** | schedule and terms |
| **Maintenance of subscriber lists** | who maintains them (both member and nonmember lists)<br>who renews them<br>who collects dues<br>postal authority requirements<br>delivery schedule for any lists maintained by the society |
| **Transfer of subscriber lists** | timing of transfer of prior subscriber lists and circulation data |
| **Transfer of funds** | method for transfer of moneys collected by prior publisher for upcoming volume |

**Table 10.1** (*cont.*)

| | |
|---|---|
| **Other fees/prices** | who sets and approves these prices |
| **Back issues** | transfer of printed stock<br>ownership of stock on termination<br>handling of claims for issues published before contract is signed (or after it is terminated) |
| **Advertising** | handled by publisher<br>approval process for adverts (content and positioning) |
| **Marketing** | handled by publisher<br>schedule for review with society |
| **Trademarks and logos** | publisher seeks right to use society marks in marketing journal<br>society does not have right to use publisher's logo or other marks |
| **Consortia and bundles** | inclusion of journal in bundled sales of publisher's list to consortia and single institutions |
| **Supplements** | terms of acceptance, pricing, financial return to society |
| **Color printing** | whether authors pay incremental costs for color illustrations in the print edition |
| **Page charge, extra page charge** | whether authors pay a charge per page, or for pages above a given number; mechanism for future adjustment |
| **Appointment of Editor** | usually appointed by society in consultation with publisher; specify term of office |
| **Editorial Board** | note size of Board and terms of office of members<br>Editor to nominate members<br>approval process for Editorial Board members |
| **Duties of the Editor** | solicitation of manuscripts<br>peer review of manuscripts<br>collection of signed Copyright Transfer/License to Publish forms<br>timely delivery of accepted manuscripts to publisher<br>responsibility to accept no more papers than can be accommodated within the page budget<br>consultative role in marketing |
| **Duties of the publisher** | copy-edit and "compose" papers<br>author proofing and correction cycle<br>print publication, distribution, and warehousing<br>online publication and customer support<br>marketing and sales functions |
| **Support for Editorial office** | outright annual office support payment |

**Table 10.1** (*cont.*)

| | |
|---|---|
| | support for Editorial office staff salary (may be a fraction of a full-time employee for a small journal) |
| | reimbursable office expense support (may specify limit on annual amount) |
| | start–up payments |
| | schedule for payments |
| | annual review, mechanism for increase or schedule for discussion of adjustments |
| | if adjusted for inflation, specify source of inflation adjustment figure |
| **Compensation for the Editor** | honorarium (i.e., fee) or royalty |
| | start–up payments |
| | schedule for payments |
| | annual review, mechanism for annual increase or schedule for discussion of adjustments |
| **Return to the society** | |
| *if* **royalty** | specify on which revenue streams royalty is calculated |
| | how share of income from bundles and consortia packages is allocated |
| | royalty percentage for each stream |
| | specify that royalties are on net cash received, after deduction of discounts and commissions |
| *if* **surplus/profit share** | specify on which revenue streams surplus/profit is calculated |
| | how share of income from consortia packages is allocated |
| | what costs are included |
| | treatment of advertising and other commissions |
| | overhead percentage and method of calculation |
| | percentage share to society |
| | what happens in case of loss in one year (e.g., carry loss forward to next year) |
| | what happens if cumulative loss at end of contractual term |
| *both* **royalty and surplus/profit share** | specify any revenue guaranteed to the society (and mechanism for annual adjustment, if any) |
| | any deductions applicable (e.g., in some contracts, member subscription fees are deducted from the money due to the society) |
| | provide sample format for royalty/profit share statement in appendix to contract |
| | specify when payment of financial return is due (tied to specific time period after close of calendar year or publication of last issue, whichever is later) |

**Table 10.1** (*cont.*)

| | |
|---|---|
| | specify when any estimates of financial return are due<br>specify when any advances are due (and basis of calculation) |
| **Society services** | specify, if any (e.g., creation and maintenance of a society web page, creation of a subject portal, cross-promotion of society to related journals in publisher's list, conference organization and/or publication, membership list management/dues collection) |
| **Handling of copyright and permissions** | who obtains signed Copyright Transfer/License to Publish agreements from authors and where these are stored<br>who registers copyright in journal (if applicable)<br>what rights are reserved to authors<br>who handles permissions requests for the journal and how any income is distributed<br>authority for the publisher to take legal action in the event that the society's copyright in the journal is infringed |
| **Other intellectual property issues** | use of society name, logo, and trademarks (if any) in marketing the journal |
| **Warranty and indemnification** | guarantees that each party can enter into the agreement, will not violate copyright or publish libelous or defamatory material, etc.<br>mutual "hold harmless" clauses based on whose action led to the breach of a warranty<br>limitations on liability |
| **Audit** | society has right to audit journal accounts<br>what can be audited<br>when (and notice period)<br>who pays for audit if errors are discovered/not discovered |
| **Notice** | who receives official noneditorial notices at both publisher and society |
| **Noncompete clause** | publisher not to launch competing title during term of contract or within X years of termination of agreement |
| **E-edition on termination** | society as owner responsible for providing continued access to online edition for existing customers<br>publisher to have royalty-free license to provide continued access for customers<br>publisher to provide society/new publisher with set of files |
| **Transition process** | reference suitable industry guidelines (e.g., Transfer Code of Practice) |

**Table 10.1** (*cont.*)

| | |
|---|---|
| **Dispute resolution** | preference for arbitration in lieu of court (note where dispute is to be arbitrated and under what rules) |
| **Renewal terms** | period of notice to be given (on either side) of intent to renew/terminate/renegotiate |
| | term for an automatic renewal |
| **Appendix** | sample format for financial report to society |
| | sample Copyright Transfer or License to Publish agreement |

(subscription-based) society-owned journal – it can easily be adapted if an OA model is preferred by the society. A sample format for the financial report to the society should be included as an appendix, along with a copy of the publisher's standard authors' Copyright Transfer agreement or License to Publish. (Table 10.2 shows a sample profit share statement for Journal D from Table 8.5 in Chapter 8, Journal finances.)

Even though an agreement may be reached in principle, it has been known for this to break down in the course of contract negotiations, and for the journal to end up being assigned to the runner-up. Thus, it is vitally important to maintain a level of flexibility in the wording of contract terms, and to be aware of which terms are negotiable for the publisher and which are not. Difficulties sometimes arise in crafting the formal contractual language regarding the timing and/or ultimate responsibility for annual price setting, the terminology used in warranty and indemnity clauses, or, with international publishers, the jurisdiction and laws under which any disputes would be adjudicated. Having alternative versions of potentially problematic clauses ready at hand will help to smooth the process.

It is essential to specify within the contract clear channels of communication between the society and the publisher, with regularly scheduled meetings to review the journal, identify problems, and arrive at solutions without the need for a formal conflict resolution process. It is also important to have a clear delineation of responsibilities and actions in the event the agreement is not renewed (a prenuptial agreement, so to speak).

At the same time as negotiating the contract, the Commissioning/ Acquisitions Editor should finalize a transition plan and timetable and let

**Table 10.2**  *Sample profit share report format for a society-owned subscription-based journal*

| Revenue | $ |
| --- | --- |
| Net subscription sales | 275,000 |
| Allocation of incremental consortia income | 10,000 |
| Net advertising sales | 8,000 |
| Offprints and reprint sales | 800 |
| Single-issue and back-volume sales | 500 |
| Pay–per-view article downloads | 1,000 |
| Rights and permissions | 7,500 |
| Other revenues | 200 |
| **Total income** | **303,000** |
| **Expenses** | |
| Editorial office support | 25,500 |
| Prepress, printing, paper, and offprints | 89,700 |
| Postage and distribution costs | 25,520 |
| Online mounting | 4,000 |
| Direct marketing | 6,000 |
| Operating expense allocation (10% of income) | 30,300 |
| **Total expenses** | **181,020** |
| Surplus | 121,980 |
| 65% of surplus to society | 79,287 |

the society know what will be needed from it and when. The goal of the transition plan is to alert the market to the change in publishing arrangements, to minimize disruption of service to authors and subscribers (both print and online), and to continue publication on schedule. Among the important issues to address are transfer of subscriber lists, alerting of subscription agents for renewals, handling of work in progress (including any shifts in third-party vendors), transfer of print stock (if any), and, most important, the transfer/conversion of the online edition to the publisher's platform (including alerting of relevant databases so that link resolvers will point to the correct location) and activation of access for existing customers. The UKSG has developed a Transfer Code of Practice (UKSG, 2008) to provide consistent guidelines to help publishers ensure that journal content remains easily accessible by librarians and readers when there is a transfer from one publisher to another.[8]

While the parties may meet, and aspects of the transition plan may be implemented, before the contract negotiations are complete, the publisher will generally hold off making any announcements or significant expenditures until the contract is signed. Refer to the sections regarding launching a journal or integrating an acquisition in Chapter 2, Managing journals, for more details on the transition process.

## Managing the society journal

While managing a society journal is similar in many ways to managing a journal owned by the publisher, it is important to remember that the publisher is not the owner and that the society will have the ultimate decision on many aspects of the journal which would be decided in-house for a wholly owned journal. For this reason, it is important for the Commissioning/Acquisitions Editor to establish and maintain regular channels of communication with the journal's Editorial office, the society, and its management staff (if any). Such communication is essential in order to collaborate in addressing editorial issues, marketing plans, price setting, product development, and a host of other issues. All of the publisher's staff who are working on the journal need to alert the Commissioning Editor as soon as possible of any problems that may arise, so that they can be dealt with proactively and not become a cause for discontent between the society and the publisher.

Some societies will default to the journal Editor as the primary point of contact with the Commissioning/Acquisitions Editor, given that the journal Editor's term of office may be longer than that of the society officers. This can lead to problems if the Editor does not pass on relevant information to the society or its management staff, or if a rift develops between the society/staff and the Editor.

While most of the contact will be of an editorial nature, there are various business- and policy-related matters that are better addressed to a representative of the society other than the journal Editor, especially if these are to do with the performance of the Editorial office. While these

---

[8] Also useful are the Guidance Notes at the ALPSP website (www.alpsp.org) which are available to staff of ALPSP member companies.

issues can be addressed to the President or a designated member of the Board, it is particularly helpful if the society establishes a Publication Committee, of which the Editor would be an *ex officio* member (but not the Chair). The Chair should be a society member with publishing experience who can offer informed advice to the officers and provide a continuing point of contact – a kind of "institutional memory" – between the society and the publisher as officers change. (Part of this role may be assigned to management staff in larger societies.)

## The renewal process

If the communication channels have been open and well maintained, the Commissioning/Acquisitions Editor should be well aware of what to expect when the deadline draws near for the society to give notice of a desire to renew, renegotiate, or terminate the agreement. Ideally, relations are good and the contract is renewed for an additional term. Even if the contract provides for automatic renewal, it is important to be aware of this deadline, and to thank the society for the renewal.

If the society serves a notice of intent to renegotiate, negotiations often move smoothly to a quick resolution. If negotiations fail, however, the society will put the journal out for tender and the current publisher may or may not be invited to bid.

In some publishing agreements with societies, publishers have inserted a clause guaranteeing them a right to match any successful competing offer if the contract were to be terminated. The advisability of such a clause is debatable. Invoking it will preserve the partnership (and revenue) for an additional term, but against the society's will. It is akin to a "shotgun marriage" and may do more harm than good in the long run.

Note that the notice arrangement is bilateral; if the publisher decides not to renew the agreement, it must provide the same period of notice to the society.

## Termination and transition

If a notice of termination is given and the publisher does not win back the publishing rights to the title through the RFP process, it will need to engage in the reverse of the transition process noted above. While it is the ultimate responsibility of the society, as owner of the journal, to provide continuing online access to the electronic edition, online subscribers expect the publisher that sold them the subscription/license to bear this responsibility. Thus, it is important that the original agreement includes a license for the publisher to continue to provide access to the journal content it has published for the society for a suitable period after termination, until the content is available from the new publisher and customers have had time to redirect their access to the new location.

Societies leave publishers for a variety of reasons. It is important to manage the departure of the society and the transition of the journal to its new publisher as professionally and expeditiously as possible. A Commissioning/Acquisitions Editor may be in the position of acquiring another society journal from the new publisher in the future. Other societies may contact the journal Editor and society officers to ask about the relationship with their former publisher when considering whom to invite to bid on an RFP. And while it is rare for a society to return to a publisher it has left, it is not unknown for the current publisher of a society journal to acquire or merge with the journal's former publisher.

## Conclusion

Publishing a journal on behalf of a society is often a mutually beneficial arrangement. Regular and efficient communication between the society and publisher, and an attitude of mutual respect, are essential for the relationship to succeed.

### REFERENCES

Morris, Sally, 2007, Mapping the journal landscape: how much do we know?, *Learned Publishing* 20: 299–310 (http://dx.doi.org/10.1087/095315107X239654)
UKSG, 2008, The Transfer Code of Practice, Version 2.0 (www.uksg.org/transfer)

### FURTHER READING

Ashman, Pete, 2009, What societies want from a publishing partner, *Learned Publishing* 22: 209–19 (http://dx.doi.org/10.1087/2009307)
Association for Learning Technology, 2011, *Journal tendering for societies: a brief guide* (http://repository.alt.ac.uk/887/)
Bull, David, and Susan Hezlet, 2000, What do societies and publishers want from publishing partnerships?, *Learned Publishing* 13: 205–7 (http://dx.doi.org/10.1087/09531510050162039)

Campbell, Robert, 2010, Publishing partnerships can help society journals, *Research Information* April–May (www.researchinformation.info/features/feature.php?feature_id=265)

International Council for Science, 1999, *Guidelines for scientific publishing*, Paris, ICSU Press (www.bodley.ox.ac.uk/icsu/guidelines.pdf)

International Society of Addiction Journal Editors, 2010, *Proposal for journal agreements with publishers and sponsoring organizations*, project proposal (www.parint.org/isajewebsite/Journal%20Agreement.doc)

Singleton, Alan, 1981, Learned societies and journal publishing, *Journal of Information Science* 3: 211–26 (http://dx.doi.org/10.1177/016555158100300502)

Ware, Mark, 2008, Choosing a publishing partner: advice for societies and associations, *Learned Publishing* 21: 22–8 (http://dx.doi.org/10.1087/095315108X248329)

# 11 Copyright and other legal aspects

While copyright provides the legal underpinning for much of what journal publishing does, it is far from being the only area of law which is relevant. Contract law governs the whole range of agreements, from full-blown contracts (e.g., between a publisher and a journal's owner, or between the publisher/owner and the Editor) to agreements with individual authors; licenses (whether for a whole country, or for an individual user), and subsidiary agreements with third parties, are contracts too. The issue of libel may arise (for example, in book reviews). Another area of law which is increasingly important, as personal records of authors, reviewers, and others are generally maintained on computer, is that of data protection.

All of these areas of the law are governed by national laws, which vary somewhat (although within the European Community they operate under the overall umbrella of European law); in this chapter we aim to bring out the main differences between US and UK/European law. Further detail of the national differences can be found at http://portal. unesco.org/culture.

## Copyright

### What is copyright?

Copyright is what it says – the right to copy. It provides the copyright owner with the exclusive right to make copies, and to permit (or not to permit) others to make copies (in whatever medium) and to "communicate them to the public" – i.e., to distribute or publish them. It also covers the right of rental or lending; performing, showing, or playing the work in public; including in a collection (e.g., an anthology); and making an adaptation (e.g., a translation). The owner of the copyright is initially the only person who is able to grant others the right to make copies, and this right may be granted on whatever terms are agreed between the parties.

He or she may, however, in turn license another person or organization – either exclusively or (less commonly) on a nonexclusive basis – to grant such rights. Only the copyright owner has the right to take action against infringement of that copyright – unless the owner has licensed someone else to act on his or her behalf.[1]

Copyright arises automatically when an original literary, dramatic, or artistic work (or, indeed, a film, sound recording, etc.) is set down in permanent form; no special steps need to be taken in order to obtain copyright protection (registration of copyright used to be required in the USA; although this is technically no longer necessary, it is still wise to register, as it will allow statutory damages to be awarded in any US copyright enforcement action).

Copyright protects the expression of an idea – in the case of a "literary work" (which doesn't have to have any literary merit!), the words in which it is recorded – and not the idea itself. In order to protect an actual idea (such as an invention), the creator usually obtains a patent.

In the case of journals, the most fundamental copyright is that of the author. In the USA, UK, and related legal systems he or she may either assign the copyright to the publisher or journal owner, or retain copyright but grant a license to publish (which is also a form of contract). However, in a number of European countries copyright cannot be sold or given away by the original owner (the implications for journal publishers are discussed below under "Contracts"). If the author is an employee and is writing as part of his or her employment, the copyright will generally belong to the employer. If he or she is a government employee, the situation is slightly different: in the USA, the work will not be subject to copyright within the United States, whereas in the UK and related legislations it will belong to the Crown, and special copyright arrangements will apply. (Copyright in government employees' work is discussed more fully below, under "Contracts.")

However, the author's is not the only copyright to consider. The journal Editor has copyright in his or her original contributions; the publisher or other owner of the journal holds copyright in the complete

---

[1] Some license agreements do provide for this right to be explicitly granted to the licensee (e.g., publisher). However, in some jurisdictions the courts would still require the author to sign a declaration and/or go through other formalities before legal action could be taken on the author's behalf.

journal (as a compilation of articles and other literary elements, as well as illustrative material); and, under UK law, the publisher even owns the copyright in the physical appearance of the printed page (the so-called "typographical copyright" – see below). Copyright in quoted extracts, illustrations, or republished articles may have a different owner, from whom permission needs to be obtained.

### The legal basis of copyright

The first fully fledged copyright law in the world was the British "Statute of Anne" in 1710, in which for the first time authors, rather than printers, were granted a fourteen-year monopoly on the reproduction of their works (Copyright Act, 1710). Other countries followed suit – the US, for example, in 1790, France in 1793, but Germany not until 1837.

Over the years, there have been a number of international treaties and agreements which have attempted to lay down a common basis for copyright. There was the Berne Convention in 1886; the Universal Copyright Convention in 1952; the Paris Act (updating Berne) in 1971, amended 1979; more than twenty other World Intellectual Property Organization (WIPO) Treaties including the 1996 Internet Treaties; and the Trade-Related Aspects of Intellectual Property Rights (TRIPS) Agreement in 1994.

However, national copyright laws – even within the European Community – are far from standardized. In the US, copyright is treated as a kind of property or economic right, which can be transferred by the original owner to others with or without payment; this used also to be the case in UK law. In most of Europe, however, it is seen primarily as a personal right of the author, as the various names for copyright (e.g., "droit d'auteur," "Urheberrecht," "derechos de autor," "auteursrecht," "diritto di autore") make clear. Since revising its legislation to come into line with the rest of Europe, the UK has had a somewhat uneasy hybrid between the two different concepts.

The US Copyright Act of 1976 was updated by the US Digital Millennium Copyright Act in 1998; this was one of the earliest attempts to bring copyright in line with the digital age. Under US law, copyright can be (but no longer has to be) registered with the Copyright Office. The author is usually the owner of the copyright; "work made for hire," which includes work prepared by an employee in the course of employment, and work specially ordered or commissioned in writing, is the copyright of the employer. Exceptions for educational uses are broader than in the UK (see below). Authors do not have "moral rights" under US copyright law (though these rights may be protected under other legislation, such as trademarks, and authors' reputation may be protected under state law).

The UK Copyright Designs and Patents Act of 1988 was updated by the UK Copyright Regulations in 2003. In the UK, there is no provision for copyright registration. As in the US, the author is usually the copyright owner. The employer owns copyright in a work created by an employee "in the course of employment." Exceptions for educational and other uses are less broad than in the US. Moral rights for authors are included.

The EU Copyright Directive 2001 represented a significant step towards recognizing the realities of the digital world within copyright legislation. It introduced two new copyrights – for online services, and for interactive on-demand transmissions. For the first, it updated the idea of publication (or, if you like, merged it with that of broadcasting) so that it could include electronic communication to the public. And for the second, it introduced a new right of "making available" (sometimes called the "access right" or "on-demand availability" right); it covers the provision of access for members of the public, who may access the work at a time and place they choose.

The Directive also made a significant change to copyright exceptions (see below); it included only one exception which every country must include in its laws – that allowing incidental copying (e.g., temporary reproduction as part of a technological process, such as caching). However, there was a list of twenty optional exceptions, broadly reflecting similar exceptions in different countries' preelectronic copyright laws; individual countries were entitled to adopt any from this list (but no others) which mirrored existing rights in their own legislation, but not to introduce any new rights or to extend them to nonprint materials. Thus, far from standardizing copyright law within Europe, the result is that the laws could still be different in every member state. The Directive also made it unlawful to circumvent technical protection measures, or to remove digital rights management information (such as the details of the copyright owner or of the actions which are/are not permitted).

The concept of copyright, enshrined in the Berne Convention, includes two key rights which are described as "moral rights" (though that's a slightly misleading phrase) – like copyright, they last for seventy years after the author's death. The two main "moral rights" are that of "paternity" – the right to be credited as the author (including joint authors) – and that of "integrity" – the right to object to "derogatory treatment" (i.e., detrimental changes which would negatively impact the author's reputation). There is also the right to object to false attribution – being named as the author when one is not (this lasts for twenty years after the death of the person to whom the work is falsely attributed).

This is what the Berne Convention says:

Independently of the author's economic rights, and even after the transfer of the said rights, the author shall have the right to claim authorship of the work and to object to any distortion, mutilation or other modification of, or other derogatory action in relation to, the said work, which would be prejudicial to his honor or reputation. (Article 6bis, Berne Convention)

However, the Berne Convention's approach has not been uniformly incorporated in national copyright legislation; in US copyright law moral rights are not recognized (except, in a very limited way, for visual art). The 2001 European Union Copyright Directive, which does reflect it, has been enshrined in law in all member countries – the last to implement it was Germany, in 2007; the UK had, in fact, previously adopted the idea of moral rights in the 1988 Copyright, Designs and Patents Act. Canada adopted moral rights even earlier, in 1931 – it was the first common law country to do so; moral rights have also been adopted in many developing countries.

The right of paternity – the right to be named as the author – only applies (in the UK) if it has been actively asserted by the author; this is usually done as part of the copyright notice. The other moral rights can be waived by contract in the UK, though not elsewhere in Europe. If one author waives his or her moral rights, that does not automatically waive the rights of any co-authors.

However, these "moral rights" do not generally apply to authors writing in the course of their employment (they do have the right of integrity, but only if they have been identified by name). Neither do they apply to publication in newspapers, encyclopedias, etc. It is not entirely clear whether or not they actually apply to articles in a journal, though it may be safest to assume that they do.

Copyright starts as soon as the "work" is recorded in permanent form, and the period for which it lasts is set down in law. It lasts for seventy years from the end of the year in which the author died (even if the author is not the copyright owner).[2] After his or her death, copyright can be exercised by the author's heirs and successors; unfortunately it is not always easy to ascertain when the author died, or to trace his or her heirs. It is not essential (though it is helpful to subsequent users) to include a copyright notice on the published work – this used to be a requirement under US law, but is no longer.

After the legal term of copyright has expired, anyone can republish the work without seeking the original owner's permission; what may not, however, be possible is simply to reproduce the original printed page. This is because (under UK law), the "typographic copyright" is itself protected for twenty-five years from the date of publication (of that particular edition), and belongs to the publisher rather than the author. It is not entirely clear whether this has any bearing on an electronic edition, where the appearance of the page (unless it is a PDF) may be changed by the user at will.

### The copyright notice

A journal should include a copyright notice, normally on its title verso page (or the electronic equivalent) though sometimes on the title page, masthead, or table of contents page. The copyright in the journal as a whole is held by its publisher (or, in some cases, sponsoring society), while that in individual articles may belong to the publisher, the author, or the author's employer – more detail is given below. A typical example is shown in Box 11.1.

In addition, each individual article should carry its own copyright notice (i.e., "Copyright © [copyright owner] [year]") in both print and electronic formats; even when the publisher (or other journal owner) holds copyright in all articles, they will be accessed and quite possibly printed out individually.

### Copyright exceptions

There are, however, certain circumstances in which the copyright owner cannot prevent someone else from making copies of his or her work; these

---

[2] Patents, by contrast, only last for a maximum of twenty years, if renewal fees are paid; at the other extreme, trademarks can be renewed for ever, again on payment of fees.

**Box 11.1** Journal copyright notice

are known as "copyright exceptions." They are not actually a right to do certain things; rather, they are a defense against the accusation of infringing copyright. These exceptions differ slightly from country to country; there are also differences between what is allowed to individuals and to libraries. However, under the Berne Convention, all exceptions have to pass what has become known as the "Berne 3-Step Test": permitted only

- in certain **special cases**
- which **do not conflict with the normal exploitation** of the work
- and **do not unreasonably prejudice the legitimate interests of the rightsholder**

In the US, there is an exception (under S107 of the 1976 Copyright Act) for "fair use" (provided the above conditions are met). There are no precise rules in the US Act about how much may be copied. It depends on four factors: the purpose and character of the use (including whether it is for nonprofit or commercial purposes), the nature of the work, the amount and substantiality of the extract, and the effect on the market. Copies may be made for purposes such as criticism and comment; news reporting; teaching (including multiple copies for classroom use, though not assembling entire course anthologies for sale to students); and for scholarship or research. Agreement was reached as early as the 1930s on guidelines for classroom use, and these fed into the 1976 legislation (www. copyright.com/Services/copyrightoncampus/content/index_class.html). Some further common ground was reached by the National Commission on New Technological Uses of Copyright Works, or CONTU, in 1978 (www.cni.org/docs/infopols/CONTU.html); one of its most useful outcomes was the "Rule of Five."[3] However, an attempt to agree on guidelines between librarians and publishers (the Conference on Fair Use, or CONFU) was abandoned without agreement in 1991.

Section 108 of the Copyright Act also makes limited provisions for libraries and archives to make copies for preservation, replacement, and patron access; in 2005/6, a group of publishers and university librarians worked together to prepare recommendations for how the law could adequately take account of digital realities (see www. section108.gov).

In the UK and Canada, there is a similar – but not identical – provision for "fair dealing." This provides a defense against claims of copyright infringement if the copies are made, within the limits of "fairness," for a list of specific purposes only: criticism or review, reporting of current events, and (noncommercial) research or private study. There are no specific guidelines as to how much of a work may be copied – it must be "insubstantial" bearing in mind both its extent and its importance. In addition, educational institutions are permitted to make copies of up to 1% of a work per three-monthly period (the Copyright Licensing Agency's licenses for schools and universities provide for much more extensive copying, in return for a fee). It is also permissible to make a copy in a format accessible to a visually impaired person, but only in the absence of a licensing scheme – the CLA now offers a (free) Visually Impaired Persons license.

UK copyright law also provides for something called "Library Privilege," entitling certain not-for-profit libraries and archives to make paper copies of journal articles for so-called "interlibrary loan" (though of

---

[3] This states that, for articles published up to five years from the date of request, a library may not request more than five articles from a particular journal in a given year, nor may it fulfill more than five requests for articles from a given title that it holds; more than this was considered to amount to substituting for a subscription.

course they are not really loaned at all, but retained by the requester) provided the user signs a declaration stating that the copy is for private, noncommercial use only. Libraries are also allowed to make copies for preservation purposes.

In the UK, provision of these copies has largely been centralized through the British Library's "Document Supply Centre." Library Privilege copies must be ordered through a library, and the requester must sign a form confirming that the purpose is noncommercial. In all other cases, items can be ordered online, for a fee; supply to all commercial customers is governed by a CLA license, and (from 2012) that to noncommercial customers outside the UK by an explicit license from the publisher. (See www.bl.uk/reshelp/atyourdesk/docsupply/industryspecificinfo/publisher/index.html.)

In Germany, a consortium of university libraries set up subito, a Europe-wide document supply service which is similar to that offered by the British Library. Some aspects of subito's service clearly went beyond what was permitted by copyright law in not obtaining permission from, or making payment to, publishers. After protracted negotiations, spearheaded by the STM Association, a resolution was reached in 2006, whereby any publisher willing to do so can sign an agreement with subito, allowing it to distribute copies under certain conditions; while the publisher sets its own fees for distribution direct to end-users, the fees for delivery via libraries are fixed.

As mentioned above, the 2001 EU Copyright Directive did not have the effect of standardizing copyright exceptions throughout the member states. However, it did narrow down the exception for research, so that commercial research was explicitly excluded. This has helped publishers in clarifying the terms under which such services as the British Library or subito can legally operate.

The abstracts of journal articles provided either by the author or by the publisher are a special case. While in other countries they are covered in exactly the same way as any other content, there is a curious twist in the UK. The 1988 Copyright, Designs and Patents Act introduced a last-minute change providing that abstracts of scientific and technical (but not medical or other) articles could be freely copied unless there was a suitable licensing scheme in place. However, despite interesting philosophical debates about whether or not readers are happy to substitute abstracts for the full articles, publishers have mostly come to the view that – especially online – the abstract is the key "hook" that draws potential readers to identify an article as being of interest. Thus, abstracts (as well as all the associated bibliographic information – "metadata") are generally made freely available, whether or not the full article is open access – the Open Knowledge Foundation provides a set of "Principles on Open Bibliographic Data" (http://openbiblio.net/principles/). They are also opened up to as many relevant search engines as possible.[4] (See Chapter 6, Marketing and sales, for more on this.)

One of the problems with the existing laws on fair use/fair dealing is that they were not really devised for the digital age, where making and distributing huge numbers of copies can be done with a key-stroke. Many publishers have attempted to address this uncertainty (as well as the confusion caused by national variations) by being specific in their licenses. For example, many licenses explicitly permit distribution within the licensed institution of copies of journal articles (and other materials) for the purposes of classroom teaching, including course packs and, frequently, distance learning.

Licenses may also specify what may or may not be done in terms of so-called "interlibrary loan." University and other libraries would (understandably) dearly love the convenience of being able to provide copies directly from their e-journals. However, many publishers (equally understandably) do not wish to allow the systematized distribution of copies of journal articles to those who request them via other libraries. Some may either forbid it, or put an (admittedly artificial) brake on it by requiring that the article be printed out first and either faxed or sent in paper format, because of the potential impact on revenues – taken to the extreme, it could render many subscriptions unnecessary.

### Reproduction Rights Organizations (RROs)

In many countries, an organization (or organizations) has been set up to protect authors' and publishers' interests, and to collect fees due to them for uses of their copyright works in circumstances where it is not really practicable for the payments to be made direct. Although they were originally established to cope with the threat posed by photocopying,

---

[4] This is not necessarily the case when an abstracting and indexing service has created its own abstracts, rather than using those in the published journal.

many have now developed, or are developing, licenses which also cover digital uses of copyright works.

In the USA, the Copyright Clearance Center (CCC – www.copyright. com) represents both creators and publishers – indeed, its board also includes librarians. It was initially conceived as a central clearing house to handle requests and payments for interlibrary loan usage beyond that allowed under the CONTU guidelines. However, the CCC has expanded to become a comprehensive licensing agency for registered copyright holders (authors and/or publishers). It offers licenses for specified uses to both commercial and noncommercial organizations; these may be on either a repertory (single annual fee covering use of a wide range of works) or a transaction (payment per use) basis. CCC has also developed RightsLink, a "plug-in" publishers can opt to add to their online platforms to facilitate the licensing of digital rights to both individual and corporate users. Royalties collected are remitted to rightsholders after deduction of a percentage to cover operating costs.

In the UK, the Copyright Licensing Agency (CLA – www.cla.co.uk) issues licenses to a variety of organizations, including schools, universities, government departments, and businesses; certain licenses for electronic uses (such as scanning) are also in place. Income from licenses is divided between books and journals on the basis of usage surveys which are carried out regularly; authors' share is paid to them via one of the CLA's co-owners, the Authors' Licensing and Collecting Society (ALCS) – but only to authors who have registered with ALCS – and the publishers' share via the other, the Publishers Licensing Society (PLS); a smaller share is also paid out directly to artists, for illustrations, via the Design and Artists Copyright Society (DACS). Thus publishers have no need to pass on any part of their PLS payment to authors or illustrators. Negotiations over the split of journals' license income between the component organizations have relied heavily on publishers' ability to demonstrate that they "own or control" (e.g., under license) the rights in all or most of the content; this is one reason why it is essential that publishers obtain, and keep records of, their author agreements.

Similar organizations (sometimes less formally known as Collection Agencies or Collecting Societies) have been set up in many other countries – see www.ifrro.org. Reciprocal agreements exist between all the major ones, so that payments are made for copying that happens in country A of works whose copyright owners are in country B.

## Contracts

### *What are contracts?*

A contract is an agreement voluntarily entered into by two (or more) parties; in many countries, to be legally binding, it must be recorded in writing, on paper, and (manually) signed.

The essence of any contract is that something (a good, a service, or the right to do something) is provided in return for something else (the "consideration"). The consideration may be a financial payment, which could be substantial as in the case of a site license; at the other extreme, no money may change hands, but a service may be provided (e.g., the services associated with publication, including providing the peer-review infrastructure, editing, typesetting, redrawing illustrations, creating the online and printed versions, marketing, sales, archiving, and, usually, supplying printed and/or electronic copies – "offprints" – for the author's personal use).

A contract – whether an assignment of copyright or grant of license to publish, or a more substantial agreement – should be written down and signed;[5] in the case of a copyright assignment or license it must be in writing, and signed by the copyright owner (who is not necessarily the author), in order to be valid. In some countries, this still means a paper document (although many publishers accept a scanned copy sent electronically); however, in the US and many European countries, online forms with electronic signatures[6] are now legally acceptable, and others will surely follow.

Contracts formalize our relationships with a whole range of business partners in the chain of journal publishing. They can, technically, override the provisions of copyright law (such as the exceptions mentioned above), and some publishers have tried to do so (for example, by prohibiting the use of the electronic journal to fulfill interlibrary loan requests) – however, this is hardly conducive to good relations with one's customers! It is a good idea to make the language of contracts as comprehensible and undaunting as possible.

---

[5] It is worth remembering that a verbal agreement to publish may be held by the courts to be binding, even if nothing was put in writing – see the case of Malcolm vs Oxford University Press (www.5rb.com/case/Malcolm-v-Oxford-University-Press).

[6] A growing number of publishers accept e-signatures, often providing text along the following lines: "By typing my name into this field, I am confirming that I am the person whose [online submission and peer review system] account is logged into, and I understand that an electronic signature is taking place and I intend to be bound by this record."

While the agreement with the original author is fundamental, there are many other contractual relationships involved in journal publishing:

- The agreement between the Editor and the publisher and/or owner (e.g., a learned or professional society).
- The agreement between the owner (e.g., society) and the publisher.
- Permissions agreements (both inbound and outbound).
- Vendor or other third-party agreements.
- Licensing agreements with third parties.

and, one of the most important:

- E-journal licenses with customers.

### The author (or the author's employer)

#### Copyright Transfer or License to Publish?

There has been much debate about whether authors should be asked, or required, to transfer copyright in its entirety to the publisher, as opposed to granting the publisher a license to do certain things. Although, when surveyed, authors often say they prefer to retain copyright, in reality publishers experience relatively little resistance to requests to transfer it; being published in a particular journal seems to be far more important to the author. Many publishers have in any case modified their agreements so that they do allow authors, within reason, to do the things that they may want or need to do, such as placing a copy (usually a prepublication version) on a personal or institutional website, or reusing all or part of the article for classroom purposes, or in their own subsequent publications (see, for example, Morris, 2009).

If the author is an employee, writing in the course of his or her work, copyright – as mentioned above – legally belongs to the employer, so the author is not in a position to transfer it. Some universities have attempted to state in faculty's contracts of employment that copyright in their works belongs to the university, although faculty have tended to resist this. Even where this is the case, however, universities rarely prevent authors from signing agreements with journal publishers. Commercial employers, on the other hand, are often unwilling to transfer copyright; they may want to be able to use the work for their own purposes.

Governments generally will not transfer copyright in their employees' work to a publisher. For US government employees, the work is not subject to copyright at all within the US. The work is, however, subject to copyright as far as other countries are concerned; for publication in international journals, a copyright agreement with the relevant government agency, and a copyright line, will therefore still be necessary (see www.usa.gov/copyright.shtml).[7] In the UK and related legal systems, copyright in the work of government employees belongs to the Crown, and special licenses apply – these are available online (see www.nationalarchives.gov.uk/information-management/our-services/crown-copyright.htm).

A slowly growing minority of publishers do not ask for copyright transfer, and instead ask authors to sign a "License to Publish" (Cox and Cox, 2008).[8] When properly drafted, such an agreement can also provide all of the rights that both parties need (see, for example, that used for the journal *Learned Publishing* – www.alpsp.org/Ebusiness/Research Publications/LearnedPublishing/LicenceToPublish.aspx). In other cases, while initially asking for copyright transfer, a number of publishers will provide a license as an alternative, on request. Although a license may be either exclusive or nonexclusive, most publishers require exclusivity for their own commercial protection. A few publishers don't obtain any written agreement from authors; however, they then have no rights at all (except, arguably, the right to publish first).

In open access publishing, the "Creative Commons" (CC) licenses, which provide for free reuse under certain conditions, are rapidly becoming the norm (see Chapter 8, Journal finances, for more details on OA). Each CC license is available in three versions – described by CC as "lawyer-readable," "human-readable," and "machine-readable." There are four licenses (and various permutations of them) imposing different restrictions and conditions: attribution to the author as the only requirement; noncommercial use only; no derivative works; and "share alike" (reuse only permitted if the same terms are offered downstream to others) – see http://creativecommons.org. Publishers may also opt to apply such

---

[7] However, any copyright material incorporated into a work of the US government (e.g., extracts or figures reproduced from copyright works) retains its copyright status.

[8] In book publishing, exclusive licenses are in fact more common than outright transfers of copyright, particularly in trade, educational, and children's publishing.

licenses to material within an article (such as figures) which they are happy for others to reuse if duly acknowledged.

Those publishers who insist on copyright transfer argue that their job is made much more complicated, particularly with regard to uses of the work which were not envisaged at the time of the original agreement, if they do not hold the actual copyright – witness the difficulties involved in creating an online archive of a journal if copyright is held by individual authors (or their heirs). However, what makes the publisher's job really complicated is having different agreements with different authors – this makes it necessary to have a record-keeping system which can keep track of every single agreement, and to which staff can refer whenever they want, for example, to grant "downstream" rights to a third party.

Copyright is in fact a divisible intellectual property (a "bundle of rights"); its ownership can be transferred in whole or in part, but the transfer must be in writing. However, journal publishers have traditionally required a full transfer of copyright from the author and have drafted transfer agreements that are all-encompassing. If the publisher agrees that the author should continue to have certain rights after a full transfer of copyright, these rights must be explicitly granted back to the author. A license to publish, on the other hand, enables the author to grant only specific named rights to the publisher; any right not mentioned in the agreement remains with the author.

The key differences between a transfer of copyright and a license to publish are shown in Table 11.1.

Whichever form of agreement is adopted, it is important to cover all of the following:

- The publisher needs to be able to defend the copyright on the author's behalf (e.g., in case of infringement).[9]
- The publisher needs to be able to sublicense to others (e.g., for translations, permissions, or aggregations).
- The author needs to be able to self-archive a version in a repository or elsewhere – this may be a requirement of his or her institution and/or the funder of the research; the publisher should be specific about which version may be deposited, and what restrictions – if any – there are on where, when, and by whom the self-archiving may be done.

---

[9] Although, as mentioned above, this alone may not be sufficient in US courts.

**Table 11.1** *Key differences between Transfer of Copyright and License to Publish*

| Copyright Transfer | License to Publish |
| --- | --- |
| © transferred to publisher | © remains with author |
| Certain (self-archiving, reuse) rights may be granted back to author | Certain (publication) rights granted to publisher |
| | All other rights (self-archiving, reuse) remain with author |
| Must be in writing and signed by © owner | May be informal if nonexclusive – though this is inadvisable |
| Necessarily exclusive | Can be exclusive or nonexclusive |

- The author needs to be able to reuse his or her work in ways that don't compete with the original publication (e.g., for classroom purposes, or included in a book).

As mentioned earlier, despite the fact that most dealings between publishers and authors take place electronically, in some jurisdictions, the agreement between the journal author (or his or her employer) and publisher still needs to be in writing, on paper; if exclusive, it must (and even if nonexclusive, ideally it should) be signed by the copyright owner, although – unlike with book publishing contracts – most publishers do not consider it necessary that the publisher should also be a signatory. If the author or employer has made any changes to the agreement, ideally these should be initialed by the publisher to indicate that it has noted and accepted the changes. Publishers must be careful to ensure that what they receive is valid under the law that is applicable to the author: an agreement (transfer or license) signed by an author who does not own the copyright in the first place (such as an employee writing in the course of his or her work) will not be valid, and strictly speaking, in a number of European countries an author cannot transfer copyright at all.[10]

What should the publisher do if the author refuses to sign? If it's the transfer of copyright that is bothering them, many publishers, as mentioned

---

[10] Germany is the most notable example, Although a License to Publish might therefore appear to be the only form of agreement which is possible, many publishers do in fact continue to ask for assignment of copyright, on the grounds that in these circumstances it constitutes a transfer of the right to commercial exploitation.

above, offer the alternative of a license to publish. Sometimes, authors are bothered by other provisions, for example the requirement to obtain (and, if necessary, pay for) permission to use others' material, or the warranty (i.e., legally binding promise) that the content does not contain anything which is libelous, illegal, or infringes anyone's copyright or other rights; usually a little explanation will set the author's mind at rest – the clearer the wording in the first place, the less need there will be for such discussions.

If the author will not sign any agreement that is acceptable to the publisher, then unfortunately there is no option but to decline to publish his or her article. Hence, it always makes sense to obtain the agreement at the beginning of the submission process, rather than waiting until the article has been accepted (it should be made clear in the agreement that it automatically terminates if the work is rejected or withdrawn).

In the case of commissioned articles, such as review articles or educational materials, in both US and UK law, copyright remains with the author, in the absence of a written agreement to the contrary.[11] It is therefore wise to seek a Copyright Transfer form or a signed commissioning contract, to make this ownership clear.

Publishers sometimes do not bother to obtain agreements from authors of short items such as book reviews or letters to the Editor; this is unwise, as the publisher does not necessarily have the right to publish the material without such an agreement. An invitation to contribute the review or letter might be argued to be an implicit contract, but this is not ideal. Some authors of book reviews and the like may want to retain the right to republish the same work elsewhere – if the publisher accedes to this, it is sensible to specify that it may only appear in a noncompeting journal, and with a full bibliographic reference to the original publication.

In the past, agreements with authors were not always explicitly obtained and recorded; this can make life difficult for the publisher when it comes to digitizing back issues of the journal to create a complete digital archive – whether this is done directly, or via a third party such as JSTOR (www.jstor. org). It may simply not be practicable to contact all published authors (even if they could still be traced), let alone third-party owners of copyright in illustrations or quoted extracts, to obtain their permission. A notice in the printed journal, and on the journal website, may be the best that can be

---

[11] For more details on US law relating to "work made for hire," see Circular 9 from the US Copyright Office (www.copyright.gov/circs/circ09.pdf).

done in the circumstances, and the publisher may simply have to take the risk that someone will object (of course, the objector's article can always be removed from the online version when necessary).[12]

### The journal Editor

Copyright subsists in the Editor's own original contributions to the journal; to the extent that this explicitly forms part of the Editor's employment by the publisher (or journal owner), the copyright belongs to the employer. It is sensible, however, to make this completely clear in the Editor's contract. If the Editor contributes free-standing articles to the journal which are subject to the normal peer-review process, however, this will not apply; in such cases, the same agreement would apply as is used for all other contributors.

The Editor also has a contract of employment with the publisher (or society or other sponsor, as appropriate). A checklist of the points which this should cover is shown in Table 11.2.

### The journal owner

The journal may be owned by the publisher or by a sponsoring organization such as a learned society (or, in rare cases, jointly by both). When a journal changes publishers, either because the original publisher wants to sell it, or because the journal's sponsoring society decides to move it, it becomes crucial to know exactly what it is that the publisher (or, if applicable, the sponsor) owns.

### *Journal title*

Titles are generally arrangements of familiar words (e.g., the *British Journal of Surgery*) and, as such, are not themselves subject to copyright. Thus there is nothing (other than good sense) to prevent someone else launching

---

[12] "Orphan works" – those whose copyright owners cannot be contacted – have been the subject of much discussion on both sides of the Atlantic; they present a particular challenge to major digitization projects such as Google Books. Solutions are being developed in many countries, specifying the terms under which orphan works may be reused; in some cases a database of orphan works is also proposed, to facilitate the identification of the copyright owner.

**Table 11.2**  *Points which should be covered in the journal Editor's contract*

| | |
|---|---|
| Journal ownership | Either the publisher or the society (joint ownership, though possible, can lead to complications). |
| Copyright ownership in the Editor's work | This should be transferred to either publisher or society. |
| Warranty | The Editor should warrant (i.e., a guarantee with legal remedy) that nothing in the journal will be illegal (libelous, obscene, or in breach of copyright). He or she should be responsible for checking all content from this point of view. The Editor may also be required to be responsible for obtaining the Copyright Transfer or License to Publish obtained from each contributor, which incorporates the same warranty, although in many cases this task is carried out by the publisher's staff. |
| Conflict of interest | The Editor agrees not to serve as Editor or Editorial Board member of a competing journal during the term of the contract (may also restrict involvement with a competing journal within a certain period of termination). |
| Editor's responsibilities | These should be clearly spelled out, and should include:<br>• Appointment (or, better, recommendation) of Associate Editors and Editorial Board members.<br>• Soliciting and/or commissioning papers.<br>• Carrying out peer review in a timely manner.<br>• Communicating with authors on publication decisions.<br>• Ensuring appropriate coverage and quality.<br>• Preparing accepted papers for publication.<br>• Staying within a page budget; accepting the appropriate quantity of material.<br>• Forwarding accepted material to the publisher on schedule.<br>• Keeping track of acceptance/rejection data.<br>• Proofreading on schedule (if required).<br>• Providing marketing advice and assistance. |
| Publisher's responsibilities | Should include:<br>• Providing, supporting, and maintaining the submission and peer-review system.<br>• Copy-editing.<br>• Design (though it would be unwise not to consult the Editor).<br>• Print buying and management.<br>• Creation, hosting of, and access to online version.<br>• Advertising sales (if any).<br>• Pricing, including licenses and discounts.<br>• Marketing and promotion. |

**Table 11.2** (*cont.*)

| | |
|---|---|
| | • Sales and license negotiation.<br>• Order processing, access management and physical dispatch.<br>• Subsidiary licensing. |
| Frequency and extent | The frequency (number of issues) and extent (number of pages or words) of the journal at the start of the contract, and the timing and mechanism for changing this in future.[a] |
| Overview of editorial structure | Number of Editorial Board members and their terms, whether there are Assistant or Associate Editors, etc. |
| Finances | Should include:<br>• Editorial expenses – what is covered, the initial amount, how and when it is paid, and how any increases would be arrived at – e.g., inflation-proofing.[b] While it is usual practice to specify a payment schedule, it is safer to relate the timing of payments to the publication of each issue in case the journal begins to run late. A possible formula for calculating any subsequent above-inflation increases could refer to the number of articles, pages, or issues processed.<br>• Editorial fee/honorarium or royalty – if a rising royalty is offered, make sure the formula is unambiguous and one that your royalties department can calculate! If it is a fee, again include the mechanism for any adjustment in future years.<br>• Start-up expenses – initial expenses during the transition from the previous Editor or for the launch of the founding Editor. |
| Expiry or termination | When the contract expires (avoid a change-over in mid-volume, as this will affect promotional materials, preprinted covers, etc.); under what circumstances it could be terminated earlier (e.g., unsatisfactory performance); what happens when it expires or is terminated; what obligations continue after termination,[c] and how the contract is renewed (e.g., automatically or by mutual agreement, and when notice must be given) |

[a] Ideally, the discussion should coincide with the pricing cycle for the coming year so that changes can be accommodated in the budget and initiated at the start of a new volume.
[b] If an adjustment is tied to inflation, the source of the inflation figure used should be clearly specified, as well as whether it is tied to the location of the Editor or that of the publisher.
[c] For example, payment of royalties due on the last volume published under the departing Editor's tenure. In addition, some conflict-of-interest clauses preclude the Editor from becoming Editor of a competing journal for a specific period after termination of the contract.

another journal under the same title. This would come to light when the second journal applied for its ISSN (see www.issn.org/2-22652 -Requesting-an-ISSN.php for how to do this), as the first title would show up in the ISSN agency's register.

In serious cases, such competition could be challenged under UK (and a few other) laws as "passing off" – trying to sell something under the pretense that it is something else. Some protection may be gained by registering the journal's title as a trademark, but this is rarely felt to be necessary.[13]

### Journal contents

Not only the articles, but also all the other journal content – including covers, title pages, abstracts, indexes, and so forth – is covered by copyright. Thus, even if authors or their employers have retained copyright in the individual articles and have instead granted a license to publish, the publisher/owner owns copyright in everything else.[14]

### Journal records, work in progress

The records (usually on computer) of authors – their submissions, correspondence, acceptance/rejection, and publication status; editors and reviewers – their workload and performance; and customers (not only library and individual subscribers/licensees, but also advertisers, third-party downstream licensees, and others) are a key asset which, in the case of a sale or transfer, the new publisher will wish to acquire.

If a journal is being sold or otherwise transferred, the Editor must naturally be informed; his or her contract may be reissued with the new publisher's name in place of the old (known as a "novation" agreement), or the new publisher may prefer to enter into a completely new agreement. Authors

---

[13] However, if you are developing a series of specialty journals derived from a more general journal, trademark protection may be needed for the "brand."

[14] However, it would not make sense for the publisher to make none of this content freely available online. The "navigational" content – tables of contents, indexes (if included), and indeed abstracts – must be available if online users are to be able to find the articles they want. Many journals also provide free access to the citations at the end of articles. In fact, some journals also make the non-research article content freely available (in some cases, such as the *BMJ*, it is the other way round – see Chapter 8, Journal finances, for more on this).

whose work has not yet been published will also need to be informed; unless their Copyright Transfer or License to Publish agreements specifically granted rights to the publisher "and its successors or assigns," new agreements may also be needed for them. It has been known for authors (or Editors, or even whole Editorial Boards) to object to a particular publisher, and to wish to withdraw if the journal is transferred to that publisher.

The publisher/owner also owns the copyright in (or, if licensed, the right to publish) the "work in progress" – all the manuscripts that have been received and have not yet been either published or rejected, including versions that are in the course of peer review, editing, typesetting, or proofreading, or which are ready for and awaiting publication – and this will also need to be covered in the agreement with any new publisher.

When a publisher undertakes publication of a journal on behalf of its owner (e.g., a society), the contract between them is, naturally, of crucial importance. The contract must, at a minimum, cover the points shown in Table 11.3. (Such relationships, and the points which the contract should include, are covered in much more detail in Chapter 10, Contract publishing.)

## Printed copies

Most journals, though not all, are still produced in print issues or, at least, in a single annual print volume. Any stocks of printed copies are also the property of the publisher (or possibly, in the case of contract publishing, the journal's owner – this will depend on the contract between them), and negotiations will need to include a way of arriving at a price for transferring them to the new publisher.

The cover and overall design and appearance of the journal are not automatically transferred to a new publisher; in some cases, indeed, this may be inappropriate if the journal followed the original publisher's "house style." This, therefore, also needs to be covered in any agreement for sale or transfer.

## The online version

The publisher will also have created an online version, hosted with its other journals (if any), either on its own system or by a third-party online host. This version may extend back many years; in addition, earlier

**Table 11.3** *Points to be included in the contract to publish on behalf of the journal's owner*

| | |
|---|---|
| The names of the parties | Publisher and society/other owner |
| The name of the publication | |
| The nature of the publication | E.g., primary research journal, review journal, educational journal |
| Ownership of the different aspects of the publication | • Copyright<br>• Mailing lists<br>• Undistributed issues<br>• Electronic files |
| The starting and ending dates of the agreement | |
| The first and last issues to be published under the agreement | |
| Warranty and indemnification | These should be balanced so that each side takes responsibility for the areas under its control |
| Dispute resolution | How any disagreements will be handled (arbitration is better than the courts); in which country (publisher's or owner's, if different) any court case would be heard |
| Renewal terms | Whether or not renewal is automatic; requirements for notice of intended termination or renegotiation |

volumes may have been digitized to create an online archive. The electronic files, the "look and feel" of the online version, and the characteristics of the particular online system (if it is the publisher's own) are all part of what the publisher owns.

Extracting the digital files and transferring them to a new publisher is not always straightforward, particularly if they are not immediately compatible with the new publisher's system; while the actual content files may be relatively easily exported, additional features and functionality may not. It is important to establish exactly what the original publisher is and is not technically able to do, and to establish a clear timetable in the agreement for those steps which are possible. It is often sensible to keep the content available on the original publisher's site for an overlap period, until the new publisher is confident that all is working smoothly; from that point onwards, it is helpful if the original publisher provides a link to the new site.

Excellent advice on the things to be done when a journal is transferred can be found on the Transfer working group website at www.uksg.org/transfer.

### Permissions

Authors often wish to use sections of text, or illustrations, from the work of others. Unless the work to be reused is out of copyright, it is essential to obtain permission for this reuse; this may have to be paid for, although a number of publishers have reached an informal reciprocal agreement about not charging each other (see www.stm-assoc.org/copyright_and_legal_permissions_guidelines.php). The use of "insubstantial" extracts (judged by importance as much as by length) is in fact allowed in many legal systems – but as there are no hard and fast rules about what constitutes an "insubstantial" extract it is never safe to assume that permission is not needed.

Most publishers ask the author to obtain (and pay for) such permission; however, authors may not realize that they have to contact the original publisher, and not just the original author or illustrator. Alternatively, they may not have obtained permission for worldwide use, or for use online – both of which are essential for scholarly journals. It is wise to ask for a copy of the letter or email in which the permission was granted, in order to make sure that it is adequate; some publishers provide authors with a model form letter to use (see Box 11.2 for an example).

When including text or illustrations which are someone else's copyright, it is important that they are accurately and fully acknowledged (some publishers will specify the exact form of words they want used). When editing an article, the Copy-Editor needs to be on the lookout for quoted extracts which do not seem to be properly credited, or which are too long to have been used without explicit permission. The checklist in Table 11.4 may be helpful when the publisher receives a request for permission to reproduce something.

When permission is granted, the permission agreement may be very brief, but it should at least make clear:

- Whether the permission is for this single use only (meaning that separate permission must be sought for any further use or edition) or – more conveniently for all – whether it applies to all editions/versions, though not to the item taken out of the context for which the original permission was obtained.

**Box 11.2** Permission request form for *Comprehensive Physiology*

### *Comprehensive Physiology* Permission Request Form

I am preparing a manuscript to be published by John Wiley & Sons, Inc., in partnership with the American Physiological Society (APS). APS is the copyright holder of *Comprehensive Physiology*. *Comprehensive Physiology* is an online-only quarterly serial reference work. Please note that John Wiley & Sons is a signatory to the "STM Permissions Guidelines," which allows gratis permissions for the reuse of figures, tables, and excerpts from publications of other signatories. A list of signatories is attached to this form.

Author(s) and Article Title _____

Estimated publication date of first issue of *Comprehensive Physiology*: January 2011.

☐ The following material will be used in my manuscript as originally published below.

☐ The following material will be redrawn or adapted for my manuscript.

I request your permission to include the following material in the above-referenced publication, in all media of expression now known or later developed and in all foreign language translations and other derivative works published or prepared by John Wiley & Sons, Inc., or its licensees, for distribution throughout the world, and also in versions made by non-profit organizations for use by blind or physically handicapped persons. Appropriate credit will be given as provided below.

Author(s) and/or editor(s) _____

Title of book or periodical _____

Title of selection _____ Copyright date _____

From page ____, line ____, beginning with the words _____

To page ____, line ____, ending with the words _____

Figure # ____ on page_____        Table # ____ on page _____

(*If necessary attach continuation sheet*)

Please indicate your agreement by signing and returning the enclosed copy of this letter to me. In signing, you warrant that you are the sole owner of the rights granted and that your material does not infringe upon the copyright or other rights of anyone. If you do not control these rights, I would appreciate your letting me know to whom I should apply.

Thank you.

Reprinted with permission from Wiley.

**Table 11.4** *Checklist for permissions*

| Who is asking? | • If it is the author – is he or she allowed to do this anyway, under the existing agreement with the publisher? <br>• If it is a university or company – is the proposed use covered by a license, either your own or one issued by a Reproduction Rights Organization such as CCC or CLA (see above)? <br>• If it is a publisher – do the STM guidelines apply (see above)? |
|---|---|
| Is the proposed use, or is the requesting organization, commercial? | If so, fair use/fair dealing exceptions will not apply. Your company may have more liberal terms for educational organizations/uses |
| Is the request for use of the whole work (e.g., article) or an extract? | If an extract is "insubstantial," it may come under fair dealing/fair use |
| In what medium will the reused content be made available? | Electronic distribution raises different, and more complex, issues |
| How many copies will be made? | It is difficult to find a satisfactory way of measuring the number of electronic "copies" |
| Is the reuse likely to compete with your primary sales? | If so, you may not wish to permit it – or you may want to charge a substantial fee |
| How much do you want to charge? | In some cases a zero or nominal charge may be felt appropriate (is it worth the cost of charging at all?); in others, a commercial rate may be applicable |

- Whether it is free of charge, and if not what is the fee and when payable.
- Whether the permission is exclusive or nonexclusive (most likely the latter).
- What territories, media, and languages are included or excluded.
- Details of the form of acknowledgment of the original publication required (e.g., "Reprinted from [Author, Title, Copyright (year)], by permission of [Publisher]").
- That the permission does not include any copyright material from other sources that may be included in the selection – it is the requester's job to identify such material and to seek appropriate permission for its inclusion.

But don't be so restrictive as to make the requester's life impossible – do as you would be done by!

The in-house permissions burden can be significantly reduced by making it unnecessary to process requests for which you are not in any case going to charge. If this is the case (for example, if you want to allow – even encourage – copying of tables of contents), it should be made very clear in both online and print editions of the journal itself; it is also important to make sure that both authors and licensees understand exactly what they or their institution can do without needing to ask for permission. It is also helpful if you make it as easy as possible for people to request permissions (and for you to respond), for example by including appropriate forms on your website.

A number of organizations have taken further steps to streamline the permissions process by the use of automation. For example, RightsLink (www.copyright.com/content/cc3/en/toolbar/productsAndSolutions/rightslink.html), an initiative of the Copyright Clearance Center, allows customers to obtain a range of permissions and other rights online at the click of a button. It is important to remember, when setting up online forms for such systems, to use language which will be meaningful to the requester, rather than publishers' jargon (e.g., what does "commercial use" mean to an author?), and not to request information which will likely not be known to the requester (e.g., circulation of the journal, or the projected date of publication of the article).

### Republished articles

As mentioned in Chapter 3, Editing, a journal's Editor may sometimes feel that there is good reason to republish an article which has appeared elsewhere: this might be a classic article, possibly many years old, from the same or another journal; it might be a translation of an article originally published in a language inaccessible to many of the journal's readers; or, less commonly, the article might originally have appeared in a publication geared towards a completely different readership.

In all such cases, of course, permission must be obtained from the copyright owner, whether this be the author or the original publisher (as well as the translator, if appropriate).[15] A full citation should be given to the article's original appearance; in the case of a straight republication, the

---

[15] If the original does not make copyright ownership clear, it is wise to contact both author and publisher if possible.

copyright notice should reproduce the original copyright notice, as a new copyright has not been created, although in the case of a translation it should say "[Original] language version copyright [year]; this [translated] language version copyright [year]."

### The publisher

Irrespective of whether or not the publisher is the owner of the journal, under UK law, it is the owner of the "typographic copyright" mentioned above. This lasts for twenty-five years from the date of publication; it may, therefore, still be in place even if the original publication is out of print. Thus, no one can reproduce the printed pages of the journal – even if the content of those pages is someone else's copyright – without the original publisher's permission. This can be important if a journal intends to reproduce the exact appearance of a "classic" article, rather than re-setting it.

### Agreements with third parties

The journal publisher enters into contractual agreements with a whole range of other people and organizations. Agreements with suppliers (such as prepress vendors, printers, distributors, and, most particularly, online hosts) are usually drawn up at the end of a Request for Proposal (RFP) process. When a publisher needs to purchase a product (e.g., paper) or service (e.g., peer-review management software and service), the publisher will put out an RFP, which spells out the publisher's needs and requirements and gives a deadline for the response from the bidders. Each response should include a statement regarding the vendor's ability to meet those requirements and pricing for each product or feature and service the publisher is requesting.

After analysis of features, quality, and price, the publisher will choose a vendor, and a contract will be drafted, usually by the vendor. The contract will typically cover the following:

- The names of the parties.
- Term. A common term for a vendor contract is three years.
- Product, features, or service description.
- Detailed price list.

- Warranty and indemnification.
- Dispute resolution.
- Renewal terms.

### The customer license

One of the most important of all the agreements into which a journal publisher enters is its license for access to and use of the online version. Written agreements were virtually unheard-of for print journals; everyone knew what was being sold, and knew (or thought they knew) what rights went with that sale – notably, the right of ownership. Thus selling, and purchasing, journals was such a simple and standardized process that it could be carried out with very little thought other than over the price.

Electronic journals are a completely different matter. Customers are very rarely buying a physical product at all (although some journal archives are provided on CD-ROM); what they are buying is, simply, rights – not copyright itself, which remains with its original owner, but the rights to do certain things; anything which is not explicitly permitted in the license (and which is not an exception under applicable copyright law, as outlined above) is an infringement of the agreement. The license therefore needs to be specific about the uses that are permitted, those that are not, and the remedies for infringement. Thus, almost all journal publishers have developed their own licenses for online journals. Unfortunately, in many cases these have become both long and complex, and the process of negotiation has therefore become extremely time-consuming, requiring the involvement of expert staff on both sides, and therefore extremely expensive in itself. Publishers are, however, learning from their discussions with customers and to some extent the language and terms of licenses are becoming more similar, and more acceptable to librarians.

The customer license may be a relatively simple (and usually non-negotiable) document covering the rights of an individual online user (often these are not signed paper documents, but online "clickthrough" agreements; some publishers, perhaps unwisely, don't bother with them at all for individual subscribers). It may be a license for all or part of an institution (for example, a department) – with one or many physical sites, and possibly including off-site users as well. Or it may be a license for a consortium – a group of libraries, or even a national license covering all academic libraries (or even all users) in a given country. And it may cover one publication, a group of publications, or all the publications from the publisher (or, indeed, from multiple publishers). It may or may not also include access to backfile content. Generally speaking, the larger the license (in terms of both content and customer[s]) the more scope there is for negotiation, not just of the price but also of the detailed terms.

In essence, the license needs to cover the following:

- The parties (publisher and licensee).
- Definitions – making sure both parties mean exactly the same thing by the terms used.
- The publication(s) – identifying not only the title but also the precise year(s) or volume(s) covered.[16]
- The authorized users – including whether or not walk-in and off-site users are permitted, and if so under what conditions.
- The authorized and nonpermitted uses (specifying which of these survive termination of the agreement – for example, the institution may be permitted to continue to access [or host locally] and use the volumes which were previously licensed).
- The publisher's and the institution's responsibilities.
- Sanctions for contravention of any of the terms of the license (e.g., in the worst case, cutting off access).
- The period covered by the license, and how it is renewed or terminated from the end of that period.
- Indemnity – the institution's undertaking to accept responsibility for the actions of its users, and the publisher's undertaking to accept responsibility for any copyright or other infringement involved in the inclusion of content in the journal(s).
- The jurisdiction under which the license is to be interpreted, and the location of the courts in which any case would be heard (normally, this is the law and the country of the publisher; however, most US state universities are not permitted to sign agreements unless US law and their local courts are specified). Fortunately, cases of disagreement over licenses coming to court are extremely rare.

---

[16] To allow for regular renewals, this may be more loosely worded (e.g., "for any year for which the customer has a paid subscription").

- Consortia and other negotiated site licenses are likely also to include the price for the current year, and any calculation model to be applied (e.g., number of users, usage stats).

Each institutional subscriber needs to agree to the terms and conditions of the publisher's license agreement; most institutional agreements are on paper,[17] with copies held by both the publisher and the library. It helps to remember that it is not lawyers but mid-level personnel working in publishing offices and libraries who are usually responsible for negotiating, if not signing, license agreements for online access. Publishers should try to use plain, understandable English that avoids legalese as much as possible; for one thing, many subscribers and licensees are not native English-speakers. Terms of use should also be reasonable – actual lawsuits between publishers and libraries over the use of online journals are rare (if not unheard-of), so extreme language anticipating worst-case scenarios is not very helpful. Lawyers are trained to anticipate the worst possible events and automatically want to say "no" to everything your customers want; moreover, they often do not understand library practices well enough to appreciate real-world behavior that cannot meaningfully be proscribed in the first place.

Years of licensing discussions between publishers and libraries have produced a fairly general consensus on standard terms, although librarians still complain about unusual, unique, and sometimes eccentric terms in some publisher agreements. They are not shy about discussing such terms publicly in Liblicense-l (www.library.yale.edu/~llicense/) and other online discussion groups. A number of model documents have been produced, in the hope that publishers will adopt their wording and definitions in their own licenses – for example, that created by Liblicense in the US (www.library.yale.edu/~llicense) and a range of model licenses at www.licensingmodels.com. The latter site, developed by publishing consultant (and lawyer) John Cox, does not require a publisher to adopt a specific set of licensing policies, but it does provide appropriate language for the policies the publisher has adopted – language with common meaning for both parties.

There is an alternative to these license agreements. Publishers and libraries (with NISO support), hoping to simplify the whole licensing

---

[17] Libraries often seek changes in the wording of the publisher's standard license agreement. Among the most common: companies that want mutual indemnification clauses, and state universities in the US, which are not allowed to accept the governing law of another state (i.e., the publisher's).

process, have collaborated in the "Shared E-Resource Understanding" (SERU) project to create a set of standard definitions of the key terms in any license, to which publishers are invited to link; then all they need to do is to exchange documents with the customer agreeing the price, the journals included, and the duration of the license. As the SERU site states, "The creation of a license is not required for the creation of a binding contractual agreement. The invoicing/purchase order/payment process is generally sufficient for the creation of a contractual relationship. Normal contract law and copyright law, of course, apply." By registering at the SERU website, libraries and publishers indicate their adherence to a set of seven "best practice" principles, equivalent to typical licensing agreement terms governing usage of electronic content.

The SERU principles omit several standard clauses in a typical publisher's license agreement, including those covering limitation of warranties, indemnification, payment of taxes, assignment of rights, governing law, and legal jurisdiction.[18] Few corporate subscribers, for whom such things as indemnification and governing law may be important, are likely to rely on SERU in lieu of a written license agreement. The SERU model is also unlikely to satisfy the needs of many consortia and other institutions with special licensing (and pricing) terms.

There have even been some experiments in doing without a license altogether – some publishers manage quite well without them (using one supplied by the customer, as a starting point for negotiation, when required), although when the *BMJ* briefly abandoned its requirement for a license, it found that some customers insisted on having one! Many smaller publishers do not in fact require their regular institutional customers to sign a license; their journal platform provider may have on the site a standard set of default guidelines for use of the material (e.g., http://highwire.stanford.edu/tfocis/guidelines.dtl).

There are two conflicting pressures on journal licenses. On the one hand, everyone wants the license to be accurate and comprehensive, so that no areas of uncertainty remain. At the same time, everyone also wants the process of licensing to be quicker, simpler, and cheaper. Ideally, computer systems would be enabled to pick up contractual terms, and

---

[18] Of course, the very existence of SERU suggests that clauses like these are unnecessary for a practical relationship between a scholarly publisher and an academic library – but each publisher will have to consult its own legal advisors to decide how important they are.

even to act on them; ONIX for Licensing Terms (OLT) is a project which is developing tools to enable publishers to express their licensing terms in a machine-readable way – see www.editeur.org/85/Overview.

It is increasingly unusual to ask individual users within an institution to "click on" an agreement accepting the publisher's terms of use, although the license may require the institution to impose certain rules upon all authorized users.

### Other licenses

Publishers may also enter into "downstream" license agreements with a range of third parties, for example:

- With a third party organizing multipublisher packages, such as BioOne (www.bioone.org), Project Muse (http://muse.jhu.edu) or the ALPSP Learned Journals Collection (http://aljc.swets.com).
- With organizations that can reach markets that the publisher cannot, such as subscription agents and content aggregators (e.g., OVID – www.ovid.com). Publishers may need to exclude certain markets; it is important to specify what data and analysis they want their partners to supply (see Chapter 9, Subsidiary income, for more information on licensing to aggregators).
- With organizations that archive electronic versions of publications (e.g., JSTOR, www.jstor.org, LOCKSS, www.lockss.org, CLOCKSS, www.clockss.org, and Portico, www.portico.org) (see Chapter 4, The production process, for more on archiving and preservation).

Many of these organizations have their own standard forms of agreement; however, it is always wise for the publisher to study the document carefully, and to discuss and if possible negotiate modification of any areas with which it is unhappy.

## Other legal areas

### Plagiarism and fraud

Plagiarism – copying someone else's words and passing them off as one's own, is an ethical issue as well as a copyright issue; as such, it is dealt with in Chapter 12, Ethical issues.

Similarly, fraud – the fabrication of research results – is dealt with in Chapter 12. Fraud can also arise on the customer side: there have been instances of subscription agents purchasing subscriptions to journals at reduced individual rates and then reselling these to institutions (see Chapter 6, Marketing and sales).

### Piracy

In some less-developed countries, cheap copies of new and recently published journals are printed and sold, undercutting the publisher's prices and providing the publisher with no income. The American Association of Publishers and the UK's Publishers Association have been especially active in identifying the culprits and working to ensure that they are stopped.

In the digital world, piracy of journal articles has become even easier and is alarmingly widespread. Some organizations target certain industries, such as the pharmaceutical industry (where articles referring to a company's own drugs are of particular interest), offering for sale single or even multiple copies of articles which have not, in fact, been authorized by the publisher. In other cases, articles are posted on unauthorized websites.

Publishers can help to reduce the likelihood of piracy by offering special pricing terms for particular countries – this is easy to effect with online journals, although of course online access may not be very widely available in some of the markets publishers would like to help. Through projects such as HINARI (see Chapter 6, Marketing and sales), many publishers offer reduced-price or even free online access to users in countries where the average per-capita income falls below specified levels – see www.library. yale.edu/~llicense/develop.shtml for a comprehensive list of such initiatives.

If a publisher comes across its (or indeed another publisher's) articles being illegally sold or given away, the company's trade association (such as AAP in the US or the PA in the UK) may be in the strongest position to mobilize action against the offender. The PA has an excellent "Copyright Infringement Portal" at www.copyrightinfringementportal.com/.

### Libel, obscenity, and blasphemy

Any false, malicious, and defamatory written statement which is published constitutes libel – if spoken, it is slander. Not only the author of the statement is liable; the publisher and printer are also jointly liable (though the printer, but not the publisher, may be able to claim that it was unaware of the content). Two of the most significant defenses against a claim of libel are that the statement is true, or that it is "fair comment" – reflecting an honestly held opinion which is based on known facts. Feelings can run high in the world of scholarly research, and libel can certainly arise in scholarly journals. For example, a book reviewer may make abusive personal comments against the author of a book, or an article author may defame another scholar.

There are also laws in most jurisdictions against the publication of statements which are obscene – offensive to public morality, particularly sexual morality – or blasphemous – offensive to religious sensibilities (no longer illegal in the UK, though it may still be elsewhere).[19] In both cases, the offense tends to lie in the eye of the beholder, which makes it difficult to pin down. Fortunately, these are less likely to occur in scholarly journals.

It is important that all those involved with detailed processing of journal articles – reviewers, Editors-in-Chief, Copy-Editors – are alert to all of these possibilities. If a potentially problematic statement is found before publication, it is prudent to ask the author to modify it. If it is published, legal proceedings could ensue.

### Product liability

In some disciplines – for example, medicine, engineering, or chemistry – there is the possibility that following published information or instructions could lead to injury or even death. While most product liability legislation concerns damage actually caused by faulty or unsafe (physical) products, it remains a possibility that an author (and indeed publisher, printer, and distributor) might be held liable in such an instance. There have been very few cases on whether product liability could apply to printed materials, and in those cases it was concluded that it did not apply, since the materials were not themselves inherently dangerous (unless they fell on someone!). Publishing a disclaimer (such as the example in Box 11.3) provides little or no defense in law; however, it may have the effect of alerting the reader to the possibility of danger.

---

[19] Given the international nature of journal distribution, offended parties may initiate legal action in jurisdictions more favorable to the plaintiff.

**Box 11.3** Disclaimer from the *American Journal of Physiology-Cell Physiology* (August 2011)

**Disclaimer**: The statements and opinions contained in the articles of the *American Journal of Physiology-Cell Physiology* are solely those of the individual authors and contributors and not of the American Physiological Society. The appearance of advertisements in the journal is not a warranty, endorsement, or approval of the products or their safety. The American Physiological Society disclaims responsibility for any injury to persons or property resulting from any ideas or products referred to in any article or advertisement.

Reprinted with permission from the American Physiological Society.

### Data protection

Legislation is in place in many countries to protect personal information about individuals; such information obviously becomes much more vulnerable to abuse once it is held in a computerized database. "Personal information," in this context, refers to any information whatever that is linked to an identified living individual – it doesn't have to be sensitive information.

The 1998 Data Protection Act brought the UK into line with the European Data Protection Directive of 1995; it was updated by the Privacy and Electronic Communications (EC Directive) Regulations in 2003. The act requires any organization that processes personal information to register with the Information Commissioner's Office, and pay for a license (see www.ico.gov.uk). Data may only be used for the specific purposes for which it was collected. It may not be disclosed to anyone else without the explicit consent of the subject; it may not be sent outside the European Economic Area (i.e., the EU member states plus Iceland, Liechtenstein, and Norway) at all, unless the subject consents and the recipient country has adequate protections in place. Individuals have the right to ask to see the information held about them (though it is permissible to charge a fee for this). Personal information must be kept up to date, and may not be held for longer than necessary.

The US does not itself have specific data protection laws, but its "Safe Harbor" framework (http://export.gov/safeharbor/index.asp), prepared in coordination with the European Commission – to which companies can sign up for a fee – guarantees that the signatory provides adequate protection for personal data from the EU or Switzerland.

### Legal deposit

Many countries require publishers to deposit one or more copies of every (eligible) published work in a national library, in order to establish a comprehensive national collection which can both be used by current researchers and be preserved for those of the future. The earliest such requirement was the French royal decree of "dépôt legal," signed in 1537, which stipulated that two copies of every book printed in France be deposited at the Chateau de Blois. Most publishers are happy to contribute a copy to their own national library, although they may balk at being asked to deposit multiple copies or even to deposit in multiple countries.

In the USA, the 1967 Copyright Act requires all publishers – including those who publish abroad, but distribute their publications in the USA – to deposit copies of each issue at the Library of Congress within three months of publication. The imposition of such a requirement on non-US publishers has been challenged, but without success. While US publishers must deposit two copies of every print work on publication, the Library's advice is that non-US publishers can safely await a request (provided they send the publication within three months of the request), and then only need to send a single copy. A working group is looking at the extension of these requirements to cover nonprint materials. One advantage of deposit is that every work that is received in response to a request is cataloged by the Library of Congress; US librarians consult this catalog regularly.

In the UK, it was agreed in 1610 that the Bodleian Library in Oxford would receive a copy of every book registered at Stationers' Hall; today's legal deposit requirements are based on the 1911 Copyright Act. UK publishers must deposit one copy of every printed book or serial with the British Library, within one month of publication; there are five other deposit libraries, in Dublin, Edinburgh, Aberystwyth, Cambridge, and Oxford, each of which may also request a copy within twelve months. They usually do so, and it is therefore more convenient and cost-effective for the publisher automatically to send a copy for each to the British Library's Copyright Agent (who will distribute them), without waiting to be asked.

The 2003 Legal Deposit Libraries Act established in principle that non-print materials (not just online resources, but also microfilm and publications on physical media such as CD-ROM or DVD) should be deposited in the same way. However, the detailed implications are complex and vary according to the type of publication; a joint group of publishing and library representatives worked out some of the details before being disbanded (as part of government cuts) in 2011. The government has consulted on the Legal Deposit Libraries (Nonprint) Publications Regulations and intends for them to come into force in April 2013. These would apply to every new nonprint publication (provided it did not replicate a print publication), and would provide for essentially the same arrangements to apply to "offline" publications as to print. For online publications, web harvesting (with access details, if needed, provided by the publisher) or, if necessary, deposit arrangements would apply; there would be restrictions on how many people may view the publication at once, and how soon after publication they may access it. (See www.culture.gov.uk/publications/9322.aspx)

## What if it all goes wrong?

Sometimes – despite their best efforts – publishers and their authors, editors, customers, or others do fall out. Recourse to lawyers should always be a last resort; often, problems can be resolved by discussion and mutual agreement.

In the case of infringing publication, either effected by one of your own authors or by someone else infringing your or your authors' rights, the first thing to do, if it is online, is to attach a note to the infringing item on the site, indicating that copyright issues have been raised in relation to the item (there is no need, at this point, to apportion any blame). It may also be wise to publish a similar note in the next available print issue. When the parties have agreed the truth of the matter, the infringing publisher should publish alongside (and linked to) the original an amended version with proper acknowledgment and an apology, if that is possible (e.g., online) or, if absolutely necessary, a retraction. Often, this is sufficient without financial compensation being demanded. Many publishers feel that it is unhelpful to the record of science for content, even if infringing, to be removed from the online record – see www.stm-assoc.org/2008_03_01_Preservation_of_the_Objective_Record_of_Science.doc. For more on the handling of plagiarism, see Chapter 12, Ethical issues.

Similarly, if an author has put his or her article online in contravention of your author–publisher agreement (copyright assignment or license to publish), all you really need to do is to ask him or her to remove it, and to replace it with the appropriate version or, if necessary, with a link to the published version (which may not, of course, be freely accessible to nonsubscribers).

Sometimes, publishers are made aware that an institution is using the publisher's materials in a way which contravenes the license that has been signed. This can be a particular problem with online journals: you may detect mass downloads, or find articles (or even passwords) being posted in a way that is not restricted to the licensed community. Once again, the best approach is to inform the institution as soon as possible and ask it to stop the abuse (they may need to investigate first to find out who is doing it). Librarians at licensed institutions are usually perfectly cooperative; of course, the publisher has the final sanction: it can cut off access. (For more on resolving license abuses, see Chapter 7, Fulfillment.)

If informal discussion fails, informal dispute resolution can be a very workable option, and a number of national publishing associations offer an arbitration service – for instance, the UK Publishers Association's Informal Disputes Settlement Scheme (www.publishers.org.uk). Arbitration is a more formal approach, but does not involve the level of costs of going to court; the parties refer the dispute to an agreed person or persons, whose decision they agree to accept.

If a problem arises which threatens to become a legal issue, you must contact your own legal experts – in-house legal staff if you have them, or the company's external lawyers if you do not. Never attempt to go it alone – the experts know how to draft letters and so forth to prevent things getting any worse! If any problem arises concerning a journal, it is important immediately to alert the journal's Editor, its owner (such as a society) if there is one, and the company's management.

However, with goodwill and good sense, and clear agreements between all parties, most problems can be avoided in the first place, and those that do arise can be settled without undue escalation.

## REFERENCES

Copyright Act, 1710, 8 Anne c. 19, *An Act for the Encouragement of Learning, by Vesting the Copies of Printed Books in the Authors or Purchasers of Such Copies, during the Times Therein Mentioned* (www.copyrighthistory.com/anne.html)

Cox, John, and Laura Cox, 2008, *Scholarly publishing practice 3*, Worthing, Association of Learned and Professional Society Publishers (www.alpsp.org/Ebusiness/ProductCatalog/Product.aspx?ID=44) – summarized in Morris, 2009 below

Morris, Sally, 2009, *Journal authors' rights: perception and reality*, London, Publishing Research Consortium (www.publishingresearch.net/author_rights.htm)

## FURTHER READING

Committee on Publication Ethics (http://publicationethics.org)

Copyright Society of the USA, Copyright Links (www.csusa.org/info_links.htm)

Jones, Hugh, and Christopher Benson, 2011, *Publishing law*, 4th edn, Abingdon, Routledge

Kaufman, Roy S, 2008, *Publishing forms and contracts*, Oxford University Press

Leaffer, Marshall A, 2010, *Understanding copyright law*, 5th edn, Albany, NY, LexisNexis

Owen, Lynette, 2010, *Clark's publishing agreements*, 8th edn, London, Bloomsbury Professional

SERU (Shared Electronic Resource Understanding), 2012, *SERU Recommended Practice (RP-7-2012)*, Baltimore, MD, National Information Standards Organization (www.niso.org/publications/rp/RP-7-2012_SERU.pdf)

UNESCO collection of national copyright laws (http://portal.unesco.org/culture)

Winternitz, Ingrid, 2000, *Electronic publishing agreements: precedents with commentary and disks*, Oxford University Press

www.library.yale.edu/~llicense/liclinks.shtml – wide range of resources on licensing

www.licensingmodels.com – suite of model licenses for various different situations, compiled by John Cox

# 12 Ethical issues

The discussion of ethics in scholarly publishing has become more common in recent years. One could argue that this is due to an increasing amount of unethical behavior by authors, who are under ever more pressure to publish often and in high-profile journals, and who may stretch or breach the boundaries of what is ethical in order to do so. One could also argue that the use of technology to create a manuscript makes it easier to copy and paste published texts, or to tweak the information shown in a figure. But at the same time, this technology makes instances of unethical conduct easier to find, because, for example, it is easy to compare two documents electronically, to open an electronic figure file to see how it was changed, or to search for text online to see if it has been copied from another source. So one could equally argue that authors are not more dishonest than they used to be, but that ethical issues are more easily, and therefore more frequently, found. More than likely, the apparent increase in cases of ethical misconduct is a combination of all of the above.

There is a spectrum of ethical issues, and some can be considered more serious than others, as will be clear throughout this chapter. They range from unintentional sloppiness, through intentional pushing of the boundaries and "researchers behaving badly," to the kind of behavior that negates published research, destroys careers, and tarnishes the research enterprise.

## How ethical issues are found

Ethical issues are often found by reviewers as they read a paper closely before it is accepted for publication. A reviewer might recognize familiar text (sometimes from his or her own publication!), especially since the reviewer may be looking at related literature as he or she reviews a paper. A reviewer might notice something unusual about a figure, or about the data. When this happens, the reviewer will usually contact the Editor of the journal to express concern. The journal may also receive complaints from authors, either during peer review or after publication. A co-author may not be happy with the order in which the authors' names are listed; or someone who should have been named as an author may complain that his or her name was left off a paper. The author may complain of being unfairly treated by a reviewer, or that his or her work is being delayed to enable a rival to publish similar work first. During production, Copy-Editors and those who work on the figures may find problems such as plagiarized text and manipulated figures. Or readers of a journal may contact the journal Editor or the publisher after a paper is published, if they notice the same kinds of problem.

Software is also used to detect certain kinds of unethical conduct automatically. Text-matching software, such as the iThenticate software used by CrossCheck (www.crossref.org/crosscheck/index.html – see Box 12.1), can be used during the review process or after acceptance[1] to find strings of text that match those in CrossCheck's large database of scholarly literature. However, the journal Editor (or an appropriate member of the Editorial office staff) then needs to decide whether the matched text strings constitute plagiarism; this highlights the fact that people are needed in the process to make judgments about ethical issues.

---

**Box 12.1** CrossCheck

Members of CrossRef, the cross-publisher reference-linking system, can join CrossCheck and use its tools to search actively for plagiarism in submitted manuscripts. CrossCheck members pay an annual fee equivalent to 20% of their CrossRef fee, and a per-document checking fee. The process is as follows:

1. The publisher allows its published content to be indexed and included in the CrossCheck database.
2. The publisher uploads a newly submitted manuscript to the web-based iThenticate system and runs a check against the CrossCheck database. The software returns a list of documents that contain significant amounts of the same text as the uploaded manuscript.

---

[1] This is often done after a paper is accepted, to avoid spending time and effort on papers that may be rejected. But some journals perform a check on all manuscripts submitted, in order to detect all cases of unethical behavior, whether or not the papers would have been accepted for publication.

## Types of ethical issue

### Authors

There are various ways that authors can behave unethically. The most common ones are described below.

### Plagiarism

Plagiarism is the use of someone else's work without attribution – in other words, passing it off as one's own. Text, figures, tables, and even ideas can be plagiarized. When a whole entity (e.g., an entire article, a figure, a table, or a dataset) is republished without attribution or permission, there may be a copyright violation as well as ethical misconduct.

When an author reuses someone else's text, any direct quotes should be put in quotation marks, and any text (or ideas) that are reused should be credited to the original source. There are no set rules about how much reused text constitutes plagiarism, and text-matching software is so sensitive that phrases that are in common use in a given academic field will be highlighted as matched text strings. This has engendered much discussion about what constitutes serious plagiarism. For instance, many journals' ethical guidelines will acknowledge that multiple papers that discuss the same method or technique will use the same or similar descriptions of it; however, some journals still expect the author to paraphrase this section (or to leave it out and reference it instead), so as not to repeat it word for word from another source. However, if a "Methods" section of a submitted manuscript is repeated verbatim, should the journal Editor treat the infraction as seriously as one in which data or more original text is plagiarized? The Committee on Publication Ethics (COPE, http://publicationethics.org/) has drafted a discussion paper on the topic to help guide journal Editors facing the plethora of matched text strings found with text-matching software that may or may not be serious cases of plagiarism (Wager, 2011).

### Auto- or self-plagiarism

When an author repeats text or data from his or her own published work in a new manuscript, it is considered auto- or self-plagiarism. As with plagiarism, self-plagiarism can occur when an author uses the same words to describe his or her previous work or a previously published technique, but it becomes much more serious when an author is trying to pass off as novel material something that is not. There are a number of ways that authors can commit self-plagiarism:

- Submitting the same manuscript to more than one journal at the same time.
- Redundant publication – submitting a published manuscript to another journal without acknowledgment of the original publication, perhaps in another language, or to a journal in another specialty, where it might be less likely to be recognized.[2]
- Including data from another paper as though the data were unique. An example of this occurs when a researcher does not repeat controls in a multipart experiment, and so includes the same control data in multiple papers. This would be unethical on its own and would also negatively affect the integrity of the paper. Data duplication can also occur when a researcher tries to "slice" one research project into too many papers, sometimes called "salami publishing" or "salami slicing."

## Data appropriation

Data appropriation is different from plagiarism; the term usually refers to the situation where unpublished data of another researcher is used and represented as the author's own. Collaborators, colleagues who are shown preliminary versions of manuscripts for feedback, and reviewers of submitted manuscripts are all privy to unpublished data. This prepublication exposure – which is a key part of the way scholarship is shared and progresses – can lead to data appropriation.

## Data fabrication

Data fabrication occurs when data are invented – either some data, which just tip the results of the research over to being positive and significant, or the wholesale fabrication of all the data in a paper. A famous case of wholesale fabrication occurred in 2006, when *Science* had to retract two papers on stem-cell research published in 2004 and 2005 (Kennedy,

---

[2] If one author of a co-authored paper submits it to a second journal without the knowledge of the other authors, this is also an authorship issue.

2006). Data fabrication is a very serious form of unethical conduct because, once discovered, it cannot be explained away by error or carelessness. However, it can be one of the hardest types of ethical issue to detect, because if research is presented in a scientifically sound and plausible way, it is very likely to pass through peer review.

## Data falsification

Falsification of data is also a very serious type of unethical conduct. It involves the manipulation of otherwise real data to make results look more positive or significant, or to make an overblown hypothesis seem more likely, and includes the omission of data that does not support the author's hypothesis.

## Figure manipulation

Manipulating figures to improve the study results shown in them has been one of the most prevalent kinds of data falsification in recently discovered ethical cases. As with plagiarism, this is partly due to the ease with which figure manipulation can be found; it is readily detectable using the software used to edit electronic figure files.

There may be some traditional reasons or longstanding habits that lead authors to consider some degree of figure "enhancement" to be acceptable. Authors have always, understandably, submitted the figures that most clearly show the results they want to show, just as in the days of non-electronic figures they chose the photo in which the contrast was just right, or included only "representative" samples of gel lanes or blots (both forms of tests used in molecular biology), or cropped photographs to eliminate "artifacts" or other elements. Then, as now, these examples would have fallen somewhere on a continuum of ethical to unethical behavior.

Now that most data is captured electronically and then put into an electronic figure file, there are many more opportunities to enhance what the reader will ultimately see. With a few key-strokes, contrast can be changed, and parts of figures can be moved, hidden, or added without degradation of the picture quality or obvious (to the reader) marks of manipulation.

However, these manipulations are often still discoverable. Reviewers looking carefully at manuscript figures have sometimes noticed image elements copied from one figure to another, but with a different orientation. But what makes figure manipulation most easy to detect is the way figures are prepared for publication by many publishers. In order to prepare for production the myriad kinds of files that authors use to submit their figures, compositors or staff in the art department are armed with powerful software that can read and "open" many graphic file types. Depending on journal rules and style, the art department may be charged with changing figure labels to a standard font or size, or may be asked by a Copy-Editor to correct the spelling of figure labels. They may also be trying to improve the resolution or quality of a figure for print or online publication. What they sometimes find may surprise a naïve author. Evidence of cutting and pasting, hiding figure elements, or changing colors or contrast in ways that unfairly enhance parts of a figure can suddenly be seen using these software packages, which are sometimes the same software packages the authors used to create and manipulate the figures in the first place.

Many editorials have been written to warn authors of the dangers of using these tools to manipulate their figures, and to give guidelines on what types of figure manipulation are and are not acceptable (Rossner, 2002; Cromey, 2010). An example of guidelines (American Physiological Society, 2007) is shown in Box 12.2.

**Box 12.2** Instructions to authors on figure manipulation, from the American Physiological Society's website

- Authors should not move, remove, introduce, obscure or enhance any specific feature within any (digital) image.
- Authors should not adjust contrast, color balance or brightness unless applied to the entire figure and disclosed in the figure legend.
- Authors should not obscure, eliminate, or misrepresent the originally-captured information.
- If parts of different gels, fields, or exposures are grouped or rearranged, then dividing lines must be used to indicate these changes, and disclosure of the arrangement must be added in the figure legend. Even if the arrangement is from the same capture, the rearrangement or deletion of lanes, fields, etc, is discouraged, but if there is any such deletion or rearrangement, it must be disclosed in the legend.

Reprinted with the permission of the American Physiological Society, August 2011.

## Animal welfare issues

Research studies involving animals must follow strict protocols involving the keeping, experimentation on, and (if necessary) euthanasia of the animals. Although reviewers and readers will sometimes contact a journal Editor if they are alarmed by something they have read in an article that they know would not have been allowed at their institution, it is impossible for reviewers, journal Editors, and journal staff to judge whether animals were actually treated according to accepted standards. That is why most journals require that authors include a statement, either as part of the submission process or in the manuscript itself, that the authors obtained approval from their governing body on animal welfare. In the US, an institution's Institutional Animal Care and Use Committee (IACUC) must give approval for the specific study. In the UK, researchers must obtain three separate levels of license from the Home Office: a personal license, a project license, and a certificate of designation for the place where the procedures are carried out.

## Human welfare issues

Research studies involving humans, human specimens, or human data must also follow strict protocols involving the experimentation itself, as well as requiring the consent and protection of the privacy of the individual. Most journals that publish human or clinical studies state that they adhere to the Declaration of Helsinki (World Medical Association, 2008) and expect authors to have done so. Many journals also require that authors include a statement, either as part of the submission process or in the manuscript itself, that the authors obtained approval from their governing body on human protocols. In the US, this is an institution's Institutional Review Board (IRB); in the UK, each university has a committee responsible for such research outside the National Health Service, while within the NHS it is governed by the Research Governance Framework for Health and Social Care, as well as the guidelines of the local trusts.

Each such governing body is concerned not only to ensure that the protocol respects the subject's welfare, but also that informed consent was obtained for that specific study, and that absolute confidentiality of all human subject information is maintained. Strict protocols are not only required for clinical studies; surveys of participants in studies conducted in the humanities and social sciences must also maintain confidentiality. Consent forms for surveys should inform the participant that the data collected will be used only for research purposes, that the data will be "anonymized" – the participant's identity will not be recognizable – and that the data will be archived so as to be used in future research, if applicable. (Van den Eynden et al., 2011)

## Authorship issues

A number of ethical issues can arise with the list of authors of an article. These include authorship disputes and inappropriate authorship, including guest authorship (a named author who has not participated in the work) and ghost authorship (an unnamed author who has). Except perhaps for data falsification and fabrication, there are no ethical issues more fraught with intrigue and emotional tension.

This is an interesting phenomenon, because there are very clear guidelines about who has the right to call himself or herself an "author" of a paper. These are often discussed in detail in the style guides developed by the primary organization(s) for the various HSS and STM disciplines. For example, the International Committee of Medical Journal Editors (ICMJE) (www.icmje.org) recommends the following criteria for authorship in its *Uniform requirements for manuscripts submitted to biomedical journals*: "Authorship credit should be based on 1) substantial contributions to conception and design, acquisition of data, or analysis and interpretation of data; 2) drafting the article or revising it critically for important intellectual content; and 3) final approval of the version to be published. Authors should meet conditions 1, 2, and 3" (International Committee of Medical Journal Editors, 2010). The *Uniform requirements* go on to say, "All contributors who do not meet the criteria for authorship should be listed in an acknowledgments section. Examples of those who might be acknowledged include a person who provided purely technical help, writing assistance, or a department chairperson who provided only general support."

However, the negotiations that go on among people who work together, collaborate, and report to each other can make moot even such clear guidelines as these. And the order in which authors are listed on the title page of a paper is often based on customs that differ across fields, and can sometimes have little to do with effort or actual contribution. In order to make the situation more transparent, some publishers thought they might move away from a list of authors to a list of contributors, with each contributor's name listed together with a description of his or her contribution (Rennie et al., 1997). The journals that use this method, however, still preserve the traditional author list on the title page of the article (which is how authors still get credit for the publication), along with a contributor list usually near the end of the article, which spells out what each author (and others who are not listed as authors) contributed to the research and the article (Bates et al., 2004).

The aim in requiring all authors to specify what they contributed to the paper is to reduce the number of cases of "honorary" or "guest" authors. Honorary authors had little to do with the research or writing of the paper, but hold some position of influence with the authors (e.g., the head of department). Guest authors also had little or nothing to do with the specific research or article, but are asked to allow their names to be added to the author list, in order to give the paper a boost of recognition or respect (and thus to improve its chances of acceptance by a reputable journal).

Explicit instructions about contributorship are also intended to help expose ghost authors. Unlike honorary or guest authors, ghost authors actually do quite a lot of work on papers – many are the sole writer – but their names are not included in the authorship list. The most egregious type of ghost authorship is when an employee of a pharmaceutical company writes, or hires someone to write, an article summarizing research done at that company. The true author remains anonymous, while the company recruits researchers outside the company to allow their names to be listed as authors of the paper (guest authors) (Ross et al., 2008; Sismondo, 2009).

*Authorship disputes.* Occasionally, an individual will contact the journal Editor or publisher complaining that a paper – either currently undergoing peer review or already published – should have included his or her name as author. Sometimes, it is the order in which the author names appear that is questioned by one or more of the listed authors. Sometimes, when all co-authors are contacted by the Editorial office acknowledging submission of a paper, one or more will respond stating that he or she is surprised to be listed, because he or she had little or nothing to do with its writing. In each of these instances, an ethical case will be opened, and the dispute will be investigated. This can often delay peer review and, thus, hold up potential publication. If the individuals cannot come to some agreement, the case may have to be turned over to the corresponding author's[3] institution for a decision, as the Editorial or publishing office has little to go on to decide the case.

## Reviewers

While late or unhelpful reviews are rarely treated in any formal sense as instances of ethical misconduct, reviewers should not break the bargain they make when they agree to review an article. In other words, they should deliver their review in a timely way, and approach the review without bias as to the author or the type of research. If a reviewer believes that he or she cannot approach the manuscript in an unbiased way, the invitation to review should be declined. Most reviewers excuse themselves if the manuscript is written by someone in their department or by collaborators or family members, in order to avoid a real or perceived conflict of interest.

When a reviewer purposely delays submitting a review for personal gain – by delaying publication of the article in order to get his or her own research published first – this becomes an ethical issue that should be dealt with by the journal.

Reviewers must be particularly careful about ethical breaches that violate confidentiality. As was stated above, misappropriation of data from a paper being reviewed is one of the most serious ethical issues that can be committed by a reviewer. Passing on a request to review a manuscript to another person, such as a graduate student or postdoctoral fellow, should only be done with the approval of the journal, and in such cases the review should not be submitted under the name of the invited reviewer. Some journal Editors will not accept reviews written by someone other than the Editor's choice of reviewer; however, others see it as valuable training of new reviewers and a way to increase the reviewer pool. Using an unpublished manuscript one has been asked to review in a journal club[4]

---

[3]  The corresponding author is the author in charge of all correspondence with the publisher, and is often, but not always, the author who submitted the manuscript.

[4]  A "journal club" is a group that meets regularly to read and critique recent scientific papers. It is used as a teaching tool for graduate and professional students to develop their evaluative and debating skills. Some publishers have developed "journal club journals" which consist of informed commentary on recent research articles in a given field.

should also be avoided, because it increases the risk of others appropriating data or ideas.

### Journal Editors

Journal Editors need to avoid the same issues as reviewers, such as conflicts of interest (discussed in greater detail below), delays in publication, breaches in confidentiality (including the confidentiality of details of ethical issues), and bias. Journal Editors can be guilty of the same kinds of bias as reviewers: biases for or against certain topics, methods, interpretation of results, or authors. But they can also act in ways that are inappropriate when showing bias towards their own journal, most frequently manifested in "tricks" used to increase a journal's impact factor.

Many journal Editors employ perfectly legitimate tactics to improve their journal's impact factor: publishing more review articles and encouraging commentaries and letters to the Editor about (and citing) other articles. Forcing – or even encouraging – authors with papers in peer review to add more citations to their journal, or publishing an annual editorial that cites every paper in last year's issues, is frowned upon. The difference here is obvious: the legitimate actions add real content to the journal, whereas the less appropriate actions do not. In fact, Thomson Reuters monitors and publishes self-citation rates, and punishes journals in which the rate exceeds the typical rate of self-citation,[5] by suppressing – essentially, not publishing – their citation data until the excessive self-citation ceases (Testa, 2008).

Some journal Editors refrain from publishing their own original research in their journals during their terms of office, in order to avoid appearing to use the journal to promote their own work. However, if the peer review is handled fairly, as described in the next section on conflict of interest, this is an unnecessary precaution. In fact, most publishers want their journal Editors to show support for their journal by submitting their best research to it. When an Editor clearly uses a journal as a form

---

[5]   Thomson Reuters considers any journal with a self-citation rate of 20% to have a high rate of self-citation, but does not make public the percentage that it considers excessive (McVeigh, 2003). This seems to be because a more subjective judgment is made when a journal is considered to have an excessive self-citation rate, based on the nature of the journal and its citation history.

of "vanity publishing," however, there is an ethical issue. An infamous case was that of the math journal *Chaos, Solitons & Fractals*, whose Editor, M S El Naschie, resigned after his rate of self-publication became excessive, causing much controversy in his field and in publishing circles (Davis, 2010).

### Conflict of interest

"Conflicts of interest … can be defined as conditions in which an individual holds conflicting or competing interests that could bias editorial decisions" (Scott-Lichter and the Editorial Policy Committee, 2009). Furthermore, even the perception of conflict should be avoided. Journal Editors, reviewers, and authors can all have real or perceived conflicts of interest. For the publisher or journal itself, real or perceived financial conflicts should be avoided.

### *Personal conflicts*

Conflicts of interest can arise from personal relationships. As stated above, reviewers and journal Editors should excuse themselves from handling submissions written by individuals close to them, or if they have any other strong biases for or against the authors or the subject of the manuscript. Some peer-review systems can automatically flag possible conflicts (e.g., author and reviewer in the same department, or sharing the same family name). If an Editor submits a paper to his or her own journal, another member of the Editorial team, or even a Guest Editor, should handle the paper, and the peer-review system should not allow the submitting Editor access to the manuscript record. To avoid the perception of conflict, written editorial policies should be in place describing how such events are handled, and these should be made public.

### *Financial conflicts*

The type of conflict of interest that attracts the most attention is the financial kind (Okike et al., 2009; Campbell and Zinner, 2010; Drazen et al., 2010; Fontanarosa et al., 2010; Rockey and Collins, 2010; Zuckerman, 2010). This is especially pertinent to journals that publish clinical studies; the goal must be to avoid the conflict or perceived conflict that can arise when an author, reviewer, journal Editor, or the journal itself is involved with or receives financial support from companies that can benefit from published research that shows their drug, instrument, or product in a positive light.

Individuals have a perceived conflict of interest when they are paid by (as employees, consultants, or speakers) or own stock in companies whose products they then use in their published research. It is not automatically assumed that these authors, reviewers, or journal Editors are biased, but the reader should be informed of the potential conflict so that he or she can read the article (or review or journal) in this context. In order to avoid the appearance of hiding potential conflicts, it is important for the journal to have disclosure policies, such as those developed by the ICMJE (www. icmje.org/ethical_4conflicts.html; Drazen et al., 2009). Authors, and in some journals, reviewers (Scott-Lichter and the Editorial Policy Committee, 2009) and journal Editors, are asked to sign disclosure forms that describe their financial relationship, if any, with relevant companies. Authors with such relationships are asked to acknowledge their funding or personal financial ties to these companies in the acknowledgment or disclosure section of the manuscript.

Some sponsored print journals are distributed free of charge, with the costs supported by advertising, a commercial sponsor, or a combination of the two. The recipients may be chosen by the sponsor, or they may register to receive the journal, in which case they will be asked to supply details showing why they qualify to receive it (these are sometimes referred to as "controlled circulation journals"). The circulation list is subject to external audit in order to qualify for special postal rates; advertisers/sponsors will also require the audit figure to verify that the numbers with desired demographics are being reached. These publications usually contain articles about recent research studies, and these articles are usually not peer reviewed. As long as it is clear that the publication is sponsored, there is no ethical issue; concealing the fact, however, is a serious breach (Rochon et al., 2002; Gallagher, 2009).

Peer-reviewed journals can be sponsored in part by industry, and again, as long as this is made clear, there is no ethical issue; this usually takes the form of sponsored supplements. Symposium proceedings are often published as a journal "supplement," printed and bound separately from the issue with which it is mailed. These supplements are usually sponsored by the same company that sponsored the symposium, and the sponsor more than pays for the cost of the supplement, in exchange for the prominent placement of its company or product names in or on the piece. As the articles in a sponsored supplement may not be peer reviewed, and can be of lesser quality than similar articles in the regular journal issues, it is wise to make the sponsorship clear on each article (Rochon et al., 1994). (Sponsored journals/supplements are also discussed in Chapter 9, Subsidiary income.)

## Dealing with ethical issues

When an ethical issue is discovered, or a question arises, it is often brought to the attention of the journal Editor or someone in the Editorial or publishing office. It is a very good idea to have a policy in place for dealing with these issues, so that the journal is not seen to be approaching them in a haphazard or *ad hoc* way. Having a written policy about how to avoid ethical issues and how they will be handled also gives the publisher something to point to if an accused individual claims he or she did not know what the rules were, or complains about the process. Many publishers ask authors to guarantee that they have not committed some common transgressions (by filling in check boxes in the peer-review system or by including statements on Copyright Transfer forms). Some examples of clear ethical policies are those of Wiley-Blackwell (www.wiley.com/bw/publicationethics/#newflowcharts), the American Physiological Society (www.the-aps.org/publications/journals/apsethic.htm), and the Society for Neuroscience (www.sfn.org/index.aspx?pagename=guidelinesPolicies_PolicyonEthics).

The Committee on Publication Ethics (COPE) has developed very useful flowcharts (http://publicationethics.org/resources/flowcharts) for handling ethical issues, which can be amended to fit a journal's preferences and personnel (see Figure 12.1 for an example).

When ethical issues are brought to the attention of the journal Editor or a member of the publisher's staff, the procedures that have been put in place must of course be followed. There are many variations among publishers regarding how and by whom ethical cases are handled. Although it is always best to have publishing staff involved in order to ensure that the publisher's policies and procedures are followed consistently, with some journals the Editor and Editorial Board and/or office handle the case, with backup – especially legal backup, if necessary – from

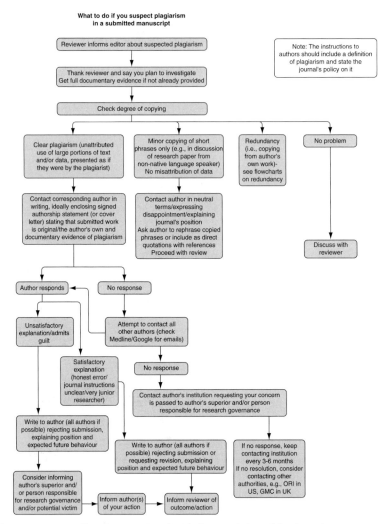

**What to do if you suspect plagiarism
in a submitted manuscript**

| | |
|---|---|
| Reviewer informs editor about suspected plagiarism | Note: The instructions to authors should include a definition of plagiarism and state the journal's policy on it |

Thank reviewer and say you plan to investigate
Get full documentary evidence if not already provided

Check degree of copying

| Clear plagiarism (unattributed use of large portions of text and/or data, presented as if they were by the plagiarist) | Minor copying of short phrases only (e.g., in discussion of research paper from non-native language speaker) No misattribution of data | Redundancy (i.e., copying from author's own work)- see flowcharts on redundancy | No problem |

Contact corresponding author in writing, ideally enclosing signed authorship statement (or cover letter) stating that submitted work is original/the author's own and documentary evidence of plagiarism

Contact author in neutral terms/expressing disappointment/explaining journal's position
Ask author to rephrase copied phrases or include as direct quotations with references
Proceed with review

Discuss with reviewer

Author responds ◄─── No response

Unsatisfactory explanation/admits guilt

Attempt to contact all other authors (check Medline/Google for emails)

Satisfactory explanation (honest error/ journal instructions unclear/very junior researcher)

No response

Contact author's institution requesting your concern is passed to author's superior and/or person responsible for research governance

Write to author (all authors if possible) rejecting submission, explaining position and expected future behaviour

Write to author (all authors if possible) rejecting submission or requesting revision, explaining position and expected future behaviour

If no response, keep contacting institution every 3-6 months
If no resolution, consider contacting other authorities, e.g., ORI in US, GMC in UK

Consider informing author's superior and/ or person responsible for research governance and/or potential victim

Inform author(s) of your action

Inform reviewer of outcome/action

**Figure 12.1** COPE flowchart. Reprinted with the permission of the Committee on Publication Ethics (COPE), www.publicationethics.org.

the publisher. Societies are likely to handle such cases in-house (some even have "ethics officers" on staff; Frank, 2011), under the direction of a Publications Committee made up of society members or some subset of that committee. Groups such as COPE will provide advice to Editors on how to handle ethical cases. The Office of Research Integrity (ORI) in the US also provides educational materials related to ethical issues, and will provide oversight of an institutional investigation.

## Investigating an ethical issue

Every ethical issue that arises will be a little different, and there are different procedures to be followed according to the type of issue. Here, the COPE flowcharts are invaluable, because they have developed one for each category of ethical issue. However, there are certain basic procedures that always apply:

1. The journal finds out about, or is informed of, a potential issue.
2. The appropriate person (journal Editor, Managing Editor, Publications Committee Chair, ethics officer) writes a nonaccusatory message to the corresponding author of the article in question to inquire about the issue.
3. If the author's answer is satisfactory, the author is thanked and the case is closed.
4. If the author's answer is not satisfactory, more evidence may be requested (e.g., correspondence among authors, permission forms, IRB or IACUC forms and/or actual protocols, versions of manuscripts, or figure files) from the author.
5. The journal Editor, publisher, or committee, armed with such evidence, can make a decision about certain types of issue. These are typically plagiarism, redundant or duplicate publication, figure manipulation, and sometimes animal and human welfare issues. If evidence of unethical behavior is clear, the issue moves to the next stage, dealing with misconduct.
6. There are other types of issue that the journal Editor, publisher, or committee cannot easily or fairly investigate. These are typically authorship issues and issues of fabricated or falsified data, and some animal and human welfare issues. In these cases, the institution of the corresponding author is asked to adjudicate the case. After turning a case over to the institution, if the publisher is not asked to provide any further evidence, the publisher may not hear anything from the institution for many months; however, the publisher should make sure that it is informed of the outcome by the institution.

## Dealing with misconduct

Once a case of author misconduct is established, the authors and the paper must be dealt with, whether the manuscript is still in peer review or the paper has been published. If the paper has been published, the scientific record also needs to be amended.

If the manuscript is still in peer review, the following choices for dealing with the authors pertain, more or less in order of severity:

- *Correction.* If the infraction is minor and truly seems to result from an author's oversight or ignorance of the rules, a strong warning may be given to the author, while allowing him or her to correct the manuscript. The manuscript will then continue through the peer-review process.
- *Rejection.* Most papers with clear evidence of scientific misconduct are rejected. The publisher may also want to consider the next two choices, depending on the type and seriousness of the infraction.
- *Informing the author's institution.* If the author's institution was not approached to investigate the ethical case, it can be informed of the journal's findings, both as a form of punishment and also to warn the institution that there may be a lack of integrity in that author's group. This should not be done lightly, because the career of every author of the paper can be adversely affected by this action.
- *Sanction.* For serious infractions, rejection of the paper may not be deemed a sufficient punishment or lesson to the offending author(s), and the journal will also have a lingering distrust of their integrity. In these cases, the authors are "sanctioned" from submitting to the journal. In other words, they are banned from submitting to the journal for a defined period (one to five years), or occasionally for life. When a journal is considering sanctions, it also looks at whether all authors of the paper share equally in the misconduct, and may sanction different authors of the same paper for varying periods of time.

When taking actions that can affect an author's career (e.g., informing his or her institution or its Office of Research Integrity [ORI], or sanctioning the author), the investigation and findings of the person (e.g., journal Editor) or group (e.g., Publications Committee) making this decision should also be reviewed by a lawyer or a governing body (e.g., a society's board or council) to help ensure that the author is being treated fairly. If an accused author threatens a lawsuit, the publisher's and (if applicable) society's lawyers must get involved – see Box 12.3.

If the article has already been published, rejection is no longer an option, but the authors' institutions can still be informed and the authors

**Box 12.3** When to involve a lawyer

There are many actions during the process of dealing with an ethical problem that can potentially damage an author's career, so a publisher may want to involve a lawyer before doing any of the following:

- Contacting an author's institution or other investigative body, such as the Office of Research Integrity (ORI).
- Sanctioning an author.
- Publishing an expression of concern.
- Publishing a retraction.
- Dealing with an Editor who is the subject of an ethical case.

can still be sanctioned. It is also important to amend the published article, so that misappropriated or falsified information does not remain in the academic record. This can be done in a number of ways (see Chapter 4, The Production process, for how these can be handled technically in an online journal):

- *Erratum or corrigendum.* If the infraction does not invalidate the soundness of the paper, it can be corrected with a published erratum. An example of this might be when an author neglects to get permission from another journal for a reprinted figure. The correction would include the citation and permission line that should have been published with the article originally, and should include an apology from the author(s).
- *Retraction.* When the integrity of the research and its results are damaged or questionable, the paper should be retracted. A retraction notice is published (ideally written by the authors, or if they will not do so, by the journal Editor or publisher), and the online version of the article is clearly marked "retracted," to prevent the article from being cited in the future. PubMed will pick up retraction notices and also mark its own record of the article as retracted.
- *Expression of concern.* A misconduct investigation can take a very long time to be resolved by the authors' institution or another investigative body, such as the ORI. If the publisher believes that the research is likely to be proved faulty, and that there is some danger in it being left unchallenged and citable while the investigation is going on, an

"expression of concern" can be published in the journal and linked to the article to alert readers and other researchers to a possible problem with the article. The expression can then later be retracted, amended, or corrected, or a retraction notice of the article can be published at a later date if suspicions are proved correct.

If there is another journal that is wronged by an ethical issue, as in cases of plagiarism, a letter from the journal Editor or publisher should be written to the Editor of the journal that was wronged, apologizing for the infraction and informing him or her of the actions taken (e.g., erratum, retraction, sanction).

Sometimes, a journal will find out about an ethical issue after the investigation is already completed by others, and corrections, retractions, and/or sanctions have been decided upon. In these cases, the journal will be informed by an author's institution, a funding agency, or the author (usually at the behest of the institution or funding agency) that a published article needs to be retracted and/or that the authors have already been sanctioned by funding agencies and other journals, effectively ending their careers as researchers. In one high-profile case, the researcher Eric Poehlman was forced to retract ten published papers, was banned for life from applying for NIH and other US government funds, and was sentenced to prison (Federal Register, 2005; Kintisch, 2005). It is important that the publisher corrects the scholarly record by publishing retractions of which it is notified.

In summary, while written ethical policies, editorials, and author-targeted seminars given by publishers or societies can help educate authors about ethical pitfalls and thus avoid the occurrence of some ethical problems, publishers should be prepared to handle ethical issues as they arise, because they will. In fact, some publishers actively look for them (for example, through the use of CrossCheck). There are many resources listed in this chapter on which to base an ethics policy, and other groups, such as COPE and the ORI, that can offer assistance, if needed, when dealing with ethical issues.

### REFERENCES

American Physiological Society, 2007, *Ethics in figure preparation*, Bethesda MD, American Physiological Society (www.the-aps.org/publications/authorinfo/ figures/fig_manip_2007.htm)

Bates, Tamara, Ante Anić, Matko Marušić, and Ana Marušić, 2004, Authorship criteria and disclosure of contributions: comparison of 3 general medical journals with different author contribution forms, *Journal of the American Medical Association* 292: 86–8 (http://dx.doi.org/10.1001/jama.292.1.86)

Campbell, Eric G, and Darren E Zinner, 2010, Disclosing industry relationships – toward an improved research policy, *New England Journal of Medicine* 12: 604–6 (http://dx.org/10.1056/NEJMp)

Cromey, Douglas W, 2010, Avoiding twisted pixels: ethical guidelines for the appropriate use and manipulation of scientific digital images, *Science and Engineering Ethics* 16: 639–67 (http://dx.doi.org/10.1007/s11948-010-9201-y)

Davis, Phil, 2010, Controversial math journal relaunches: new editors, focus on rigorous review, *Scholarly Kitchen*, March (http://scholarlykitchen.sspnet.org/2010/03/18/chaos-relaunches/)

Drazen, Jeffrey M, Peter W de Leeuw, Christine Laine, Cynthia Mulrow, Catherine D DeAngelis, Frank A Frizelle, Fiona Godlee, Charlotte Haug, Paul C Hébert, Astrid James, Sheldon Kotzin, Ana Marušić, Humberto Reyes, Jacob Rosenberg, Peush Sahni, Martin B Van der Weyden, and Getu Zhaori, 2010, Toward more uniform conflict disclosures: the updated ICMJE conflict of interest reporting form, *Journal of the American Medical Association* 304: 212–13 (http://dx.doi.org/10.1001/jama.2010.918)

Drazen, Jeffrey M, Martin B Van der Weyden, Peush Sahni, Jacob Rosenberg, Ana Marušić, Christine Laine, Sheldon Kotzin, Richard Horton, Paul C Hébert, Charlotte Haug, Fiona Godlee, Frank A Frizelle, Peter W de Leeuw, and Catherine D DeAngelis, 2009, Uniform format for disclosure of competing interests in ICMJE journals, *New England Journal of Medicine* 362: 1896–7 (http://dx/doi.org/10.1056/NEJMe0909052)

Federal Register, 2005, Case summary – Eric T Poehlman, *Federal Register* 70: 15092–5 (www.gpo.gov/fdsys/pkg/FR-2005-03-24/html/05-5876.htm)

Fontanarosa, Phil B, Annette Flanagin, and Catherine D DeAngelis, 2010, Implementation of the ICMJE form for reporting potential conflicts of interest, *Journal of the American Medical Association* 304: 1496 (http://dx.doi.org/10.1001/jama.2010.1429)

Frank, Martin, 2011, We must do better!, *Physiologist* 54: 43–5 (www.the-aps.org/publications/tphys/2011html/April/opinion.htm)

Gallagher, Richard, 2009, For shame, Merck and Elsevier: everyone makes mistakes – it's how you handle them that matters, *The Scientist* 23: 13 (http://classic.the-scientist.com/2009/06/1/13/1/)

International Committee of Medical Journal Editors, 2010, *Uniform requirements for manuscripts submitted to biomedical journals*, updated 2010 (www.icmje.org/urm_main.html)

Kennedy, Donald, 2006, Editorial retraction, *Science* 311: 335 (http://dx.doi.org/10.1126/science.1124926)

Kintisch, Eli, 2005, Researcher faces prison for fraud in NIH grant applications and papers, *Science* 307: 1851 (http://dx.doi.org/10.1126/science.307.5717.1851a)

McVeigh, Marie, 2003, *Journal self-citation in the Journal Citation Reports*, Thomson Reuters (http://thomsonreuters.com/products_services/science/free/essays/journal_self_citation_jcr/)

Okike, Kanu, Mininder S Kocher, Erin X Wei, Charles T Mehlman, and Mohit Bhandari, 2009, Accuracy of conflict-of-interest disclosures reported by physicians, *New England Journal of Medicine* 361: 1466–74 (www.dx.doi.org/10.1056/NEJMsa0807160)

Rennie, Drummond, Veronica Yank, and Linda Emanuel, 1997, When authorship fails: a proposal to make contributors accountable, *Journal of the American Medical Association*, 278: 579–85 (http://dx.doi.org/10.1001/jama.1997.035500700710410)

Rochon, Paula A, Lisa A Bero, Ari M Bay, Jennifer L Gold, Julie M Dergal, Malcolm A Binns, David L Streiner, and Jerry H Gurwitz, 2002, Comparison of review articles published in peer-reviewed and throwaway journals, *Journal of the American Medical Association* 287: 2853–6 (http://dx.doi.org/10.1001/jama.287.21.2853)

Rochon, Paula A, Jerry H Gurwitz, C Mark Cheung, Jason A Hayes, and Thomas C Chalmers, 1994, Evaluating the quality of articles published in journal supplements compared with the quality of those published in the parent journal, *Journal of the American Medical Association* 272: 108–12 (http://dx.doi.org/10.1001/jama.1994.03520020034009)

Rockey, Sally J, and Francis S Collins, 2010, Managing financial conflict of interest in biomedical research, *Journal of the American Medical Association* 303: 2400–2 (http://dx.doi.org/10.1001/jama.2010.774)

Ross, Joseph S, Kevin P Hill, David S Egilman, and Harlan M Krumholz, 2008, Guest authorship and ghostwriting in publications related to rofecoxib: a case study of industry documents from rofecoxib litigation, *Journal of the American Medical Association*, 299:1800–12 (http://dx.doi.org/10.1001/jama.299.15.1800)

Rossner, Mike, 2002, Figure manipulation: assessing what is acceptable, *Journal of Cell Biology* 158: 1151 (http://dx.doi.org/10.1083/jcb.200209084)

Scott-Lichter, Diane, and the Editorial Policy Committee, 2009, Council of Science Editors, *CSE's white paper on promoting integrity in scientific journal publications*, 2009 update, Reston, VA, Council of Science Editors (www.councilscienceeditors.org/i4a/pages/index.cfm?pageid=3331)

Sismondo, Sergio, 2009, Ghosts in the machine: publication planning in the medical sciences, *Social Studies of Science* 39:171 (http://dx.doi.org/10.1177/0306312708101047)

Testa, James, 2008, Playing the system puts self-citation's impact under review, *Nature* 455: 729 (http://dx.doi.org/10.1038/455729b)

Van den Eynden, Veerle, Louise Corti, Matthew Woollard, Libby Bishop, and Laurence Horton, 2011, *Managing and sharing data*, UK Data Archive, University of Essex, May (www.data-archive.ac.uk/media/2894/managingsharing.pdf)

Wager, Liz, 2011, *How should editors respond to plagiarism?*, COPE discussion paper (http://publicationethics.org/files/COPE_plagiarism_discussion_%20doc_26%20Apr%2011.pdf)

World Medical Association, 2008, *Declaration of Helsinki: ethical principles for medical research involving human subjects*, Ferney-Voltaire, France, World Medical Association (www.wma.net/en/30publications/10policies/b3/17c.pdf)

Zuckerman, Joseph D, 2010, Accuracy of financial disclosures reported by physicians, *New England Journal of Medicine* 362: 470 (http://dx.doi.org/10.1056/NEJM c0911065)

## FURTHER READING

COPE (Committee on Publication Ethics) resources (www.publicationethics.org/resources); COPE flowcharts (http://publicationethics.org/resources/flowcharts)

Hames, Irene, 2007, *Peer review and manuscript management in scientific journals: guidelines for good practice*, Oxford, Association of Learned and Professional Society Publishers/Wiley-Blackwell

# 13 The future of scholarly communication

## Scholarly communication

The primary objective of a scholar's work is to answer questions or solve problems. The nature of the questions or problems may be very different in the sciences and the humanities, but the underlying objective is the same.

This work, however, achieves nothing unless it is communicated. Scholars communicate with each other in order to test and develop their ideas, as well as to set down a personal marker for their discoveries and insights. They do this in a whole spectrum of different ways, ranging from the completely informal (e.g., face-to-face, telephone, or email "conversation") to the completely formal (e.g., publication in a journal article or book). And formal publication is itself only a means to an end – that of getting the author's work accepted by others, and eventually integrated into the body of the world's knowledge.

More than a decade ago, publisher Arthur Smith (Smith, 2000) nicely described the range of ways in which scholars communicated in the past, and might do in the future – see Figures 13.1 and 13.2. He illustrated how publication in a journal is just one stage in a sequence which moves from the author's first, preliminary private communications to the eventual adoption of his or her findings by the wider world.

Smith's view of the potential impact of electronic media (shown in Figure 13.2) was remarkably prescient. While the stages of communication, and the degrees of completeness/formality, have remained the same, the advent of online means of achieving these ends has placed increasing control in the hands of authors and their institutions, particularly at the stage of "communication."

As this shift continues, the ubiquity and ease of other modes of communication – including social media, which barely existed when Smith wrote his paper – are bound to impinge ever further on the role and importance of scholarly journal articles.

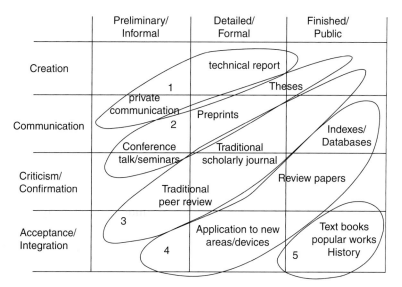

**Figure 13.1** Scholarly communication – the past (Smith, 2000). Reprinted with the permission of ALPSP.

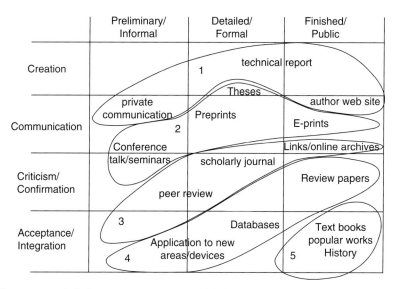

**Figure 13.2** Scholarly communication – a possible future (Smith, 2000). Reprinted with the permission of ALPSP.

## The drivers of change

A number of different pressures have combined to drive the changes we have seen – and will continue to see – in scholarly communication.

## Economics

As was outlined in Chapter 1, Introduction to journals, the number of journals has increased remarkably consistently over nearly 350 years. This mirrors the growing output of journal articles, which must result either in the expansion of existing journals or in the creation of new ones. This output mirrors the growth in the number of researchers, which in turn reflects (particularly since World War II) the growth in expenditure on research and development (R&D); the ratio between the number of papers and the number of researchers has remained remarkably constant over many years (Mabe and Amin, 2001; Mabe, 2003).

While investment in R&D is demonstrably good for the economic health of a national economy (May, 1998), the resultant growth in the number and/or size of journals has been less welcome, since the budgets provided for libraries to acquire this ever-expanding wealth of information have long since ceased to keep pace with research funding. Librarians have been forced to make difficult choices about what to buy and how to buy it (e.g., subscription/license, or single articles on demand), and what not to buy at all; they have also joined forces in buying consortia, to strengthen their hand in negotiations with publishers.

At the time of writing (2012), many countries with a strong tradition of research and publication are experiencing economic difficulties, in some cases exacerbated by the impact of natural disasters, and it is not obvious when (or even whether) the financial climate will improve. Funding for research itself is being squeezed, and the library funding for the acquisition, access, and preservation of that research is in serious trouble.

Publishers, too, are feeling the economic pressures; as library funds become ever tighter, it has become increasingly difficult to launch new journals, at least under the existing subscription/license model which is funded on the "reader side," by library acquisitions (and any personal subscriptions). Full or partial "author-side" funding, through page, color, submission, publication, or other charges, is one way of addressing this problem, though it only scales with R&D funding if the charges can be paid out of the research grant (or directly by the funder), which is not always the case (see Chapter 8, Journal finances, for more extensive discussion of the "author-side" funding model, the commonest way of achieving what is often known as "Gold open access").

Some commentators have long felt that the subscription/license model would eventually prove unsustainable, as the gap between the literature to be acquired and the money available to acquire it continued to widen. A "catastrophic" change – in the literal sense of "sudden and violent change of state" – is, they would say, inevitable. Will alternative business models be sufficient to avert this catastrophic change? If both authors and readers continue to want the value that is added to articles by the publishing process, the costs of that process still have to be paid for, whether by the library, the research funder, or someone else; other, better targeted ways of paying for content (e.g., article by article, or on the basis of usage) would still have to cover the same costs. Unless we can find a completely different way of carrying out the processes of scholarly communication – one which costs a whole lot less than the current one – the financial dilemma will not go away.

## Technology

We should not forget that changes in printing technology made a huge difference to scholarly communication long before the advent of computers, let alone the Internet. Indeed, the first published journals were themselves the successors of correspondence between scientists on the one hand, and meetings of learned societies and the like on the other; with the advent of printing, it became possible to widen the scope of both, although it was not until 200 years later that printed journals were born. In 1620, Francis Bacon wrote that printing was one of the inventions that had "changed the whole face and state of things throughout the world" (Bacon, 1620).

Subsequent developments made it possible to print large quantities more economically, made color illustrations affordable, and made extremely small print quantities also financially viable.

In 1959, Xerox's development of the photocopier made it quick and easy to generate multiple copies, while the same company's development of a convenient fax machine a few years later enabled instant transmission of written communications over distance. Both created alarm in the minds of publishers and other copyright owners, as making unauthorized copies became so easy that it rarely crossed users' minds that they might be contravening copyright by, for example, photocopying articles for classroom use, or faxing an article to a corporate researcher.

However, it was the development and popularization of the personal computer in the 1970s, and later its convergence with communications technology, that brought about the most dramatic changes. Communication of scholarly work can be virtually instant, irrespective of distance; at the same time, much informal communication is no longer preserved in the way that letters were, and the long-term preservation of even formal communications (such as journals) presents considerable (and potentially costly) challenges, as discussed in Chapter 4, The production process.

Contrary to the hopes of many, however, electronic publishing has not slashed the overall costs of producing, or of acquiring, journals (see discussion in Chapter 1, Introduction to journals). And it has made theft of the content so easy – whether it be sending a copy of an article to an electronic discussion list, or cutting and pasting text into one's own work – that publishers have to wonder whether they will suffer the same fate as the recorded music industry, which lost millions in revenue because of so-called "file sharing."

## *Scale*

In the thirteenth century, St Albert the Great was described as "doctor universalis" – "the teacher of everything there is to know"; the single term "philosophy" (or "natural philosophy") described all scientific knowledge. However, even in 1255 it was becoming increasingly difficult to know everything: "the multitude of books, the shortness of time and the slipperiness of memory do not allow all things which are written to be equally retained in the mind" (Vincent of Beauvais, 1255). And 500 years later, the mathematician and philosopher Denis Diderot wrote:

As long as the centuries continue to unfold, the number of books will grow continually, and one can predict that a time will come when it will be almost as difficult to learn anything from books as from the direct study of the whole universe. It will be almost as convenient to search for some bit of truth concealed in nature as it will be to find it hidden away in an immense multitude of bound volumes. (Diderot, 1755)

The steady expansion of research outputs mentioned above presents the reader with an increasingly intractable problem – that of information overload. In the 1950s, it was estimated that some 90% of all the scientists who had ever lived were alive (and, in many cases, researching and publishing) (Oppenheimer, 1958). It has been estimated (Jinha, 2010) that some 50 million learned articles have been written since journals first began back in 1665; and thanks to a wealth of projects to digitize older material, a significant proportion is available online. There is no way that an individual can read and internalize even a tiny fraction of the available literature. Scholars are having to read more and more articles, but must spend less and less time on each article (King and Tenopir, 2006).

Of course, disciplines have become more and more specialized (some would say narrow): while it is not possible to read everything that has been written about music, perhaps it is at least possible to read everything that has been written about the music of Hildegard of Bingen. This comes at a cost, however − cross-fertilization across disciplines can lead to refreshingly new insights, but it is increasingly difficult for a scholar to be a true polymath, whose knowledge stretches across many fields.

The ever-increasing number of potentially relevant articles means that efficient means of identifying and accessing the most relevant ones are increasingly important (CIBER, 2009). The tremendously powerful online search tools which are now available to us make it very easy to find information on almost any topic; it is hardly necessary to provide an index for a journal, as readers can simply search the full text of the content (and a number of publishers have stopped providing indexes for this reason).

While specialized services such as Google Scholar (http://scholar. google.com) enable scholars to focus their searches on the academic literature, some still use a general search engine. Specialist A&I databases appear to be the most popular route, followed by specialized and then general search engines (Gardner and Inger, 2012). In any case, few searchers go beyond the first couple of pages of search results (Rieger, 2009). Thus, while searching is easy, it is something of a blunt instrument. Google and other search engine providers are continuously improving the sophistication of their search algorithms − but can they actually replicate the skills of the information scientist?[1]

The value of "route maps" has thus increased steadily, as the problem of information overload has grown. The scholar may rely on expert opinion, such as the title-level filtering that occurs when a journal is selected for inclusion in bibliographic or citation databases (hence the importance, to publishers, of getting their journals into these as soon as possible after

---

[1] Most readers are not expert searchers; setting up a really accurate search, and then refining it as required, is a skill which many librarians have almost given up trying to teach their patrons.

launch). Or he or she may rely on the selection and comment of a particular expert author whose review article identifies the most important articles on a specific topic (with links, more often than not, to the original articles discussed); the extent to which review articles are both downloaded and cited is an indication of how popular they are. Publications such as *Computing Reviews* (http://computingreviews.com) develop the idea of the review journal by using a large panel of peer-nominated experts to select, summarize, and recommend individual published articles; those in biology and medicine from Faculty of 1000 (http://f1000.com) go a step further, giving each article a rating and explaining its importance.

However, other readers' opinions – as indicated by their actions – have become an increasingly important pointer for online readers: as with the "likes" on services such as YouTube, both citations and downloads by others provide strong indicators of the potential usefulness of a given article. Some services, such as Google Scholar and Scopus, already indicate the number of citations which an article has received (see Chapter 5, Journal metrics, for more detail); it seems highly probable that the number of downloads might also become a publicly available metric. And from there, it is a short step to using this information to present the most popular articles in response to a search,[2] or to offer Amazon-style recommendations: "people who read this article also read this." Possibly this signals a decline in respect for the role of the "expert" (as for authority in general), which may have ramifications for the "expert" status of journal peer reviewers and editors in future. (But is popularity the same as importance? It could become increasingly difficult to go against the grain of popular opinion – which is what the great thinkers have always done.)

### Globalization

For centuries, the volume of research literature has increased fairly steadily; however, that could be changing. Countries with enormous populations – such as India and China – have reached a stage in their development where R&D funding has become extremely significant; this results, inevitably, in

---

[2] Citations are already one component of Google Scholar's algorithm for determining the ranking of articles in the search results listing.

an outflow of journal articles, the best of which are of high international quality. It is important to the researchers and their funders that their work reaches the maximum international audience, and thus a growing proportion is published in English, either in locally published journals or in international journals. Many British and US journals report a steep increase in submissions (made much easier, especially for authors on the other side of the world, by online submission systems), with a significant and growing proportion from these countries. So it is possible that the steady growth in the number of articles and journals discussed earlier may be about to increase dramatically – which will, of course, exacerbate the information overload mentioned above.

At the same time, providing access to the journal literature to readers around the world is made both easier – with electronic journals – and more difficult – because of widely differing Internet infrastructure. As discussed in Chapter 6, Marketing and sales, publishers have made great efforts to ensure that journals are available either free of charge, or at a much reduced price, to readers in countries with limited funds. The fact that publishers can generally tell in what country an online user is based, monitor usage, and shut down access when they detect abuse makes such provisions both easier to achieve and much less risky than the longstanding practice of offering specially priced print copies for specific (underdeveloped) markets, which are sometimes found being resold elsewhere at full price. But the fact that journals are available online is of no help if you live in a country where the telecommunications infrastructure is unreliable or nonexistent, or where the hardware is not widely available.

One can perhaps envisage a future in which the price paid by any customer is tailored precisely to the customer's location and indeed other characteristics (e.g., member of a society, previous contributor to the journal, teacher, student, etc.). In the not too distant future, every Internet user could have a personal profile which contains all such information, and to which services can respond appropriately.[3]

---

[3] The Shibboleth system, which can be used to enable subsets of a university's population to access specific resources (http://shibboleth.internet2.edu), OCLC's EZproxy (www.oclc.org/ezproxy) and other initiatives are under way.

## How change has affected journals

### Changes for authors

The transition to online publication from the late 1990s onwards has been the most dramatic change to affect scholarly journals. However, the use of personal computers from the 1970s onwards had already enabled one key change. Authors' work could be submitted in electronic format (initially, of course, on floppy disks – later online), thus obviating the need for rekeying at the publisher's expense. What is more, with personal computers, more and more scholars were typing their own work, rather than having it typed by a secretary. Thus, the author had much more direct input into what eventually appeared in the published journal (apart, of course, from editorial and copy-editing changes).

From the point of view of the author and Editor, online journals have made the process of submission, through peer review to eventual acceptance or rejection, much easier (at least, with the better systems) and, in principle, accessible irrespective of the user's location. They have streamlined the mechanics of the process, removing the need to send paper copies via the postal system, with the attendant costs in both time and money, although of course the key functions – peer review, editing – still have to be done by human experts (even if they work on-screen).

Also from the point of view of the author, "publication" with a small "p" (a distinction made by Blume, 1998) – simply making one's work accessible to the public – has become extremely easy to achieve. The author can post his or her thoughts, notes, or articles on the Internet – on a personal or institutional blog or web page, or in a more formal institutional or subject-based repository. Others can respond informally or more formally, and the author may choose to modify the original posting accordingly, as the dialogue evolves. So far, at least, this form of publication has not supplanted formal Publication (with a capital "P"), although for a minority of articles (about 12% in 2009, according to Björk et al., 2010) the two coexist.

The ability to modify one's published work in the light of others' feedback or new information offers authors wonderful new flexibility – their ideas no longer have to remain set in stone. But this is both a blessing and a curse; the reader cannot be certain whether what he or she is looking at (or linking to) now is the same as the version the reader, or the author who cited it, had in mind. Ways of recording the changes that have been made, and of identifying, in a reader-friendly way, the version being looked at, are essential (Morris, 2005; National Information Standards Institute and Association of Learned and Professional Society Publishers, 2008 – see Chapter 4, The production process, for more on this).

## Changes for readers

From the point of view of the reader, journals are (more or less) straight-forwardly accessible at the desktop. This access may appear to be seamless and free of charge if the reader's institution has a subscription or license, or if the content is in fact available without any reader-side payment (indeed, the reader may understandably be unaware of the difference; Morris and Thorn, 2009). If not, credit cards and micropayments make the threshold easy to cross in practical (though not necessarily financial) terms. Browsing the list of contents of the reader's favorite journals is still surprisingly common, but searching is becoming both easier and (relatively) more precise (CIBER, 2009); and if the reader searches for articles on a given topic, rather than browsing a given journal, the journal itself is a much less important starting point. Having found an article of interest, too, the reader can navigate within the article, and from it to other cited articles.

In the 1960s, the Internet visionary Ted Nelson envisaged a truly hyperlinked world of information:

1960 – It occurs to me that the future of humanity is at the interactive computer screen, that the new writing and movies will be interactive and interlinked. It will be united by bridges of transclusion [the inclusion of a document or part of a document into another document by reference] . . . and we need a world-wide network to deliver it with royalty. (Nelson, 1994)

Nelson feels that the World Wide Web is but a trivialization of this grand idea (Xanadu, 2011) – but perhaps we are edging nearer to it.

## Business models

As was discussed in Chapter 8, Journal finances, electronic journals also opened up a far wider range of possibilities for business models – ways of paying for publications (and generating enough profit or surplus for those involved to keep on doing it). Subscriptions from individual institutions to individual publications have to a considerable degree given way to licenses, either from individual institutions or from groups of institutions (right up to whole countries), for anything from a single publication to the entire output of one or indeed multiple publishers. And purchasing individual articles, or potentially even parts of articles, is also now technically so straightforward that requests for so-called "interlibrary loan" copies (which have an administrative cost to both the requesting and the supplying institution) are becoming increasingly unnecessary.

Author-side charges, in the form of page charges and color charges, had long been a feature of the journal business model, particularly for society journals. However, the introduction of journals which are completely free to the reader, and are entirely funded by author-side charges (sometimes combined with other sources of income, including subsidy), is a phenomenon only made possible by online journals. It is possible because the incremental cost of making the journal, or article, available to one more user is relatively trivial. Hence we now see thousands of open access (OA) journals listed in the Directory of Open Access Journals (www.doaj.org), and it has been suggested that there are many more that have not yet been included in the list, particularly if they are not published in English. In addition, we find many journals carrying a mixture of OA and non-OA content; many more make all their content freely available after a period, sometimes as short as six months but more commonly one or two years.

The future landscape of business models – if it does indeed remain possible to fund, one way or another, something approximating to the current journal publication process – may well contain a complex patchwork of different models, and combinations of all of them, perhaps including some we haven't thought of yet. What is key, however, is that readers will undoubtedly want their access to articles to be completely seamless, with any licensing or payment thresholds dealt with in the background, or – if the reader has to make a purchase decision – as simply as possible. The way that online customers can buy music downloads might provide one useful model for the future.

### Preservation

Another issue with which publishers and librarians have to grapple is that of long-term preservation of the content of e-journals. Ink on paper, given the right sort of paper and correct storage conditions, can last for a very long time. Print publications are produced in multiple copies, which are likely to be stored in many different locations, so that if one library goes up in flames or is destroyed by flood, other copies will remain elsewhere. And because the publications are two-dimensional, it is not an insuperable challenge to make a copy when the original is in danger of becoming too fragile to use.

E-journals are a different matter. They may not always be stored in multiple locations; some publishers are very reluctant to permit local hosting, although many have signed up to LOCKSS, CLOCKSS, Portico, and similar digital preservation projects (www.clockss.org; www.portico.org; see Chapter 4, The production process). And they are not two-dimensional – at the very least, they likely include internal and external links, and they may also include interactive content, video, or other non-two-dimensional material. But we know how fast information and communications technology changes, and how rapidly both hardware and software become obsolete – remember the BBC's "Domesday Project" in the 1980s, intended to be a successor to the original 1086 Domesday Book census of England, but recorded on LaserVision disks which are now unreadable.[4] With a change of software, the more complex features of online journals may be difficult or impossible to preserve, even if the basic content can be migrated to a different system. While this issue will surely be solved eventually, it presents huge challenges to the many people working on it, and both the solution (or solutions – it may be unwise to put all our digital eggs in one basket) and its future implementation will continue to require major funding.

## ... and what hasn't changed

Curiously, despite all these changes, the form of most journals has changed surprisingly little; indeed, a number of e-journals still look and behave exactly like their print counterparts. Although some journals have embraced a variety of features which are made possible by online technology – navigation within and between articles, linked citations,

---

[4] In 2011, a team at BBC Learning converted the entire project to web-based formats now available as "Domesday Reloaded" (see www.bbc.co.uk/domesday).

nontextual content (e.g., interactive data, 3-D rotatable diagrams, video clips), post-publication discussion – the journal still goes through exactly the same underlying processes.[5] Articles are submitted, screened, peer-reviewed, revised, accepted, edited, and published as part of a collection (issue, volume) under the general banner of "*Journal X.*" We still find a table of contents; we still find the same article structure: abstract, introduction, materials and methods, results, analysis, discussion, conclusions, with a list of references at the end.

It was mooted as long ago as 1999 that journals could exist as mere "overlays" to articles placed in repositories such as ArXiv; the idea was that relevant teams of experts (perhaps from learned societies) should review articles from repositories, and identify those worthy of inclusion in a particular "overlay journal" (J Smith, 1999; A Smith, 2000). Various projects are under way, such as RIOJA (Repository Interface for Overlaid Journal Archives, www.jisc.ac.uk/whatwedo/programmes/reppres/tools/rioja.aspx), and OJIMS (Overlay Journal Infrastructure for Meteorological Sciences, www.jisc.ac.uk/whatwedo/programmes/reppres/sue/ojims.aspx), but as yet we are aware of no examples of active overlay journals that draw entirely on repositories;[6] one problem may be that there seems to be no place for the constructive review and revision cycle of conventional journals, and another that reviewers and editors are less motivated to participate than they would be if focused on a "real" journal.

Similarly, open or "community" peer review – where readers' comments on the initially posted version can help to shape the final version – has been adopted by only a few journals (*Electronic Transactions in Artificial Intelligence* [www.etaij.org] and *Atmospheric Chemistry and Physics* [www.atmospheric-chemistry-and-physics.net] were among the first). However, an experiment by *Nature* along similar lines received very little use (*Nature* Debates, 2006); it appeared that too few readers had the time or inclination to contribute constructively. It would seem, too, that

---

[5] To date, authors have been relatively slow to take up the options of submitting nontextual material with their papers – perhaps because of the amount of additional effort involved. However, the enthusiastic adoption of YouTube suggests that this may soon change.

[6] There are, however, journals such as the American Academy for the Advancement of Science's *Knowledge Environments* Virtual Journals (http://stke.sciencemag.org/about/) which draw on articles in existing journals, as well as other material.

authors prefer – and expect – to have their work commented on pre-publication only by invited experts. A different form of open peer review, in which reviewers are named, but are still selected by the journal's Editorial team, has been adopted, apparently successfully, by journals including *BMJ*, the *British Journal of Psychiatry*, and the *Journal of the Royal Society of Medicine*.

## How change has affected scholars

The astounding development of the scale and power of computing, and its rapid convergence with communications technology, is transforming the way that scholars are able to work – the kinds of research they can do, how they do it, and how they communicate with each other about it.

Vast amounts of observational data in a wide range of fields, from astronomy and physics to sociology and literature, can be collected, manipulated, combined, and analyzed – if necessary using multiple computers around the world (Borgman, 2008). For example, in the area of ecology, scientists around the world collect, share, and use data on climate, earthquakes, and many other aspects of our environment. Sociologists are able to use vast quantities of population data (the American Sociological Association, for example, includes "data sharing" in its code of ethics – www.asanet.org/cs/root/leftnav/ethics/code_of_ethics_table_of_contents). Similarly, astronomers and astrophysicists collect and analyze data from strategically placed radio-telescopes in many countries (and, indeed, the "seti@home" project, http://setiathome.berkeley.edu/sah_papers/woody.php, invites the public to put their personal computers at the service of the massive analysis required to detect any signs of potential extraterrestrial intelligence). Indeed, it could be argued that some areas of science have moved from the traditional model of gathering data in order to test a hypothesis, to one of first gathering as much data as possible, mining it to see what patterns emerge, and only then forming hypotheses about what these patterns might signify.

Gathering and working on huge amounts of data can require huge teams of researchers, and an increasing number of research teams are widely distributed across many different centers and even countries, reporting and discussing their work (thanks to digital communication) in real time. In high-energy physics, for example, collaborations can involve as many as 290 authors (over 13% of articles in this field have more than six), quite possibly from ten or more countries (Mele et al.,

2006). One study found that multinational authorship of journal articles published in leading journals ranged from 13% in surgery to 55% in astronomy (Abt, 2007).

Communication of one's findings beyond the research team used to be limited to presenting one's ideas at conferences (first possibly as a poster, and later as a full paper), and in "Q&A" and informal discussions with other delegates; distributing preprints to those who asked for them; and eventually publishing a paper in a peer-reviewed journal. Most of these stages, it will be noted, involved one-way, more or less formal communication.

However, communication is so easy that it is becoming less and less necessary to be formal about it – whether speaking or writing, much communication is more a form of conversation. Information is transmitted in short chunks, and increasingly rarely as a long, extended argument. The informal stages outlined in Figure 13.2 above are becoming far more important, while – some would argue – the formal stage of publication is being eroded. Informal, generally two-way modes of "chat" through blogs (e.g., www.scienceblogs.com), wikis (e.g., www.sklogwiki.org, www. quantiki.org, pronetos.com), bookmarking sites (e.g., www.citeulike.org/, http://del.icio.us/, and www.connotea.org/), and the like are being adopted and adapted by research communities, in many cases without the involvement of publishers. In such fora, discussion of one's ideas and work is continuous, and the ideas and suggestions of others can sometimes make a real difference to its direction and outcome.

## ... and what hasn't changed

Oddly enough, scholars do not seem to be publishing articles any less, or differently, than in the past (Ware and Mabe, 2009; RIN, 2009). When they have so many other means of communication at their disposal, why might this be?

The importance of published articles on one's curriculum vitae does not seem to have diminished: "peer-reviewed prestige publications are the 'coin of the realm' in tenure and promotion decisions" (Harley et al., 2010). If anything, as pressures on scholarly posts and on research funding increase, the value of publication for authors may have grown. And not just any published articles – they must be published in peer-reviewed journals, the more highly regarded the better. "Publish or perish" is alive and well.

The "canonical" functions of journals (discussed in Chapter 1, Introduction to journals) would seem to be as important to scholarly authors as ever:

- Registration – putting down a personal/team marker as the first to come up with a particular finding (i.e., priority). Speed of publication is therefore highly important, particularly in fast-moving and competitive fields; online publication of an accepted, but unedited, version is of particular value to authors in these areas.
- Dissemination – making the work not just available, but discoverable. Authors want their work to come up (and to be readily accessible) whenever one of their peers searches for items on the same topic, whether the searcher already knew of the article's existence or not.
- Peer review – both in the sense of quality control, and of quality improvement; the process must be both fast and honest.
- Archiving – researchers want their work to have permanence, and to remain discoverable and retrievable by current and future scholars.

Despite the much more relaxed norms of information-sharing which are emerging on the web, scholars still have a strong proprietorial feeling about their own work; this relates not only to their articles, but (perhaps even more strongly) to the underlying data. While researchers would like immediate and unimpeded access to other researchers' data, they are very clear that they want to restrict access to their own data, at least until their work is published (Piwowar, 2011).[7]

Readers, too, have changed their behavior less than one might think. While many scholars are now obtaining information from an ever wider range of sources, across the informality/formality spectrum, and while they discover articles in different ways (search engines, citation rankings), they still appear to value published journal articles as a definitive source of information (Ware, 2010). It would seem that the signals attached to a published article (e.g., that it has been peer reviewed, that it has been selected by a well-reputed journal) are at least as valuable as they ever were (Tenopir et al., 2010) – perhaps, with the increasing problems of overload, they may become even more necessary.[8]

---

[7] In the case of commercially funded research, the funder may want to keep the data permanently confidential.

[8] CrossRef has recently launched CrossMark (www.crossref.org/crossmark/index.html), enabling publishers to attach a symbol to each individual article, indicating that it is a publisher-maintained document; clicking on the symbol enables the reader to find out

## The role of journal publication

Publishers cannot assume that journals as we know them will retain their key position in the scholarly communication landscape of tomorrow. While, for now, the key functions of registration, certification, dissemination, and preservation may seem to be as important as ever, the reasons for this may be changing. Increasingly, the primary reasons given by researchers for publishing formal articles in journals include a wish to benefit, in career terms, from the journal's reputation (Rowlands and Nicholas, 2005), and to ensure long-term preservation of their work (Housewright and Schonfeld, 2008). At the same time, researchers are also using a variety of other means to disseminate their work to their own peer group. In some fields, such as computing, other forms of publication – in this case, conference proceedings – are preferred because of their immediacy; in economics, leading authors are moving away from top journals, possibly bypassing formal publication altogether and posting directly on the web (Ellison, 2007).

The journal itself – as an "envelope" containing a collection of articles which are related in terms of topic, perspective, quality, etc. – may be becoming less and less important. While the "brand" of a particular journal still provides useful signals to potential readers about what to expect of an article published in it, the journal is no longer the most common starting point when a researcher is looking for articles on a topic. Increasingly, the individual article is the primary unit of information. What, therefore, will happen to the journal as "brand"? It may need to be transformed into a different kind of indicator (or set of indicators) of topic, perspective, quality – and perhaps more besides – which conceivably might not be exclusive: one article might carry a variety of indicators from different sources, rather than just the "brand" of a single journal. And if that happens, at what stage, and by whom, does the quality control and improvement get carried out?

More fundamentally, journals – as we currently know them – have a number of weaknesses which may mean that they will satisfy the needs of scholars less and less well in future.

whether the article has been peer reviewed, as well as whether there have been any changes since publication.

## Speed

Compared with the gamut of informal and immediate means of communication accessible to scholars, even the fastest journals are slow. The processes of peer review and editing – filtering, selection, and improvement – take time, however slick the underlying systems. Even making articles available immediately after acceptance, and before final editing and publication, does not entirely remove the delay.

## Static version

Not only publishers but also authors and readers set great store by the "version of record" (see, for example, the ALPSP/NISO project on Versions of Journal Articles, www.niso.org/committees/Journal_versioning/JournalVer_comm.html). However, this is not necessarily the way that scholars actually operate, nor how their work develops over time. A researcher may add his or her own or others' new findings; the analysis may be refined or even overturned in the light of subsequent comments and discussion. Perhaps in future it will become unrealistic to expect the account of a researcher's work to be fossilized, as it were, in amber?

## Limited mode of communication

Journal articles are one of the few pieces of the communications jigsaw that continue to consist of one way communication (conference presentations, books, and podcasts are others). In the real world, communication is a complex process. It happens in many different forms, from informal to formal; it is multidirectional; and it links with other communications in both the past and the future.

## Linearity

Scholars and research teams do not, in reality, work in isolation; thus, their work does not in reality exist as a discrete, linear contribution to their field, even though journal articles necessarily present it in this way. Their work is likely to form part of a network of information, closely related to other people's work, and to be developed over time through the participation of many others – all of whom will be communicating in a wide range of modes. Information, as Ted Nelson realized (Nelson, 1994), is not really linear – it is part of a vast, interconnected web.

## A vision of the future?

Let us imagine the scholar of the year 2060. She speaks to her paperback-sized BrainBox™: "What's been done in the last five years on reversing the symptoms of Alzheimer's?" A voice responds: "Thirty-nine articles, ten datasets, fifty communication streams – what do you want to see?" The scholar replies, "Give me the details of the top five articles." The screen displays the bibliographic details, plus number of downloads and citations, for five articles. She selects article number three, and the display changes to the section headings of the article. The scholar says "abstract" – then "conclusions," then "methods." She decides she wants to see the data, so she says "data" and is presented with a toolkit for searching and manipulating the authors' vast dataset. Then she wants to look at what other people have said about the work, so she says "follow-up," and gets a thread of video discussion posts. She posts a short public video comment of her own; she also records some private notes; one of the earlier commentators immediately comes back to her and they start an interesting discussion.

If this seems overly speculative, imagine what people in 1945 made of Vannevar Bush's predictions (Bush, 1945):

Consider a future device for individual use, which is a sort of mechanized private file and library. It needs a name, and, to coin one at random, "memex" will do. A memex is a device in which an individual stores all his books, records, and communications, and which is mechanized so that it may be consulted with exceeding speed and flexibility. It is an enlarged intimate supplement to his memory.

. . .

The owner of the memex, let us say, is interested in the origin and properties of the bow and arrow. Specifically he is studying why the short Turkish bow was apparently superior to the English long bow in the skirmishes of the Crusades. He has dozens of possibly pertinent books and articles in his memex. First he runs through an encyclopedia, finds an interesting but sketchy article, leaves it projected. Next, in a history, he finds another pertinent item, and ties the two together. Thus he goes, building a trail of many items. Occasionally he inserts a comment of his own, either linking it into the main trail or joining it by a side trail to a particular item. When it becomes evident that the elastic properties of available materials had a great deal to do with the bow, he branches off on a side trail which takes him through textbooks on elasticity and tables of physical constants. He inserts a page of longhand analysis of his own. Thus he builds a trail of his interest through the maze of materials available to him.

While our future scenario – like Bush's – may be wrong in detail, it is hard not to imagine that, in the foreseeable future, research data, the articles that present and discuss that data, and other related communication streams (such as blogs, messaging, voice, and video) will be easily connected for the benefit of scholars – and that the details of how it has all been paid for and by whom will be completely invisible to the user.

## Is there a place for publishers (and librarians)?

Both publishers and librarians are merely intermediaries between scholars who wish to communicate with each other; our respective tasks (which are increasingly converging) are, on the one hand, to facilitate the transmission of the author's message and, on the other, to facilitate its retrieval by readers, both now and at any time in the future. We cannot assume that the publishers (or librarians) of today automatically have a role in the scholarly communication of tomorrow.

There will surely be a place, however, for intermediaries who are able to provide valuable services to the world of scholarly communication. A number of publishers, and nonpublishers, are already engaged in exciting experiments to develop a range of new features and tools to support researchers' new working patterns (for example, Elsevier's "Article of the Future" [www.cell.com/ – see Marcus, 2010] or Nature Network [http://network.nature.com]). Journals (or whatever their successors are called) will need to integrate text, data, sound, and images (including 3-D and video); they will need to link related content together seamlessly; they will need to bring together formal and informal modes in a continuum of instant, multidirectional communication. It must be intuitively easy both to find content and to access it. And all this will need to be affordable.

This kind of development is a challenge even for large, well-funded publishers; it requires not only deep pockets, but also new skills – from television, video, and games, for example, rather than traditional publishing (and people with such skills are expensive!). The smaller, predominantly nonprofit publishers who make up the majority may not have the resources to invest – and to go on investing, for this is not a one-off project – in radical innovation and experimentation. And long-established publishers of all types risk being held back by the innate conservatism of their organizations – the "if it ain't broke, don't fix it" mentality. This could mean that new players, from outside the familiar ranks of either publishing or librarianship, are best placed to step in.

So where do we start? Even in the early stages of a career in journal publishing, it is essential never to lose sight of the fact that, as publishers, we are there to serve the communication needs of the scholarly community. If we stop serving those needs adequately, scholars will turn elsewhere. Keeping close to the particular part or parts of the scholarly community that we aim to serve – understanding what they are trying to do, and how they are trying to do it, while keeping an open mind about how they can best be helped to do it in future – is undoubtedly the key.

## REFERENCES

Abt, Helmut A, 2007, The frequencies of multinational papers in various sciences, *Scientometrics* 71:1, 105–15 (http://dx.doi.org/10.1007/s11192-007-1686-z)

Bacon, Francis, 1620, *Novum organum*, Liber I, CXXIX, London

Björk, Bo-Christer, Patrik Welling, Mikael Laakso, Peter Majlender, Turid Hedlund, and Guðni Guðnason, 2010, Open access to the scientific journal literature: situation 2009, *PLoS One* 5(6): e11273 (http://dx.doi.org/10.1371/journal.pone.0011273)

Blume, Marin, 1998, What constitutes "publication" in electronic media?, *AAAS/UNESCO/ICS workshop on developing practices and standards for electronic publishing in science*, Washington, DC, American Academy for the Advancement of Science (www.aaas.org/spp/sfrl/projects/epub/ses1/Blume.htm)

Borgman, Christine, 2008, Data, disciplines and scholarly publishing, *Learned Publishing* 21: 29–38 (http://dx.doi.org/10.1087/095315108X254476)

Bush, Vannevar, 1945, As we may think, *Atlantic Monthly* July (www.theatlantic.com/past/docs/unbound/flashbks/computer/bushf.htm)

CIBER, 2009, *E-journals: their use, value and impact* (final report), London, Research Information Network (www.rin.ac.uk/system/files/attachments/Ejournals_part_II_for_screen_0.pdf)

Diderot, Denis, 1755, *Encyclopédie*, Paris (http://diderot.alembert.free.fr/)

Ellison, Glenn, 2007, *Is peer review in decline?*, National Bureau of Economic Research working paper (http://econ-www.mit.edu/files/906)

Gardner, Tracy, and Simon Inger, 2012, *How readers discover content in scholarly journals*, Renew Training (www.renewtraining.com/How-Readers-Discover-Content-in-Scholarly-Journals-summary-edition-pdf)

Harley, Diane, Sophia Krzys Acord, Sarah Earl-Novell, Shannon Lawrence, and C Judson King, 2010, *Assessing the future landscape of scholarly communication: an exploration of faculty values and needs in seven disciplines*, Center for Studies in Higher Education, UC Berkeley (www.escholarship.org/uc/cshe_fsc)

Housewright, Ross, and Roger Schonfeld, 2008, *Ithaka's 2006 studies of key stakeholders in the digital transformation in higher education*, New York, Ithaka (www.ithaka.org/ithaka-s-r/research/faculty-surveys-2000-2009/faculty-survey-2006)

Jinha, Arif E, 2010, Article 50 million: an estimate of the number of scholarly articles in existence, *Learned Publishing* 23: 258–63 (http://dx.doi.org/10.1087/20100308)

King, Donald W, and Carol Tenopir, 2006, *The use, usefulness and value of libraries to social scientists, scientists and medical professionals* (presentation), Alexandria, VA, Special Libraries Association (http://units.sla.org/division/dsoc/Conference%20Archive/DWKing.ppt)

Mabe, Michael, 2003, The growth and number of journals, *Serials* 16: 191–7 (http://uksg.metapress.com/content/f195g8ak0eu21muh/fulltext.pdf)

Mabe, Michael, and Mayur Amin, 2001, Growth dynamics of scholarly and scientific journals, *Scientometrics* 51: 147–62 (http://dx.doi.org/10.1023%2FA%3A1010520913124)

Marcus, Emilie, 2010, 2010: a publishing odyssey (editorial), *Cell*, 140: 9 (http://dx.doi.org/10.1016/j.cell/2009.12.048)

May, Robert, 1998, The scientific investments of nations, *Science* 281:5737, 49–51 (http://dx.doi.org/10.1126/science.281.5373.49)

Mele, Salvatore, David Dallman, Jens Vigen, and Joanne Yeomans, 2006, Quantitative analysis of the publishing landscape in high-energy physics, *Journal of High Energy Physics* 12: S01 (http://dx.doi.org/10.1088/1126-6708/2006/12/S01)

Morris, Sally, 2005, *"Version control" of journal articles*, Baltimore, MD, NISO (www.niso.org/workrooms/jav/Morris.pdf)

Morris, Sally, and Sue Thorn, 2009, Learned society members and open access, *Learned Publishing* 22: 221–39 (http://dx.doi.org/10.1087/2009308)

National Information Standards Institute and Association of Learned and Professional Society Publishers, 2008, *Best practices for journal article versions*, Baltimore, MD, NISO (www.niso.org/publications/rp)

*Nature* Debates, 2006, Overview: *Nature's* peer review trial (www.nature.com/nature/peerreview/debate/nature05535.html)

Nelson, Ted, 1994, *Interesting times*, Sausalito, CA, Mindful Press

Oppenheimer, J Robert, 1958, The tree of knowledge, *Harper's Magazine*, 217: 55–60 (http://harpers.org/archive/1958/10/0008834)

Piwowar, Heather A, 2011, Who shares? Who doesn't? Factors associated with openly archiving raw research data, *PLoS One* 6(7): e18657 (http://dx.doi.org/10.1371/journal.pone.0018657)

Rieger, Oya Y, 2009, Search engine use behavior of students and faculty: user perceptions and implications for further research, *First Monday* 14: 12 (http://firstmonday.org/htbin/cgiwrap/bin/ojs/index.php/fm/article/view/2716/2385)

RIN, 2009, *Communicating knowledge: how and why researchers publish and disseminate their findings*, London, Research Information Network (www.rin.ac.uk/system/files/attachments/Communicating-knowledge-report.pdf)

Rowlands, Ian, and David Nicholas, 2005, *New journal publishing models: an international survey of senior researchers*, London, CIBER (www.homepages.ucl.ac.uk/~uczciro/pa_stm_final_report.pdf)

Smith, Arthur P, 2000, The journal as an overlay on preprint databases, *Learned Publishing* 13: 43–8 (http://dx.doi.org/10.1087/09531510050145542)

Smith, John W T, 1999, The deconstructed journal – a new model for academic publishing, *Learned Publishing* 12: 79–91 (http://dx.doi.org/10.1087/09531519 950145896)

Tenopir, Carol, Suzie Allard, Ben Bates, Kenneth J Levine, Donald W King, Ben Birch, Regina Mays, and Chris Caldwell, 2010, *Research publication characteristics and their relative values*, London, Publishing Research Consortium (www.publishingresearch.net/PRCTenopiretalWord2010ResearchPublicationCharac teristics_000.docx)

Vincent of Beauvais, 1255, *Speculum maius*

Ware, Mark, 2010, *Access vs. importance: a global study assessing the importance of and ease of access to professional and academic information* (Phase 1 results), London, Publishing Research Consortium (www.publishingresearch.net/documents/PRCAccessvs ImportanceGlobalNov2010_000.pdf)

Ware, Mark, and Michael Mabe, 2009, *The STM report: an overview of scientific and scholarly journals publishing*, Oxford, International Association of Scientific, Technical & Medical Publishers (www.stm-assoc.org/2009_10_13_MWC_ STM_Report.pdf)

Xanadu, 2011, Project Xanadu website, http://xanadu.com/

## FURTHER READING

Campbell, Bob, Ed Pentz, and Ian Borthwick (eds.), 2012, *Academic and Professional Publishing*, Oxford, Chandos Publishing

Cope, Bill, and Angus Phillips (eds.), 2009, *The future of the academic journal*, Oxford, Chandos Publishing

Nielsen, Michael, 2011, *Reinventing discovery: the new era of networked science*, Princeton University Press

Paquet, Sébastien, 2002, *Personal knowledge publishing and its uses in research*, weblog posting, October 1 (http://radio.weblogs.com/0110772/stories/2002/10/03/ personalKnowledgePublishingAndItsUsesInResearch.html)

Porter, Sandra, 2007, *Science in the blogosphere*, Presentation at the ALPSP International Scholarly Communications Conference, April (www.alpsp.org/Force Download.asp?id=428)

Rowlands, Ian, Dave Nicholas, and Paul Huntingdon, 2004, *Scholarly communication in the digital environment: what do authors want?*, London, CIBER (www.ucl.ac.uk/ ciber/ciber-pa-report.pdf)

*The Scientist*, 2012, Whither science publishing? *The Scientist*, August 1 (www.the-scientist. com/?articles.view/articleNo/32378/title/Whither-Science-Publishing-/)

# Appendix 1

# Glossary

**abstract**   A short summary (usually by the author, often within a set word limit) of the content of an article, usually published at the head of the article and generally freely available even when the article itself is not. Also third-party summaries included in some abstracting and indexing services (q.v.). A structured abstract is an abstract with distinct, labeled sections, often mimicking the IMRAD heading sequence (q.v.).

**abstracting and indexing (A&I) service**   A database and/or publication of bibliographic information, with or without summaries, about the scholarly literature in a given field (e.g., Mathematical Reviews) or a related set of fields (e.g., Inspec); a few cover extremely large sets of journals (e.g., Scopus, Web of Science). A&I services now find themselves competing with general search engines such as Google and Bing.

**acceptance rate**   The percentage of submitted papers that are accepted for publication. A high-profile, high-impact journal may have an acceptance rate of less than 10% due to a high volume of submissions far in excess of the available page budget. Many specialty journals have an acceptance rate of between 40% and 60%.

**acid-free paper (sometimes known as permanent paper)**   Paper made for archival purposes. The specifications for manufacture are laid out in American Standard ANSI Z39 1984 and cover neutral pH, alkaline reserve, chemical finish, tear resistance, and fold endurance.

**Acquisitions Editor**   Another term for Commissioning Editor (q.v.).

**aggregator**   An organization bringing together content from multiple sources into a single, searchable database (see list in Appendix 3, Vendors).

**archive**   Journal content, usually going back to the first issue, stored and preserved in print or electronically. An online archive may consist of retrodigitized print issues published before the journal went online (sometimes sold as a one-off package), electronic files generated in the course of online publication, or a combination of both.

**archiving**   The long-term storage of material; in this case, the storage of journals, their articles, and all parts of the articles, in print or electronic form.

**Art Editor**   Staff person at a publisher or compositor who edits author figures in preparation for publication.

**arXiv** (http://arxiv.org)   The first "preprint archive" (q.v.), for articles in high energy physics and related areas. Originally established in 1991 by Paul Ginsparg at Los Alamos National Laboratory and subsequently moved to Cornell University. Operates very light review to ensure appropriateness before accepting articles.

**ASCII**   American Standard Code for Information Interchange. ASCII codes represent text as displayed in computers. Each symbol in the 128 character ASCII code consists of seven data bits and one parity bit for error checking.

**Associate Editor**   A specialist in one or more subfields covered by a journal, who is responsible for handling articles in those subfields, or from specific regions, or specific article types, for the Editor-in-Chief. Sometimes called Assistant Editor, Decision Editor, or Section Editor.

**audit**   Periodic analysis of various elements of journal performance. The audit may be internal, for the publisher's own assessment of the health of the journal, or external, done for the owner of a journal published under contract.

**Audit Bureau of Circulation (ABC)**   (www.accessabc.com) Nonprofit association of advertisers, agencies, and publishers that provides verified figures for print circulation, readership, and website activity of publications.

**author-side fee**   A payment made by (or on behalf of) the author for publication of an article, in order that the article be freely available when published; a common model for funding OA journals. Also applies to page charges, color printing support, or submission fees sometimes charged to authors by subscription journals. Also called author fees.

**backfile**   Usually refers to online journal volumes published before the current subscription year.

**back-issue/volume sales**   Sales of single issues or whole volumes of a print journal published prior to the current subscription year.

**batching**   In journal production, the act of holding manuscripts or pieces of manuscripts until a certain number or an issue's worth are available before moving it to the next production step.

**Berne Convention**   1886 convention which first laid down a common international basis for copyright.

**Berne three-step test** The three conditions in the Berne Copyright Convention which must be met for any use of copyright material to qualify as "fair use," "fair dealing," or similar terminology permitting use without permission from or payment to the copyright owner. The three conditions are: the use must be a special case (i.e., not systematic); it must not conflict with the normal exploitation of the work; and it must not unreasonably prejudice the legitimate interests of the rightsholder.

**bibliometrics** The study of information (such as journals) by quantitative methods (such as citation analysis).

**Big Deal** Term used to describe licensing agreements in which a library or consortium of libraries purchases access to a publisher's entire online portfolio, which might include hundreds of journals across dozens of disciplines. Such deals make available content that the library/libraries had not previously subscribed to for very little additional cost; this only became possible with electronic distribution.

**bit map** An array of pixels which together make up an image for screen display or printing out.

**bleed** Illustration or advertisement which extends beyond the trimmed edge of the printed page.

**brand/branding** The particular combination of editorial, design, and other features that distinctively identifies a journal and/or a publisher's imprint.

**break-even point** The point at which a journal's net income covers both direct and indirect expenses.

**BRIC** Acronym for "Brazil, Russia, India, and China" – the four most important developing markets.

**browser** Generic name for search/view software needed to access the World Wide Web, such as Internet Explorer, Firefox, or Safari.

**bulk sales (also known as special sales or commercial reprints)** Sale of a quantity of an article or journal issue to one customer, for redistribution to its clients for advertising purposes.

**bundle/bundling** The packaging of journals together, usually less-desired journals with those that are most desired, in order to add value to the higher-priced desired journals and increase the usage (and therefore value) of the less-desired journals. This term is also used to describe the inclusion of both print and online versions of the journal in one subscription price.

**business model**    The method of doing business by which an enterprise plans to sustain itself; the way an enterprise expects to generate sufficient income to cover costs and ongoing obligations and stay in business.

**Business Publications Audit (BPA)**    (www/bpaww.com) Nonprofit organization owned by advertisers, publishers, and agencies, which provides verified circulation figures for business and consumer publications.

**calendarization**    A projection of an annual budget line item that allocates receipts or expenses in given periods (e.g., monthly or quarterly).

**Carnegie classifications**    (http://classifications.carnegiefoundation.org) A framework for classifying US colleges and universities according to their size, setting, focus, and activities, developed by the Carnegie Foundation.

**cascading style sheets (CSS)**    A type of style sheet used to run against a DTD (q.v.) to format a document coded in a markup language (e.g., XML).

**case report**    An article type that reports on one or several cases of a medical condition in order to illustrate a clinical technique or diagnosis.

**cash flow**    The timing and flow of money into and out of the enterprise.

**circulation**    The number of print copies of a journal that are distributed, whether they are sold to subscribers, provided as a benefit of society membership, or given away for free. Readership is higher than circulation because a single copy can be shared by many readers. In the online world, readership is more directly measured by usage, represented by the number of views, the number of downloads, the number of unique visitors, and similar metrics.

**citation**    A reference in an article to another article (or other published – or occasionally unpublished – source) to support the author's statements. With the use of DOI (q.v.) a growing number of citations in online journals link directly to the cited item.

**claims**    With print journals, it is the report by a customer of missing or damaged issue(s). With online journals, it is usually a complaint about lost access for one or more IP addresses (q.v.).

**classified advertising**    Advertising in print journals (usually charged by the word or line) for job vacancies and the like; increasingly displaced, in all but the most frequent journals, by online alternatives.

**click-on**    Acceptance of an agreement (such as online terms and conditions of use) effected by clicking an "I agree" button on a web page.

**clickthrough**    The process of a user "clicking" an online advertisement and being taken to the advertiser's website. Clickthrough counts provide a measure of the effectiveness of an online advertisement.

**closed peer review**   Peer review that is done confidentially, in which the reviews are seen only by the authors of the paper being reviewed, the Editor(s), and sometimes the other reviewers of that paper. Usually, the identity of the reviewers is also kept confidential to the authors and other reviewers. See also single-blind peer review and double-blind peer review.

**commentary**   An editorial-style article that most often comments on another article in a journal.

**Commissioning or Acquisitions Editor**   The person in the publishing office who is responsible for researching, developing, and launching new journals, and often has continuing overall responsibility for their management.

**conflict of interest**   The real or perceived condition of bias on the part of an author, reviewer, or Editor based on his or her personal or financial relationship with an author, product, or company featured in an article.

**consideration**   Payment (not necessarily financial) in return for something else (e.g., publication of an article in return for transfer of copyright).

**consortium (plural: consortia)**   A group of libraries or other organizations that band together in pursuit of a common purpose. Library consortia have dramatically changed the market for scholarly journals by negotiating with publishers for better prices and more favorable access policies. In a closed consortium, each member must participate in the negotiated deal. In an open consortium, each member is free to opt in or out of the negotiated deal.

**content management system**   Any system that manages the editing and version control (q.v.) of documents and other content items. In the context of scholarly journal publishing, it usually refers to a system that specifically manages the version control and digital preparation of manuscripts and other parts of journal articles.

**contract publishing**   Publishing a journal on behalf of another party, such as a scholarly society.

**controlled circulation**   A business model used for some magazines and journals, which are distributed free to "qualified" readers (by virtue of their job descriptions, membership in a society, responses to a survey, etc.); the number of recipients is externally audited, and is very important to advertisers. The publications are usually supported by advertising. or by a commercial sponsor. See also sponsored publication.

**Copy-Editor**   A person who prepares manuscripts for publication by ensuring that the manuscript is consistent with house style and is free of spelling and grammatical errors.

**Copyright, Designs and Patents Act (CDPA)**   The UK Copyright Act of 1988 and its revisions.

**copyright notice**   Notice placed in the front matter/prelims (q.v.) or online masthead/information page of a journal, stating who owns the copyright in the journal as a whole and (if different) in the individual articles, together with the date. Also notice placed on individual articles giving copyright owner and date (important as articles are increasingly seen in isolation from the journal itself). Also similar notice placed on a journal or other website.

**Copyright Transfer agreement**   Form which a journal contributor (or other copyright owner) is required to sign, transferring copyright in an article to the publisher – certain rights may be granted back to the original owner. See also License to Publish.

**CRC (camera ready copy)**   The final proof of type and artwork (as it is to appear on the printed page) that is photographed for making printing plates. Sometimes referred to as a mechanical. The use of CRC to create printing plates has been displaced by computer-to-plate technology.

**Crown copyright**   Copyright held by the Crown in UK (and commonwealth) publications authored by Crown (i.e., government) employees. Special arrangements pertain for the use of such material.

**CTP (computer-to-plate)**   The process by which a final electronic file is used to create printing plates without the need for CRC or an intervening photographic process. Sometimes referred to as direct-to-plate.

*Current Contents*   (http://thomsonreuters.com/products_services/science/ science_products/a-z/current_contents) Current awareness database published by Thomson Reuters, containing complete tables of contents, bibliographic information, and abstracts from the latest issues of leading scholarly journals.

**data appropriation**   A type of ethical misconduct in which a researcher misappropriates unpublished data of another researcher and publishes it without permission.

**data fabrication**   A type of ethical misconduct in which data in an article is invented to support the researcher's conclusions.

**data falsification**   A type of ethical misconduct in which data in an article is manipulated or misrepresented.

**data protection**   Legislation (varying in detail from country to country) restricting the use that may be made of personal information gathered about individuals.

**delayed open access**   The practice, in subscription-based journals, of making the content open access (q.v.) after a period of time, ranging from a few months to, most commonly, a year or more.

**deposit library**   The library (often a national library) or libraries in which publishers are required to deposit one or more copies of their published works, in order to establish a national archive or to meet copyright registration requirements.

**Deputy Editor**   An Associate Editor who acts as a second-in-command to the Editor-in-Chief. May or may not be the Editor-in-Chief's designated successor.

**Digital Millennium Copyright Act (DMCA)**   1998 US legislation, updating the 1976 Copyright Act, designed to bring copyright law into the Internet age.

**direct expenses**   The costs of goods and services directly related to a particular product. See also indirect costs.

**direct mail**   Marketing materials sent by post to potential buyers or users of a product, designed to elicit an order or other "direct" response. Once the primary way that publishers advertised new journals to libraries and authors, direct mail today is usually complemented with less expensive online marketing tools.

**disclaimer**   Statement (providing limited legal protection) sometimes placed in medical or technical journals, disclaiming the publisher's responsibility for accident or injury resulting from any errors in the content.

**distribution**   With print journals, the number of journals delivered to subscribers. With online journals, the nearest equivalent is the number of users reached, but this is harder to quantify.

**document delivery services**   Services delivering print or electronic copies of individual journal articles to customers, for a fee; in most cases the fee includes the publisher's copyright fee, which is remitted to the publisher either directly or via a Reproduction Rights Organization (q.v.).

**DOI (Digital Object Identifier)**   A unique identifier for content, including articles and their parts (graphs, charts, multimedia), providing a persistent link to content (or information about content) even if the destination page changes web location. The DOI database is maintained by CrossRef (see Appendix 2, Resources).

**double-blind peer review**   Form of peer review in which the identity of the authors is kept from the reviewers and vice versa. See also single-blind peer review.

**dpi (dots per inch)**   A measure of the dot/pixel density of a printed or online image. Grayscale images are reduced to different sized dots for printing; the more dots (or pixels) per linear inch, the sharper the image (but the greater the size of file it requires).

**DRM (digital rights management)**   Systems for controlling the use and/or distribution of digital content on the Internet and other electronic media.

**DTD (document type definition)**   An SGML model of the structure or content of a document (or group of similar documents). This model identifies the tags that will be used in the document, and the permissible relationships between the information elements identified by the tags.

**EDI (electronic data interchange)**   Structured transmission of data between organizations by electronic means (e.g., of journal subscription orders/renewals between libraries and subscription agents, or subscription agents and publishers).

**Editor-in-Chief**   The lead Editor of a journal, who is ultimately responsible for its content and scope.

**editorial**   An introductory article commenting on one or more articles in the journal issue or on a more general topic of interest to its readers. Often written by the Editor-in-Chief or an Editor of the journal, or less frequently by an invited author.

**Editorial Assistant**   An administrative assistant to an Editor, who coordinates the peer review of a journal (and may have other functions).

**Editorial Board**   A group of specialists in a field covered by a journal, who act as consultants to the Editor(s) on its scope and direction, and are often required to review submissions to the journal.

**embargo**   Period of time before content is allowed to be made available outside the journal; can apply to the time delay after publication required by a publisher before its journal (or other) content can be made available in an aggregated product, or the time delay which authors are required to honor before self-archiving their articles. Can also apply to the time before publication noted in a press release that must be honored by journalists before reporting on content that will be published in the near future.

**ERM (electronic resource management)**   Systems used by libraries to manage their electronic information resources.

**erratum** or **corrigendum**   A correction to a published article.

**EU Copyright Directive**   2001 Directive of the European Union, requiring all member states to update their copyright laws to take its provisions into account; the last country to do so was Germany, in 2007.

**even working**   A total number of pages in a print publication which can be produced entirely by printing signatures (q.v.) of the same number of pages (e.g., signatures of sixteen or thirty-two pages, making up an issue of sixty-four pages).

**extent**   The number of pages in a printed (or PDF) publication; the number of words is a more meaningful measure for online publications in formats such as HTML, though account also needs to be taken of figures and tables.

**fair dealing**   UK legal definition of the circumstances in which copyright material may be copied and used without permission from or reimbursement to the copyright owner.

**fair use**   US legal definition of the circumstances in which copyrighted material may be copied and used without permission from or reimbursement to the copyright owner.

**first copy cost**   The costs incurred to produce the first copy of a print journal.

**fixed costs**   The costs incurred to produce a journal that do not vary with the number of users or volume of sales. See also variable costs.

**fixed-date archive**   Journal backfiles (q.v.) covering a fixed period, usually retrodigitized, sold as a single archive package for a one-off fee.

**frequency**   Timing of publication of journal issues (e.g., quarterly, monthly, weekly). Ceases to be relevant if an online journal publishes article-by-article.

**front matter**   Introductory pages of a printed publication (e.g., title page, title verso [containing copyright and other information], table of contents). In the UK often referred to as prelims.

**FTP (file transfer protocol)**   Internet standard enabling a client-server system to transfer files.

**gateway**   Same as portal (q.v.).

**ghost authorship**   A type of ethical misconduct that involves unattributed authorship, especially when the only authors listed are guest authors.

**Gold open access**   Unrestricted access to an entire journal provided by the publisher (often funded by author-side publication fees).

**Green open access**   Unrestricted access to individual articles deposited by their authors (sometimes called "self-archiving") on a website or in an institutional or government-run repository.

**guest authorship**   A type of ethical misconduct that involves inviting or paying (usually well-known) researchers to be listed as authors of a paper they did not write or conduct the research for.

**Guest Editor**   Person who edits a special section of a journal, or who steps in to handle papers submitted by the Editor-in-Chief or Associate Editors.

**GUI (graphical user interface)**   User interface allowing computer users to interact with on-screen images rather than text commands.

**half-life (citation half-life)**   Figure used in *Journal Citation Reports* (q.v.) to indicate how long content is cited after publication; the median age of articles in a given journal that were cited in the year in question. Thus, half of all citations were to articles younger than the citation half-life, and half to articles older.

**half-tone**   Illustration created by dots of varying size (or, in the online equivalent, pixels), giving the impression of continuous tone.

**Harvard reference style**   One of the most frequently used styles for references (particularly in HSS journals): name and date in text, bibliographic details (in alphabetical order by author) at the end of the article or chapter. The style used for this book. See also Vancouver reference style.

**home page**   The main or initial page of a website; also, the default page which appears when a browser is opened.

**honorarium**   Fee (often a nominal amount) for services such as editing a journal; the same as any other fee for taxation purposes.

**honorary authorship**   The practice of allowing a person with authority over the authors of a paper (e.g., department chair) to be listed as an author even though he or she did not write or perform the research. Can amount to a type of ethical misconduct. See also guest authorship.

**host (hosting)**   Electronic service for mounting online journals (or other content) from multiple publishers, usually with a standard look and feel and common features.

**HSS/H&SS**   Humanities and social sciences, as compared to STM (q.v.).

**HTML (Hypertext Markup Language)**   Markup language used to prepare a document for viewing over the World Wide Web.

**HTTP (Hypertext Transfer Protocol)**   The networking protocol (or standard) underpinning the operation of the World Wide Web.

**hybrid journal**   A subscription-based journal that makes certain articles free (open access) upon the payment of an author-side publication fee. It may be possible for subscription prices to be held down if the OA uptake is high enough.

**hyperlink (hypertext link)**   A displayed text or graphic with an embedded macro identifying the location of the web page that the user will reach when he or she clicks on the link.

**IACUC (Institutional Animal Care and Use Committee)**   In the US, a committee at a researcher's institution that approves the protocols of animal studies.

**impact factor (journal impact factor)**   A measure of how often a journal is cited, and thus of its "impact" in the research community. The impact factor of a given journal in a given year is the number of citations received in that year to any article published in the previous two years, divided by the total number of citable items published in those years.

**imposition**   Arrangement of page images on a printing plate in a sequence which will read consecutively when the printed sheet is folded for binding.

**IMRAD**   An acronym for a common method of structuring a scientific article. The letters stand for Introduction, Methods, Results, and Discussion.

**incidental copying**   The making of a transient copy of copyrighted material as an integral part of some technical process (such as caching or making backup copies) – usually permitted by law.

**incremental archive**   Journal backfiles that are licensed as a complete online archive (often incorporating retrodigitized preonline issues), with the previous year's content being added annually. See also fixed-date archive.

**indirect costs**   Also referred to as "overhead." The costs that cannot readily be allocated to a particular product. These are the "costs of doing business."

**institutional membership**   In the context of OA journals, a form of subscription entitling the institution's faculty and students to discounted or waived publication fees.

**institutional repository**   An often (but not necessarily) freely accessible online database set up by a university or other institution, containing digital copies of articles and other intellectual output from that institution. Authors may self-archive (q.v.) their journal articles there.

**intellectual property (IP)**   The author's or owner's rights in a literary or artistic creation; protected by copyright. Can also refer to a trademark (q.v.).

**interlibrary loan (ILL)**   Originally, the physical loan of books or other items between libraries; in the case of journal articles, requests have long been satisfied by the supply of photocopies (which the borrower is not required to return). The potential supply of electronic copies rather than photocopies is a cause of some concern to publishers and is the subject of much discussion with library organizations.

**intermediary**   An organization mediating between the provider and the customer. Generally taken to refer to subscription agents or aggregators; but in fact publishers and libraries are also intermediaries, between the author and the reader.

**IP address**   Internet Protocol address; every computer connected to the Internet has one. Institutions register their IP address ranges with publishers, which is how users are authenticated when they try to access the publisher's content.

**IRB (Institutional Review Board)**   In the US, a committee at a researcher's institution that approves the protocols and conduct of human studies.

**ISI (Institute for Scientific Information)**   Organization, founded in 1960 by Eugene Garfield (the pioneer of citation indexing) and now part of Thomson Reuters, which indexes articles in and citations to a large number of journals, and publishes the resultant data in the *Journal Citation Reports* (q.v.).

**ISSN (International Standard Serial Number)**   Standard unique identification number provided by the relevant national agency for each serial publication (corresponding to the ISBN for books). The agencies recommend that publishers obtain a separate ISSN for online version and print version; an ISSN-L (linking ISSN) links together ISSNs for the same resource in different formats.

**jobber**   A middleman or wholesaler. In publishing, often refers to book or back-issue wholesalers and other suppliers to the trade.

**journal**   A serial publication containing primarily original research in a field, normally peer reviewed. It may also publish review articles, case reports, educational articles, reviews of books or other media, letters to the editor, and news reports in the field.

**Journal Archiving and Interchange Tag Suite (JATS)**   The DTD (q.v.) commonly known as the NLM DTD, created by the National Library of Medicine as a standard DTD for STM journal content.

**Journal Citation Reports (JCR)**   Annual publication by Thomson Reuters, providing a range of statistical information about its listed journals (including impact factor and citation half-life), based on citation data. *Science Citation Reports* covers over 8,000 journals, while *Social Science Citation Reports* covers over 2,650 (there is some overlap). See also citation, half-life, impact factor.

**journal club**   A group that meets regularly to read and critique recent papers (usually in STM journals), often used as a teaching tool for graduate and professional students to develop their evaluative and debating skills.

**journal of record**   The edition (i.e., print or electronic) that the publisher deems to be definitive in the case of any difference between the two; normally, the electronic version.

**keywords**   Terms used in, or describing the coverage of, an article. Increasingly, rarely used at the head of an article, but may be included in its metadata (q.v.) to improve search results.

**LAN (Local Area Network)**   Computer network connecting computers in a limited geographical area, e.g., university building or company office.

**LaTeX**   A document markup language and document preparation system for the TeX (q.v.) typesetting program; widely used by academics in mathematics, physics, and related areas.

**launch**   Publication of the first issue of a new journal, and all the marketing and other activity that goes on around it.

**legacy content**   Preonline print journal content, which has often been retrodigitized to provide an online archive.

**legal deposit**   Deposit of one or more copies of every publication in the national or other deposit library (q.v.), as required by law in many countries.

**libel**   False and malicious statement which is published (whereas slander is spoken).

**library privilege**   UK legislation permitting libraries to carry out certain activities with respect to copyright material – e.g., copying for preservation purposes – without seeking permission. Similar rights exist in many national legislations.

**license agreement**   Legally binding agreement between the publisher and library or, less frequently, individual, governing the terms (sometimes including price) and conditions under which access to the content is granted. Larger licenses (for many journals and/or many libraries) may be negotiated between publisher and customer; smaller ones generally are not.

**License to Publish**   Agreement which journal contributors are required to sign, granting the publisher all the rights necessary to publish the work, but retaining copyright and all other rights not explicitly granted. See also Copyright Transfer agreement.

**link resolver**   Library software that directs users from a public online link to content that the user has a right to access, normally by virtue of an institutional subscription.

**list**   The list of journals (and, sometimes, books) handled by an Acquisitions Editor, or the entire list of journals and/or books produced by a publisher.

**list rental**   The sale of a publisher's list of subscribers, members, or other contacts to a third party for commercial use, normally on a one-time basis. In some cases, the publisher may not actually hand over the list (or labels derived therefrom), preferring to keep the list confidential and carry out the mailing itself on the client's behalf. Such use is subject to data protection (q.v.) provisions.

**make-ready**   Setting up printing equipment for a specific job.

**Managing Editor**   Person who oversees the day-to-day running of the journal.

**margin**   Profit expressed as a percentage of the revenue.

**marginal cost**   For print, the incremental cost of printing, servicing, and mailing one more print subscription. For online, the variable costs of adding access and customer support for one more online user.

**memex**   Machine envisaged by Vannevar Bush in 1945, the function of which was a precursor of hypertext.

**metadata**   Data about an information resource that helps users identify and retrieve the information. Bibliographic information found in a library card catalog or a journal database is a type of metadata.

**mobile apps**   Application software designed for handheld devices such as mobile phones. In the context of journals, applications allowing users to access some or all journal content on their mobile devices.

**moral rights**   Term in EU copyright law, now incorporated into the legislation of all member states, describing key rights which inhere in the creator whether or not he or she is the owner of copyright. The main ones are "paternity" – the right to be credited as the author – and the right to object to "derogatory treatment" (detrimental changes which would negatively affect the author's reputation).

**NLM DTD**   Same as Journal Archiving and Interchange Tag Suite (q.v.).

**nondisclosure agreement (NDA)**   An agreement between two organizations to hold confidential any business information disclosed by either party, for example, financial data shared during the journal acquisition process.

**nonprofit/not-for-profit**   Term used for an (often charitable) organization, such as a learned society, which does not distribute profits to shareholders; instead, any surplus is reinvested in furthering the objects of the organization.

**novation agreement**   New agreement replacing the existing one under the same terms but with one or more different parties, for example, the agreement with an Editor-in-Chief if a journal changes hands.

**OCR (Optical Character Recognition)**   Automatic conversion of images of text into digital characters.

**offprint**   Additional sheets produced when a journal issue is printed, which are bound up to make copies of individual articles for supply to authors or others. See also reprint.

**offset**   Printing process using an intermediate medium to transfer the image from the printing plate onto the paper.

**ONIX for Serials**   A set of standards for communicating machine-readable information about journals.

**OPAC (Online Public Access Catalog)**   Database of content held by a library (or group of libraries), which has generally replaced the old card catalogs.

**open access (OA)**    Free and unrestricted access to content (mostly used with reference to journal articles). See also Green open access, Gold open access, and hybrid journal.

**Open Data**    Free and unrestricted access to the data resulting from research studies; generally supported by publishers, but in practice not always by the researchers. Requires standardization of data formats if the data is to be truly interchangeable.

**open peer review**    A form of peer review in which submitted articles are made publicly available and are subject to open comments (which are also public), either after or instead of formal closed peer review (q.v.). The same term is sometimes used for regular peer review in which the names of both author(s) and reviewer(s) are disclosed to the other.

**ORI (Office of Research Integrity)**    The office of the US Department of Health and Human Services that oversees and directs research integrity activities.

**origination**    The first phase of production, from the author's edited work to a form from which published copies can be made. Sometimes known as prepress.

**overhead**    Same as indirect costs (q.v.).

**overlay journal**    A journal consisting of a personal or organized selection of articles from an existing (generally open access) source or sources, such as a repository.

**parent–child relationship**    Term used to describe the relationship between parts of an institution (e.g., main and departmental libraries); essential information when negotiating a site license (q.v.) for one or more entire institutions.

**parser**    See SGML parser.

**passing off**    Presenting a product or service as if it is something else (e.g., by using the same or a very similar title).

**patient consent**    The signed consent which must be obtained from an individual whose image or medical records are to be used in a publication.

**patron-driven acquisition**    Letting actual usage of journal content by patrons drive the decision to purchase or renew a journal subscription, rather than basing acquisition decisions on the professional opinion of the faculty or librarian. This can take several forms, such as evaluating usage statistics to guide renewal decisions, or adding a subscription based on ILL demand or turnaways (q.v.), or acquiring a journal because document-delivery fees have approached or exceeded the cost of a subscription.

**PDF (Portable Document Format)**   File format originally created by Adobe in 1993, and used as an open standard for exchanging documents independently of software, hardware, and operating systems. Produces effectively an electronic replica of print.

**peer review**   The system by which a submitted article is reviewed by independent experts (the author's peers) to help the Editor reach a decision on publication.

**perfect binding**   Binding in which pages are held together by glue on the roughened back edges, rather than sewn or wire-stitched.

**permissions**   The granting of permission (often, but not always, for a fee) to a third party to reuse an extract from an existing copyright publication.

**perpetual access**   Arrangement allowing subscribers continuing access to the online journal content to which they have already subscribed, after the subscription ends. Sometimes known as perpetual rights.

**piracy**   In the context of journals, unauthorized duplication and/or distribution of complete journals or journal articles.

**pixel**   Picture element – the smallest element of a displayed electronic image.

**plagiarism**   Passing off another's work as one's own.

**portal**   A web page intended to be a central point of entry for a topic, with links to a wide range of content from various sources.

**PostScript**   Page description language from Adobe which is device-independent. It enables pages to be compressed, transmitted, and displayed on Adobe Acrobat.

**prelims**   Short for preliminaries; same as front matter (q.v.).

**prepaid article bundle**   A method of paying the publisher up-front for a set number of individual article downloads, by establishing a deposit account that is debited each time an article is downloaded.

**prepress**   Same as origination (q.v.).

**preprint**   A version of a journal article prior to publication; most commonly taken to mean the version submitted to the journal, before peer review or editing.

**preprint archive**   Freely accessible online database storing journal article preprints either in a particular subject (e.g., arXiv, q.v.) or for a particular institution (see institutional repository). See also Green open access and self-archiving.

**preservation**   The storage and maintenance of online content (including electronic journals, their articles, and all parts of the articles) in a way that will allow it to be read and used beyond the lifetime of current hardware, media, and software.

**press release**   An announcement released to the media and to influential persons, intended to generate awareness and news coverage. In the journals field, may be about a new journal launch, a significant change (e.g., of publisher), or a particularly newsworthy article.

**Production Editor**   The person in the publisher's office responsible for coordinating all parts of a manuscript (text, figures, tables, etc.) through the production process.

**profit**   The difference between income and expense; sometimes referred to as surplus. Gross profit is the difference between net income and direct expenses. Net profit is the difference between net income and the sum of direct and indirect expenses.

**publicity**   The dissemination of information about a journal, author, article, publisher, etc., usually via press releases, advertising, and social media.

**reader-side fee**   Term sometimes used (in contrast to author-side fee, q.v.) to describe the business model whereby access to an article or journal is gained through a payment made on behalf of (or occasionally by) the reader – e.g., a library subscription or pay-per-view purchase.

**reference**   The same as citation (q.v.).

**rejection rate**   The percentage of articles submitted to a journal that are rejected; the converse of acceptance rate (q.v.).

**renewal rates**   The percentage of prior-year subscribers who renew for the current volume.

**repository**   An often (but not necessarily) freely accessible online database storing journal article reprints (and sometimes other content). May be subject- or institution-based.

**reprint**   A copy of a journal article separately reprinted after publication of the journal issue (sometimes with a special cover); usually produced in quantity for commercial clients (e.g., pharmaceutical companies). With digital printing technology, reprints are increasingly also used for authors' copies in place of offprints (q.v.).

**Reproduction Rights Organizations (RROs)**  National organizations set up by rightsholders, which issue licenses and collect and redistribute fees for copying of copyright works; examples are CCC, CLA, Access Copyright, CAL (see Appendix 2, Resources).

**Request for Proposal (RFP)**  A formal detailed description of the requirements of a journal's sponsor to a publisher (e.g., for contract publishing, q.v.), or of a publisher to a vendor (e.g., for online hosting services).

**research and development (R&D)**  Systematic research, often undertaken by commercial organizations or governments, and generally directed toward the development of usable applications.

**retraction**  Formal withdrawal of an article. The marking of a journal article with a retraction notice informs readers that the study should not have been published due to error or ethical problems.

**revenue**  Income attributed to a product. Gross revenue is the total income before any deductions; net revenue is the total income less any discounts, commissions, currency conversion fees, or other deductions taken before the money is received by the publisher.

**review article**  An article summarizing the work done in a field of research. Sometimes called a literature review; review articles often have long reference lists.

**Reviews Editor**  The Editor who solicits people to write reviews of relevant books, videos, software, online resources, etc., for a journal.

**rolling backfile**  Subscription model which includes access to a given number of years' online backfiles with the current year's subscription. Access to an incremental archive (q.v.) may exclude those volumes included in the rolling backfiles, to avoid duplication.

**RTF (Rich Text Format)**  Document file format designed for cross-platform document interchange. RTF contains tagged typographical information which typesetters can use, but no structural information (unlike HTML/XML).

**saddle-stitched binding**  Binding that involves stapling along the center-fold or spine of a publication. It is appropriate for publications that have too few pages for perfect binding (q.v.).

**salami publishing**  (Sometimes called "salami slicing.") Dividing up the results of a single research study to form many separate journal articles instead of a single report; this practice is frowned upon.

**sanction**   To ban an author or authors from submitting to a journal for a specified period after they have been found guilty of ethical misconduct.

**scholarly communication**   The whole system of communication among scholars, encompassing the full range of both informal and formal communication; publication forms just one part of this.

*Science Citation Index*   The largest of Thomson Reuter's indexes of articles and citations, used to calculate journal impact factors (q.v.) for science journals. Originally produced by ISI and now part of Thomson Reuters. There is also the *Social Sciences Citation Index* and the *Arts and Humanities Citation Index*; the latter is not used to calculate JIFs.

**scope (or aims and scope)**   A succinct description of the subject coverage and article types that a journal carries or intends to carry.

**search engine marketing**   Ways of increasing the online visibility of a product or service in the results list of a search query. For example, paying a fee to have the website appear – usually identified as an advertisement – above or beside the top search results (paid placement); paying for an advertisement which comes up alongside content which includes relevant terms (contextual advertising); or paying for a website to be included in a search engine's index (paid inclusion – not all search engine providers allow this).

**self-archiving**   Deposit of copies of journal articles (or other content) by, or on behalf of, authors in freely accessible institutional or other repositories (or, less commonly, on the author's own web page). Many, but not all, journal publishers permit authors to self-archive the accepted manuscript version of their articles; some funders make it a condition of their grants that authors self-archive the published version.

**self-plagiarism**   Repeating text or data from the author's own published manuscript in a new manuscript, and passing it off as new and original.

**serial**   Any publication (journal, magazine, newsletter, etc.) issued in successively numbered parts and intended to be continued indefinitely.

**serials crisis**   A term coined to describe the increase in number and price of journals starting in the 1970s, making it difficult for libraries, whose budget increases did not keep up with the increases in funding for scientific research, to provide their patrons with the journals they required.

**SGML (Standard Generalized Markup Language)** International standard for the markup of text. A language for describing both the structure of documents or information and a tagging scheme to delineate that structure within text.

**SGML parser** SGML software product that verifies DTDs against the rules of SGML, and also checks a tagged document against the rules of its DTD.

**sheet–fed press** Printing press in which the paper is fed in precut sheets, in contrast to a roll of paper, as in a web press (q.v. web).

**SI** Abbreviation for Système internationale d'unités – the internationally agreed system of metric units.

**signature** Folded section of pages from one printed sheet.

**single–blind peer review** Form of peer review in which the identity of the reviewers is kept from the authors, but the authors' identity is known to the reviewers. See also double-blind peer review.

**single–user license** A license granted to an individual subscriber to access an online journal. Access is usually based on a username/password system.

**site license** License for online content, whether a single journal or a group of journals with or without other content, which provides access rights to users on a physical or virtual site (e.g., a university campus and its associated network).

**social media** Web-based and mobile tools allowing individuals to interact with each other; may be associated with an organization or publication (e.g., a blog linked to a journal).

**sponsor** (a) An organization (such as a learned society) which lends its name to and often owns a journal, even if that journal is published on the sponsor's behalf by another publisher. (b) A commercial organization, such as a pharmaceutical company, that financially supports the distribution of a journal or a journal supplement as a form of marketing.

**sponsored publication** A publication – which may be a magazine, journal, or journal supplement – that is distributed for free to "qualified" readers (by virtue of their job descriptions, membership in a society, responses to a survey, etc.) and financially supported by a commercial organization whose services, products, or brand are highlighted in the publication. See also controlled circulation.

**Statistics Editor** An Editor appointed to review the statistical content of papers, either as part of the peer-review process or after acceptance by the journal.

**STM**    Science, technology, and medicine, as compared with HSS, q.v. Alternatively, may refer to the International Association of STM Publishers – see Appendix 2, Resources.

**submission rate**    Statistic indicating the number of articles submitted for publication on a monthly or annual basis; analysis may also include details of the geographical source of the articles. A sharp increase or decrease, or a change in the geographical mix, may require action by the publisher. See also acceptance rate.

**subscription agent**    Intermediary from whom libraries purchase journal subscriptions from multiple publishers, and publishers receive orders from multiple customers.

**SuperJournal project**    (www.superjournal.ac.uk/sj/) Pioneering UK research project which ran from 1996 to 1998 and looked at the features which would make electronic journals successful. It correctly identified, among other things, the importance of reference linking, which is now facilitated by the DOI (q.v.).

**tag**    Marker inserted in a document to identify the type of information contained in that part of the document.

**Technical Editor**    A higher level Copy-Editor, who has enough expertise to improve the clarity of the authors' language and to ensure consistent and accurate use of technical terminology.

**TeX**    A typesetting system with particular capabilities for composition of complex mathematical formulae. See also LaTeX.

**text-matching software**    Software that compares a manuscript against published content looking for matching text strings and therefore potential plagiarism.

**TIFF**    Tagged Image File Format – graphic file format developed by Aldus and Microsoft that compresses bit-mapped information.

**tipping point**    The point at which small changes cumulate sufficiently to initiate a large change (popularized by Malcolm Gladwell in his book *The tipping point: how little things can make a big difference*, New York, Little, Brown, 2000).

**ToC (table of contents)**    The listing of all the articles and other items included in a journal issue, which generally appears at the front of a print issue (sometimes also on the front or back cover), and on the issue web page for an online issue.

**toll-free/toll-paid**    Terms sometimes used by open access supporters in reference to the subscription barrier to access.

**trademark**  Legal protection against passing off (q.v.) which can be obtained (for a fee) for a distinctive name or symbol identifying an organization, product, or service.

**trial access or trial subscription**  Temporary access to an online journal, given to interested potential customers in the hope that they will then subscribe.

**turnaway**  A visitor who tries to gain access to a journal and is "turned away" because he/she is not covered by a subscription. Turnaway data are often used to try to convince a librarian to subscribe to the journal. In COUNTER reports, a turnaway refers to a user at a subscribing institution who is denied access because of limits on the number of allowed concurrent users.

**turnover**  Another term for (generally annual) revenue (q.v.).

**twigging**  Often used to describe the branching of a discipline into subdisciplines, giving rise to new journals, or the equivalent division of a journal into separate more specialized sub-journals.

**typographic copyright**  Twenty-five-year copyright protection for the "typographic arrangement" – the actual typeset pages of a publication; only applies in the UK, and unclear how – if at all – it applies to online publications.

**Unicode**  A platform-independent standard for digital representation of the characters used in all of the world's languages. Unicode is developed and maintained by the Unicode consortium (www.unicode.org).

**unit cost of production**  The cost per copy produced, i.e., the total production cost divided by the number of copies produced. Only meaningful for print publications.

**unit cost of sales**  The cost per copy sold, i.e., the total production cost divided by the actual number of paid subscriptions.

**URL**  Universal Resource Locator – the computer code for a web address.

**US Copyright Act**  Legislation passed in 1976, and updated by the Digital Millennium Copyright Act (q.v.) in 1998.

**US government works**  Works written as part of the author's employment by the US government or its agencies; these are in the public domain within the US, but are still subject to copyright protection elsewhere.

**Value Added Tax (VAT)**  Tax added to prices of many goods and services (including publications) in European Union countries. Some countries charge a reduced rate (in the case of the UK, a zero rate) on print publications, but online publications are generally charged at the full rate, which can lead to pricing complications.

**Vancouver reference style**   One of the most frequently used styles for references (particularly in STM journals): numbered sequentially in the text, bibliographic details (in numerical order) at the end of the article or chapter.

**variable costs**   Those costs that vary with the number of copies or users.

**vendor**   Third-party supplier of services (e.g., printer, online host, aggregator). A partial list of vendors is included in Appendix 3, Vendors.

**version control**   The issue of identifying and managing the many different iterations through which a journal article may pass between first draft and publication (and beyond). The ALPSP/NISO Journal Article Versions project (www.niso.org/publications/rp/RP-8-2008. pdf) is an attempt to codify the different versions and recommend practices for publishers.

**version of record**   The version of a journal article which is deemed (generally by the publisher) to be the definitive one, after all pre-publication corrections and editing; it may be indicated by the "CrossMark" symbol (see Appendix 2, Resources).

**virtual journal**   Topic-based collection of fulltext links to articles in multiple journals from the same or (with appropriate agreements) different publishers.

**WAIS (wide area information server/service)**   Client-server text searching system that searches index databases on remote computers, using the Z39.50 standard (q.v.).

**WAN (wide area network)**   Telecommunication network linking users in discrete geographical locations (e.g., a university or company network).

**web**   Common name for the World Wide Web. Also printing term for the continuous roll of paper used on a web-fed press, as opposed to a sheet-fed press, q.v.; suitable for larger printruns.

**work in progress**   Items intended for publication in the journal, on which work has been started (e.g., editing, composition, printing) but which have not yet been published.

**work made for hire**   US legal term for an item written by an employee in the course of and as part of his or her job, in which the copyright belongs to the employer.

**WYSIWYG**   What You See Is What You Get – computing display system in which the text and graphics are displayed on-screen in exactly the same way during editing as in the final product.

**XML (Extensible Markup Language)**   An open standard for a set of rules to encode documents in machine-readable form.

**Z39.50**   ISO standard for an information retrieval protocol for inter-system searching.

# Appendix 2

# Resources

CONTENTS

## Organizations

Publishing trade associations

*International*

**Association of Learned and Professional Society Publishers**
(ALPSP) (www.alpsp.org)

> International trade association representing primarily nonprofit
> publishers. Provides advocacy, practical information and advice,
> education (many journals courses in the UK and USA), annual
> conference, research, and cooperative initiatives. Publishes the jour-
> nal *Learned Publishing*.

**International Association of Scientific, Technical & Medical
Publishers (STM)** (www.stm-assoc.org/)

> International trade association for academic and professional pub-
> lishers (despite its name, not just in STM disciplines). Provides

information, education (including journals courses), annual General Assembly (at Frankfurt), and advocacy.

**International Federation of Scholarly Publishers**
(www.scholarly-publishing.org/)

Umbrella grouping of associations which represent (solely or primarily) nonprofit publishers. Provides liaison and information exchange between its member associations; represents its members on the Council of the International Publishers Association.

**International Publishers Association (IPA)**
(www.internationalpublishers.org/)

The umbrella organization for national and international publishing associations; campaigns actively for copyright, literacy, and freedom to publish.

**Open Access Scholarly Publishers Association (OASPA)**
(www.oaspa.org/index.php)

Organization founded in 2008 to represent the interests of OA journal publishers in all disciplines through an annual conference, advocacy programs, and involvement in industry standards and the development of business and publishing models.


*National*

**Association of American Publishers (AAP)** (www.publishers.org/)

Covers all areas of publishing; the Professional/Scholarly Publishing division (PSP) (www.pspcentral.org) covers journal-related issues through its Journals Committee. Provides advocacy and educational events; PSP has its own annual meeting.

**Association of American University Presses (AAUP)**
(http://aaupnet.org/)

Covers university and other nonprofit presses. Provides advocacy and information.

**Publishers Association (PA)** (www.publishers.org.uk/)

Covers all areas of the industry in the UK; journal-related issues are covered by the Academic and Professional division, which has a Serial Publishers Executive. Provides advocacy and information. Particularly active against piracy.

See also the full list of IPA member associations at www.internationalpub lishers.org/index.php/home-mainmenu-1/ipa-membership/ipa-members

## Publishing-related organizations

**Book Industry Communications (BIC)** (www.bic.org.uk/)
Promotes supply chain efficiency in all sectors of the book (and journal) world through e-commerce and the application of standard processes and procedures.

**Chicago Collaborative** (www.chicago-collaborative.org/)
A working group of publishers, editors, and librarians committed to working together on the challenges facing scholarly communication.

**CLOCKSS (Controlled LOCKSS)** (www.clockss.org)
A not-for-profit joint venture between leading publishers and research libraries to build a sustainable, geographically distributed dark archive with which to ensure the long-term survival of web-based scholarly communications.

**COPE (Committee on Publication Ethics)** (publicationethics.org/)
Membership forum for editors and publishers of peer-reviewed journals to discuss all aspects of publication ethics. Provides advice on how to handle cases of research and publication misconduct.

**Council of Editors of Learned Journals** (www.celj.org/)
Membership organization of editors of scholarly journals in all disciplines. Provides information, education, and annual meeting.

**Council of Science Editors (CSE)** (www.councilscienceeditors.org/)
Membership organization of editorial professionals in the sciences. Provides practical information and advice (including the journal *Science Editor*), and annual meeting.

**COUNTER (Counting Online Usage of NeTworked Electronic Resources)** (www.projectcounter.org)
An international initiative to set standards for consistent and comparable recording and reporting of online usage statistics. Produces Codes of Practice, and cooperates with other organizations to develop usage-related research and services.

**CrossCheck** (www.crossref.org/crosscheck)
Initiative of CrossRef (q.v.) to establish a database of member publishers' scholarly content, across which members can search to identify potential instances of plagiarism

**CrossMark** (www.crossref.org/crossmark)
Initiative of CrossRef (q.v.) to enable publishers (or others) to attach a logo to the definitive version of an article or other content on the web.

**CrossRef** (www.crossref.org)

Organization run by Publishers International Linking Association, Inc. (PILA), which is funded by leading publishers. Provides a collaborative linking service (using DOIs) and is working on a range of related projects.

**EDItEUR**(www.editeur.org/)

The international trade standards body for the global book and serials supply chains.

**European Association of Science Editors (EASE)**
(www.ease.org.uk/)

Membership organization of individuals involved in science communication and editing. Provides practical information (including the Science Editor's Handbook), education, and triennial General Assembly.

**Frankfurt Group** (www.sub.uni-goettingen.de/frankfurtgroup/)

European forum for discussion of issues affecting academic and research information; members include representatives of publishers, vendors, rights organizations, libraries, and research centers. Produces joint position statements on a variety of topics.

**International Committee on EDI for Serials (ICEDIS)**
(www.icedis.org/)

Organization consisting of business and technical representatives from leading publishers and subscription agents. Works on the specification, development, testing, and implementation of EDI (see Glossary) standards for journal subscriptions and licenses.

**International Digital Object Identifier Foundation (DOI)**
(www.doi.org/)

The consortium (consisting of commercial and nonprofit partners) that manages the DOI system for identifying content objects in the digital environment.

**International Network for the Availability of Scientific Publications (INASP)** (www.inasp.info/)

Charitable organization working with various partners to support global research communication through innovation, networking, and capacity strengthening, focusing on the needs of developing and emerging countries. Sponsors the Programme for the Enhancement of Research Information (PERii), through which many publishers provide free or low-cost access to developing countries.

**International Society of Managing and Technical Editors (ISMTE)** (www.ismte.org/)

> An organization of journal Editorial office staff, providing networking, training, and an annual meeting.

**National Federation of Advanced Information Services (NFAIS)** (www.nfais.org)

> Global, nonprofit membership organization for all those who create, aggregate, organize, and provide access, navigation, and use of information. Provides education, advocacy, and a forum in which to address common interests.

**National Information Standards Organization (NISO)** (www.niso.org/home/)

> US organization that develops information industry standards and best practices, many of which are subsequently adopted internationally.

**North American Serials Interest Group (NASIG)** (www.nasig.org/)

> Membership organization of individuals involved in the serials information chain. Provides leadership on industry standards and other issues, and an annual conference.

**Publishing Research Consortium (PRC)** (www.publishingresearch.net/)

> International group of trade associations and individual publishers. Supports global research into scholarly communication in order to enable evidence-based discussion. Growing number of reports, and links to other important research into publishing.

**Publishing Training Centre** (www.train4publishing.co.uk/)

> Provides a wide range of training courses in the UK, including a few on journals.

**PubMed Central (PMC)** (www.ncbi.nlm.nih.gov/pmc/)

> Freely accessible repository of biomedical and life sciences journal literature at the US National Institutes of Health's National Library of Medicine (NIH/NLM). Contains both published articles deposited by their publishers (with an access embargo [see Glossary] if required), and article versions self-archived by authors. Recipients of NIH grant funding are required to deposit the final, published version of the resultant article(s); many publishers cooperate in enabling this.

**Research4Life** (www.research4life.org/about.html)

> Public–private partnership of the UN, Cornell and Yale Universities, and the STM association, which runs three programs – HINARI,

OARE, and AGORA – providing researchers in developing countries with free or low-cost access to the scholarly literature.

**Society for Editors and Proofreaders** (www.sfep.org.uk/)

UK membership organization for editors and proofreaders. Provides information and well-respected training courses.

**Society for Scholarly Publishing (SSP)** (www.sspnet.org/)

A nonprofit organization with membership open to individuals and organizations involved in all aspects of scholarly publishing (publishers, editors, librarians, vendors) – journals loom large. Provides information and education through conferences, educational seminars, and an annual meeting. Supports the popular blog, The Scholarly Kitchen.

**Subito** (www.subito-doc.de/)

Document delivery service, based in Germany, providing electronic copies of journal articles. After lengthy discussions with publishers, these copies are now licensed and generate a modest fee to the copyright owner.

**Thomson Reuters** (http://thomsonreuters.com)

Publisher (among many other resources) of the annual *Journal Citation Reports*, which assign an impact factor (see Glossary) to over 10,000 indexed scholarly journals.

**UKSG (formerly UK Serials Group)** (www.uksg.org/)

Membership organization for the whole scholarly information community – librarians, publishers, intermediaries, and technology vendors. Provides information, education, and an annual conference. Publishes the journal *Insights* (formerly entitled *Serials*).

**Ulrich's Periodicals Directory/UlrichsWeb** (www.ulrichsweb.com/ UlrichsWeb/faqs.asp)

International bibliographic database providing the most comprehensive information on journals published throughout the world.

**World Association of Medical Editors** (www.wame.org/)

Membership organization of editors of peer-reviewed medical journals, fostering international cooperation. Provides information resources.

## Learned society organizations

**Academy of Social Sciences** (www.acss.org.uk/)

UK organization of learned societies and individuals in the social sciences. Provides advocacy and meetings.

**American Council of Learned Societies (ACLS)** (www.acls.org/)
> Organization of learned societies in the humanities and social sciences. Provides advocacy, education, publications, collaborative initiatives, and fellowships.

**American Institute of Physics (AIP)** (www.aip.org)
> Not-for-profit membership corporation of numerous learned societies in the physical sciences. Provides a publishing platform for its members, as well as advocacy and other services.

**American Society of Association Executives (ASAE)** (www.asaecenter.org/); partnered with European Society of Association Executives (ESAE) (www.esae.org/)
> Organization of individuals and industry partners involved in managing trade associations, membership societies, and voluntary organizations. Provides education, information, and research.

**Council of Engineering and Scientific Society Executives (CESSE)** (www.cesse.org)
> Organization of professionals working in membership organizations in science and engineering; separate tracks for CEOs, finance, marketing, meetings, etc. Provides advocacy and education, with an annual conference.

**Federation of American Societies for Experimental Biology (FASEB)** (www.faseb.org/)
> Coalition of twenty-four US scientific societies in biological and biomedical sciences. Provides education, advocacy, and society services.

**Foundation for Science and Technology** (www.foundation.org.uk/)
> UK organization providing a neutral platform for debate of policy issues relating to science, engineering, or technology. Also provides a support service and information for learned societies.

**International Council for Science (ICSU)** (www.icsu.org)
> Organization of national scientific bodies and international scientific unions. Provides advocacy and advice.

**Professional Associations Research Network (PARN)** (www.parnglobal.com/)
> Organization of professional associations, offering information, research, and education.

**Society of Biology** (www.societyofbiology.org/)
> UK organization of both learned societies and individuals in the biological sciences. Provides advocacy and bursaries.

## Copyright-related organizations

**Access Copyright** (www.accesscopyright.ca)
> The Canadian Reproduction Rights Organization (see Glossary). Licenses content on behalf of Canadian authors and publishers, and international content to Canadian customers.

**Authors' Licensing and Collecting Society (ALCS)** (www.alcs.co.uk)
> British collecting society for all writers, including journal authors. A co-owner of the Copyright Licensing Agency (q.v.), from whose licenses it receives a share of revenue for disbursement to its members.

**British Copyright Council** (www.britishcopyright.org)
> National consultative and advisory body representing creators, publishers, and those who manage rights in all types of copyright work. Provides advocacy and a discussion forum.

**CISAC (International Confederation of Societies of Authors and Composers)** (www.cisac.org)
> Umbrella organization of national authors' societies, working towards increased recognition and protection of authors' and other creators' rights.

**Copyright Agency Ltd (CAL)** (www.copyright.com.au)
> The Australian Reproduction Rights Organization (see Glossary). Licenses reproduction rights and covers copyright issues.

**Copyright Clearance Center (CCC)** (www.copyright.com/)
> The US Reproduction Rights Organization (see Glossary). Licenses print and electronic reproduction rights on behalf of rightsholders; offers licenses internationally, and is open to non-US publishers.

**Copyright Licensing Agency (CLA)** (www.cla.co.uk/)
> The UK Reproduction Rights Organization (see Glossary). Licenses print and some electronic reproduction rights on behalf of UK rightsholders.

**Intellectual Property Office** (www.ipo.gov.uk/)
> Official UK government body responsible for IP rights in the UK.

**International Federation of Reproduction Rights Organizations** (www.ifrro.org/)
> Umbrella organization of national RROs. Also facilitates international distribution of payments collected by individual RROs.

**Library of Congress (LOC)** (www.loc.gov/)
> As well as being the national and legal deposit library of the USA, LOC also includes the Copyright Office (www.copyright.gov/), which is responsible for the national copyright system.

**Publishers Licensing Society (PLS)** (www.pls.org.uk/)
> One of the partners in the Copyright Licensing Association, representing the interests of UK publishers.

**World Intellectual Property Organization (WIPO)** (www.wipo.int)
> Agency of the United Nations, dedicated to developing a balanced and accessible international intellectual property system.

See also the list of the International Federation of Reproduction Rights Organizations members at www.ifrro.org/RRO.

## Library organizations

**American Library Association (ALA)** (www.ala.org)
> National library organization, aiming to promote library service and librarianship.

**Association of Academic Health Sciences Libraries (AAHSL )** (www.aahsl.org)
> Supports academic health sciences libraries through education programming, advocacy, and benchmarking.

**Association of Research Libraries (ARL)** (www.arl.org/)
> Organization of US and Canadian research libraries. Provides advocacy and information, including excellent statistics.

**British Library** (www.bl.uk/)
> National and legal deposit library for the UK. Very actively involved in developing systems for long-term preservation of digital publications.

**Canadian Library Association (CLA)** (www.cla.ca)
> Leading library association in Canada; runs an annual conference.

**Charleston Conference** (www.katina.info/conference/)
> Annual conference on issues in book and serial acquisition for librarians, publishers, and vendors.

**Chartered Institute of Library and Information Professionals**
(www.clip.org.uk)

> Professional body for UK librarians and information scientists (formed from merger of Library Association and Institute of Information Scientists). Provides advocacy, education, and information; publishes the monthly magazine *CILIP Update* and various books (under the Facet imprint).

**Council on Library and Information Resources (CLIR)**
(www.clir.org/)

> US organization funded by libraries, publishers, and others aiming to transform the information landscape to support the advancement of knowledge.

**Digital Preservation Coalition**
(www.dpconline.org/graphics/index.html)

> UK organization of library and allied organizations. Supports a number of projects addressing the challenges of digital preservation.

**European Bureau of Library, Information and Documentation Associations (EBLIDA)** (www.eblida.org/)

> Independent umbrella organization of library, information, documentation, and archive associations and institutions in Europe. Provides advocacy, information, and meetings.

**International Coalition of Library Consortia (ICOLC)**
(http://icolc.net)

> Informal group of library consortia. Provides information and meetings (generally private, although publishers and vendors may be invited to make a presentation).

**International Federation of Library Associations (IFLA)**
(www.ifla.org/)

> Organization of national and local library bodies. Provides advocacy, information, and an annual conference.

**LIBER – Europe (Ligue des Bibliothèques Européennes de Recherche)** (www.libereurope.eu/)

> Organization of national, university, and other libraries in Europe. Provides advocacy and information.

**Library and Information Statistics Unit**
(www.lboro.ac.uk/departments/dils/lisu/)

> Research and information center for library and information services, based at Loughborough University. Collects, analyzes, and publishes UK library statistics.

**Medical Library Association (MLA)** (http://mlanet.org/)

US nonprofit organization for information professionals and institutions in the health sciences, offering advocacy and education. Annual meeting is well attended by publishers and vendors.

**Museums, Libraries and Archives Council (MLA)**
(www.mla.gov.uk/)

UK government-funded organization aiming to promote best practice in museums, libraries, and archives.

**National Acquisitions Group (NAG)** (www.nag.org.uk/)

Organization of UK librarians, publishers, and intermediaries. Provides advocacy, information, and education.

**OCLC (Online Computer Library Center)** (www.oclc.org/)

Organization of libraries, museums, and archives. Provides advocacy, research, and standards initiatives.

**Research Support Libraries Group (RSLG)** (www.rslg.ac.uk/)

Strategic advisory group on research support libraries, funded by the four UK higher education bodies, in collaboration with the national libraries.

**Scholarly Publishing and Academic Resources Coalition (SPARC)**
(www.arl.org/sparc/); **SPARC Europe** (www.sparceurope.org/)

Alliance of US and European academic and research libraries respectively, focusing on stimulating the emergence of new scholarly communication models, particularly open access.

**Special Libraries Association (SLA)** (www.sla.org)

International association for information professionals working with specialized collections in corporate, academic, and government settings. Provides information, education, annual meeting.

**Standing Conference on National and University Libraries**
**(SCONUL)** (www.sconul.ac.uk/)

Organization of all university and national libraries, and many in higher education colleges, in UK and Ireland. Manages reciprocal access and borrowing schemes. Provides advocacy and information (including statistics).

**UKOLN: the Office for Library and Information Networking**
(www.ukoln.ac.uk/)

UK research organization aiming to inform practice and influence policy in the areas of digital libraries, information systems, bibliographic management, and web technologies. Provides information (including *Ariadne* magazine) and education.

## Other organizations

**Association of Subscription Agents and Intermediaries (ASA)**
(www.subscription-agents.org/)

> International organization of subscription agents and other interme-
> diaries in the information chain. Provides advocacy, information,
> meetings, and an annual conference.

**BioOne** (www.bioone.org)

> Not-for-profit organization providing an aggregation of research
> journals, mostly published by small learned societies, in the bio-
> logical, ecological, and environmental sciences.

**British Educational Communications and Technology Agency
(BECTA)** (www.becta.org.uk)

> Coordinates educational and technological developments across the
> compulsory and post-compulsory educational communities.

**Centre for Information Behaviour and the Evaluation of Research
(CIBER)** (www.ucl.ac.uk/silva/publishing/research)

> Unit with the Department of Information Studies at University
> College London, focusing on research into scholarly information
> use, particularly issues such as open access publishing, institutional
> repositories, and user metrics.

**Committee on Data for Science and Technology (CODATA)**
(www.codata.org/)

> Interdisciplinary committee of ICSU (see above) which works to
> improve the quality, reliability, management, and accessibility of
> scientific and technological data.

**GeoScience World** (www.geoscienceworld.org)

> Nonprofit corporation formed by a group of leading international
> geoscientific societies. Provides aggregation of journal and other
> content for geoscientists.

**International Council for Scientific and Technical Information
(ICSTI)** (www.icsti.org/)

> Organization of bodies that create, disseminate, and use scientific and
> technical information. Provides advocacy, information, and research.

**International Organization for Standardization (ISO)** (www.iso.ch)

> Nongovernmental organization providing a network of national
> standards organizations; provides consensus on international stand-
> ards emerging from those developed nationally.

**Joint Information Systems Committee (JISC)** (www.jisc.ac.uk)
> Body funded by the UK's national university funding councils and the government. Funds major projects on innovative use of digital technologies; also provides the university network, JANET.

**Project MUSE** (Johns Hopkins University) (http://muse.jhu.edu/)
> Library/publisher collaboration offering an online database which provides fulltext subscription access to over 400 scholarly journals in the humanities and social sciences.

## Journals, magazines, newsletters, and blogs

(★ = freely available online)

*Against the Grain* (www.against-the-grain.com)
> Bimonthly journal for librarians, publishers, and vendors.

*Alertbox*★ (Jakob Nielsen) (www.useit.com/alertbox)
> Biweekly column by Internet technology guru Jakob Nielsen.

*ALPSP Alert* (ALPSP) (www.alpsp.org/Ebusiness/ResearchPublications/ALPSPAlert.aspx)
> Monthly electronic newsletter summarizing important developments in the world of publishing and related technology. Available to all employees of ALPSP member organizations.

*Ariadne*★ (www.ariadne.ac.uk)
> Web magazine (published January, April, July, and October) for information professionals in archives, libraries, and museums.

*The Content Wrangler*★ (Scott Abel) (www.thecontentwrangler.com)
> A repository for information about enterprise content management (white papers, articles, book reviews, research).

*Copyright and New Media Law* (www.copyrightlaws.com/the-copyright-new-media-law-newsletter)
> Quarterly newsletter on copyright law, compliance, management, and licensing issues.

*D-Lib Magazine*★ (www.dlib.org)
> Bimonthly electronic publication focusing on digital library research and development.

*European Science Editing* (EASE) (www.ease.org.uk/journal/index.shtml)
> Quarterly publication containing articles, meeting reports, and reviews. Free to EASE members.

***First Monday*** ★ (www.firstmonday.org)

A peer-moderated publication on Net culture and structure.

***Information Research*** ★ (http://informationr.net/ir)

Peer-reviewed journal publishing the results of research across information-related disciplines.

***Information Today*** (www.infotoday.com/it)

Weekly newspaper covering news and trends in the information industry. Selected content available free of charge.

***Information World Review*** (www.iwr.co.uk)

European fortnightly electronic newsletter for information professionals in all sectors. News stories available free of charge – editorial content on subscription.

***Insights*** (formerly *Serials*) (UKSG) (www.uksg.org/insights)

Four-monthly journal on a wide range of topics of interest to the information community. Retitled from 2012.

***Journal of Electronic Publishing*** ★ (www.journalofelectronicpublishing.org)

Irregularly published journal publishing research and discussion about contemporary publishing practices, and their impact on users.

***Journal of Informetrics*** (Elsevier) (www.journals.elsevier.com/journal-of -informetrics)

Quarterly refereed journal on quantitative aspects of information science.

***Journal of Scholarly Publishing*** (University of Toronto Press) (www.utpjournals.com/jsp/jsp.html)

Quarterly journal covering a wide range of topics on both book and journal publishing across all disciplines (but primarily humanities).

***Learned Publishing*** (ALPSP) (www.learned-publishing.org)

Quarterly peer-reviewed journal on all aspects of scholarly publishing (main emphasis is journals). Free to all employees of ALPSP member organizations and SSP members.

***Links and Trends*** ★ (Mary Waltham) (www.marywaltham.com/links_and _trends.html)

Regularly updated site with links and comments on topics of particular interest to publishers.

***Logos: Forum of the World Book Community*** (Brill) (www.brill.nl/logos)

Quarterly journal publishing articles on all aspects of the book (and occasionally journal) world.

*Managing Information* (www.managinginformation.com)
> Monthly magazine covering all areas of information, knowledge, and records management.

*Publishing Research Quarterly* (Springer) (www.springer.com/social+scie nces/journal/12109)
> Quarterly peer-reviewed journal carrying research and analyses on the full range of the publishing industry.

*Scholarly Communications Report* (www.scrpublishing.com/index.php? id=10)
> Monthly newsletter (except for July) for publishers, intermediaries, and library managers.

*Scholarly Kitchen*★ (SSP) (http://scholarlykitchen.sspnet.org)
> Moderated, independent, and often controversial blog on topics of interest to scholarly information professionals.

*Science Editor* (CSE) (www.councilscienceeditors.org/i4a/pages/index. cfm?pageid=3307)
> Quarterly publication for professionals concerned with publishing in the sciences; research articles are encouraged. Free to members of the Council of Science Editors.

*Serials Review* (Elsevier) (www.sciencedirect.com/science/journal/00 987913)
> Quarterly peer-reviewed scholarly journal on all aspects of serials information.

*Seybold Report* (www.seyboldreport.com)
> Twice-monthly newsletter covering new developments in printing and publishing technologies.

*SPARC Open Access Newsletter*★ (Peter Suber) (www.earlham.edu/~pet ers/fos/newsletter/archive.htm)
> Monthly newsletter covering issues to do with open access and free online scholarship, written by one of its most cogent advocates.

## Websites and email lists

*American Scientist September 98 Forum* (Stevan Harnad) (http:// listserver.sigmaxi.org/sc/wa.exe?SUBED1=september98-forum&A=1)
> Email discussion list on open access issues, moderated in a somewhat partisan way.

***Digital curation and preservation bibliography*** (Charles W Bailey Jr) (http://digital-scholarship.org.dcpb/dcpb.htm)

> Frequently updated listing of English-language articles, books, and other sources on digital curation and preservation.

***Directory of Open Access Journals (DOAJ)*** (www.doaj.org/)

> Regularly updated listing of "Gold" (i.e., fully, immediately free content) OA journals.

***Institutional repository and ETD*** [electronic theses and dissertations] ***bibliography*** (Charles W Bailey Jr) (http://digital-scholarship.org/iretd/iretd2011.htm)

> Frequently updated listing of English-language articles, books, and other sources on institutional repositories and electronic theses and dissertations.

***Liblicense*** (Ann Okerson) (www.library.yale.edu/~llicense/index.shtml)

> Useful site with a variety of resources including model licenses and listing of projects for providing free or low-priced access to journals for readers in less-developed countries. Also runs a neutrally moderated email discussion list on library licensing and related issues.

***Publishing Research Consortium*** (www.publishingresearch.net/)

> Site contains reports of all the studies funded by the PRC, and links to a wide range of other high-quality studies on scholarly publishing.

***Scholarly Electronic Publishing Bibliography*** (Charles W Bailey Jr) (www.digital-scholarship.org/sepb/sepb.html)

> Frequently updated listing of English-language articles, books, and other sources on scholarly electronic publishing.

***SCImago Journal and Country Rank*** (www.scimagojr.com/)

> Portal that presents journal and country scientific indicators developed from information in the Scopus database; provides tools to assess and analyze scientific domains.

***SHERPA/RoMEO*** (www.sherpa.ac.uk/romeo/)

> Listing maintained by University of Nottingham which lists publishers' self-archiving policies for a large number of journals.

***Transforming scholarly publication through open access: a bibliography*** (Charles W Bailey Jr) (http://digital-scholarship.org/tsp/transforming.htm)

> Frequently updated listing of English-language articles, books, and other sources on open access.

# Appendix 3

# Vendors

CONTENTS

Note that the following lists of vendors are by no means comprehensive; inclusion or exclusion has no significance with regard to recommendation or otherwise. Both SSP and ALPSP provide listings on their websites of those of their members who provide services in all the categories below, and more.

## Authoring and citation management systems

**CiteULike** (www.citeulike.org)
**Connotea** (www.connotea.org)
**EndNote** (www.endnote.com)
**Mendeley** (www.mendeley.com)
**NoodleTools** (www.noodletools.com)
**RefWorks** (www.refworks.com)
**Zotero** (www.zotero.org)

See also Wikipedia's useful table comparing different reference management systems at http://en.wikipedia.org/wiki/Comparison_of_reference_manage ment_software.

## Online submission and peer-review systems

**AllenTrack** (Allen Press) (www.allentrack.net/description.asp)

**Bench>Press** (HighWire) (http://highwire.stanford.edu/publishers/ benchpress.dtl)

**EdiKit** (Berkeley Electronic Press) (www.bepress.com/edikit.html)

**Editorial Manager** (Aries Systems Corporation) (www.editorialman ager.com)

**eJournal Press** (www.ejournalpress.com)

**Open Journal System** (Public Knowledge Project) (http://pkp.sfu.ca/ojs/)

**Rapid Review** (Cenveo Publisher Services) (www.rapidreview.com)

**ScholarOne Manuscripts** (ScholarOne) (http://scholarone.com/prod ucts/manuscript/)

**XpressTrack** (www.xpresstrack.com)

See also Mark Ware, *Online submission and peer review systems*, Worthing, Association of Learned and Professional Society Publishers, 2005, and listing at www.arl.org/sparc/publisher/journal_management.shtml.

## Word to XML text conversion systems

**eXtyles** (Inera preediting software) (www.inera.com)

**W2XML** (docsoft) (www.docsoft.com/)

**YAWC Pro** (XML Workshop) (www.xmlw.ie/)

See also list at www.xmlw.ie/aboutxml/word2xml.htm.

## Hosting platforms

**Atypon** (www.atypon.com/)

**HighWire** (Stanford University) (http://highwire.stanford.edu/)

**ingentaconnect** (Publishing Technology) (www.ingentaconnect.com/)

**MetaPress** (EBSCO) (www.metapress.com)

**Open Journal System** (Public Knowledge Project) (http://pkp.sfu.ca/ojs/)

**Pinnacle** (Allen Press) (http://allenpress.com/services/onlineservices/ pinnacle)

**Silverchair Information Systems** (www.silverchair.com)

**Sirius** (Portland Press) (www.portlandpress.com/pcs/services/ejournals.htm)

See also Mark Ware, Journal publishing systems: outsource or in-house?, *Learned Publishing* 20(2007): 177–81 (http://dx.doi.org/10.1087/095315 107X205093).

## Aggregators

**Dialog** (ProQuest) (www.dialog.com/)
**EBSCOhost** (EBSCO Publishing) (www.ebscohost.com)
**Factiva** (http://global.factiva.com)
**Gale** (Cengage Learning) (www.gale.cengage.com/product_sites/index.htm)
**JSTOR** (www.jstor.org)
**LexisNexis** (law; Elsevier) (www.lexisnexis.com)
**Ovid** (health; Wolters Kluwer) (www.ovid.com)
**ProQuest** (www.proquest.co.uk/)
**WilsonWeb** (H W Wilson) (www.hwwilson.com/ftabsind_alpha.cfm)

## Abstracting and indexing services

**Astrophysics Data Service/ADS** (astronomy and physics; SAO and NASA) (http://adswww.harvard.edu/)
**CABI** (applied life sciences) (www.cabi.org)
**Chemical Abstracts/CAS** (chemistry; American Chemical Society) (www.cas.org/)
**CSA Illumina** (formerly **Cambridge Scientific Abstracts**) (sciences; ProQuest) (www.csa.com)
**Education Resources Information Center/ERIC** (education; US Department of Education) (www.eric.ed.gov)
**Google Scholar** (http://scholar.google.com)
**Inspec** (physics, electrical engineering, computer science; Institute of Engineering Technology) (www.theiet.org/publishing/inspec)
**Mathematical Reviews/MathSciNet** (American Mathematical Society) (http://ams.org/mr-database)
**PsycInfo** (psychology; American Psychological Association) (www.apa.org/pubs/databases/psycinfo)
**PubMed/Medline** (medicine; National Library of Medicine) (www.ncbi.nlm.nih.gov/pubmed)
**Scopus** (Elsevier) (www.scopus.com)

**Web of Knowledge** (Thomson Reuters/ISI) (http://wokinfo.com)
**Zentralblatt für Mathematik** (mathematics; FIZ Karlsruhe) (www.
zentralblatt-math.org/zmath)

## Subscription agents

With the exception of China, India, and Japan, we have not included
agents serving individual countries.

**Allied Publishers Subscription Agency** (India: www.apsaonline.net)
**Basch Subscriptions Inc.** (www.basch.com)
**CEPIEC** (China: www.cepiec.com.cn)
**CNPIEC** (China: group.cnpeak.com)
**EBSCO Information Services** (www.ebsco.com)
**Global Information Systems Technology (GIST) Pvt. Ltd** (India:
www.gist.in)
**Globe Publication Pvt. Ltd**. (India: www.globepub.com)
**Harrassowitz** (www.harrassowitz.de)
**Huber & Lang** (www.huberlang.com/subscriptions)
**Karger Libri** (www.libri.ch)
**Kinokuniya** (Japan: www.kinokuniya.co.jp/en/)
**Maruzen** (Japan: www.maruzen.co.jp/corp/en/
**Prenax Global** (www.prenax.com)
**Swets** (www.swets.com)
**Teldan** (www.teldan.com)
**USACO** (Japan: www.usaco.co.jp/about_usaco/index_e.html)

For full list of members of Association of Subscription Agents and
Intermediaries see www.subscription-agents.org/directory.

## Sales agents

There are many agents working in individual countries such as India, Korea,
Poland, etc. The list below generally includes agencies that cover broader
regions. Several subscription agencies listed in the section above also provide
marketing and sales services for publishers.

**Accucoms** (Swets) (global) (www.accucoms.com)
**Arabian Advanced Systems** (Middle East) (www.aas.com.sa)

**Burgundy Information Services** (Europe, Turkey) (www.burgundy services.com/pages/publishers.html)

**The Charlesworth Group** (China) (www.charlesworth.com/~marketing)

**DA Information Services** (Australia) (www.dadirect.com)

**Dot.lib** (Latin America) (www.dotlib.com)

**Dragonfly Sales and Marketing Consulting** (global) (www.dragon flypubservices.com)

**eLicensing** (Europe) (dc.elicensing@orange.fr)

**EMpact Sales** (global; EBSCO) (www.empactsales.com)

**iGroup** (China, India, Southeast Asia) (www.igroupnet.com)

**Informatics India Ltd** (India) (www.informindia.co.in)

**Integrated Information Network** (Middle East) (www.iingroups. com)

**Publishers Communication Group** (US, Europe, South America; Publishing Technology) (www.pcgplus.com)

**Shinwon Datanet** (South Korea) (www.shinwon.co.kr)

**Systems Link International** (Latin America) (www.systemsint.info)

**TechKnowledge** (Middle East) (www.techknowledge.me)

**TSP Diffusion** (Francophone countries) (www.tsp-diffusion.com)

**Wize Nordic** (Scandinavia) (www.wizenordic.com)

**Worldwide Information Services** (Southern Africa) (www.wwis.co.za)

## Distribution houses

**Allen Press** (http://allenpress.com/services/distribution)

**Macmillan Publishing Solutions (MPS)** (www.macmillanpublishingsolu tions.com/Solutions/fulfillmentsolutions/fulfillmentsolutions.aspx)

**Portland Customer Services** (Biochemical Society) (www.portland press.com/pcs/services/journals.htm)

**Turpin Distribution** (www.turpin-distribution.com)

## Publishing consultants

**Chain Bridge Group** (www.chainbridgegroup.com)

**Morna Conway** (www.mornaconway.com)

**Phil Davis Consulting** (http://phil-davis.org/)

**Nick Evans** (http://uk.linkedin.com/pub/nick-evans/2/b27/626)

**Norman Frankel** (www.linkedin.com/in/normanfrankel)

**Greenhouse Associates** (www.greenhousegrows.com)
**Informed Publishing Solutions, Inc.** (www.ipsig.com)
**Informed Strategies** (www.informedstrategies.com)
**Simon Inger Consulting** (www.sic.ox14.com)
**Kaufman Wills Fusting & Company** (http://kwfco.com)
**Maverick Outsource Services** (www.maverick-os.com)
**Meyers Consulting Services** (www.bmeyersconsulting.com)
**Catherine Nancarrow** (www.linkedin.com/pub/catherine-nancarrow/
    4/360/a66)
**PSP Consulting** (www.pspconsulting.org)
**Publishers Communication Group, Inc.** (www.pcgplus.com)
**Chris Rawlins** (www.linkedin.com/pub/chris-rawlins/4/841/186)
**Shift Media Ltd** (www.shift-media.co.uk)
**TBI Communications Ltd** (www.tbicommunications.com)
**Sue Thorn Consulting Ltd** (www.suethorn.org)
**Tou-Can Marketing** (www.tou-can.co.uk)
**Mary Waltham** (www.marywaltham.com)
**Mark Ware Consulting** (mrkwr.wordpress.com/mark-ware-consulting)
**Anthony Watkinson** (www.stm-assoc.org/people/anthony-watkinson)

## Document delivery suppliers

**Access/Information** (www.access-information.com)
**ArtRieve** (www.artrieve.com)
**Biodox** (www.biodox.com)
**BNA Plus Document & Research Services** (www.bnaplus.com)
**British Library Document Supply Services** (www.bl.uk/articles)
**CourtLink Document Retrieval/ChoicePoint Washington
    Document Service** (legal; LexisNexis) (http://courtlink.lexis
    nexis.com)
**Information Express** (www.ieonline.com)
**Infotrieve** (www.infotrieve.com)
**Linda Hall Library** (www.lindahall.org/services/document_delivery)
**Michigan Information Transfer Source (MITS)** (www.lib.umich.
    edu/mits)
**NRC-CISTI** (NRC Canada Institute for Scientific and Technical
    Information) (www.nrc-cnrc.gc.ca/eng/ibp/cisti.html)

**Petroleum Abstracts Document Delivery Service (PADDS)** (www.pa.utulsa.edu/services.mhtml)

**Reprints Desk** (www2.reprintsdesk.com)

**The Research Investment, Inc.** (www.researchinvest.com/document_ delivery.htm)

**Research Solutions** (www.researchsolutions.com)

**TDI Library Services** (www.tdico.com)

**US Document Retrieval Service (USDRS)** (legal) (www.usre trieval.com)

**Wisconsin TechSearch** (http://wts.wisc.edu)

# INDEX